THE HEARTLESS MURDER OF NETTIE SACHS

AND THE SURVIVAL OF HER AMERICAN DREAM

DR. ROBERT V.V. HURST

Library of Congress Control Number: 2017916307

ISBN: 0-9791361-4-8
ISBN-13: 978-0-9791361-4-6

First Edition Printed in the United States

DEDICATION

This book is dedicated to my grandmother, Nettie D. Sachs, who died 20 years before I was born. I learned to know her through writing this book. Researching her life allowed me to see a woman who loved her children and became educated at a time when women did not have the right to vote. She navigated the social role of an educated woman in a man's world long before the role of women was redefined as it has been today. She took advantage of what America had to offer and lived the American dream. Education was her ticket to prosperity, but so was marrying a successful husband. She did both. Her life was cut short by others' greed, but her 37 years on earth were filled with more experiences than most people would see in a normal lifetime.

TABLE OF CONTENTS

PREFACE

My research on the family started in 1983, some 34 years before I wrote Nettie's story and two years after the death of my father, Bernard. While I was attending a meeting in St. Louis, Missouri, I remembered that it was at Washington University there where my grandfather had received his medical education.

I called the school and was transferred to the archives department, where they found my grandfather's transcripts from college. They also had letters written in his own hand to the dean; the school required all medical students to write letters to the dean saying they were ready to graduate. I shared these letters from my grandfather with my family, but at that time I had no intention of writing a book about the family. What I did do, though, is read these letters from time to time, knowing there was more to the story.

In May of 1991 I visited my aunt, Pearle Baskin, in Tacoma, Washington. She was then 81 years old and a widow living alone. All her life she had never spoken of her mother's death or her stepfather. She was a socialite in the area and felt the story of her past would not be an asset. She never told her children the story, withholding it from them even as adults.

She must have mellowed, though, for during our lunch she told me in great detail about her stepfather, Harry Diamond, and the day he shot her mother. She remembered every detail. After all those years she chose me to reveal her story. At the time, I didn't know why, but now I think I do. The story must be told. Pearle died eight years later.

I didn't feel the drive to find the "real" story until six years ago when I had the chance to reread some articles, saved in a school notebook given to my father by his cousin in 1923, about the death of his mother, Nettie Diamond. I also discovered that my father, Bernard Hurst, died exactly 58 years to the day after the death of his mother.

Some things are not coincidence, as a friend of mine, Gail Johnson, likes to point out. She has a special awareness of other forces and told me Nettie's story must be told—the truth should come out, perhaps the reason why Pearle felt I should be told the story. Writing this story has been a journey for me into the history of my family and that of the United States. It has given me an insight into the life of my grandmother, a woman I never knew. My father was 10 years old when his mother was murdered, leaving him and his siblings orphans (my grandfather had died when my father was 3 years old).

My research took me to Europe and I learned in detail about the life of the Jews under the tsars of Russia, the reason for their immigration to America. I also learned in greater detail the history of our country from 1897 to 1923, a period that covered two wars and the building of American industry to compete with the rest of the world. America's growth did not come easily, as immigration and race relations were issues then as they still are today.

Being orphaned so young, my father never had much to say about the family except that his father had died after an operation and his mother had been shot and killed by his stepfather. He knew he had aunts and uncles and cousins in both New York and Houston but never remembered meeting them. He and I would do maintenance on the "Drugstore," a building that was still in the family, where he was born, and which had served as his first home when the family lived on the second floor. He would tell me stories about his life there, and I got to experience the view from the roof where he and his brothers played. I did wonder about my grandparents.

I remember that each spring our family would go to the cemetery and plant flowers on the graves of Nettie and Sam. I never questioned why they were not buried together, but rather in different areas of the cemetery, but I now understand the Jewish law. We never visited Harry Diamond's grave, which was not near Nettie's. My father always told the story of how as kids they waited in the car while his mother was buried and that someone came by and gave them candy bars. I could imagine the car by the curb, just like my Dad remembered that day in 1923.

One day, while I was painting the back stairs with my father, an elderly man came by and said that my grandfather was a great doctor and had cured him of an ailment as a child. After my father died, I came into possession of a folder that was a 10th-grade school project done by one of his cousins, Joe Herskovitz, in 1923. It was a compilation of newspaper articles about the trial of my step-grandfather, Harry Diamond, and the murder of my grandmother. This fueled my search for more information about the details of my grandmother's life.

My father had always been curious about his family and eventually tracked down a branch of the family that lived in Houston. This was the family of his mother's older brother, Edward Sacks (he spelled his name differently). Nettie traveled from New York to Houston to live with her brother and care for her niece after Edward's wife died of yellow fever in 1898.

When Dad was attending a convention in Houston he picked the name Sacks from the phone book and made a call to a possible relative. Luckily, he found his first cousin Seymour, who coincidentally had been born the same year he had been.

Dad's relatives in New York, however, were still a mystery. It was through the work of my researcher, Pam Hines, that we stumbled across a second cousin, Ann Mitnick, granddaughter of my father's Aunt Rose. Ann was the New York connection.

We were now able to start to put the pieces of the family together. My great-grandmother, Mary Sachs, lived with this branch of the family until her death. Stories from their early days in America and the old country were passed down through the generations, eventually to her great-granddaughter, Ann, who lives in California with other descendants of this branch of the family. California is also the residence of one branch of the Herskovitz family, my grandfather's side. These were the decedents of my grandfather's "sister" Ettie, who was actually his first cousin. She was raised as their sister—the only girl among three boys—after the death of her mother, the sister of Pearl (Pepe) Herskovitz.

My search for Nettie's story has taken me from Lithuania to New York, Houston, St. Louis, Chicago, Los Angeles, San Francisco, and Sacramento. Along the way, I have met relatives I never knew and heard stories I had never heard. I have found photos more than 100 years old that few in the family had ever seen. Mysteries of the family's early days in America have been solved. What was once thought to be a small family has grown larger over the many generations here in America.

Nettie's American Dream lives on.

ACKNOWLEDGMENTS

Washington University in St. Louis, Missouri, where my grandfather received his medical education, was the starting point for my research 34 years ago. I received help from Philip Skroska and Paul Anderson, Washington University Medical School archivists. They sent me the actual university catalog showing the coursework and professors who taught my grandfather.

Nettie's education was another starting point, and I found Jennifer McGillan, archivist at Columbia University. She helped me with the class lists and coursework that Nettie had to accomplish. She also had the work schedules for the students and requirements for entrance and graduation.

New to genealogy research, I hired American Ancestors to begin the search. I especially needed information about Nettie's first child, who was born in St. Louis. An American Ancestors genealogist uncovered that birth record in some old hand-written books of local births. This finding started to unravel the questions about Nettie's life in St. Louis. Ceri Stevens of the Missouri Mental Health Department; David Lossos, a St. Louis genealogist; and Cynthia Miller, researcher with the St. Louis Public Library, were additional sources of St. Louis information.

Tara Parks, deputy clerk of courts for Crown Point, Indiana, was an invaluable resource for all the legal information on Nettie's estate and the many articles about the trial published in local newspapers. Her skills at finding information from the files, some more than 100 years old, was truly a lucky break for me, finding Tara. Maybe it wasn't by chance: Tara gave me the impression that she too wanted to get to the truth behind Nettie's story.

Stephen G. McShane, archivist/curator of the Anderson Library of Indiana University, shared with me photos of people and buildings from the 1920s. The collection he maintains helped me put a face to the time period. David S. Hess, librarian with the Gary (Indiana) Public Library, added additional information to the story.

My friend Richard Moore helped me in my search for information on Campion Academy, a Jesuit school in Wisconsin. This is where my father and his older brother Lloyd were sent to school after their mother was murdered. It was his information that put me in touch with David P. Miors, Ph.D., Mary Struckel, and Mary C. Ganser of the Midwest Jesuit Archives in St. Louis. They had student lists and much more information, all saved from more than 90 years ago.

Indiana University in Bloomington was where all the Herskovitz boys went to college. My friend Dr. John Barbour helped me locate the people who found information from the athletic department. It was Molly Wittenberg, the records manager for the Indiana University Archives, who dug deep for the information on Bernard and Cecil's athletic activities. She found previously unseen photos of both of them. These photos I have shared with family members.

Family members contributed much to this story. Many had only foggy memories of stories passed down from their parents. Others, like my cousins Dr. Stephen and Dr. David Hurst, had written transcripts from interviews with their father, Lloyd Hurst. This helped me confirm and cross-check information from various sources but also shed light on Nettie's children's struggle to survive and pursue the American dream. My cousins in Houston, Edwin and Diane Sacks, and their aunt, Shirley Furman, shared photos and information on their branch of the family. Dr. Richard Hurst gave me additional information about his father, Dr. Cecil Hurst. Louise Walsh and Neil Hillel, both grandchildren of Ettie Hillel, my grandfather's "sister" cousin, shared family photos from 1902. These photos have never been seen by much of the family. Babs Maza, though not a family member, is the granddaughter of Anna Cohen Fishman, Nettie's closest friend. She raised Pearle after Nettie died and looked after the other children. Babs was also a teacher at Washington Elementary, the school where my father Bernard was principal.

I was able to track down Michael Shafer, the grandson of the founder of Shafer Motors, the auto agency where Nettie bought her 1923 Hudson that played a central role in her murder. Gastroenterologist Dr. Dennis Berk helped with my understanding of Nettie's wounds and medical procedures at that time.

Pamela Dudley Hines, researcher and genealogist, knows more about our family than most of us. Without her help, this book would not have told the true story of Nettie and her life. Pam searched the newspaper archives and any lead, how seemingly small, to uncover pieces of the story that would have gone missing. It was Pam who found Ann Cohn Mitnick, my second cousin. Her grandmother, Rose Cohn, was Nettie's older sister. Our great grandmother, Mary Sachs, lived with this branch of the family until her death. Many of the stories were found here, safe with Ann. Ann also cared for her aunt and uncles later in their lives and found them a rich source of information. It was Ann's search for more information that led her to Pam, and a mutual friendship has developed.

Jennifer Arnoult, my secretary and all-around right hand, has put up with the interruptions that writing this book over the past six years has caused in the office. It is Jennifer who is credited with the title for the book, one that tells Nettie's story. She has shared with me the unmasking of information about Nettie's life as we have seemed to turn up page after page of interesting and sometimes unbelievable information. Pam Hines would confirm the stories, finding the hard print in the newspapers. Learning the history of this period has been fascinating to both Jennifer and me. It was with her help that I was able to reconstruct the events of Nettie's last day with maps and photos.

This book would never exist if it were not for my editor, Jill McLain. Jill took the job as editor, and I'm not sure she knew how much help the author would need. Nevertheless, she stuck with me, correcting my grammar and punctuation. More than that, she did the layout, combining all the photos and footnotes in their proper places. She too got to see Nettie come alive in the book. Editor Judi Bredemeier got the last look at the book before publication. She took on the job as "clean-up" editor and helped the book tell Nettie's story. Amber Colleran, my graphic artist, composed the artwork for our cover. It sets the tone and the century for Nettie's book. How Amber does this is a mystery to me. She gets it just right. It was her job to take photos over 100 years old and make them work in the 21st century. My thanks to all of them for a job very well done.

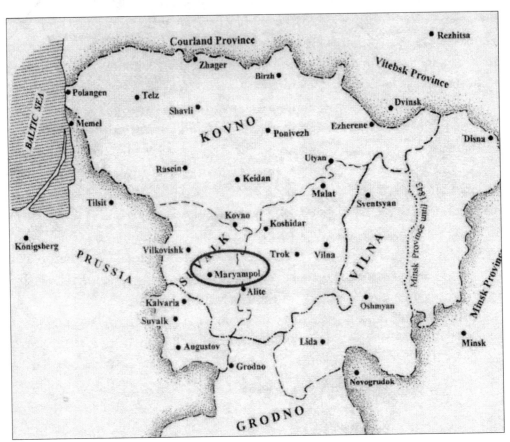

1885 Map of Lithuania and Poland. *Courtesy of Google Maps*

Nettie's
Mariampole,
1885-

Today was one of those welcome days at the start of spring when the sun was bright and seemed to light up everything with its warmth after a very cold winter. Mariampole was a city in the Pale of Settlement,[1] which was an area of Poland, Latvia, Lithuania, Ukraine, and Belorussia where the Jews of Eastern Europe were forced to live from 1791 to 1917. This is now the eastern part of Poland, but it had been annexed by Russia in the late 18th century. Mariampole lay on the banks of the Sheshupe River, surrounded by forested hills. The main road into town connected St. Petersburg to Warsaw. It was a prosperous town as compared with most in the Pale.

The smaller surrounding towns were called *shtetls*, and it was the goal of the Russians to keep the Jewish population isolated and impoverished in these little towns. The main street in Mariampole was cobblestone, which provided the storekeepers and housewives some relief from the mud and dirt—a constant problem on the side streets. For the years prior to 1881, when the liberal tsar, Alexander II, was ruling Russia, the Jews in these settlements were given greater control over their lives. His goal was to emancipate the serfs, starting in 1861. After the tsar's assassination in 1881, he was succeeded by his son Alexander III, who had never been schooled to become a tsar. It was his older brother, Nicholas, who had been groomed to rule, but unfortunately Nicholas died suddenly in his 20s and Alexander was called upon to lead Russia.

---

1 The Pale of Settlement was the term used to describe an area where the Jews were allowed to live. Loosely, it means fence. The areas along the Pale were porous and fluid, as many families lived on the border and would cross over to other countries, albeit illegally, to obtain goods.

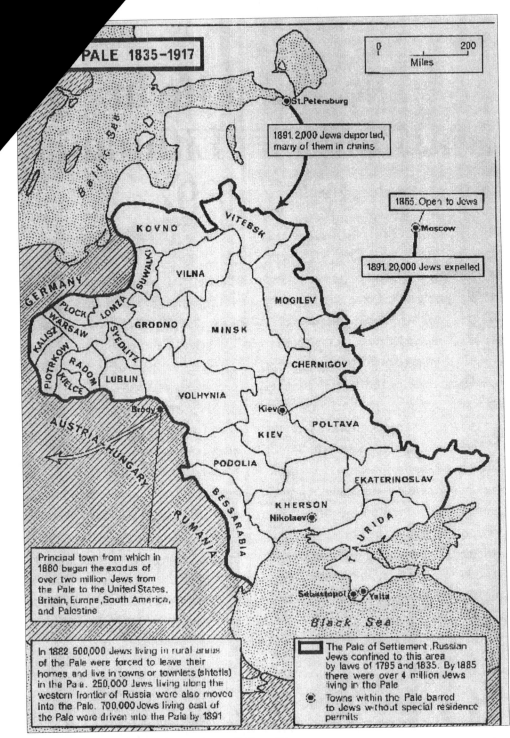

PALE 1835-1917

1891. 2,000 Jews deported,
many of them in chains

1855. Open to Jews

●Moscow

1891. 20,000 Jews expelled

Principal town from which in
1880 began the exodus of
over two million Jews from
the Pale to the United States,
Britain, Europe, South America,
and Palestine

In 1882 500,000 Jews living in rural areas
of the Pale were forced to leave their
homes and live in towns or townlets (shtetls)
in the Pale. 250,000 Jews living along the
western frontier of Russia were also moved
into the Pale. 700,000 Jews living east of
the Pale were driven into the Pale by 1891

The Pale of Settlement, Russian
Jews confined to this area
by laws of 1795 and 1835. By 1885
there were over 4 million Jews
living in the Pale.

● Towns within the Pale barred
to Jews without special residence
permits

Map of the limits of the Pale. *Courtesy of Wikipedia*

Alexander's policies were the exact opposite of his father's, and he decided that he wanted the Jews to be eliminated or assimilated, which created violence in the Pale between the Jews and Gentiles (non-Jews). This escalated in the years 1881 through 1884. Nettie Sachs was born in 1885, a year after the assassination of Tsar Alexander II.

In 1884, Tsar Alexander III died of kidney disease at the age of 49, just three years into his reign. He had, however, already set in motion severe restrictions on the Jewish people with the enactment in 1882 of the May Laws, which forced the Jews out of the cities and into the shtetls. Here they lived side by side with the Russian serfs—who, though uneducated, had more power than the Jews. The May Laws regulated Jews by taxing every aspect of Jewish life, from a tax on Sabbath candles to a tax for wearing a *yarmulke* (skullcap). Jewish boys were drafted into the army for six-year terms; if they were tall, this could happen as young as age 13. Entrance into any school was greatly restricted; only 3 percent of the students could be Jewish. Although the Jews had lived in this area for over 200 years, they were thought to be aliens. Speaking their own language, Yiddish, and believing firmly in the traditions of their religion made for a strained relationship with their Russian neighbors. These were the conditions under which Nicholas II assumed the role of tsar after the death of his father, Alexander III, who had called him a "girly girl," because his mother doted on him after his older brother died in infancy.

Nicholas II[2] was overwhelmed by the task of ruling and just continued his father's policies, adding further rules and laws against the Jewish population. He expanded the May Laws of 1882 that controlled all aspects of Jewish life and imposed on Jews taxes and penalties that were not assessed to the Gentile population. He seemed to look the other way when pogroms[3] occurred throughout the Pale.

Nettie was a very special child to the Sachs family in many ways. She was unexpected, as her brothers and sisters were all at least 10 years older. Mama Mary was 36 and Papa Sam was 44 when she was born. Her brothers and sisters—Edward, Fannie, Nathan, and Rose—left for America when Nettie was only four years old. Edward had finished his forced service in the Russian Army, and both he and his siblings left to find a better life

---

2   Nicholas II was the last tsar of Russia. Unable to manage the country or command the army during WWI, he was forced to abdicate during the Russian Revolution of 1917. He and his family were executed by Bolsheviks on July 16, 1918.

3   Pogroms were organized raids on the Jews in the towns of Russia starting in 1881. Jewish property was seized and destroyed, women were raped, and others were killed while the authorities watched and some participated.

in America. Mama and Papa didn't have the money to go with them but said they would come later.

Papa was one of 11 tailors in town. Laws that prohibited certain professions and trades for Jews resulted in many having the same trade, and fierce competition kept income low and the poverty level high. The Jews were not allowed to trade or work outside the Pale, as the Russians didn't want the competition. Papa Sachs was lucky; many of the police and soldiers wanted him to do their uniforms, as his needlework was judged the best in town. Nettie—who loved the rich red of the special fabric that was used for the parade super vests and the fine green wool used to make uniforms for the Imperial Army Heavy Cavalry Guards, the Cuirassiers—collected the scraps and used them to accent her otherwise-plain black or brown dresses and found the flat silver tress with red borders especially good for making hair bows. In return for Papa's good work, the police and army officers would give him warning when the tsar's men were about to start a raid on the homes and businesses of the Jews in town.

A raid orchestrated by the tsar or a pogrom would target all or parts of the Jewish community, and the police were instructed to look the other way. All possessions of the Jews were fair game for the rioters, who at first were just looters, but began to kill as they got more agitated. All it took was a little vodka and the apocryphal story that the Jews used Christian blood to bake their bread.

The Sachs' older children escaped this period of violence but said they would send money after they got jobs in America. Growing up, Nettie would get letters from them about how wonderful things were in America. She and her best friend, Anna Kalish—a tall, slender girl with light brown hair and hazel eyes—would play dress-up and pretend they were wealthy Americans or Maria Alexandrovna, the wife of Nicholas II, using their shawls as make-believe fur coats. Anna's father was a cobbler, one of many in town, and his shop was next door to Nettie's father's tailor shop. Anna was the third child of six—and the only girl. She loved being around Nettie, as life was always an adventure.

They would play in the lilac fields in May and swim in the river in the summer. In the winter, they would tie pieces of wood to the bottoms of their boots and skate on the frozen river. The world was a make-believe place when Anna was with Nettie, and they could ignore all the taunts and insults from the Gentiles. All the rules and pogroms from Tsar Nicholas II directed at the Jews and the name calling by the Gentile children seemed like minor inconveniences.

Nettie's Life in Mariampole

It was the spring of 1896. Nettie had just turned 11 years old, and the signs of young womanhood could not be ignored. She was already five-foot-four, with a sturdy build—four inches taller than her mother. Her crowning glory was a thick head of black hair. She had brown eyes and a peaches-and-cream complex-ion that made her face glow.

Market Square in Mariampole. *Courtesy of Elaine Gordon*

Mama joked and said Nettie was lucky her hair was so thick, as it kept her warm during the cold Russian winters. Mama said it was like she was wearing her own mink hat. This was one of the few times that Mama showed her sense of humor. Her name was Mary, but she was nothing like the Mary portrayed in the Bible. Barely five feet tall, she had a wiry build, dark black eyes that could see right through someone, and hair was pulled back in a tight bun behind her head. Mary was a strict disciplinarian and would not put up with any foolishness. This came from a life of hard work, and raising a family on what a tailor could earn was difficult. She never seemed to tire, and it may have been the work that distracted her from dwelling on her situation in life. None of this rubbed off on Nettie. From an early age, she wanted to be the center of attention and have fun. She and Mama were always at odds. Nettie was also a bit of a flirt. She would walk around the market square with Anna and talk to all the merchants, flashing her smile and showing her infec-tious personality. Some would reward her with little gifts, which would only encourage her to be more outgoing. The girls loved walking around the square with its multitude of merchants, both Jewish and Gentile. Today was Friday, the last day of the week's work for the Jewish merchants. It was also bath day for everyone. First the men and then the women were called to the bathhouse, just off the market square. There was a lot of activity that day. The smell of the horses and the sounds of the people speaking both Russian and Yiddish created a rhythm of sight, sound, and smells. The seasons determined what would be in the market, whatever was ripe in the fields or was brought from the Baltic Sea only

40 miles to the east. They visited the market square after school and were always looking for something different and new. They would tell their fathers who they had met. When their shops closed, they would all walk home together.

New Peddler in the Market

This day, the girls noticed a new merchant in the square, a peddler they had never seen before. His cart was pulled by an old white horse with a sway in its back that looked like a jump rope almost touching the ground. The cart itself was in very bad shape; its wooden wheels seemed ready to fall off. On the side of the cart was painted "Reuben Finkelstein *Fayn Skhoyre*" (fine goods). Gathered around the cart were at least seven children, the oldest a boy of at least 13, as he was dressed like the other men with his prayer shawl around his waist. The clothes that the other children wore looked worse than hand-me-downs. Nothing seemed to fit, and if Nettie didn't know better, she would have thought them beggars.

The merchandise in the cart was a potpourri of old cooking utensils, prayer books, house shingles, and pieces of wool cloth.

"Hello," said Nettie, who was never bashful about meeting new people.

The older boy looked at her with a surprised look on his face. "Where is your father or mother?" he asked.

"Why?" said Nettie, who didn't like the tone of the question from a boy who was not as tall as she. He was no man, she thought. He was beardless. He had a swarthy complexion, dark brown eyes set very close together, and thin lips that parted very little when he spoke. He seemed to be hiding behind them and was waiting for an opening to get the upper hand in the conversation.

"Girls are not supposed to talk to men they don't know. Only adults can do that."

"Who says?" Nettie shot back at him.

"It's written in the Talmud[4] that women are to serve men and be silent."

Nettie would have none of this and said, "What is your name?"

---

4 The Talmud is a body of Jewish civil and canonical law. This consists of the combined Mishna (instruction) and oral law written before the third century CE. The study of the Talmud was restricted to the men only and not taught to the women.

Wooden houses in a shtetl in Lithuania. *Courtesy of Wikipedia*

"Joseph Finkelstein." "Well, Joseph, I don't believe you, and I will talk to whomever I like. You are new to our marketplace, and here we can talk to anyone. What town did you come from, Joseph?"

"Kaunas," he said. "There we didn't have girls who were so disrespectful, and they knew their place. By the way, the color of ribbons on your hat and dress is against the law." Nettie was always adding little accents to the uniform she wore (a brown dress, apron, and little stiff hat), using leftover fabric from Papa's work sewing military dress uniforms, most of which were scarlet red.

"Not here," Nettie said. "Come on, Anna. *Az me redt a sach, ken men zikh oisreden a narishkeit.* (When one talks too much, one talks foolishness.) Let's find someone who is not so serious and wants to have fun."

Anna was used to Nettie and her straightforward approach to people, never fearing the consequences of her actions. She just watched and kept silent in the exchange between Nettie and Joseph. The two girls walked away, leaving a confused Joseph and his family. Nettie was definitely different from any girl he had ever known, he thought as he watched the girls walk off giggling to themselves. Anna said, "I think Joseph likes you, Nettie."

"I don't think so. We are so different. He is so traditional, and I'm not. Besides, I am not interested in a poor peddler's son. Did you see the things they were selling?"

"Your papa says speaking up to men is going to get you in trouble. Just be careful who you talk to."

Nettie ignored what Anna had just told her. All her life, Nettie had heard "keep quiet, and don't talk to strangers," but when the topic came up, she automatically tuned it out.

"Anna, those kids look like they need some help," she said. "Do you think they are living in the square behind their wagon?"

"That's you Nettie, always thinking you have to put your nose into other people's business," said Anna.

"I'll ask Papa tonight at Sabbath dinner. He always knows what is going on in town. Everyone talks at the tailor shop."

The Sachs house was just like all the others on their dusty side street. It was built with the timber from the surrounding woods. The trees were cut and left to dry and age in one of the many squares, and then the men would cut them into planks with saws and axes for house building.

The foundation was raised on bricks, usually about three steps high, leading to a little porch in front of the main entrance. There were two *kayles* (barrels) at the front door—one for rainwater, the other for pickled herring. Inside the front door was the kitchen, with a brick and earthen stove used to heat the house at night and in winter. Below the brick fireplace was a chicken coop, with fresh eggs always handy. Off the kitchen area was a larger room with a table and kerosene lamp hanging in the center of the room over the table. On one wall was a folding bed that turned into a bench when closed. Along the wall of the living room were pictures of the *mishpokhe* (family).

There was also a wall clock that was wound by weights on a chain, a sofa that served double duty as a bed, a chest of drawers, and a wooden clothes closet. Another tile oven was used to heat this area of the house. The bedrooms were off the living room—one for the parents, one for the girls, and the other for the boys. The walls of the rooms were calcimined or covered in paper. On her walls, Nettie had pictures of America sent by her brothers and sisters. All their postcards were pinned to the walls. The most commanding portrait was that of Tsar Nicholas II, which hung prominently in the living room for the police to see that the Sachs were loyal subjects. This did not always work, but a bribe would do wonders to bypass many of the laws.

Help for the Newcomers to Town

Nettie and Anna finished their walk around the market square and came back to the side where their fathers' shops were located. They parted ways as Anna went into the cobbler shop and Nettie into the tailor shop. "Papa," Nettie said as she burst through the door, "did you know there's a new peddler and his family in the market?" Before he could reply, Nettie said, "The children look like they could use some better clothes. I think they are living behind their wagon."

Papa looked up from his stitching and gave her a look that said to be quiet, because a customer was in the shop and this was not the time or place to discuss the issue. Nettie knew better than to pursue the issue and just made herself busy picking up the bits and pieces of the fabric that lay on the floor. They would talk on the way home.

As Papa closed the shop, he took her hand and they started the walk home. This was always a special time for Nettie, as she had Papa Sam all to herself. Papa was still spry at age 56, though all the bending during his stitching had given him a curve in his back, so that as they walked, he was not much taller than Nettie. His hair and beard were a mixture of black and white, and Nettie thought he looked handsome. He was the kind one in the family, someone she could go to with any problem. Papa would listen patiently while the animated Nettie told her story. He tried to live his life by the Jewish law but knew that Nettie was a free spirit—nothing like the other four children—and he just hoped for the best. He had stopped trying to change her years ago.

"Who is the peddler, Papa? Can we help them?"

Papa, in his quiet voice, said, "I heard they just got here from another town with only the shirts on their backs. They were run out of town because they were working with the police to turn in other Jews who were breaking the tax laws. This had been going on for some time, as no one could figure out who was telling the police. The police paid them to inform on their neighbors. I will bring up their situation with the council. We will see what we can do to get them a place to live."

The council was a mutual aid society set up by the synagogue to help people in times of need. Misfortune could be around the next corner for any family, so this extra help was much appreciated. The money was usually paid back when the crisis was over.

Papa said, "For the time being, be very careful. *A volf farlirt zayne hor, ober nit zayn natur* (a wolf loses his hair but not his nature). I think I can find some material to make the children some better clothes."

"Thank you, Papa," said Nettie, seeing the true meaning of *tzedakah* (charity) in her father's actions.

"Nettie, let's have the council give them the clothes. It is better if they don't know they were from us," he cautioned her.

Nettie, knowing that the little children would be taken care of, relaxed and agreed.

Nettie Dreams of Joseph

The sound of Joseph's voice woke Nettie up from a sound sleep. He was saying, "Girls are supposed to obey boys; it says so in the Talmud."

Thank goodness it was only a dream, but that day she told Anna about the dream.

"Anna, what is it that the boys are learning at the *yeshiva* (Jewish boys' school) that is not taught to us at our school? All we ever learn are languages and embroidery. You have brothers; have they told you anything?"

"Nettie, it's forbidden for women to study the Talmud," said Anna. "My brothers tell me nothing."

"I have an idea," Nettie said.

Anna knew the look when Nettie had an idea for a new adventure. Her eyes would get a special sparkle, and her movements got very animated.

"Let's dress as boys and go to the *yeshiva* and see what they are learning."

"Not me," Anna said, with expressions of fear in both her face and voice. "That is a crime, Nettie. If anyone found out, the rabbi would punish our families."

"Oh, you're just a spoil sport. How bad could it be? Tell me, Anna, don't you want to know too? I will get some of your brother's clothes, cut my hair, and look like a boy. Who would know? I can go as your brother's cousin from another town. I want to know if it is truly written that girls have to do what boys say."

Anna's eyes looked Nettie up and down. "We can cut that thick long black hair, but I think you will need more than a prayer shawl to cover what's happening to your chest."

"I'll cut my hair short and wear a cap. We can use an old bedsheet to wrap around my chest."

"OK, let's do it," said Anna in agreement.

Nettie Asks Anna's Brothers for Help

This was not going to be easy, and they had to plan out everything carefully. First, they had to enlist Anna's brothers. Because they all liked the vivacious Nettie, it should have been easy. It was not. The brothers knew that any girl learning from the Talmud would be considered a witch, and a severe penalty would ensue. Nettie and Anna had to promise the boys that they would have nothing to do with the scheme.

Anna's oldest brother, Daniel, was off serving in the tsar's army. He was drafted when he was 13—big for his age, but the oldest and a son, so he had to go.

The next in line was Abraham, just two years older than Nettie and Anna. He was always very quiet and had difficulty playing the role of older brother while Daniel was off in the army. He was small for his age and had been successful in avoiding the draft, as he looked too young to serve.[5]

Anna's two younger brothers, Yosef and Michael, were not yet in the *yeshiva* but in a *cheder* (Jewish elementary school), so they would not be involved in the plan.

The story the girls would tell was that Nettie, now known as Aharon, was Abraham's cousin from Prienai, a town 25 miles to the east. He would be here for a week and did not want to miss his studies. Abraham was not convinced about this plan. He had always secretly liked Nettie but never knew how to approach her. Now she would be wearing his clothes. This was too much for him to comprehend.

"Please, Abraham, would you do this little thing for us?" Anna said, as Nettie leaned over and placed her hand on his arm. The sensation startled him, and he could feel his face flush with excitement. So this was why they kept the women separate from the men in the synagogue?

"OK, I'll do it," he said, without thinking of the consequences.

Nettie squeezed his arm a little tighter. All this touching was prohibited and foreign to him, but he liked it.

The Plan

The plan was for Nettie to leave her house and come to Anna's to change her clothes before leaving for the *yeshiva*. At the end of the day, she would change back into her own clothes and walk home. The first order of business was to cut Nettie's hair. She would tell her mother that it was the new American style. With a cap on her head, long socks, and pants held up with suspenders, she could pass as a boy.

---

5   It had become the custom to not record dates of birth so as to not inform the authorities that a boy was of age to enter the military. This is why many birthdays were not celebrated, or if they were, it was on the various Jewish holidays.

The First Day at the *Yeshiva*

The day arrived, and with her new hairdo, Nettie left her house to go to Anna's to change into her brother's clothes. Mama had prepared her dinner of *schmaltz* (chicken fat) on bread, a little fruit dessert, and some juice.

Then it was off to school with Abraham. Nettie's hands were sweating a bit as they neared the *yeshiva*. She could feel her heart pounding in her chest… *Was this really the right thing to do?* she asked herself. It was too late, as they were already at the door. There greeting them was Rabbi Ebersmann, a tall, thin man with a full black beard and the long customary black coat and hat. He had never married and was so thin that every wife in town would invite him over for the Friday Sabbath meal just to try to fatten him up.

A very imposing figure, Nettie thought, as he towered over the two of them saying, "Who do you have with you today, Abraham?"

"This is my cousin Aharon, from Prienai. He will be visiting this week. Would it be OK for him to study with our group?"

"That would be fine," the rabbi said. "By the way, Aharon, how is my old friend Rabbi Ginsburger doing in Prienai?"

"Just fine," said Nettie. "He sends his regards." Nettie couldn't believe this lie came so effortlessly to her. This might be easier than she thought.

As the boys filed into the building, she noticed Joseph Finkelstein and a few other boys from the town. They were all seated at long tables facing the rabbi. She could feel the sheet tight against her chest, hoping it would not give way.

This first day went very smoothly. Lots of stories were told by the rabbi, and the students had to determine if the people were judged as good or bad.

There was always a lesson to be learned from every story. When it came time to have dinner, she and Abraham sat apart from the other students. Joseph and his friend Dov, a little worm of a boy, came by and wanted to talk.

"My cousin is very shy," said Abraham, as Nettie sat there eating her food with her cap pulled down tight over her head.

"I hear the boys are not very smart in Prienai," said Joseph.

"Yeah, that's what I heard too," said Dov.

"Leave us alone," shot back Abraham, surprising himself that he was so forceful. With that, the taunting boys moved away to another area of the yard.

"Thanks," said Nettie. "I really don't like that Joseph, and it looks like Dov is his puppet."

"Yes, they have been best buddies since Joseph showed up in town," said Abraham.

Finally the day was over, and off they went toward home. On the way, Nettie held Abraham's hand, whenever anyone was not looking. He liked the feeling and wanted to do anything Nettie would ask him.

The Second Day at the *Yeshiva*

The next day started out just like the first, but it was not going to end as pleasantly. The morning started out with a question-and-answer session.

Usually Rabbi Ebersmann would turn the question around so that whoever asked it would have to answer it. If not, he would give background information to help with the answer.

"Now, Aharon," he said to Nettie, "what question do you have that has no answer?"

Now was the time, she thought, if ever there was one—and it was the reason she was here in the *yeshiva*. "Rabbi, why is it that women must obey men? I thought it says in the Bible that all are created equal?"

A hush fell over the room. Who was this Aharon boy that would challenge the core teachings? Had Nettie wandered into unspeakable territory, or was the question thought to be too simple? She noticed out of the corner of her eye Joseph and Dov whispering to each other.

Rabbi Ebersmann turned the question back with, "Tell me what it says in the Bible about the creation of man and woman."

Nettie was ready for this, as she had been asking and studying this question.

"Rabbi, it says in chapter 1 of Genesis that God created man in his own image—male and female created at the same time. In chapter 2, it says that a rib was taken from Adam, from which he made Eve. She shall be called woman because she was taken out of man."

Rabbi replied: "In the Talmud, it says she was made from a hidden part of the man's body so she would be modest. This is the reason women are looked at as lower than men. Because Eve ate from the tree of knowledge and persuaded Adam to do so, she was punished with the pain of childbirth and was obliged to submit to her husband's rule. Man's role is public, and the woman's role is considered private. Women are responsible for making a good Jewish home. They are not counted as part of a *minyan* (the minimum number of men needed to make up a prayer service). Does this answer your question, Aharon? Let's see a show of hands. All those who see men as superior to women, raise your hands."

Only Abraham and Aharon kept theirs down.

"Time for dinner, students."

As Nettie and Abraham sat in their corner of the courtyard, they were approached by Joseph and Dov. "I don't think your name is Aharon," Joseph said, while Dov pulled off Nettie's cap, showing her entire face.

"I knew it," Joseph said. "You are Nettie, the tailor's daughter. Now you are really in trouble. How much money do you have?"

"Why?" Nettie asked.

"Because for five rubles, I won't have Dov tell the rabbi."

Nettie was ready: "We bribe Gentiles, not Jews. Come on, Abraham, we are going home."

"Dov, go tell the rabbi we have had a girl in the class," said Joseph.

The Plot Exposed

"I knew that having Joseph in the class was going to be trouble," said Nettie. "Can you believe he wanted a bribe?"

Abraham was silent as they walked home. *What is going to happen to us now? Why did I let this girl talk me into this scheme? Was this what happened to Adam when Eve gave him the apple?* The walk home seemed to go on forever.

Nettie asked Abraham, "Why did you not raise your hand when the rabbi asked if you thought all girls were inferior?"

"I don't know; I guess I just wanted to support you."

He really didn't know why he didn't raise his hand. Did Nettie have him mesmerized just like it warned in the Talmud? Men just can't concentrate when women are around. They are too distracting, especially Nettie.

Arriving at his house, they were met by Anna. "What happened? Why are you home so early?"

"We were found out by that peddler's son, Joseph," said Nettie. "He had his buddy Dov turn us in to the rabbi, but we left before anyone could talk to us. He also wanted a bribe to keep quiet, but we were not paying a bribe."

"Let's get you changed and back to your house before the rabbi gets here," said Anna.

She was right. It didn't take long before both houses were visited by Rabbi Ebersmann. He was very upset but tried to be calm when he said that it is considered witchcraft for women to learn from the Talmud and that he would have to take this problem up with the council.

Nettie quickly dashed into the house and went right to her room.

Mama was preparing supper. When the rabbi came to the door, she was quite surprised. Nettie heard muffled conversation, and then Mama called her from her room. "What do you have to say for yourself, Nettie Dora?" (Mama used Nettie's middle name only when she was very angry.) "Do you have an apology for the rabbi?"

"I'm sorry, sir, but I had questions that I could not answer and thought the answers might be at the *yeshiva*."

"What you did was very wrong and broke many of our sacred rules between the roles of men and women. In the future, should you have a question come directly to me, and I will try to guide you to the answer."

"Yes, sir," Nettie said. "Can I go to my room?" With a nod from Mama, she knew the answer was yes and went directly to her room.

Mama wondered what she was going to tell Papa about Nettie's little experiment.

"So that's why you cut your hair?" asked Mama through Nettie's closed bedroom door. "I thought you told me it was how the ladies in America wore their hair? Sometimes I think you're a little *meshuga* (crazy). Did you find the answer to why women must obey men?"

"I'm not sure," was Nettie's muffled reply.

"You know the rules, and that is why in the synagogue, the women are kept separate from the men"

"I can't believe that God made that rule."

"Quiet," Mama said in a hushed voice. "Don't let anyone know that you think like that, or you'll get into trouble."

It didn't take long for the news to get to Papa. This was not the first time he was called before the rabbi about something Nettie had said or done. This time, it was really serious. Jewish law said that a woman who reads from the Talmud is a witch. Nettie had never seen Papa so upset. This infraction of Jewish law had never happened in their town. Everyone had mixed feelings about the punishment for the crime. Papa did try to explain that controlling Nettie was like training a cat to fetch firewood, but his attempt at humor went nowhere. The council seemed to understand but decided to remove him from the Council of Elders, a very prominent position in the Jewish community. Mama was livid, and Nettie stayed in her room without *ovntbroyt* (supper).

The fact that Joseph, the peddler's son, was involved and tried to take a bribe seemed to fall on deaf ears. Papa understood the Finkelstein people were not to be trusted.

Papa Dies

Nettie's life took a tragic turn in the summer of 1896. Growing up and beginning to become a woman was an exciting time. She already was a master in the kitchen and prepared most of the meals for the family. She was fluent in five languages: Russian, English, French, German, and of course, Yiddish, her first language. As a woman, there was no further she could go with her formal education. She did have books and could study at home, though. Medicine had a great interest to her, and she thought maybe she would work with the town doctor as an assistant. She would be better prepared when she went to America. Her brother Edward and the others had sent some money, but it was never enough with the increase in taxes and rules put in place by the tsar. Papa was now 58, a ripe old age for a tailor whose fingers were not so nimble and whose eyesight was failing. Fewer people came to his shop, and his contract to make uniforms for the Russian Army was given to another tailor who had the money to bribe the official.

That was the summer day when all of Nettie's plans died. Nettie now worked at home helping Mama. Her days as a schoolgirl were over. Today, Papa didn't come home from the shop. She and Mama got worried and rushed down to the square and his tailor shop. They found Papa slumped over in his chair, scissors and fabric still in his hands. Now their lives would really change.

New Plans for Nettie

After the burial, Mama took Nettie aside: "Nettie, baby, I must tell you that without your father's income, we have little savings to live on. I think I need to tell the *shadchen* (matchmaker) that you are available. A good husband would provide for us."

"Mama, I want to go to America."

"There is no money, Nettie, and the small sums that the children have been sending us I have been using to pay for food, taxes, and rent."

Nettie was old enough to understand the gravity of the situation. She also knew that her dream of going to America was now just a dream. She didn't like the idea of having to get married, but that is what the Talmud said was the duty of every woman: to be a man's wife and care for him and his home and children.

Nettie had developed into a beauty. Her body had the most beautiful womanly curves, and at five-foot-four (tall for a Jewish girl in Lithuania), she carried herself with a regal posture. She had a slim waist and a fully developed bosom that even her shapeless black dress could not hide. She was always getting looks from more than just the boys in town, and she knew it. If she was going to get married, it would be on her terms. She had the right to turn down matches, and she would use that right. No peddler for her. She could love a rich man as easily as a poor one.

The Matchmaker

Moshe Goldstein was going to be the one. Nettie had turned down six offers, and the matchmaker was getting a little worried that there would not be a match for her. Without a match, she would not get paid. So when Nettie decided on Moshe, everyone was happy. Moshe was a 25-year-old widower, 13 years older than Nettie. His first wife had died during a breech birth, along with the child. He was a money lender and was now living with his widowed mother. He could offer Nettie and Mama a good life, maybe even a fur coat! Nettie thought for a minute about her mother and mother-in-law, Lena, living in the same house, but then necessity makes strange bedfellows.

Moshe was not a big man, just an inch or two taller than Nettie. He had black hair and green eyes, like a cat. Looking into them, she felt he could see what she was thinking, which was a little scary for Nettie at first, before she could see past that stare. What she really loved about him was that he saw all the injustice that the Russians were capable of inflicting on the Jewish people.

Moshe felt the pressure from the non-Jews who were his customers and didn't like the idea that they had to go to a Jew for funds. Those feelings could be traced back to the assassination of Alexander II, where it was falsely rumored that he had been killed by a Jew. Many money lenders at that time were forced to forgive the loans from non-Jews or face the consequences from the next tsar, Alexander III. Moshe, unlike his father, would stand up to the Russians, and that is what sealed the deal with Nettie. He was a man she could look up to.

The Wedding, Spring 1898

It was Friday morning, and Anna was at Nettie's house when Anna squealed, "They're coming down the street!" She waved her hand at Nettie to look out the window.

"Oh no," said Nettie. "I'm not ready. I can't go like this."

"Quick, get your shawl. I'll pack your bag," Anna said, as she ran from the front room to Nettie's bedroom. What she saw was a group of men carrying a chair on a wooden platform coming straight toward the house.

This was the start of the wedding week, which was always a surprise to the bride. Tradition dictated that once the bride was selected, her future husband had to provide a house that would be suitable for his bride but only after his father said it was ready. This could take years, and during the engagement, the groom was expected to help the bride's family but he would see his bride only a few times during this period, and never alone.

Moshe already had his house. It was a two-story structure just off the main square. The office was downstairs; the living quarters were above it. Since his father was no longer living, it was up to him to decide when the time was right, and now it was. Anna and Nettie had talked many times about what it would be like to lie with your husband. Jewish law was very specific that the husband was in charge.

"At least this won't be his first time," both girls said at the same time.

"Oh, Nettie, you are going to have to tell me all about it."

The procession snaked around the streets, Nettie being carried high in the chair. Anna was right behind them carrying a suitcase with the wedding dress and anything else Nettie might need. They had plenty of time to plan, as Jewish tradition at the time forbade Moshe to spend time with Nettie. He did send the family money but could not see Nettie on a regular basis. He honored the wedding contract, the *ketubah* that both of them had signed. The procession ended at Moshe's place of business just off the main square. This was also the house he shared with his widowed mother. On the ground floor was the office but also a kitchen, dining area, and a bedroom. Moshe would be staying at the house of his friend. Nettie, Anna, and both Nettie's mother and mother-in-law would occupy the house.

"Anna, go see if the bathhouse is ready for the women," said Nettie.

The community bathhouse was on the other side of the square, and Nettie had to visit the *mikvah* (ritual bath) before her wedding day. This bath was an act of purification. The men were busy constructing the *chuppah* (wedding canopy). This symbolized a new home being built by their marriage. Tables were being set up to hold all the food the guests would bring. A marriage was a celebration for the entire Jewish community, and everyone was invited. Nettie and Moshe had signed the ketubah shortly after Nettie had accepted him as her betrothed. Normally it was a year or more before the marriage, but since Moshe was a widower and already had a home for Nettie, there was no need to wait. Eight months after the contract was signed was appropriate. Anna's father, Neche, would be part of the ceremony in the absence of Papa Sachs. Tonight they would celebrate the Sabbath[6] at Anna's house and then go to the synagogue.

Friday Night

All Friday afternoon, Nettie, Anna, Mama Mary, and Lena were preparing the house for the upcoming wedding. It was a short walk to Anna's house before sundown. There, everyone was waiting for them. Mama and Nettie had not observed a Sabbath with a man at the table since Papa had died. The ladies all took turns doing the man's blessings. This was a more normal Sabbath meal. All the boys were there, even Daniel who had just returned from his six years in the Russian Army. His younger brother, Abraham, the one Nettie had persuaded to help her infiltrate the *yeshiva*, was there and was just as shy as ever. This Sabbath meal would be special, as it was the last one Nettie would observe as a single woman. This also was the beginning of the 24-hour fast before her wedding.

After the meal, the group walked to the synagogue for the Friday-night service. They all filed in—the women on one side, and the men on the other. Nettie caught the eye of Moshe, and he gave her a wink. Talking with the bride-to-be was prohibited, but maybe a wink on the night before your wedding was OK. The last announcement by the rabbi was an invitation to the congregation to attend the wedding of Moshe Goldstein and Nettie Sachs.

Nettie just beamed hearing her name spoken from the *bimah* (stage).

---

6   Sabbath is the Jewish tradition of resting on the seventh day of the week in honor of the creation of the earth, where God made the heavens and earth in six days and rested on the seventh. The celebration begins a few minutes before sunset on Friday evening until Saturday night. The women light candles, and then four blessings are given. The first blesses the children, and the husband honors his wife. The second blessing is for the wine. Third is the ritual hand-washing, and last is the blessing of the *challah*, a six-stranded bread loaf. This Sabbath observance was looked down upon by the Gentile population, who could not understand how people as poor as the Jews could skip two days of work, as by law they could not work on Sunday.

Last Night as a Single Woman

Walking back from the service, they noticed the *chuppah* (wedding canopy) was in place. The decorations and all the tables and chairs for the guests would be set up the next day with the help of Moshe's Gentile friends, as neither he nor any other Jews could work on the Sabbath.

When they returned to the house, Mary took Nettie aside and said, "I have a gift for you." There on the table was a cardboard box tied with a bow. "Go ahead and open it," Mary said. With that, Nettie tugged on the bow and opened the box. Inside was a black wig, a *shaytl* that Nettie would have to wear when outside the house.[7]

"Thank you, Mother. I had forgotten all about it." She took it out of the box and tried it on. "How do I look, Anna?"

"Beautiful" was her reply. "It looks almost like your own hair."

That night, Nettie and Anna stayed together in Moshe's house and talked throughout the night. Nettie was prepared to do all the womanly tasks and couldn't wait to sanctify the marriage. Tomorrow would be a day neither wanted to forget.

The Wedding Day

The wedding day began with the skies being a little overcast, and then it began to rain. Just the lightest of showers that made the spring flowers soak up the life-giving water, the ground took on the earthy odor of fertility one smells after a spring shower, signifying winter is over and spring has begun. The rain would not dampen Nettie's day and a new chapter in her life.

The girls looked out the window and watched the people getting things ready for the ceremony. Moshe had arranged for the food, and it was being cooked all day under the supervision of Lena and Mary. They had adjusted Nettie's wedding dress the afternoon before so that all was ready for the hour after sundown. Rabbi Ebersmann was to conduct the ceremony.

---

7   The tradition of covering a married woman's head and hair dates back many centuries. The term *tzniut* means modesty and describes a group of laws concerned with modesty in dress and behavior. It has its greatest influence within Orthodox Judaism. The *shatyl* (wig) or *tikhlach* (head scarf) was used to cover the hair to indicate that the woman was unavailable, as it was felt that uncovered hair could be sexually alluring. This practice was rarely adhered to in 20th-century America, but it is making a resurgence with some Orthodox women. Men are not required to cover their heads except when performing some religious acts or at meals. This is when they would wear a *yarmulke* or a hat; some men wear both.

The Ceremony Begins

It was an hour after sundown, and the girls could see Venus in the twilight left by the setting sun. Everyone was ready, and down the aisle walked Moshe and Anna's father, Neche. *Moshe is so handsome*, Nettie thought. *What a lucky woman I am to find a wealthy, handsome husband.* When they reached the bridal canopy, Mama and Lena escorted Nettie from the house to the canopy. Nettie circled Moshe three times, representing the three virtues of marriage: righteousness, justice, and loving kindness.

Rabbi Ebersman recited the two blessings—one over the wine and then the betrothal blessing. Moshe tasted the wine first; then Nettie tasted it. Moshe slipped the gold band over Nettie's right index finger. It was time for the seven blessings, which the rabbi recited, and then Moshe and Nettie drank the wine. With the formal part of the wedding completed, a wine glass was placed on the ground in front of Moshe. With a mighty stomp of his right foot, he shattered the glass[8], all the guests shouted *mazel tov* (congratulations), and the musicians played *freylekhn* (cheerful melodies).

The new couple, now Mr. and Mrs. Goldstein, walked down the aisle receiving good wishes from all their friends and visitors. They headed into the house for the *yichud* (private time for the bride and groom to be alone for the first time for 15 or 20 minutes after the ceremony). This is a necessary part to complete the wedding. Some people think this is the first time the couple would be intimate, but that's not always the case.

When they entered the house and went into the back bedroom, Nettie was smiling in anticipation that something special was to happen. The look on Moshe's face told her this was serious.

As they sat on the side of the bed, Moshe said, "Nettie my beloved wife, I have something to tell you that I have kept to myself since we signed our marriage contract. I don't have to tell you that these are dangerous times we live in. What I haven't told you is that when the pogroms started in 1881, our family was targeted. In 1884, when we were living in Kaunas, our family was attacked. My older sister and I watched as they killed our father with a hoe and they raped our mother."

Moshe continued, "I was 12, and my sister Lyova was 14. We hid in a wardrobe that had a false back on it, but we could see through a hole what went on. They ransacked the house, as they knew money and jewels were hidden there as collateral for loans. Then they

---

8   This custom of breaking the wine glass has a number of varied interpretations. The most common is that it represents the destruction of the Temple in Jerusalem, which we must not forget.

set fire to the house. We got out with just the clothes on our backs. It was my uncle here in Mariampole who took us in. Mother has never really gotten over the injustice of it. As soon as she could, she sent my sister to America for a better life. I took over my uncle's business when he passed away. Of course, you know about my first wife. Why do I tell you this? Be careful and watchful of those around you."

Moshe also said, "Many people in this town would like to be free of their debts with the destruction of our family. The pogroms of the past are about to begin again, as there is a lot of unrest in Russia. I will show you later how we will not be passive like my father but will protect ourselves. Be alert, and know that not everyone is your friend—Gentile or Jew."

He kissed her gently. She could feel the passion in his kiss and knew that there was more to come.

"Let's go out and join the celebration. We are to have fun tonight!"

Those were just the words Nettie wanted to hear, and she was ready for the party.

Their marriage fast was over. They came out the door hand in hand as the guests were already dancing. Everyone shouted *mazel tov*, and the party began. They were seated in a place of honor. The dancing was directly in front of them. The women danced with women; the men danced with men. The sounds of the violin, clarinet, and flute were both melancholy and, at times, exciting. The rhythms changed from slow to fast as the dancers kept pace with the music. Interspersed with the music was the wedding banquet.

There was *cepelinai*, a potato-based dumpling dish, along with beef, lamb, chicken, rabbit, and duck. There was *balandeliai*, cabbage leaves stuffed with meat and then braised. Appetizers included *zrazai* (beef rolls), gefilte fish, marinated herring, and smoked eel. Hot *borscht*, or beet soup, was on the menu, too.

For dessert, there were poppy seed rolls, but the crowning glory was the *sakotis* cake of many layers filled with jam, vanilla, chocolate, and rum. Rounds of toasts to the bride and groom ensued, with a hearty *l'chayim* (to life) shouted by all the wedding guests after each toast.

Nettie Breaks the Rules

Tradition says that the bride should be veiled throughout the wedding celebration, as it is not her beauty but the quality of her character and spirit that are important. For Nettie, removing the veil was a practical issue, as she wanted to see her guests and the veil was just in the way. Anna was by her side and pointed out the Finkelstein family, who came empty-handed to the wedding. Usually guests would bring a food item for the celebration.

All they saw was the family eating with plates piled high.

"That Joseph Finkelstein thinks he's a *macher* (big shot), but he and his family are really *gonifs* (thieves or scoundrels)," Anna said.

Nettie ignored her and went over to the younger Finkelstein children, grabbed their hands, and danced with them. Then she went over to Anna's brother Abraham and took him out on the dance floor. A hush fell over the celebration, but the music didn't stop. This was unheard of, a man and woman dancing who were not married. Lifting the veil was bad enough, but dancing with an unmarried man?

Rabbi Ebersmann just shook his head, as his thoughts went back to the time Nettie spent two days masquerading as a boy in the *yeshiva*. "I sure hope Moshe knows what to expect from his bride," he said for anyone who could hear him above the music.

Fortunately, the music drowned out his words. Joseph Finkelstein looked on, still not understanding Nettie but drawn to her nevertheless. Now that she was a married woman, the door was closed to him, but something inside said their lives were somehow intertwined. On into the night, the party went until everyone was tired and a little tipsy from all the wine. A few stragglers were left when Mama and Lena walked back to their old house to spend the night. This left Moshe's house all to the newlyweds.

Anna left with her brothers after giving Nettie a big hug and whispering in her ear, "Have a wonderful night."

The Wedding Night

The newlyweds entered the house and closed and locked the door behind them. They could still hear a few of the guests outside. No one had to rise early tomorrow, as it would be Sunday. One of the tsar's orders was that Jews were banned from working in the market on Sunday. It was a Christian worship day that they had to observe.

Together, Nettie and Moshe ascended the stairs to the second-floor bedroom. Lena had been using this room, but it was now the master bedroom. The ladies had redecorated the room, and in keeping with the wealth of Moshe, they spared no expense.

In one corner was a dressing screen with a wardrobe next to it. There was a matching one in the other corner. Each of them retired behind their screens to take off their wedding clothes and dress into their bed clothes. Nettie had a special camisole for the occasion. Between their dressing screens were two wash basins and a pitcher of water. Nettie used one of them to wash and then applied a special perfume that she and Anna had picked out.

Moshe was in a black nightshirt that extended to his ankles with buttons down the front. "I hope you are not nervous, Nettie. There's nothing to be afraid of."

"I'm not nervous, Moshe. I know what a wife's duty is but only wonder why they call it a duty."

He took her in his arms and held her close as they kissed again, but this time they held it longer. She could feel his body through his nightshirt and started to feel the strangest warmth come over her body.

They kissed again, and Nettie closed her eyes and let the feeling course throughout her body. Moshe kissed her neck, and his hands moved about her body. He relaxed his embrace and they each entered the bed from opposite sides. Nettie sunk deep into the goose-down-filled mattress. Hers at home was nothing like this. Beneath the mattress was a series of ropes that crisscrossed the frame, which gave the bed its firmness.

Moshe turned to her in the bed and began kissing her again while one hand was ever so gently unbuttoning her camisole to reveal her breasts. *Oh my God, why am getting so hot?* Nettie thought as she threw back the covers.

Moshe was now caressing her breasts, as they seemed to be getting larger and her nipples became erect. She could now feel his body next to hers. This is the part that Anna had told her about. After all, she had four brothers.

Without removing his nightshirt, he lifted up the bottom of her camisole and his nightshirt as he rolled on top of her. Instinctively, Nettie opened her legs and allowed him to penetrate her, slowly at first, and then deeper and harder. Nettie was expecting pain, but she experienced nothing but pleasure. She lost all inhibitions and started to move her hips in unison with his. Their breathing became faster and faster. When she felt she was about to burn up, she felt the warmth inside her. Moshe rolled to his side of the bed. *Oh my*, she thought, *this is wonderful.* And then they drifted off to sleep with their arms around each other.

They woke with the morning light streaming in the window. Nettie wanted to experience again that feeling she had last night, and Moshe was more than willing to oblige. This time, it would be in the daylight, and Nettie could see his *schmekel* (penis), the source of her pleasure. This second time was better than the first. Being a wife would not be a chore for Nettie.

Mrs. Goldstein Meets the Public

The next seven days were just a blur for Nettie. Every night, they had dinner at the home of a different friend of Moshe's. She hadn't realized how influential he was in their town, and it made her feel good that she had made the right choice. At 12, she acted older than her years, with her regal posture and the ability to make friends. This was not an act, but it sure felt like acting as Moshe would tell her about the people they were to meet each night. They even had dinner with the chief of police. He was a client.

Moshe kept saying, "Not everyone we meet is really our friend. Watch and learn." This caution fell on deaf ears as Nettie was having too much fun with everyone.

She did have time to talk with Anna, who couldn't wait for the details of the wedding night. "Oh Anna, it was the most wonderful feeling. I am so glad it was not his first time. Have you been talking to the matchmaker?"

"I'm not as bold as you, Nettie, and I haven't even filled out yet. What man would want me?"

"Don't be silly, Anna, there is someone out there for you; you'll see."

"Guess who's moving into your old house, Nettie?"

"The Finkelsteins."

Life as Mrs. Goldstein

The rest of spring and summer just flew by. Having a home just off the market square made it easy for Nettie to shop, and now she had enough money for anything she wanted. Two days a week, she helped the local doctor in town—something that always was an interest to her. He was training her because as a Jew, the system denied her an education.

Mama Mary had moved into the house. She and Lena shared the downstairs bedroom. They all shared in the kitchen duties, which relieved Nettie of most of the cooking. Moshe had the best of all possible situations—three women all waiting on him. Nettie wrote letters to Rose, her sister in New York, and learned that she had also married.

Rose's husband was a furrier, a trade he had learned when he lived in Lithuania. Nettie wondered if she would ever see her again.

Unrest in the Town

It was now late August, and all the harvest festivals were being celebrated. This was the time that the peasant population did a lot of drinking and was a fine time for the politicians to provoke them to violence. The recipient of the violence would be the Jewish population, a perfect distraction for the failed policies of the Russian government to be blamed on the Jews.

Moshe got word from the chief of police that a bureaucrat in Moscow wanted an incident to happen in their town and that Jewish businesses would be targeted. This is just what he had been telling Nettie. He had showed her where all the money and other property was hidden in various places in the house. He also showed her two revolvers he had taken in as collateral on a loan. They were Smith & Wesson revolvers used by the Russian Army. He would not let the vandals hurt his family. Because he knew the attack was to be the night of the full harvest moon, he had Nettie take most of the money and jewelry to Anna's house for safekeeping.

The Attack

It was Friday night, and the Sabbath meal was over. Everyone knew this was going to be the night. The moon rose full in the east and cast its light on the front of their house. They had boarded up the front windows and closed the wooden shutters on the second floor. Fire was always a concern, as most buildings were wood with wooden shutters. Moshe's building was built with brick on the first floor, but the second was wood, and they did have wooden shutters.

Mama Mary had consented to stay at Anna's house. Lena and Nettie would not leave Moshe alone. Lena had been through this before. Nettie had heard about these pogroms but had never experienced one. The excitement overcame her fear. "I'm your wife, Moshe. I will not leave your side."

Both she and Lena were upstairs but could see the street through the holes in the shutters. They had one of the guns; Moshe had the other. He was seated in the middle of the room behind the reinforced front door. In the alley behind the building his horse and buggy waited, just in case an escape was necessary. Moshe thought, though, that maybe gunfire would drive the raiders away, if all they wanted to do was provoke an incident and cause some property damage,

By 10 o'clock, the crowd was sufficiently drunk to believe the lies that would incite them to violence. "The Jews have been using the blood of peasant children to make their bread," one of the instigators yelled, as the mob coalesced from the various taverns around the square. No one had any torches, as the moon gave them plenty of light to find the Jewish businesses. The mob was bent on getting as much Jewish personal property as they could. They knew there would be no prosecution from the authorities. All Jewish property was unprotected by the police.

Nettie could see them coming across the square and whispered to Moshe downstairs, "They're coming directly toward us." They were now close enough that Nettie could see their faces. Many she recognized as merchants she had known and shopped with. *How could this be?* she asked herself. *I thought they were our friends.*

"Kill the Jew; get the money lender" was the cry from the crowd. Now Nettie was frightened. This was not just an unruly mob. These people meant to hurt someone.

Blam-blam! Something heavy was being slammed against the front door.

The whole building seemed to rock, but the front door held.

They were hitting the shutters on each side of the door trying to get in. It was only a few minutes, but it seemed longer as the mob picked the paving stones from the street and hurled them at the building.

Crash! Pieces of glass went everywhere as a stone came through the front shutter and window. Nettie peeked out the hole in the upstairs shutter. She couldn't believe who she saw. It was Joseph Finkelstein dressed in peasant clothing. He had a gun in his hand, and he handed it to another man. Just then, the front door collapsed into the front room.

Moshe fired one shot in the air, hoping to scare the mob off. It didn't work.

Bang, bang came the reply to Moshe's warning shot, which echoed through the house. These shots were aimed at him.

"I'm hit!" he yelled to Nettie and Lena. "Use your gun!"

Nettie then heard *bang, bang, bang, bang,* as Moshe got off four more shots before he clutched his stomach and fell onto the floor. Nettie had never fired a gun, and before she could pull the trigger, Lena took it out of her hand and fired at the men as they burst through the open door. Two shots were fired, and one man lay on the floor in front of Moshe. Nettie recognized him as the man Joseph Finkelstein had given the gun to.

All the gunfire seemed to disperse the crowd for the moment, and both Nettie and Lena rushed down the stairs to Moshe. He was still alive, but just barely. The shot had entered his stomach, and he was bleeding to death.

"Leave me," he said. "Get the buggy and get away from here."

"We won't leave you," Nettie said. "You are my husband. I will die with you. I love you."

Lena was looking out the door as Nettie cradled Moshe's head in her lap. She kissed him on the forehead, and with that he took one last breath and lay limp in her arms.

"We have no time," Lena said. "We must go now, or we will be next." She gave her son a parting kiss, and then out the back door they went, still carrying the gun.

The buggy ride to Anna's house seemed to take forever. Nettie could hear the mob in her house tearing it apart to find money or anything of value. She knew now they must flee the town. They must break the Sabbath rules,[9] but this was an emergency.

---

9 Keeping the rules meant no work could be done on the Sabbath. This included cooking, lighting candles, or driving a team of horses, as Nettie was forced to do in order to escape.

CHAPTER 2

The Escape to America

When they got to Anna's house, everyone could sense the worst had happened. Nettie burst through the door, but her voice was amazingly calm. "They broke into the house and killed Moshe. We think we killed the man who did it, but in the commotion, we can't be sure." They all knew there would be no justice for a Jew who killed a Gentile. "We have to leave town now. The police will be looking for us, so we must get away tonight." It was now 11 o'clock. The moon was casting an eerie light over everything.

"Who's coming with me? Lena? Mama?" It was Daniel, Anna's older brother, who spoke first. "I always wanted to see America. This must be the time."

"Good," said Nettie. "Wear your army uniform. That should help if we are stopped."

Abraham, who was about to be conscripted into the army, asked if he could come too.

"Of course, you can." Nettie gave Abraham's father, Neche, 300 rubles to pay the government for his escape from serving in the army. She also gave him 200 rubles to have a fitting burial for Moshe and a felt bag with gold coins and jewels to bribe the officials when they started asking questions.

"This is way too much," said Neche. "I don't need all of this."

"Take it. I am taking your two oldest sons. How can I ever repay you?" Nettie said through her tears.

"I can't live in this town if you're gone," said Anna. "I'm coming too."

"We all can't go in my buggy. I'm sure they will be looking for it. Let's hitch up my horse to the milkman's wagon and leave him our buggy and 50 rubles to buy a new one."

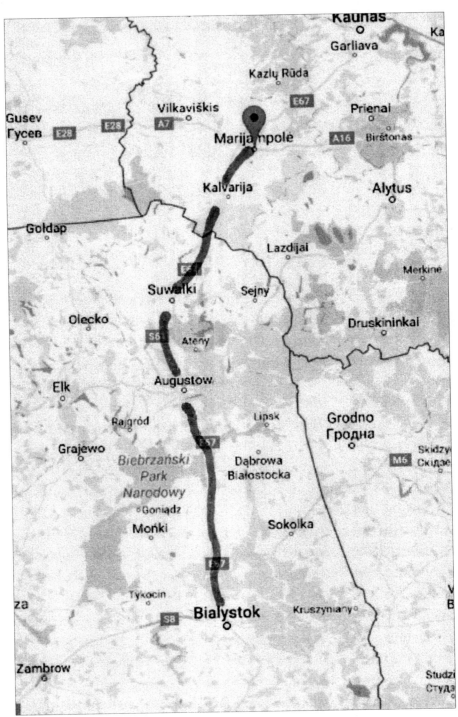

Escape route to Bialystok. *Courtesy of Google Maps*

Daniel then took control of the situation. His six years in the Russian army made him very aware of the tactics of the police and the Okhrana, the secret Russian police who were usually behind the attacks on the Jews. They could still hear the mob and started to smell fire, as the mob was completely out of control. It was the Sabbath. Most of the Jewish families were home behind locked doors.

Abraham and Daniel left to go down the street and hitch up the horse to the milkman's wagon while Nettie, Anna, Lena, and Mary packed as many provisions as they could. Nettie would disguise herself as a boy to further confuse the authorities if they should get stopped. Out came the scissors, and off went her hair.

The boys were back, and everyone piled into the wagon as they took the back streets out of town.

"We must head for the German border. They will be looking for us at every train station in Lithuania and on the main roads," Daniel said.

As the cart bumped along the ruts in the dirt road, Anna, Lena, Mary, and Nettie (now dressed in Abraham's clothes, looking again like a young boy) settled down into the hay in the back of the wagon.

Nettie had two satchels of money, gold, and precious stones that Moshe had moved to Anna's house. She would now give everyone a part of the treasure, just in case they were robbed. Someone might go undetected, and they would still have enough money for the journey to Hamburg and America.

In Lena's bag was the gun she had used, still with four bullets. She handed it up to Daniel and said, "Let's go to Bialystok where I have a cousin. Her husband is a tailor. We can trust them to help us get a train to Hamburg."

After a pause, Daniel said, "It sounds like a good plan, as the authorities will be way ahead of us if they use the train. It goes through Bialystok. We must be careful."

It was going to be a long night. Daniel was taking the back roads in hopes that they would not encounter anyone. It was 10 miles to Kalverija, then 20 miles to Suwalk. The moon was now overhead. Nettie thought, *Will we make it to America? If we get caught, we will surely be executed or thrown into prison.* The events of the night and the bumping of the cart soon put her into an uneasy state of sleep, awaking whenever one of the cart wheels got out of the rut in the road and jarred the cart back into line.

Lena and Mary hardly had time to think about their present situation. What had Nettie gotten them into this time? Would she not know how serious this was until it was over? Lena was making plans in her mind to see her daughter Lyova. She had sent her to

America so many years ago. Mary would be reunited with her sons, Edward and Nathan, and her daughters, Fannie and Rose. She had thought she would never see them again.

Escaping through the Night

It was only 10 miles to Kalvarija, and their cart rolled into town at 2 a.m. This town was much smaller than Mariampole. They all knew someone here but dared not stop. Besides, it was now Sunday and no longer the Sabbath. Jews would not want to break the Russian rules and work on Sunday. It would be better to move on toward Bialystok. No one was in the square as they quietly rolled through. They felt they went unnoticed. That was good, especially if the police had been notified.

They would soon be approaching an old border post left by the Russians since the partition of Poland in 1835. It had been 60 years, but governments do some strange things, and it was just another way to control the movement of the Jews. After the old border post, it would be 15 miles to Suwalk. This was going to be their first real test. All of them had passports of some type. Nettie, now posing as a boy, did have a passport for someone named Aharon.

It was now about 3 a.m. as they approached a tiny hut. To their amazement, the officer was outside sleeping in a chair. It was such a mild autumn night that he must have just dozed off. Their first thought was to slowly drive through the crossing. Just then, the officer's dog let out a yelp and he awoke.

Still half asleep, he said, "Who goes there?" looking up at Daniel in his Russian uniform with Abraham by his side.

Daniel said, "Sergeant Volkov, I have orders to take this Jew to Suwalk."

"Why are you traveling tonight? It's the Sabbath." The guard was unaware of the time and that it was now Sunday.

"Got to get him there before the Sabbath is over—something about a service. You know how these Jews love their traditions."

The women were huddling under the straw in the back of the wagon. Nettie's heart was pumping so hard and fast, she thought the sound of it would give them away.

"Let's see his passport."

Abraham pulled out his passport card, and sure enough it matched and even had something on it about the *yeshiva*.

"That's a mighty fine horse you have there for a rundown cart."

"Russian infantry horse. We didn't have a cart and this Jew has connections, so we just hitched it up to the only cart we could find." With that, Daniel flipped him a five-ruble gold coin. And with a salute to each other, they were on their way to Bialystok. Only 15 miles to Suwalk and time to plan their next move.

They could tell the horse was getting tired. At Suwalk, they would have to find new transportation.

It was Sunday. No Jews or Gentiles would be moving about the town. This meant that Daniel had to be resourceful and find what the group needed even though the shops and stalls were closed. Although finding a new team and cart could be difficult, he knew how to use the power of his Russian uniform. The sun was rising, and everyone got out of the cart before they entered town, taking all their provisions.

Off Daniel went in his Russian uniform. The group settled under a large oak tree to eat a breakfast of bread and cheese. *This was like the Bible story Exodus*, thought Nettie, *when the Jews left Egypt with the pharaoh's army chasing behind them.*

In a few hours, Daniel was back with a two-horse team and better wagon with springs. "It's amazing what a Russian uniform and rubles can do, even if it's only a noncommissioned officer." He also had a pile of clothing for everyone to dress themselves as Polish peasants.

Nettie loved the fact that she could dress in something different. The women could leave their long black dresses behind.

"We need to bury the old clothes," Daniel said. "If anyone comes by, they won't know we were here. That includes your wigs, ladies, and your yarmulke, Abraham. We can't dress like Jews."

"Can we wear our scarves over our heads?" asked Lena and Mary.

"Yes, I guess so. Most of the peasants have head scarves, especially the older women."

Back into the wagon everyone went—and then into the square, where no one could now tell they were Jews on the run. Their time here would be limited, so they just picked up what they thought they would need for the 75-mile trip to Bialystock: blankets, food, and more clothes, as well as feed for the horses. Very few businesses were open on Sunday. It was against the law. Because they looked like peasants, others were willing to help them, no questions asked. It would take two days, even with the two-horse team, to reach Bialystok.

Day 2 of the Escape

Daniel was really tired after the long trip during the night and needed to rest in the back of the wagon. Nettie and Anna were driving the wagon now that they were out of town.

"Just follow the signs to Bialystock," Daniel said, as he and Abraham dozed off in their new peasant clothes.

They took turns driving the team all that next day, passing through the shtetls of Olecko, Elk, and Ostroleka. Passing the farmers' fields and orchards, Nettie tried to embed the images in her mind, for she knew this would be the last time she would see this part of the world. Occasionally, they would let the horses rest while they picked plums, pears, and apples from the tree branches that hung over the roadway. Nettie would feed the horses apples, a treat for helping them escape. On these back roads, they saw but a few passing carts.

That night, Daniel located an isolated grove of trees where they hid the wagon and horses. A small brook ran outside the grove, and they washed and let the horses drink. Using extra blankets, Daniel and Abraham fashioned a tent that stretched from the wagon to several of the trees. No fire tonight. Only cold bread, cheese, and some herring. As the sun was setting, they heard the clatter of horses' hooves coming from the direction where they had just been.

Louder and louder they sounded. The little group huddled closer together under the trees and hoped their horses would not give them away. Daniel counted, one, two, three, four, up to eight riders, who came into view through his hidden position in the trees. Mosin-Nagant rifles were slung across their chests and red uniforms. The last rays of the setting sun reflected off their Shashqua sabres.

"Cossacks," Daniel whispered back to the group. "They must be on a mission. The army uses them only when they want a violent end."

LEFT: Amur Cossacks. *Courtesy of Grandpa Family Archive, cc by-SA3.0*
RIGHT: Cossaks on horseback. *Wikimedia Commons/Public Domain in the United States*

Anna whispered, "Do you think they're looking for us?"

"Maybe, but I don't want to find out."

They all clung tightly to the trees until the hoof beats could no longer be heard above the babble of the brook. Daniel still had one of the guns, but with only four bullets left, it would be no match for the Cossacks.

The Second Night Together

That night, the moon rose—but not quite full as the night before. It was a clear autumn night, and their light peasant clothing was no match for the night chill. They lay on the ground using the straw from the wagon as a mattress. Covering the group of six with the remaining blankets was a bit difficult unless they all stayed close together. Nettie ended up next to Daniel. She could feel the warmth of his body next to hers. Everyone slept soundly in the open air. Nettie could see the stars around the edge of the blanket tent. *This all happened so fast*, she thought. *What a wonderful adventure.* And then she drifted off to sleep.

Dreaming, Nettie found herself next to Moshe and embraced his body—only to wake Daniel, who thought, *They haven't finished the* Kol Nidre *(prayer for the dead)—and certainly the mourning period—and Nettie is breaking more rules.* He did not release her embrace, as the warmth of her body was both exciting and calming at the same time. Nettie awoke the next morning to find herself embracing not only Daniel but Abraham as well. Both men got up quickly and tried to appear like nothing happened. They all knew this was against Jewish law.

The Road to Bialystock

On the road to Bialystok, Lena told them of her cousin Dori Lebovitz whose family fled Kaunas in the pogrom of 1884. Their family had come to Bialystok, as it had one of the largest Jewish populations in the Pale. Lena had visited her only once, taking the train from Mariampole. Dori's husband was a tailor whose services the group would need.

This would be the last day in the wagon, as they should reach Bialystok in the early evening. Lena knew the address but not how to get to the house. Daniel was encouraging: "I will find it, the corner of Polna and Czysta, near the cemetery. That should be easy."

A wagon full of peasants in the Jewish sector of town would be a little suspicious. The women would have to cover themselves with the blankets and straw.

"Look, Anna, we're in a tent," Nettie said. Her old playful self was coming back as she felt she was nearing freedom.

Safe at Last ... Maybe

It was dusk when they entered the outskirts of town. There were enough people on the street to ask directions. Daniel hailed an obvious Jewish merchant walking home, and in his best Russian, he asked, "Where are Polna and Czysta streets?" What luck. It was only two miles away and in the direction they were headed. Polna Street was wide—and a good thing, too, as the wagon and team took a wide berth turning the corner. There it was, right on the corner like Lena had said. There was even a tailor sign on the gate. They knew they were in the right place.

Dori and Zev Lebovitz

Daniel asked Lena to come out from under the blankets and had the others stay down. Lena walked up to the door and knocked. Dori may not recognize her in her peasant clothes and certainly wouldn't be expecting a visit.

Her husband, Zev, answered the door with an expression as if he had seen an apparition. "Lena, is that you? Dori, come quick! It's Lena Goldstein. We heard that there was trouble in Mariampole and a money lender was killed." Bad news traveled fast in the Pale.

"Yes, Dori, it was Moshe who was killed. A peasant man as well."

"We have had the police in town asking questions. They are stationed all around the train station," Dori said. "Who is with you?"

"There are six of us," replied Lena.

"Quick, get them all inside and put the wagon and horses out of sight in the back."

The women all scurried into the house as Zev showed the boys where to put the wagon and team. Once the escapees were inside, Dori and the ladies prepared a hot meal for the group and listened to the details of their story. Nettie, the recent widow, was the center of attention. With her hair cut short and wearing boys' clothes at first, Dori thought she was a boy.

"So beautiful and young to be a widow," said Dori.

They all agreed that German passports and money would be needed. Zev agreed that they should be dressed like middle-class Germans to help in their escape to Hamburg and then their passage on a ship to America.

"We have spies here among the Jews. They work with the police. Everyone should stay inside and not draw any attention until you are ready to leave," said Zev. Nettie had a flashback to her wedding night, when Moshe had said, "Don't trust anyone, Jew or Gentile. They may not be your friends."

"Zev will start making your clothes tomorrow," said Dori, "and the men will take turns going to the money lender to exchange your money for German marks. Zev also knows a passport maker who for the right price will make everyone German passports and give you new names for the journey to Hamburg."

Everyone could speak German, as that was the basis for Yiddish, so they practiced their accents so that no one would suspect them of being Jewish.

The next day, the wagon and horses were sold in the market. Daniel had kept his Russian Army uniform, so again it was put to good use. Zev and Dori went to the train station twice to buy the six tickets to Hamburg without raising any suspicions. They felt the police presence everywhere, or were they just nervous? If caught, they would suffer the same fate as the fugitives.

Two days later all was in order. Splitting into three groups—Daniel and Mary (now Otto and Bertha Schmidt), Abraham and Anna (Charles and Ida Peterson), and Lena and Nettie (Emily and Walter Schuster)—they set out on foot to the train station. Dressed in their German clothes, Lena and Mary both had hats that covered their hair and made them more comfortable. Both the boys had hats, as well as Nettie, who was now wearing boys' clothes, including three-quarter-length pants and a cap to cover her hair. Carrying their new names and German passports, each had enough marks for the journey and beyond.

The Train Station

Arriving at the station, they saw only one policeman. He seemed preoccupied with a very attractive passenger. The train was supposed to arrive at 9 a.m. from Grodno. As it rumbled into the station from out of nowhere, a dozen police arrived and began checking everyone who departed from the train. Everyone was asked for their identification as they boarded the train. Speaking only perfect German, everyone made it. The cars were arranged in compartments with two benches facing each other.

There was a corridor that ran the length of each car. The group separated into three different compartments. When asked for food, they ate only German food. Although it was not kosher, it would help with their disguises. The next test would be at the German border at Poznan.

The Train Trip to Hamburg

Prussian S3 DR6 Class 13.0 engine.
Courtesy of Unbekant German Wikipedia by Pyxly

This train had the latest engine on the line. It used the latest steam locomotive S2/PKP, Class PD1, which could reach a speed of 62 mph, making the miles fly by. It was 80 miles to Warsaw, and then 175 miles to Poznan. There would be another passport check there as they left the Pale and entered German territory.

It was afternoon when the train stopped at Poznan. The German security police came on board and began checking passports. The group had rehearsed what they were to say. All said they lived in Hamburg but were visiting Bialystok. Daniel had been to Hamburg twice while in the military. He gave everyone as much information as he could remember. Anna (now Ida) could pass as German with her very light brown hair. Nettie coached her how to play up to the officers by batting her eyes and looking away from them as if she was embarrassed.

When an officer approached Nettie, he eyed her up and down and looked at the passport. "Walter Schuster, is it?"

"Yes, sir, it is," Nettie replied.

"Tell me, how old are you Walter?"

"Fifteen, sir."

The officer seemed to have more than a casual interest in Walter. Thinking that Walter looked a little feminine for a boy, the officer removed Nettie's hat and then squeezed her arm.

"You need to be doing more work, Walter. How do you expect to get muscles like mine?"

He gave her a wink and then left the car.

Lena breathed a sigh of relief. The boys looked very German, with Daniel's beard trimmed short and Abraham appearing to be escorting his sister. It was early evening now, and they were quickly covering the 175 miles to Berlin and then the 150 miles to Hamburg.

Hamburg at Last

It was 10 p.m. when they pulled into the station at Hamburg.

They agreed it would be best to spend the night in the station and then look for lodging and the steamship office in the morning. Each group separated and slept on different benches so as not to draw any extra attention.

At first light, they were out of the station and met outside. They headed in the direction of the Elbe River, where all the steamship companies kept their headquarters. They found that the earliest passage to America and New York was three weeks away. They bought second-class tickets and headed into town to find a place to stay. The steamship company had boarding houses. They felt that it would be too dangerous to make friends and that Nettie, still posing as a boy, would have a lot of trouble in an all-male facility.

They did not forget that they were still on the run and that the Russian authorities would work with the Germans to find them. Luckily, they found several rooms for rent only a mile or so from the river. Here they would stay and wait for the departure of their ship and fill out the necessary paperwork and medical exams before they would be able to board the ship *Pretoria*. The second-class tickets cost $40 each ($1,096 in 2017 dollars); they still had plenty of money for the trip and bribes if needed.

Escape route from Mariampole to Hamburg. *Courtesy of Google Maps*

Three Weeks in Hamburg

After they settled in to their new rooms, Nettie became uncharacteristically quiet. Anna tried to cheer her up but to no avail. Surely the Russians were on their trail? The whole group was beginning to get more anxious every day.

It was Daniel who gave them hope and uplifted their spirits. "If they are still looking for us, don't you think we would have seen something in the papers or wanted signs in the railway stations? The fact that we got our steamship tickets without incident was surely a good sign."

The next few weeks saw the town fill with immigrants to fill the departing ships. Nettie and the family spent most of their time off the streets in their rented rooms, staying well clear of any Jewish immigrants on the chance that someone would recognize them.

Daniel exchanged more of their money, and Lena's cousin had warned them to get only German gold marks, which would be worth more in America. Anna and Nettie did a little shopping. They had so little that a few small suitcases would do. Neither of them had been in such a large town in their lives.

"Look, Anna, the dresses are so colorful compared with our black and brown dresses at home."

"How do they get into those dresses? Have you seen how small the waists are?" observed Anna.

"They must use those corsets to get such small waists. I can't wait to get a dress like that when I get to America," Nettie replied.

The Medical Exam

They did have to fill out more paperwork for the steamship line. They had to get vaccinations, haircuts, and physical exams. There was now a fine of $100 ($2,740 in 2017 dollars) levied against the steamship company for each person who could not pass a medical exam in America. The steamship companies were not taking any chances.

At the physical exam, Nettie was going to have trouble passing as a boy. It was Daniel who came to her rescue with both a bribe and an explanation that Walter was very shy and just could not undress or take the disinfectant shower.

Having second-class tickets gave them much more leeway than if they were traveling steerage class. Steerage passengers had their luggage disinfected with steam, which ruined most of their clothes. They would often be quarantined several days after their vaccinations just to be sure they were not sick.

A Letter to America

All this time gave Nettie the opportunity to write to her sister Rose in New York.

Dear Rose,

I have so much to tell you. First, I am finally coming to America. However, the circumstances are very complicated. My husband, Moshe, was killed in a pogrom in our town, and we think we killed one of the men in the mob. We left town in the middle of the night, and I am with Lena, my mother-in-law; Mama Mary; and three from the Kalish family: Daniel, Abraham, and Anna.

We are traveling as Germans with new names: Schmidt, Peterson, and Schuster. I am Walter Schuster. That's right … I'm posing as a boy, so don't let anyone know until we clear immigration. Our ship is the Pretoria. We sail October 1 from Hamburg and should arrive in New York on October 9. We are second-class passengers. We do not have to go to Ellis Island but will be dropped off, they say, at a pier where the steamship office is, in Hoboken, New Jersey.

Please be there to meet us.

Your loving sister, Nettie

Other ships destined for other ports were leaving with the mail. The mail would reach America before they would. They all studied the 31 questions they might be asked by the immigration officers before boarding the ship: name, age, sex, marital status, occupation, nationality, ability to read and write, and physical and mental health, and they had to show them at least $25 ($685 in 2017 dollars), the minimum for immigration to America.

They could only hope that they were not identified as wanted by the Russian authorities and not allowed to leave, but sent back by the immigration officers as being on the undesirable list. Whenever anyone saw a policeman or army officer, their level of anxiety rose. People were coming from every part of the Pale—some by foot, others by train. Everyone had stories about America, with the streets paved in gold. In America, all religious beliefs were welcome, and the opportunity for education and work was based only on your ability to work hard.

All Aboard the Ship to America

Finally the day arrived that they got to board the ship and see their cabins.

They had three cabins—Lena and Nettie in one, Daniel and Mary in another, and Abraham and his sister, Anna, in the third. Nettie's posing as a boy made her see how differently the men were treated from the women.

Each room had hot and cold running water. They did share a bathroom but had their meals in the dining room—far different from those traveling in steerage.

Steerage class had bunks two high, but they were wide enough for five people. They were divided into three groups: single men in the front of the ship, families in the middle, and single women in the aft section. Each section had a separate entrance from the upper deck. The rooms were large, with 20 to 50 people in each. It was called steerage, as it had been used as a livestock cargo area below the main deck.

USS *Pretoria*, 1897, 561 feet by 62 feet. *Courtesy of Wikipedia*

The area started out clean, but most passengers became seasick, and the smell of vomit never left the area. The steerage area covered the whole width of the ship and was lighted only by the portholes.

The bunks had a "donkey's breakfast"—a mattress filled with straw, a blanket of horse hair, and a life vest for a pillow. There was one bathroom for each section with only cold water, and it was shared by over 100 people.

Most bathrooms stopped working two days into the trip. Most Jewish passengers did not eat the food that was provided by the steamship company. They brought with them herring, as it was kosher and clean. To get away from the smell, steerage passengers would prefer to stay on the deck. The steerage deck was aft of the smokestacks. They had to dodge hot embers and breathe the black smoke from the engines that would envelop this deck, but it was better than the smell in steerage.

The first- and second-class passenger section was much cleaner, as the cabins were above the deck with a better view of the ocean. The deck was free of the effect of the engines and a great place to be on the good days. Nettie's group had to eat unkosher food that was prepared by the ship's cooks. Their group dare not eat any kosher food. It might give them away as being Jewish. Nettie told them that God would understand and that they hadn't gotten this far without His help.

Life on the Ship: Nettie Meets Sam

It was Abraham who had a problem with the food. He first said it was seasickness. Later, he admitted that just the idea of eating *traif* (unkosher food) made him sick. He could have eaten the kosher food, but that would have given them away. He did get by eating some of the kosher food, telling his tablemates that he just wanted to try everything and found the kosher food to be very good. This plan seemed to work for everyone in the group.

It was on the open deck the second day that Nettie met Sam. He said he was traveling with a friend who was in steerage. Sam had lived in the Pale in Buzau, Romania. He was attending school in Budapest. His father was a miller but did not want to leave his hometown. His mother, one sister, and one brother had left for America earlier this year. He stayed to finish the semester at school. The first thing Nettie noticed was Sam's reddish hair and blue eyes.

"Hello," Nettie said, as she approached him.

Sam looked startled. *Who was this Gentile that was talking to a Jew?* "Hello to you," he said, with a Yiddish accent to his German. *Maybe I made my first Gentile friend and I'm not even in America yet,* Sam thought.

Nettie had noticed him alone in the dining room of the ship. Throwing all caution to the wind, she decided to strike up a conversation even though the group thought it best to keep to themselves. Nettie could not be quiet. Sam had been reading his *Emigrant's Interpreter,* the booklet that helped immigrants learn English.

"What's the book you're reading?" Nettie asked Sam.

"The *Emigrant's Interpreter.* I'm trying to learn as much English as I can before we get to New York."

"Maybe we can study together." She sat down next to him in a chair facing toward the ocean, giving them both an ocean view.

"My name is Walter Schuster," said Nettie. The sound of her name seemed foreign, but she had to get used to it. "What's yours?"

"Sam Herskovitz," he replied.

The sound of his name brought back memories of her father, Sam. So much had happened since his death.

"Can you speak Yiddish?" Sam asked.

"Sure, we lived next door to some Jewish people in my hometown. As a little girl, I learned their language. What do you want to do when you get to America, Sam?"

"Go to school to become a doctor. I heard it's a lot easier to get into a school in America than in Romania. My older brother wants to become a lawyer, and my sister a nurse. My mother is already in New York and has a boarding house there. What about you?"

"I have two sisters and two brothers already in America. I want to go to school too. There is so much to learn. I was helping out the doctor in my hometown before we left. I think it's great to help people when they're sick."

It was obvious that Sam and Nettie were about the same age. This helped, as they became best of friends throughout the voyage.

"Let's try to learn some English words, Sam. How about bathrooms, *lades* (ladies) and *zents* (gents)," she said, not knowing that her accent was a Yiddish one.

It was now time for Sam to try a few: "*Von, two, tree*" was his addition to the lesson.

Nettie then tried a phrase: "*Vot's de madder?*"

Sam added,

"*Vill you dansh mit dot feller* (will you dance with the feller)?"

Nettie replied, "*Eshcoosh me* (excuse me), *do vou destan how to dansh* (do you understand how to dance)?"

This was harder than they thought, so they settled for single words.

"*Veenda* (window), *cush* (cash), *sobvay* (subway), and *shpeak* (speak)," were Sam's additional words.

Nettie decided to change the subject when she said, "I understand if you can't speak English very well, they call you a *greenhornish* (greenhorn)."

"I guess we have a lot of work to do. I don't want to be called green," Sam said.

They both laughed.

Mama Mary Finds a Rabbi

Nettie was not the only one making friends. Mother Mary was chatting it up with a widowed rabbi who was also traveling in second class. Benjamin Rabinowitz had lost his wife to cancer this past year. He felt it was time to emigrate to America. He was from a little town in Lithuania and had secured a position as rabbi in a synagogue in New York City. He was a tall man in his early 50s with a full head of white hair; his beard was tinged with white streaks. He was a little overweight, but the twinkle in his eyes and his friendly smile were his weapons against all the injustice he found in the world. He was immediately attracted to Mary. Her stiff posture and apparent cold nature seemed to pose a challenge to the friendly rabbi. He felt everyone was God's child and had a good soul. *It will be a challenge to show this German lady who probably looks down on Jews that we're not all that bad.*

"May I ask your name, madam?" He sat down next to her in the dining room.

Quite startled and remembering their plan to speak German and not reveal their identities, she quickly said, "Bertha," in a brisk tone still, looking down at the food in front of her.

"Happy to make your acquaintance. I'm Benjamin Rabinowitz, on my way to New York where I have a job as a rabbi."

All this was said in Yiddish. Without thinking, she answered him in Yiddish, much to the concern of Daniel, who was sitting next to her. "We are also going to New York. This is my son Otto."

The rabbi extended his hand to Daniel in front of Mary, and they shook hands. The rabbi began, "It's been a long trip getting to the ship. I recently lost my wife, so it's a bit lonely for me. I would very much like to be your friend during this voyage. How did you learn to speak such perfect Yiddish?"

"We lived next door to a Jewish family that was very good to us, and we learned from them." This was the same explanation Nettie used when talking to Sam, and they hadn't even rehearsed it.

"Wonderful," said Benjamin. "Speaking Yiddish will be so much easier for me."

All this talking made Daniel very nervous. *Will our identities be found out by talking to strangers?* He was worried, but this would turn out to be a minor concern. It would be Nettie who would cause him the greatest worry.

Sickness on Board the Ship

It was two days into the voyage when Sam said to Nettie, "My friend from school, Sol Goldenstein, is traveling in steerage."

Nettie was at first taken aback by the similarity to her name. (She was now a Goldstein.) She asked Sam for the name again just to be sure she heard him correctly.

"I wonder if we can go down to see him. I know that they don't let the steerage passengers up here, but what about us going down there? They have a sentry at the top of the stairs. Surely they would let us go down to steerage."

This was not to be the case, as every means of access to the upper deck was guarded. The sentry had orders that no one but the crew could go down to steerage: a perfect challenge to two inquisitive teenage immigrants.

That night, Nettie talked with Anna about going with them to the steerage area.

"There you go again, Nettie, Don't you know what a risk you are taking for yourself and the rest of us?"

"What do you mean, Anna? What harm would it do to outsmart the guards and see the steerage area and find Sam's friend?"

"If you get caught or get into trouble, you could expose all of us. Please don't go, Nettie."

Nettie just had to see what was going on in steerage. The next day, the plan was hatched as Nettie and Sam sat together at the midday meal. "Sam, let's take some food from our dining room to your friend. I know the food must be awful down there. We can watch the sentry. When he leaves his post, we will be ready to go down the stairs to the lower deck. Let's get in one of the lifeboats so we can watch him."

The two had saved some food from lunch and wrapped it in napkins. They found the closest lifeboat to one of the stairs going down to the lower deck. They lifted the corner of the canvas cover and slipped inside, leaving just a little corner open for them to see the sentry.

Another adventure, thought Nettie. *Sam is so much fun.*

Within minutes, they had their chance, as the sentry left his post.

"*Mach shnel* (hurry up)," whispered Sam.

The two of them clamored down the stairs, taking two at a time. Once on the lower deck, the fetid odor of vomit wafted up through the hatches from the steerage areas. Many passengers were on the deck breathing the fresh salt air, even though it was mixed at times with the black smoke from the smokestacks. Most travelers were recovering from their seasickness. Many had anticipated the problem and brought with them preventive remedies: apples, patent medicine, lime drops, and even raw onions. None of them worked.

Moving to the forward deck, the two of them looked for Sol in the men's area. When they couldn't find him on the deck, they found the stairs leading below deck. The men's area was poorly lit with the half-light coming in through the portholes. The stagnant smell of too many bodies, vomit, and no ventilation was almost overwhelming to both of them.

Sam called out, "Sol Goldenstein?"

A faint answer came from the other side of the cabin: "I'm over here. Is that you, Sam?"

There they found Sol on a bottom bunk doubled over in apparent pain. He was a very thin boy with a sallow complexion. Nettie was not sure if it was the light or his illness that made him look so pale.

"What's the problem, Sol? Seasickness?" Sam asked.

"Oh, the pain is terrible. I thought it was seasickness, but it's getting worse and won't let up," Sol replied.

"Have you called for the doctor?"

"Yes, but he says there is nothing he can do but give vaccinations."

"Sol, this is Walter Schuster. We brought you some food from our dining room. Can you eat anything?"

"No, but thank goodness you are here. No one will help me."

Nettie was thinking, back to the time when she was working with her town doctor. "Where does it hurt, Sol?" she asked.

"Right here." Sol pointed to his bellybutton. "The pain goes from here down my right side."

Nettie also noticed his stomach was swollen. She held her hand to his forehead. It was hot with fever. "Sam, I think he has what my doctor called appendicitis. Sol, have you ever had an operation on your appendix?"

"No. Is that what you think is my problem?"

"I don't know, but we will get the doctor down here to help you. Right, Sam?"

"Yes," Sam replied. "Is there anything you need before we go find the doctor?"

"Just get him here quick," Sol pleaded.

The Ship's Doctor

Off the two of them went, now on a mission to help Sol.

"How bad can it be?" Sam asked Nettie.

"If his appendix bursts, it could kill him. I don't know if that's the problem, but if it is, he will never make it to New York. We have six more days at sea."

Getting back to the upper deck was not as easy as getting down was. The sentry just would not leave his post. Because of the emergency, they took the chance and went up the stairs.

"Where do you two think you are going? Get back down in steerage where you belong," he ordered.

Nettie stood at her full height and said, "There's a passenger down here that is very sick. We're on our way to get the doctor."

"I've heard that excuse before. Everybody is sick down there, and that is where you two are going." The sentry stared down at them.

"Oh no, we're not," piped up Sam. "My friend may be dying, and we are going to get help."

The guard was getting a little perturbed by these two unruly teenagers and decided to teach them a lesson. "It's up here you want to go? Then come with me. We're going to see the captain." With that, he grabbed them both by their collars and pulled them up the top three stairs. Then he took them to the quartermaster's deck. This was fine with Nettie, as she knew the captain of the ship had the power to make all the decisions—even life and death.

The sentry knocked on the captain's door. The first mate who was with the captain answered the knock and asked, "What's the problem, sailor?"

"I've got two kids here that were trying to get out of steerage. They say their friend is sick."

From the back of the cabin, they heard a voice say, "Let them in."

With a little shove, the sailor pushed them through the door, which closed behind them. The cabin was dimly lit with a light swaying over a table in the center of the room where a map was placed. On one side of the table was a middle-aged man with a white beard and eyes that seems to reflect the light. In his mouth was a pipe that was unlit. He held it as if he was smoking.

"What's this all about? You have a friend that is seasick?"

"No sir." Nettie was feeling like she was back at the *yeshiva*, posing as a boy and answering questions from the rabbi. "We think he has appendicitis."

"Everyone is seasick their first two days. What makes you so sure its appendicitis?"

"I used to work for a doctor, and Sol seems to have all the right symptoms."

"Has the ship's doctor seen him?"

It was Sam's turn now to answer: "He has, sir, but said he couldn't do anything. We were on our way to find him when the sentry brought us here to you."

The captain seemed impressed with the sincerity of these two boys to help their friend. He turned to the first mate. "Bring the doctor in here." The captain didn't know much about his new senior medical officer, but he did know he was somehow connected with the owners of the steamship line.

Off went the first mate. When the door closed, the captain said, "Sit down, boys, and tell me where you are from and how you know this boy that is sick."

Nettie was feeling comfortable now so lapsed into her talkative self, not letting Sam get a word in. "I'm from Germany, and Sam is from Romania. He went to school with Sol, the boy that's sick, but we are both traveling in second class. We waited till the guard was off his post and went down to check on Sol."

Just then, the door opened. In came the first mate with the doctor. Dr. Zimmer was not much taller than the two of them. He was clean-shaven with blond hair. He looked about the age of Nettie's late husband, Moshe. Dr. Karl Zimmer was the last and eighth child of his father, a wealthy banker in Germany. Karl was a bit of a playboy, and his father had sent him off to England to apprentice to become a surgeon. (In the late 1800s, physicians were university-educated, but a surgeon needed only to find another surgeon willing to train him.) After Karl passed his exam with the help of his father's purse, he came back to Germany and continued his irresponsible behavior. His father then contacted Adolph Hallie, a banker who helped start the Hamburg American Steamship line. He had Karl installed as the ship's doctor on the *Pretoria*.

What a way to see the world, thought Karl, *and have easy access to the ship's liquor supply.*

Karl had a frightened look on his face as he faced the captain. Did the captain know he had been drinking?

"Do you know anything about a boy in steerage that is sick?" asked the captain.

"There're lots of them with seasickness, Captain."

"These boys say their friend has something called appendicitis. What do you know about appendicitis?"

"Not that much, except that there's a surgery that can remove it when it swells up and causes severe pain."

Nettie couldn't keep quiet. "If it bursts, Sol can die. We can't let that happen, Captain." The tone of her voice seemed to catch the captain off guard.

"Bring the boy up to the infirmary, Doctor, and let's see what you can do. We have six more days before we reach New York and a hospital."

The look of relief that washed over both Nettie's and Sam's faces was obvious to the captain. They had made a friend who could help Sol.

"It's almost time for supper. You two go back down to your deck. You can visit your friend later in the infirmary," said the captain.

Nettie's Actions Worry the Group

The two of them left the captain's quarters and headed back to their cabins to get ready for supper. When Nettie entered her cabin, she had a welcoming committee: Daniel, Rose, Anna, Abraham, and Lena. Daniel was the first to speak: "Where have you been all afternoon, Nettie? We were worried about you."

"Sam and I had the most interesting time. We tricked the guard and went down to the steerage deck to check on Sam's friend, Sol. It looks like Sol is really sick. When we were trying to find the doctor, the guard caught us and took us to Captain Smith's cabin. It was really beautiful with fine furniture and …"

Mary cut her short: "Do you realize what you have done? You have put all our lives in jeopardy. Someone could have found out you're a woman in disguise and then the whole story would come out. They would send us all back, and who knows what would happen to us? What did you tell them?"

"Nothing. Hardly anything. We just wanted to help Sol. I think he has appendicitis."

Daniel was holding back his rage, as he knew it would do no good to threaten Nettie. She was a free spirit but didn't and couldn't gauge her actions, especially when they meant helping someone.

"Please try to keep a lower profile, especially around the crew and captain," cautioned Daniel.

"I promise, everyone, I will be extra careful," Nettie said.

Anna knew it was just words, and Abraham remembered how he got into trouble trusting her when she went to his school dressed as a boy. Lena was none too sure about her daughter-in-law, but all pledged to be more careful. Nettie reminded Mary that her friendship with Rabbi Rabinowitz could be just as dangerous. They all left the room, one at a time, so other passengers would not connect the group together.

Dinner at the Captain's Table

At dinner, they took their respective places. Nettie looked around for Sam. He was nowhere in sight. To their horror, Captain Smith came over to Nettie and her mother-in-law Lena and invited them to sit at the captain's table. Daniel gave a stern look to Nettie. Anna was so nervous, she dropped her fork on the floor. Abraham thought he might throw up, and it wasn't caused by eating non-Kosher food. He excused himself from the table but returned later. Mary was too busy talking to Rabbi Rabinowitz to notice what was happening. When she did look up, she saw Nettie and Lena with the captain. She averted her eyes so as not to bring the rabbi's attention to what was happening.

When they were seated at the captain's table, the captain said, "Mrs. Schuster, you must be very proud of your son. I think he has saved a life on my ship today." He said this with a smile. The ends of his white mustache curled upward.

"How is Sol now?" Nettie asked.

"He's in the infirmary," said the Captain, "resting much better I hope. The doctor administered a compound. He thinks it's just constipation. You can visit him tomorrow."

"What a relief," said Lena.

"Walter is always helping people, so it's no wonder that he got involved."

"Where's your friend, Sam?" asked the captain.

"I don't know, but I'll check after supper," replied Nettie.

The first mate approached their table and whispered something in Captain Smith's ear. Then he said, "Schuster family, I must go to the bridge—something about weather. Enjoy your meal."

To everyone's relief, he left with no more questions. Daniel looked over and also breathed a sigh of relief. After dinner, Nettie went to Sam's cabin and knocked on the door. "Are you all right, Sam?" she asked, talking through the door.

"Come on in," was the faint reply. As she opened the door, she found Sam lying on the bed with a glass of milk beside him.

"What's the matter, Sam? I hope you don't have what Sol has," said Nettie.

"No, it's just my stomach, I get these attacks once in a while. After I drink some milk, they seem to go away. Maybe it was too much excitement this afternoon. Thanks for checking on me, I'll be OK in the morning," replied Sam.

"Did I tell you the captain invited mother and me over to his table? He said the doctor thinks Sol has constipation, and then he had to leave—something about the weather," Nettie added.

"That sounds better for Sol. Let's check on him tomorrow," Sam weakly replied.

Nettie wanted to stay and comfort Sam but knew it was the wrong thing to do. After all, she was supposed to be acting like a boy.

The Third Day at Sea

That night, the ship pitched and rolled like a wagon hitting ruts in the road and then bouncing out of them, only to hit another rut. *This must have been the bad weather the captain was informed of last night at dinner*, thought Nettie.

The seas were high, and occasionally a wave would break across the bow as the ship pitched downward into the valley made by the waves. Sheets of rain were hitting the porthole window of their cabin and woke Nettie and Lena. A knock on their cabin door was a crew member who advised them to be careful and not go out on the deck. "Stay in your cabin as much as you can. The captain says we are in the path of a hurricane, and things won't get much better for a few days."

The ship's top speed was 13 knots. Even with its twin screws turning at full speed, it felt at times the ship was going backward. The captain maneuvered the ship directly into the waves and headwind. This was the remnants of a hurricane that had gone up the east coast of America. It then headed out across the Atlantic as it dissipated in the cooler waters. For those passengers who had just recovered from their seasickness, the rolling of the ship was surely a test for their stomachs they did not want.

Nettie was on a mission today. She had to check on Sam, and together they had to check on Sol in the infirmary. She dressed and covered herself with a yellow windbreaker made out of oilcloth, then made her way to the dining room. It was nearly empty. There, sitting alone at a far table, was Sam. What a relief. He seemed to be better, and when he saw her, he waved her over.

"Feeling better, Sam?" Nettie asked.

"Yes, much better today. My stomach pain is gone," said Sam, placing a hand on his stomach.

"I can't believe you're eating on this rolling ship," said Nettie as she sat down next to Sam.

Just then, his glass of milk slid down the table. Nettie stopped its slide and handed it to him.

"When do you want to go to the infirmary to see Sol?" Sam asked.

"I'm ready whenever you are," Nettie replied.

Sam finished what he could of his breakfast, as his plate seemed to have a mind of its own with every roll of the ship. The two of them ate off the same plate. One held it while the other took a few mouthfuls of food. The other diners were having similar problems keeping their food on the table and not the floor.

"Ready to go," announced Sam, as he rose just a bit unsteady on his feet. "We have to go up a deck to the infirmary. It's on the aft part of the ship."

As they left the dining room, a gust of wind ripped the door out of Sam's hand and it slammed against the wall of the dining room.

"Hold on, Walter," Sam hollered over the sound of the wind. "This is going to be a wet and windy trip."

Nettie found his hand, and together they moved toward the metal stairs that led to the upper deck. Sam started up the ladder first, with Nettie close behind him.

Occasionally, the wind pushed them into each other. Nettie wasn't sure if Sam felt the softness of her bound breasts as he fell back against her. She really didn't have time to worry. It was all they could do to get up the stairs fighting the wind, rain, and pitching ship. Creeping along the cabin wall holding on to whatever they could, they finally got to the door of the infirmary. Opening it on the pitching ship was all the two of them could handle. Bang! The door slammed shut behind them. Each looked down at their hands to check for any missing fingers.

In the Ship's Infirmary

They found themselves in a waiting room area staffed by one of the medical personal. The area beyond the waiting area was divided into two separate clinics. One was for the men; the other for the women. Each had about 20 beds.

"We're here to see Sol Goldenstein," they said in unison. The orderly motioned to the door that said *Men's Clinic*. As they entered the room, they saw the beds bolted to the floor, with curtains separating the beds, hanging and swaying from the ceiling. There, at the end of one row of beds, was Sol, not looking much better than he had when they found him in steerage. Sitting next to his bed was Dr. Zimmer with a bottle of liquor in his hand, its contents down to the halfway mark.

"Well, look who just dropped in, Sol? Your friends," he said with a slur that could only be the result of the liquor he had consumed. For each patient brought to the infirmary, he had to write a lengthy report and have it ready for the port authority upon arrival in New York. He was never looking for more work, and these boys were not making his job easier.

Sol opened his eyes to see his friends. In a very weak voice, he said, "Thank you for helping me. I hope they will still let me into America."

"Is the pain any better since you got to the infirmary?" asked Sam.

"No, the doctor gave me some cocaine, but I threw it up," Sol said.

Sam and Nettie looked down at Sol's stomach and saw where he pointed to the area of pain. It was on the lower right side of his belly button. They could both see a swelling.

"Doctor, have you ruled out constipation?" asked Nettie.

"Yeah, I think you kids were right. It's appendicitis," he said.

"Have you done that operation before?" inquired Nettie.

"No, I saw one once, but it was not on a ship going through a hurricane."

"How long before you think you can do it?" Nettie asked.

"The captain says it will be two more days before we get through this stuff; it will put us behind schedule getting into New York.[1] He really needs this done in a hospital, not on a ship, but I don't think he can hold out that long. I don't have anyone here who has seen this operation, so I'm counting on you two to help me."

He looked directly at Nettie, who had told the captain she worked for a doctor who had done the operation. That wasn't *quite* right. She had worked with a doctor who sent patients with this problem to another city for the operation. If it meant saving Sol's life, she would do it—and Sam would help too.

"OK, I just hope it doesn't burst before we have a chance to get it out," the doctor said.

---

1   Ships at this time did not have any way to communicate with shore—only with ships in the area that were visible. There was no telegraph, but they could use flags to pass information to and from passing ships. Weather conditions were the most important information, but medical problems could also be relayed to other ships.

The two of them then devised a plan to stay with Sol and rotate with each other until the time of surgery. If it did burst, the doctor would have to operate to put a drain in the area to get as much of the infection out of his body as possible. Sam would take the first watch, Nettie would relieve him later. She had to go back to her room to check on the others and the storm. When Nettie got back to her room, she had another welcoming committee. Everyone was there, and they wanted to know what she had been doing. She told them about Sol at the infirmary and that they planned an operation as soon as the ship was through the storm and in calmer water.

Daniel was the first to speak: "Nettie, you know how sensitive our situation is. If anyone finds out you're not a boy, everything is lost. What if you have to undress to get into some surgical gown for the operation? I want you to be prepared for anything that might happen. All of our lives depend on you."

"I'll be careful, Daniel, but I can't let this boy die. He and Sam are depending on me too."

With that, the group left the cabin, one at a time—some going to the dining hall, others to their cabins. The next two days seemed to drag by. Sam and Nettie took turns staying with Sol. On the fifth day out to sea, still five days from New York, the storm had abated and the seas became calmer. It was time to do Sol's surgery.

The Surgery

Sam had just finished his shift and told Nettie that the doctor was planning the surgery after the noon meal. Nettie thought, *I'm not sure I should eat anything, as the first sight of the incision might make me vomit or pass out.* She just had some water. They both went back to the infirmary, and Dr. Zimmer seemed a little on edge. Nettie moved closer to him to smell his breath. The last thing she wanted was a drunken doctor doing the surgery. To her relief, she smelled no liquor.

The medical staff had gowns ready for Nettie and Sam and tied them in the back over their clothes. Then they had them do a thorough washing of their hands before they entered the makeshift surgery area. All was ready. Even Sol seemed relieved that something was going to happen to help him with his pain. They put a strap around his chest and one around his legs. Each arm was then strapped to the table. Dr. Zimmer's assistant placed a mask over Sol's face to apply the ether, one drip at a time. The area around the swelling of his appendix was draped off and disinfected. All of Dr. Zimmer's instruments were soaked in disinfectant solution.[2] The first stage of anesthesia was the loss of consciousness. The second stage was the excitement stage and the reason for the leather straps to control his spastic movements. The third stage showed slower respiration and heartbeat. Eye movement slowed, then stopped, and Sol was now ready for his surgery. Dr. Zimmer picked up his scalpel and made the first incision directly over the mass that was protruding from the abdomen. Nettie and Sam were standing side by side with towels and gauze to clean away the blood or pus that came from the wound as he cut deeper into the abdominal wall. Nettie felt a bit dizzy and leaned against Sam. She wasn't sure if it was the bleeding or a whiff or two of the ether. Sam didn't look too steady himself. Dr. Zimmer carefully separated the external oblique aponeurosis as well as the internal oblique muscle. Just then, part of the appendix popped up through the opening he had created in the abdominal wall.

This made it easy for him to suture the base of the appendix where it protruded from the large intestine before cutting it free. Just as it was cut free and the doctor lifted it out with his forceps, it burst. Pus went everywhere, soaking the drapes around the open wound. Quickly Sam and Nettie added alcohol and carbolic acid to their cloths and gauze and tried to clean the area.

"This was too close to a rupture," Dr. Zimmer said in a monotone. He was already closing the incision one layer at a time until he was doing the final stitches.

"Was this like the operations you had seen when you were working for your doctor, Walter?"

"Oh yes, but you did it much faster," answered Nettie.

As Sol was coming out of the anesthetic, he was given morphine for the pain. Sol was a bit out of it, but he knew the operation was over.

---

2   The surgeon on an immigrant ship had to deal with flu, diarrhea, constipation, and lice. At times, there would be outbreaks of measles, diphtheria, smallpox, or whooping cough. He also attended births and deaths and had to oversee the stores and daily food rations and routines to keep the ship clean. The ship's surgeon would have to supply his own instruments. Dr. Zimmer, having been trained in England, was well aware of both ether and chloroform, which had been used by Queen Victoria to ease the pain of childbirth. Both drugs had their good and bad points. Ether was very flammable but safer for the patient. Chloroform was quicker but had a better chance of killing the patient by a poorly trained assistant improperly applying the anesthetic.

"Will they let me into America now that I don't have an appendix?" he asked. Everyone started to laugh, including Dr. Zimmer. "They don't check you for parts. I think you will pass the test," he said.

The next days were critical ones, as the chance of infection was very high.[3]

"He will spend the rest of the voyage here in the infirmary. We will transport him to the hospital when we get to New York. Lucky for him, he will skip Battery Park[4] and disembark in New Jersey with the first- and second-class passengers.

The rest of the trip was uneventful. The weather cleared and the ship seemed to make up the time it lost as it went through the hurricane. It had been thrown off course by the storm. The eight-day voyage turned into ten. The little group relaxed a bit now that Nettie had calmed down and was not getting into any more trouble. Sol continued to heal but did have bouts of fever from time to time. Nettie's mother, Mary, known on the ship as Bertha Schmidt, was spending most of her time in the company of Rabbi Rabinowitz. This seemed to bother Daniel, but there was little he could do about it. The rabbi was impressed with Bertha, as she understood the Sabbath service. She said she used to attend her neighbors' on Sabbath night. Anna came out of her shell a bit. All this talk of getting caught and being sent to prison was a depressing thought that haunted her. She now hung out with Nettie and Sam.

---

3   Infection was the greatest concern for surgery in the 1800s, as the first antibiotic was not invented until 1911. In England, Dr. Joseph Lister, a renowned British surgeon, had championed the use of a "clean" surgery room using carbolic acid as a disinfectant for both the instruments and the wound. This technique greatly increased the success of surgery. He assisted in operating on the appendix of King Edward VII just days before his coronation in 1901.

4   In June of 1897, the buildings at Ellis Island burned to the ground. It would not reopen until 1900. Steerage passengers would be offloaded at the steamship company's dock and loaded onto barges to go through immigration at Battery Park. This immigration station took the place of Castle Garden until Ellis Island was ready. Battery Park was located on the most southern tip of Manhattan. When the immigrants arrived, they were put through a three- to four-hour medical exam. Each immigrant was accompanied by an interpreter when passing by the doctors. The doctor had a piece of white chalk to mark on the immigrants' coats for further inspection. The eye doctors were looking for trachoma, which could cause blindness and death. The doctors used a button hook under the eyelid to look under it. An infection meant deportation.

Laughing and talking made everything much better. They were still two days out from New York. That night there was a full moon. Its magic brought everyone out on deck to watch it rise and see its reflection dance on the water.

Nettie moved closer to Sam as they leaned against the rail of the ship. *How I would like to let him know I'm a woman,* she thought.

Anna was on his right side and said, "Sam, is it true what that say about the moon?"

"What do you mean?" asked Sam.

"Well, being from Romania you must have heard about werewolves and the full moon," added Anna.

Nettie didn't like the direction of this talk. *Anna is getting too much of Sam's attention. She's now flirting with him, and that's my area. Oh, how I wish I could show him I'm a woman.* Mary and the rabbi were also on the rail and much closer together than ever. The moon was having its effect. Nettie felt left out.

Arriving in New York City, October 11, 1897

It was the morning of October 11 when the *Pretoria* anchored outside New York in the harbor. There they anchored and waited for the port authorities to board and medical personnel to give them clearance to enter the inner harbor. The cutter soon arrived, and the authorities came aboard. Dr. Zimmer was there to answer questions from the medical officer about any communicable diseases that he was treating in the infirmary. This is when the first- and second-class passengers would get their medical interrogations, which consisted of only a few questions. Everyone in their group passed.

With the all clear, the authorities returned to their cutter, and the tugboats came alongside to escort the ship into the inner harbor. With little puffs of white smoke coming from their stacks, they looked like toy boats alongside the larger *Pretoria*. As the ship began its move into the harbor, everyone was on deck straining to see through the fog that hung over the harbor.

Sam, Nettie, and Anna were on deck to see Lady Liberty, her torch held high, rising above the fog that had settled around her waist. It was an uplifting sight to all on the ship.

"This is like a dream," Nettie said, "I can't believe we made it. The *Golde Madina* (the golden country). I can't wait to see if the streets are really paved with gold."

"Don't believe everything you hear," Sam whispered in her ear.

"I can't wait to see my mother," said Sam. "She runs a boarding house in Manhattan." Nettie answered, "My sister is supposed to meet us. They live in Manhattan too."

As they neared Ellis Island, the fog seemed to lift and they could see the damage that the fire of June 14 had caused. Everything had been burned to the ground.[5] They were standing near the bow of the *Pretoria* and could see both sides of the harbor. The tugs were guiding the *Pretoria* toward the mouth of the Hudson River, passing Governors Island and the East River.

"Look to right," Anna said as she pointed up the East River. "There's the Brooklyn Bridge."[6]

"That must be Manhattan. All I see are buildings and chimneys," shouted Nettie over the blast of the ship's horns. They approached the company pier at Hoboken, New Jersey.

After the *Pretoria* docked, a barge came alongside the ship and the steerage passengers were offloaded, as was their baggage. Dr. Zimmer had the crew separate the luggage for all the infirmary patients and put them on a special barge for the trip to the Battery. It would be an easier trip to the hospital from the immigration depot at the Battery. They would already be in Manhattan. A transformation seemed to come over Dr. Zimmer since the surgery on Sol. They had not seen him with a bottle the rest of the trip. He was much friendlier to the boys every time they saw him. He looked so much more confident.

Sol Leaves the Ship

Nettie and Sam caught up to Sol as he was being carried from the ship to the barge. "What hospital are they taking you to?" they asked in unison.

"The doctor said Bellevue. It's in Manhattan. He wants to make sure I don't have any infection and said the steamship line will pay my bill. He's going with all of us to the hospital."

Sam got Sol's contact information from his uncle. "I'll get in touch with your Uncle when we get settled and find out how you're doing in the hospital," said Sam.

"That will be great. I can't wait to see you both when I'm up and walking again," Sol said.

---

5   The buildings were built with Georgia pine, not brick. Ellis Island would not reopen until December 1900, but with fireproof brick buildings. The steerage passengers would now go through immigration at the barge office. It was located at the most southern tip of Manhattan.

6   When completed in 1883, the Brooklyn Bridge was the longest suspension bridge in the world: 1,595 feet wide, with towers 276 feet above the water.

Nettie's Group Leaves the Ship

Once the steerage passengers and their baggage were offloaded, immigration officers boarded the ship. Everyone lined up and had their papers ready. The first- and second-class passengers were hardly given a second look by the immigration officials, much to Daniel's relief. These were the passengers with money and usually were well connected to family in the states. There would be no paupers or beggars in this group.

As they walked down the gangplank, Nettie strained her eyes looking for her sister, Rose. Mama saw her first. She was holding a baby in her arms. This was Mama's third grandchild, William. Rose was wearing the latest of fashions with an hourglass waist and puffy sleeves. On her head was a hat with ostrich plumes. As they came down the gangplank, the group surrounded Rose, her husband, and her baby with hugs and kisses.

Rabbi Rabinowitz was with the group, and with the chatter of Yiddish, it became obvious to him that Mama Mary (Bertha Schmidt, as he knew her), must be Jewish.

Ambulance to Belleview Hospital, New York City, 1897. *Courtesy of Wikipedia*

"Yes, it's true," Mary told him. "It's a long story, and I now will have time to tell it to you. Please come with us to Manhattan, and then you can find your congregation." A little bewildered and confused, he accepted the invitation.

Lena found her daughter Lyora and her husband as well as Lena's first grandchild in the crowd. The boys, Daniel and Abraham, stayed close to Nettie's family as Nettie and Anna excused themselves and went into the ladies' toilet at the steamship office.

"I can't wait to remove these chest bindings and be able to breathe. Six weeks was long enough to be a boy." Nettie took off her hat, fluffed up her hair a bit, and unbuttoned the top two buttons on her shirt.

"You're not going out there like that, are you, Nettie?" said Anna.

"What do you mean?" replied Nettie.

"I mean with your hair uncovered and your shirt unbuttoned." Anna was shocked.

"Just watch me, Anna. I'm in America now, not in Lithuania. I'm free of all those old customs once and for all. I wonder what Sam is going to think."

"Let's find the luggage and Sam," suggested Nettie.

Out they went to the luggage platform. It wasn't long until they saw Sam's reddish hair bobbing among all the others.

"There he is," Anna pointed down from their perch on the baggage platform.

Nettie dropped down into the crowd and worked her way directly behind Sam, tapping him on the shoulder. As he turned, she said, "Remember me? Walter?"

Sam couldn't believe his eyes. This was no Walter—not with all those curves. "What happened to Walter?" Sam said with a smile on his face.

"I left Walter in the ladies' toilet. I'm Nettie, and I'm not from Germany. I'm from Lithuania, and I'm Jewish too." She then grabbed Sam and kissed him on the lips, pressing her whole body against his. In the melee of the luggage confusion, no one else seemed to notice, but Sam sure did.

Nettie confessed, "I've been wanting to kiss you all during the time we were on the ship. I hope I didn't startle you." Well, she did, and Sam was speechless. No woman would ever kiss someone in public like this. She certainly was different.

He got his baggage and found his mother, Pearl, who went by the name Pepe. His brother Marcus and sister Ettie were with her. Ettie was really Sam's first cousin. Ettie's mother was Pauline Kohn who died during her birth. Pepe and Pauline were sisters. Pepe brought Ettie into the Herskovitz family and raised her like a daughter. It was easier for Ettie to use the Herskovitz name than her birth name, Sibalis. Ettie was almost 3 years older than Sam.

"Mom, I would like you to meet, uh, uh, Nettie, I think."

"Pleased to meet you, Nettie. Are you going to Manhattan?"

"Yes, my sister and her husband are here, so I guess we will all be crossing the river together." There was a ferry landing next to the steamship pier at Hoboken, ready to take the new immigrants across the Hudson River to Manhattan.

Nettie's brother-in-law, Philip, and Sam moved into the group. "It's time to move the party along, *mach shnel* (let's get going.) Let's get everyone to the ferry. I have a special treat for you on the other side."

Just then, a man stood up on the baggage platform. He was wearing a very official-looking uniform and holding a megaphone to his mouth. He announced, in both English and German, "Would Walter Shuster please report to the immigration office inside the Hamburg Steamship Building."

LEFT: Rose and Philip Cohn. *Courtesy of the Ann Cohn Mitnick collection*
RIGHT: Pearl "Pepe" Herskovitz, 1902. *Courtesy of Louise Walsh*

Nettie looked at Anna. Anna looked at Nettie. A look of fear crossed Anna's face. Daniel broke away from the family and came up to the two of them. He had not seen Nettie out of her disguise, and a look came over him as well. "What do you think they want?" was his first question.

"Did anything seem out of the ordinary when you were asked questions by the immigration officer on the ship?"

"No, Daniel, everything went smoothly—not a hint of a problem."

"Did anyone see you change in the toilet besides Anna?" Daniel asked.

"I don't think so, but I just couldn't stand the wraps anymore." That was really a lie. She wanted to show Sam she was a woman before she lost him to New York.

"OK, then, it's too late for you to change back to Walter. Let's hope no one in Hamburg figured all this out and then telegraphed Immigration before we got here. I don't think Immigration could work this fast, even if someone on the ship knew about your disguise. Sure hope Dr. Zimmer didn't notice you were not a boy."

"Oh, Daniel," Nettie said, "you worry too much. I promise whatever they ask me, I will never say I knew you or anyone else before we got on the ship. You and your family have done so much for me. I would never betray you."

Once again, the man with the megaphone was asking for Walter Shuster. Nettie approached the platform by herself, looked up, and said, "I can help you find Walter Shuster. Where should he go?"

"Just have him go to the door at the end of this building, Miss."

Nettie moved out of the crowd of baggage seekers and found the door to the steamship office. There was no way she could pass for Walter now. How stupid to throw everything away just to impress a man. Why hadn't she waited? When she entered the building, there was a sign over a corner office that said Immigration. She opened the door. There sat an officer in his mid-20s, very well groomed, with a handlebar mustache. The nameplate on the desk read "Gustaf Klien."

In perfect German, he said, "I can see you're not Walter Schuster," giving her a broad smile and a wink.

Nettie could feel his eyes moving over her body, coming to rest on the cleavage of her bosom. "That's right, officer. I'm his sister. How can I help you?"

"He must have dropped his Immigration papers. Someone found them in the ladies' toilet and brought them to me. He may need them in the future."

Nettie could tell he understood what was going on. Her pants were not those of a girl. Neither was her blouse. *But why was he overlooking the situation?*

"Thank you very much, officer, I will take them to him."

"I didn't catch your name, Miss," Gustaf said.

"It's Hilda Schuster," said Nettie.

"Where will you be staying in New York? I would like to show you the town." Nettie now knew why he was letting this issue slide. Things were now on her terms.

"We haven't settled on a spot yet, but give me your address. When I get settled, I will send you a note and you can show me the town."

This was such unusual behavior for a woman, and it took him completely off

LEFT: Ettie Herskovitz Hillel, 1902. *Courtesy of Louise Walsh*
RIGHT: Marcus Herskovitz, 1902. *Courtesy of Louise Walsh*

guard. A big smile crossed his face as he wrote his address. Nettie breathed a sigh of relief. He handed her both Walter's immigration papers and his name and address. *Did he really know?* thought Nettie. *I think he did, but the lure of things to come was too great for him to take any action.*

Nettie took the papers and tucked his note into her bosom. "I'll keep this close to my heart," she said, and then held out her hand. He held her hand in his as he kissed it.

"Hope to see you soon, Hilda," Gustaf said.

With that, Nettie smiled, turned, and left the office.

If I can get the attention of a man with only these clothes of a boy, just what could I do dressed as a woman?

As she emerged from the office, she could see the family huddled in a group. She approached them and said, "OK, everyone, it's off to Manhattan."

Anna looked a mess. She didn't know if she should laugh or cry.

Nettie knew Daniel needed an explanation. Looking at him, she said, "Walter dropped his immigration papers in the ladies' toilet. Someone found them and turned them in to Immigration. Hilda, his sister, picked them up."

Daniel knew right away that not many men could keep up with Nettie's level of deception. So now it was Hilda. He shook his head. How does she do it?

"OK, everyone, let's see the treat that Philip has planned for us."

CHAPTER 3

New York City and Life in America

Nettie looked over the Hudson River at Manhattan on the other side. She couldn't believe how many buildings she was seeing. These buildings were as tightly packed as trees in a forest. This place was nothing like the dreary old country she came from. Everything was alive and seemed to be moving all at once.

With all the commotion, they almost forgot to go to the money exchange before they took the ferry to Manhattan. They were in luck. They had only German gold marks, each of which was worth 25 cents. The paper marks were worth almost nothing. Nettie made sure everyone had enough money. She kept the precious stones to sell later if needed.

Daniel and Abraham promised to pay her back, but Nettie said, "The money is yours. You helped me escape to freedom. I feel I owe you more."

With that done, it was off to the ferry and the ride to Manhattan. Crossing the Hudson, they told everyone about Sol's appendix operation on the ship and what a

Electric taxi, New York City, 1897. *Courtesy of Wikipedia*

close call he'd had. No one mentioned a word about why they changed their names and why Nettie was traveling as a boy. The fact that they had so little luggage was also a question that needed an answer. The explanation would come later. Her sister Rose knew a little of the story. Nettie had written her a letter from Germany. The details would have to wait.

Rabbi Rabinowitz was still in shock from finding that Mama Mary was Jewish. Now the woman he had fallen in love with on the ship was truly marriage material.

When everyone got off the ferry, they said goodbye to Sam and his family. Nettie kissed him on the cheek this time and promised to keep in touch. Addresses were exchanged, and then Sam and his mother and brother were off to Allen Street. Lena went with her daughter's family to another address on the Lower East Side.

"This way," called Philip, as he motioned them to two of the most unusual carriages they had ever seen.

"These are the first electric taxis in New York. They just got 13 of them this year, and I've rented two of them for our afternoon tour. Put your bags in the front, and hop in."

Philip, Nettie, Anna, and Abraham took the lead taxi. Rabbi Rabinowitz, Daniel, Rose, the baby, and Mama Mary took the second taxi.

"I am going to take you on a tour of the Lower East Side. I lived here when I first landed 15 years ago." Philip was proud of his success in New York. Starting without anything but a knowledge of tailoring, he had risen to the level of clothing manufacturer/retailer of women's clothes and furs. By a combination of hard work and thrift, he worked his way out of the tenements of the Lower East Side. He was one of the many immigrant success stories. The taxis looked like mini buckboards put together in reverse. The driver was perched high up on a bench in the back, while four passengers sat in the cabin in the front. They put their few bags in, and off they went. They turned onto West Street, which ran parallel to the Hudson River, and then they turned left onto Canal, then left again onto Essex Street. Nettie couldn't believe how quiet the taxi was—just a little hum of its electric motor. They turned left again onto Hester Street.

The people in the streets stopped and stared at the strange carriages as they maneuvered through the narrow streets, around horse carts, push carts, and street vendors. They saw a man dressed all in white picking up horse droppings, a seemingly never-ending job. Philip was taking them on a tour of his city.

Jewish market, New York, 1900. *Courtesy of www.nycvitageimages.com, H.A. Dunne & Co.*

"There," he said, pointing to a tenement[1] building on the right side of the street, "that was my first home here in America." It was a five-story red brick building, with many of the bricks missing. From the first floor to the fifth was a metal fire escape. It was also being used as a laundry line and icebox. Many people put food outside their apartments to keep from spoiling. They had no refrigeration. People seemed to ooze from every opening and window.

---

1 The principle of the tenement was to house as many people as possible in the least amount of space. The lots were 25 by 100 feet. Buildings were five to six floors without elevators. Each floor had four apartments, so a five-story building could house 20 families. Hall toilets had to be provided on each floor. The cost for such a building was about $25,000 ($625,000 in 2017 dollars). Many families rented out their flats to additional boarders as they became boarding houses, so the number of people in a building could rise substantially.

"Some of these flats are boarding houses where as many as 15 people sleep," Philip called out, so that the occupants in the following taxi could hear.

Every street seems to have a different character with different voices and languages at each intersection. Ludlow Street. Orchard Street, where a school was being built. They saw row upon row of tenement buildings with no space between them. Nettie could hear the voices of the pushcart peddlers hawking their wares, selling everything imaginable.

"Anna, this is like our Market Square back home, only much, much bigger," said Nettie.

In front of all the buildings were outdoor stalls. Some were blocked by horse-drawn wagons, which made the street even narrower. Nettie just realized it was Sunday. Back home, Jews were not allowed to work because it was a Christian day of rest. Things were different here in America. Then they crossed Allen Street.

"Anna, wasn't this where Sam was going to live with his mother?" Nettie asked.

"I hope he doesn't have to share his room with 14 other people," Anna said, reflecting on what she just heard from Philip. *Guess they were poorer then they let on*, thought Nettie. No fancy dresses here. The women were wearing simple dresses, but very few were dull black and brown like the ones back home. Lots of women were without hats or scarves, showing their own hair. On the corner was the first Romanian-American Synagogue. It had Moorish-style windows. *This seems very strange*, thought Nettie. *I wonder if this is where Sam is going to attend services.*

Third Street elevated train, 1890, New York City. *Courtesy of www.flickr.com/photos/ newyorktransitmuseum/3442386092*

Eldridge Street, Chrystie Street, The Bowery, Mott Street, and Mulberry Street.

"Look, Nettie, it looks like they are getting ready for a party on this street."

Philip, their tour guide, had the answer: "They're getting ready for Columbus Day tomorrow. This street is the Italian section of town."

"It looks like fun. I haven't been here a day, and I found an American party. I just love America," Nettie said as a smile lit her face.

The taxis then turned right on Centre Street and another right on East Houston Avenue. A few blocks down, they came to a halt at the corner of Ludlow Street, outside the Iceland Delicatessen.[2] It was now about two in the afternoon.

Philip knew these new Americans were hungry. "Everybody out," he announced. "I hope you're hungry, because if not, you won't be able to finish your lunch."

"Look, Anna, there's a steam train way up there on a track." Nettie pointed above their heads.

"Oh my, does that looks dangerous," said Anna fearfully.

"Not to me, Anna. I can't wait to ride one," Nettie shot back.

It was 2 o'clock, but still the restaurant was crowded. As they entered, the attendant handed them a ticket.

"Don't lose your ticket," Philip warned them. They went to various food stations and picked out what they wanted.

At each station, the amount would be added to their ticket. When finished, it was added up. Philip took all the tickets to the cashier and paid.

Abraham couldn't believe his eyes. There in front of him at every station was a banquet fit for a king. He saw corned beef, pastrami, egg cream sodas, half-sour and dill pickles, salami, smoked salmon (lox), bagels, herring, caviar, *knishes* (handmade buns with fillings of mushroom, spinach, potato, or sweets), *matzo* ball soup, chopped liver, liverwurst, brisket, roast beef, tongue, potato pancakes, *blintzes* (cheese with fruit), noodle *kugel*, and cheesecake. There at the last station were *bialys*.[3] This brought back memories of Bialystok, the starting point on their train trip to Hamburg and then America. They had traveled far to a new world since escaping from Mariampole.

"At last, kosher food. Maybe I can gain back some of the weight I lost on the ship."

None of this banquet of food was lost on Rabbi Rabinowitz. *Here in America, I have found the land of plenty and a new family. What a blessing,* he thought. Abraham pulled a

---

2   Established in 1888 by the Iceland brothers. Willy Katz joined them in 1903, and it became Iceland & Katz. Willy's cousin Benny joined them in 1910, buying out the Iceland brothers to officially form Katz's Delicatessen. It became a hangout for actors from the Yiddish theater and remains a favorite and famous New York eatery today.

3   The *bialy* comes from the town of Bialystok, the starting point of their train trip. The *bialy* is a bagel, but instead of a hole, there is a depression that is filled with garlic and onion.

yarmulke from his pocket that he had not thrown away, like his brother had, and put it on before eating. Before they began their meal, the rabbi had to make a toast to their host Philip. "May Philip live a hundred years, it should be written."

"*Mazel tov*," said the group.

After dinner, it was off to the Garment District, where the Cohns lived above their factory and clothing store. Nettie's sister Rose said, "Nettie, you, Anna, and Mama are going to love the place. We have the whole third floor of the building. We're not in such cramped quarters as the people are on Allen Street."

The taxi driver called down: "How far are we going? I only have enough battery for 13 more miles."

"OK," Philip said, "go to Fifth Avenue and West 43rd. Let's go to the temple first."

Up Fifth Avenue they went, seeing larger buildings and some magnificent hotels. At 33rd Street, they saw the Waldorf Hotel.

"Isn't this wonderful, Anna?" said Nettie. "No clip clop of the horses, and so smooth is the ride."

Anna was again speechless. *Have I entered another world? This is so different. I just can't adjust as fast as Nettie.*

"Here we are, sir, Fifth Avenue and 43rd Street, Temple Beth El."

"Thank you for the tour and taking me to my destination," Rabbi Rabinowitz said. "I know they will take good care of me."

"Oh no," said Mama Mary, "We must make sure they have a place for you to stay."

"Look, they have built a *sukkah* on the side lot," the rabbi noticed. "I can't believe I forgot the date. Today is the first day of *Sukkot*,[4] the fifth day after *Yom Kippur*. How could I forget?" Then it dawned on him. This little group all seemed to come down with sea sickness at the same time on the ship. The ship was five days out on Wednesday, October 6, *Yom Kippur*, a day of fasting. How did he not figure this out? Anyway, here he was, starting his new position as head rabbi on the first day of *Sukkot*. The next seven days would be a feast and a good time to meet the congregation.

_____

4   *Sukkot*, also known as the Feast of the Tabernacles, is observed in the Fall. This celebrates the harvest and serves as a reminder of the time the Jewish people wandered the desert for 40 years after their exodus from slavery in Egypt, building *sukkahs* to give them temporary shelter. *Sukkot* celebrants eat meals in the *sukkah*. Another tradition is waving the *etrog* and the *lulav*. The *etrog* is a citron, related to a lemon; the *lulav* is made of myrtle twigs, willow twigs, and a palm frond.

Coming out to greet them was the president of the congregation, Emanuel Goldberg. By 1897, Temple Beth El had a congregation of the most successful Jewish immigrants. Most were German and had come to New York around 1840. This group was trying very hard to assimilate in America.

"You must be our new rabbi, Benjamin Rabinowitz. I see you are in good company. Philip Cohn is one of our founding members. Hello, Philip."

"Yes, I am Rabbi Rabinowitz," he said.

"I trust your trip over was a good one?" asked Mr. Goldberg.

"There was a little problem with a hurricane for a day or two. That's why I'm late," answered the rabbi.

"Let me take you to your quarters. I think they will suit your needs," said Mr. Goldberg.

Mama Mary followed them into the temple and the rabbi's office. A door at the back of the office opened into a beautifully appointed apartment.

"Is this to your approval, Rabbi?" asked Mr. Goldberg.

"Yes, it will do just fine," he answered.

Mama Mary also approved.

"Will you return here tonight for services?" he asked Mary.

"Of course. I don't want to miss your first day on the job. I will see you tonight."

Philip and Rose's Home

Everyone got back in the taxis, and they headed home to Ninth Avenue and 35th Street, just five or six blocks away. It was a three-story red brick building. On the side of the building in white letters it said "Greenbaum and Cohn Women's Clothing." Greenbaum had been a partner in the business, but Philip had bought out his interest.

On the first floor was a retail women's dress shop. On the second floor were the cutting room and seamstresses. On the top floor, the family living quarters. As they entered the apartment, they were met by Christina, their Swedish live-in maid. She didn't appear to be much older than Nettie and Anna. She had a sturdy build with braided blond hair that she wore coiled around her head.

"Christina has all your rooms ready for you. I'm afraid she doesn't understand Yiddish. She can speak a little German, and she's learning English. When we heard you were coming, we added a few more bedrooms."

Rose showed the boys their room. Her mother and the girls would each have their own rooms. Their few suitcases were unloaded, Philip paid the taxi drivers, and everyone tried to settle in.

Anna turned to Nettie and said, "That Philip sure is a *mensch*.[5] How lucky can Rose get?"

"You're right about that, Anna," said Nettie.

Rose took charge and said, "It's time for the three of you to look like women from New York. We are going downstairs to pick out your outfits for tonight. Philip, see what you can do for Daniel and Abraham. We don't want any of our guests to look like *greenhorns* at the temple."

This couldn't have been better news for Nettie, as all she had was boys' clothing. It was time to dress like a woman. Downstairs they went. Rose opened the shop.

"Oh my," were the first words out of Nettie's mouth. "Look at all the dresses and the colors—every color of the rainbow. I never knew so many styles of dresses existed. And hats too. They're beautiful."

They were all still wound up from the trip and seeing things in New York that were beyond their imaginations.

Rose was now giving the directions. "First we have to get everyone a corset to get that hourglass figure."

"I don't know about that," said her mother. "Do I have to?"

"Yes, Mother," replied Rose. "You want to win that rabbi over, don't you? Just wait till he sees you in your new dress. We only have the best corsets here, all with metal clasps. This little piece of equipment, you don't want to fail. Next are corset covers and drawers. Anna, you're going to need some bust pads until you fill out. Nettie, with that *zaftig*[6] figure, you won't need any padding. Look over here. These dresses and jackets will be perfect for tonight."

Nettie picked out a pastel pink dress with green trim and flounces of beige and ivory silk chiffon. It had small, puffy gigot sleeves. She found some lace-up boots and a hat with a bow and feathers. After they were all dressed, Rose pronounced them fit for New York society. Gath-

---

5   *Mensch* is a Yiddish term used to describe a very good man, a person of high values and character, an individual recognized for noble values or action.

6   *Zaftig* is a full-figured woman, very buxom.

ering their clothes, they returned to the apartment. Here they found Daniel and Abraham in their new suits. Philip had a friend of his open his men's shop and got the boys all new clothes.

They had on three-piece suits, each consisting of a sack coat, matching waistcoat (vest), and contrasting trousers. Their shirts were striped and had their collars turned over and pressed into wings. Their dress shirts had stiff fronts with shirt studs. A four-in-hand necktie surrounded each boy's collar and was attached with a stickpin. On their heads were bowler hats. They both looked quite handsome.

"What a transformation," Nettie said. "You really look like New York gentlemen." After a little nap, they all dressed. Then Philip had his coachman bring the carriage around, and off they went to the temple.

Sukkoth Service at the Temple

When they arrived at the temple, there was already a crowd. As they entered the sanctuary, there were introductions all around for the newest additions to the Cohn family. Nettie was finding it difficult to walk in her new corset and found herself standing very upright but moving in a most unusual manner. As people were finding their seats, she noticed that this Reform temple[7] was not the Orthodox synagogue she had known in her town. Here the pulpit faced the congregation and was not situated in the center of the congregation. There was a choir, and there were musical instruments, including an organ. The whole family was able to sit together in family pews, with the women not separated from the men. All this equality really made an impact on Nettie, but Anna and Abraham found it a little uncomfortable. There on the pulpit was Rabbi Rabinowitz, and Mama Mary couldn't take her eyes off him.

This modern service was quite new to Mama Mary and all the new immigrants. There was music and singing, and the women and men worshiped together.

---

7   Judaism has three divisions of worship: Reform, Conservative, and Orthodox. These divisions, although all Jewish, observe the faith at different levels of the traditional worship. The Reform movement has a liberal interpretation of the religion, while the Orthodox is the most traditional. Conservative is in between. Reform describes their place of worship as a temple, while the Conservative and Orthodox use the term synagogue. The Reform movement began in Germany in 1840 during the time of the Jewish Age of Enlightenment (1700 to 1900). These Reform Jews mingled freely with Gentiles (non-Jews) and prided themselves on assimilation into the community. David Einhorn was a leading figure in the American Reform movement. In 1897, these Reform Jews were assimilating into New York society.

Nettie liked the idea that things were different here in American and that traditions were not so restrictive. Women were treated on a level closer to that of men.

Daniel, Anna, and Abraham were feeling a bit out of place with the singing and the women being seated with the men. The religious service was conducted mostly in English, not Yiddish. After the service, the congregation all moved to the social hall where the *Oneg Shabbat*[8] was held. Although this wasn't a Friday night Sabbath service, it was a special one.

It was the first day of *Sukkot*, a harvest festival. The food of the harvest was in abundance at the buffet table. This was also the time for Philip to show off his family to the congregation. Nettie, of course, stood out with her regal posture and new clothes. Anna, being blond, was also the focus of attention of the single men.

The rabbi and Mama Mary were acting like a rabbi and his *rebbetzin* (rabbi's wife). Both of them met his new congregation.

"Hello," Nettie heard in her left ear. Upon turning around, she saw a handsome man in a blue cutaway suit, starched white shirt, four-in-one necktie, and patent leather shoes. His hair was cut short but slicked back along the sides. His eyes were a pale blue, and his smile was as warm as his hello.

"I'm Elliot Molinsky. You must be Nettie. So glad they didn't keep you in the old country." Nettie caught only a bit of what he said, as it was all in English and the words just came too fast for her.

"Glyad to meech you," she said in her best English. "Could you pleees shpeak in Yiddish? My englese is not too goot yet."

"Of course. With a woman as beautiful as you, I would speak in any language," he said in perfect Yiddish. A smile came to Nettie's face, as she could feel the power of her attraction over this man. "I would like you to meet my partner, Michael Nagle." Nettie turned to see a dark-complexioned man about her height with thick black hair and a stocky build. The cut of his jacket was doing nothing for his short, bulky stature. His head appeared to rest on his shoulders without a neck. He had a floppy bow tie.

He looks like a bear in a suit, thought Nettie. With this image, a smile came over her face as he said, "Nice to meet you, Nettie. I'm Michael." Nettie then had the presence of

---

8 The *Oneg Shabbat* (joy or delight) is the social gathering after the Friday-night service in the Reform temple or after the Saturday-morning service in the Conservative or Orthodox synagogue. It's a time to meet the congregation, talk with old friends, and make new ones. Food prepared by the sisterhood of the temple is the unifying theme. People greet each other and eat. It is the welcome mat for the congregation, especially for newcomers.

mind to turn and introduce Anna, who was the exact opposite of Michael. With Anna being tall, thin, and blond, the two made for quite a contrasting couple. Daniel wasn't far away, as he felt the responsibility to look after his little sister.

"I have an idea," Elliot said. "Tomorrow is Columbus Day, and the four of us could go down to Mulberry Street and see how the Italians throw a party. Are you ladies up for a gay time?"

Nettie's eyes got bigger. Of course, she was ready for a party—on her second day in America. "Yes," she said.

Daniel, hearing this, said, "Anna can't go unless Abraham and I come with her."

"That's OK," said Elliot. "With six of us, it will be safer. We'll be able to watch out for the pickpockets and other thieves. They come out in droves when there's a party with fresh greenhorns[9] in town."

"It's a date, then. We'll come by Philip's place around 10 o'clock tomorrow. We can take the 3rd Avenue Elevated down to the Lower East Side. It's a short walk over to Mulberry Street."

Everyone was in agreement. Anna noticed that Rose and Philip appeared to be giving Elliot and Michael the cold shoulder. Nettie was unaware of anything going on around her except the gaze and the attention of the men.

"Time to go," Rose announced, as the food was picked over. She knew the group was tired. As they rode back to the apartment, Nettie and Anna were all abuzz about the two young men who had invited them to the Columbus Day celebration. Rose and Philip were quiet—just a little small talk about their accommodations and how everyone was tired.

Columbus Day on Mulberry Street

The next morning, the girls were up early. They had to go downstairs to the store to pick out their outfits for the trip to Mulberry Street.

"Go with something less full in the skirt," suggested Rose. "There will be crowds of people, and a smaller skirt will take up less space and be easier when you ride on the train."

The men were there at 10 o'clock sharp with a two-horse carriage and driver. "Is everyone ready?" Elliot called out. The group came down the stairs, and Elliot's mouth dropped

---

9   Greenhorn was the term older immigrants would give to the new ones who had not learned the customs and ways of America. They were an easy mark for all kinds of scams, from knockout drops (chloral hydrate put in drinks) to moll-buzzers (pickpockets who targeted women) to footpads (muggers on foot).

Mulberry Street Market, New York City. *Courtesy of www.wdl.org/en/item/158, H.A. Dunne & Co.*

open as he saw Nettie in a walking suit of gray corded silk with a yellow silk panel down the front and yellow silk under large puff sleeves with rows of navy beaded decoration, all on a white silk background and a high collar. Perched on her head was a hat with contrasting bows that were tied under her chin. Her corset accentuated her zaftig figure.

"It sure didn't take you long to adjust to America's fashion," Elliot said, as he helped her into the carriage.

Michael helped Anna in, and Daniel and Abraham got in the back. It was a mile to the 3rd Avenue Elevated. There they would have to climb up three flights of stairs to the station. As they waited on the platform, they could hear the steam engine before they saw the train.

Anna confided in Nettie, "I'm not so sure I'm going to like this."

"Just stay close to me and everything will be fine. This will be fun." Nettie was always up for a new adventure.

They boarded the train, Elliot and Michael paid the fares, and off they went to Houston Street and Lower Manhattan.

"We're here," Elliot called over the sound of the train and the voices of people exiting, all on their way to the Columbus Day celebration. "Hold my hand, Nettie. I don't want to lose such a pretty thing on your second day in America."

When he took her hand, she could feel a surge of energy enter her body. The touch of a man reminded her of Moshe on her first night after the wedding. It was like a switch turning on something deep within her body, and she loved it. She had never seen so many people crowding together. She held her purse tightly by its strap with one hand and Elliot's hand with the other.

"It's just two short blocks to Mulberry Street. Everyone stay close together."

As they approached Mulberry from its north end, they could hear the bands and smell the food cooking in outdoor stalls.

"Here we are," shouted Elliot, over the noise of the crowd. "Let's keep walking till someone sees some food they want to try."

The street lamps were decorated with red, white, and green tinsel. Italian flags of the same colors were in front of all the buildings and storefronts.

"Hey, mister, you gunna bey a flag for a penny?" The voice seemed to come from the street. There looking up at them was a little girl no more than four or five years old with a handful of tiny American flags.

"Sure will," Elliot said. "Got to get into the holiday spirit." With that, he gave the little girl a quarter and got six flags.

"Thanks, mister," she said.

"Keep the change," replied Elliot.

He turned to Nettie and said, "You think she's having fun? She may be homeless, or worse, put on the street by a gang to hustle the visitors. It's as bad for her as it is for the garment workers. They get a dollar a day for 12 hours of work." This was news to Nettie, who thought, *I've heard stories about the treatment of immigrants, but now I'm seeing it firsthand.*

Nettie wanted to change the subject and get back to the purpose of their outing, so she quickly pointed to a display of pastries and said, "Oh, Elliot, what is that over there?" She had spotted a plank counter under a canvas awning, brimming with cannoli shells filled with cream and dipped in chocolate, sfogliatelle pastry filled with ricotta, and biscotti with nuts. "Let's have our dessert first. It all looks so good."

"Is it kosher?" asked Abraham.

"Of course," answered Nettie. "We are close to the Jewish district, so it must be kosher."

Daniel, hearing this logic, just rolled his eyes thinking, *there she goes again.* Abraham bought the explanation and dived right in to all the food like he hadn't eaten in a month.

This was partially true, as he had hardly eaten on the ship during their trip from Germany. On down the street they went, smelling the fragrance of the cooking food, hearing the music and the chatter of many languages. The universal language of food and friends gave everyone a light spirit. People were on the rooftops of the buildings. Every once in a while, they would hear a toast to "Cristoforo Colombo." Everyone in the street would answer back, "To Cristoforo Colombo."

They were about halfway down Mulberry Street when Anna let out a squeal. "Nettie, look over there. See that red hair; is that Sam?" Sure enough, it was Sam and his brother Mayer and sister Ettie. It was only his second day in America. His brother and sister decided they would walk over from Allen Street and see the celebration. If it weren't for Christopher Columbus, they wouldn't be in America.

Mayer saw their group first and pointed them out to Sam: "Aren't those the ladies you came over with on the ship?"

"I think so, Mayer," answered Sam. This was so confusing. *How could she find another man so fast? She will be hard to forget.*

"Looks like she hasn't wasted any time in finding company," Mayer replied.

"Let's go," Sam said. "I've had enough of this celebration already."

"What's the matter? Little brother afraid of the competition?"

"No, I have other things to do like check on Sol at the hospital and get ready to apply for school."

Upon seeing Sam, Nettie thought, *I wonder how Sol is in the hospital. Weren't we supposed to visit him?*

Meeting Sam with Elliot would be very uncomfortable. "No, I don't see him, Anna."

With that, Sam disappeared in the crowd. He had seen who he thought was Nettie and Anna with other men. How could he forget the two of them? With Anna's blond hair, she stood out in the crowd. Nettie's kiss at the steamship depot was still fresh on his lips.

The six of them moved down the street. They found sausage and pepper sandwiches and torrone with honey and almonds. As they passed the Bowery section, Elliot pointed out a Bowery boy. He wore a pearl gray derby tilted over one ear, a suit with a loud check pattern, a tight coat worn over a pink striped shirt, black flared trousers, silk vest, and flared box overcoat. His boots were high-heeled calfskin and his hair was oiled and slicked back. He was ready for a night on the town. He called his woman "me rag" or "me bundle." She was wearing a tight jacket; a corseted, waist-length bedraggled shirt; and a hat perched on her head with a broken ornamental feather. They had a hard walk, or a swagger called "spieling." These different ways of dress were intriguing to Nettie and Anna. Evening was coming quickly this autumn day. As the sun set, the fireworks began lighting up the sky.

As they approached Canal Street, Elliot said, "This is where we get back to the 3rd Avenue Elevated and head home. Further down Mulberry Street is an area called Mulberry Bend. This was one of the worst slums in town, called Bandit's Roost. It bordered the Five Points area where gangs ran the show. The whole area was demolished last year. They are turning it into Columbus Park. The police have little control down there, where the Gopher gang rules. One of our own also operates there—Monk Eastman,[10] a Jewish gangster with the Allen Street Cadets. I think Michael knows more about Monk Eastman than he is willing to tell. Right, Michael?" Michael just nodded his head.

Nettie thought, *who are these two men*, but then let the thought go.

Anna was glad that her brothers Daniel and Abraham were with her. Back on the train, Anna felt a little more at ease on the ride home. *Could I be getting Americanized so soon?* Being with Nettie always opened up new experiences for her, and for that she loved Nettie for making her step out of her shell. Because of her adventurous spirit, Nettie wasn't always aware of her current situation and the danger around her.

First Weeks in America

The next few weeks were a whirlwind of activities for Nettie and Anna. Both Michael and Elliot seemed determined to show them all of New York City: Central Park, Brooklyn Bridge, the Waldorf Hotel, the Fifth Avenue Hotel. (It had the first elevator in the country.) They were introduced to and dined with many of the boys' friends, though it

---

10 Edward "Monk" Eastman, 1875–1920, was born in lower Manhattan as Edward Osterman. He was raised by his grandfather on the Upper East Side after his father left the family when Edward was 5 years old. He was raised with two older sisters and one younger. He was the only boy in the family. His grandfather set him up in the pet store business, as he was always fond of animals, but a life of crime was his pursuit, and he was first arrested in 1898 for larceny. He was nicknamed Monk for his simian ability to climb walls and swing through windows. During this period, he belonged to a gang of pimps and thieves known as the Allen Street Cadets. He wore a derby hat two sizes too small for his head and always was accompanied by his pigeons. At five-foot-six, he became a bouncer and worked closely with politicians in "getting out" the vote. His greatest rival was Paul Kelly, leader of the Five Points Gang.

was difficult to understand what they were saying. Michael and Elliot would translate to Yiddish for them.

None of this was sitting well with Nettie's sister Rose. "We need to talk about your friends, Nettie," Rose said, as she pulled her aside after breakfast one morning. "I don't know if you know, but Elliot and Michael are union organizers. They are trying to form a union of Ladies Garment Workers. If this happens, Philip's business will be hurt when strikes are called and wages go up."

"What does that have to do with me, Rose?" Nettie asked.

"The other garment makers have seen them here at our store. They have been asking Philip questions as if he's involved in the union movement, which he's not."

"I really don't care what Elliot does, Rose. He's showing me a good time in the city and has been kind to both me and Anna. Do you prefer I meet him somewhere else and not have him come to the house?"

"That would be unheard of, a lady unescorted on the street being picked up by a man. There's a word for that kind of woman. I've been talking with mother, and she thinks it's time for you to go off to a finishing school. The rabbi was told of one on Long Island that all the Jewish families use. You will learn English and all the customs and manners of the upper-class women."

"I don't know, Rose. I think I'm doing quite well as I am."

Nettie then confided in Anna and told her what Rose had said.

"I don't want to cause any trouble here," said Anna. "Rose has been nice enough to give me and my brothers a place to stay. If it means I don't see Michael anymore, then that's how it's going to be."

Nettie shot back, "I think she's just jealous of me getting a *mensch* like Elliot."

"I don't know, Nettie. I think he is more of a *macher*[11] than a *mensch*. You've only been in this new country for three weeks. I think Rose knows more about what is going on than you give her credit for."

"All I know, Anna, is that I'll not stop seeing Elliot and his friends."

"Nettie, do you know what his friends are saying about you when we are at supper?" asked Anna.

"I don't know, but they smile a lot and seem to be making jokes."

---

11 *Macher* means big shot, an important person.

"Nettie, those jokes are about us. We don't know what fork or knife to pick up. We can't read the menu or even make conversation with these people. I think we are being paraded around and shown off for some other reason. You know many of them can speak Yiddish but only speak English around us. They do this so we don't know what they're talking about."

"I think you are being silly, Anna. Elliot tells me he has never met anyone like me."

"I heard it slip out one night that you were married in the old country and your husband was shot and killed. I thought we took an oath to never tell anyone about our past. It's not going to take much to put the story together that we're on the run. They may turn us in to immigration for the money!" said Anna, with a frightened look on her face.

"You're letting your imagination run wild, Anna. I didn't tell him that much."

"Be careful when he gives you that second glass of wine," Anna warned.

Union Problems

That night, everyone could hear a heated discussion between Rose and Philip. No doubt it was about Nettie and her unionizing boyfriend. "We can't just throw her out on the street, Philip. She's my sister."

"I'm getting pressure from the other garment makers that Elliot and his boys are just too cozy with us. You know he has connections with Monk Eastman and his friends. They're people we don't want to cross paths with."

"I'll talk with Nettie again in the morning. We will work something out."

The morning came, but Nettie was in no mood to talk to Rose. She just sat around the house playing with the baby, waiting for a messenger to bring a note from Elliot. It came that afternoon. Nettie wrote him back that Anna would not be coming but that she would meet his carriage up the street. Later that evening, she left the house on her own. Daniel watched from an upstairs window and saw her get into the carriage that he knew was Elliot's.

"Daniel, don't you think we'd better find out where Nettie is going? Anna says Elliot lives at the Windsor Hotel on Fifth Avenue and 46th Street. Maybe she's going there. I'll ask Philip's driver to take you there," said Mama Mary.

"I'll see what I can find out, but you know how bad is my English. Maybe my army training will help me. I know how to be observant."

Nettie Learns about the Union

"What's the matter, Nettie?" Elliot asked, as she got in the carriage.

"If you really want to know, my sister and brother-in-law think you are in some kind of union movement. They say it will hurt their business, and they want me to stop seeing you."

"I think getting a union will help their business. If all their workers are happy to come to work, they'll be more productive," answered Elliot.

"So you *are* working for a union?"

"Not exactly. We are trying to form a union to help the Jewish immigrants get a better start in this new world and not be exploited by greedy American capitalists, making money off their hard work," explained Elliot.

"I don't want to talk about this, Elliot. It's too depressing. What have you planned for us tonight?" Nettie loved to change the subject.

"When you said Anna would not be coming, I thought a quiet dinner at my hotel, just the two of us. What do you say?"

"Fine, Elliot. Maybe a little wine will help me forget all this nonsense about unions."

Daniel Meets an Old Friend

Philip's coachman dropped Daniel off about a block from the hotel entrance and said he would wait for his return. Daniel starting walking toward the entrance, as the hotel covered the entire block. He nodded to the doorman as he entered the lobby. The ceiling was at least three stories tall with arched columns. It looked more like the inside of a church. The floor was a polished stone—so smooth that he could see his reflection off the floor. The reception desk was a dark oak, as were the tables and overstuffed chairs in the lobby.

Daniel took a seat in the lobby and pretended to read the newspaper that was on the table next to his chair. Out of the corner of his eye, he watched the people come and go, listening to them talking. English was still very new to his ear, but he did catch a few words and phrases. Just then, he heard someone speaking Russian, in a voice familiar to him. Looking across the lobby, he saw a familiar face wearing a doorman's uniform. It was Asa Zimmerman, one of the Jewish conscripts who served with him in the Russian Army. He couldn't believe his good luck.

Standing up, Daniel walked toward him, putting himself in Asa's line of vision, as he was talking to another doorman. When Asa saw Daniel, he stopped his conversation and turned to meet him and gave him a bear hug. "I can't believe it's you, Daniel."

"Nor can I believe it's you, Asa."

Asa was built like Daniel, or maybe it was the time in the Russian Army that gave them both that solid muscular look of a wrestler.

"Daniel, if you can wait a few minutes, I'll have another break in my shift and we can get a drink at the bar."

"Sure, I'll wait right over there in that chair."

They had served in the same unit for several of their years in the army. Being Jewish, they were both passed over for promotions but stuck out the duration of their time, as they had no other options. Because of their time in the service, Daniel and Asa had a bond that few men would ever have.

Finishing his shift, he came over to Daniel. "Let's go have a drink. I have about 20 minutes before I go back on duty."

They walked over to the lobby bar. It was empty except for the bartender and one man at the end of the bar.

"What will you have, gents?"

"How about a beer for my old army buddy," Asa said.

"What army?" asked the bartender.

"The Russian Army," answered Asa.

"Well, the drink is on the house. Here's to Mother Russia," as the bartender lifted his glass for a toast. "May she die a slow death."

The bartender was another Russian immigrant, just like Asa. Immigrants from different areas seemed to follow others for employment, and this hotel had a lot of Russian Jews.

"How long have you been in America, Asa?"

"About eight months. How about you, Daniel?"

"Only four weeks," answered Daniel.

"That explains why you're not speaking English. I had a hard time with the language, but now I really can speak it. I know you are not staying at this hotel. I know everyone who comes and goes. Why are you here?"

"I'm checking up—or should I say following?—a young lady that came over with our group. She met a man that the family thinks is not good for her, and they asked me to follow her tonight."

"What's the man's name, Daniel?"

"Elliot Molinsky."

"That's not good. Your family has a right to be worried. He's a very powerful man with a lot of friends that are gang members down on the Lower East Side. I see them here from time to time. They are tough looking fellows. I think I saw Mr. Molinsky tonight. He brought a very attractive young lady into the hotel. In fact, I think they are in the dining room."

"Did she have thick black hair, and was she jabbering away in Yiddish?" asked Daniel.

"Yes, you described her."

"Her name is Nettie Sachs, and our families are very close. Should anything bad happen to her, I would feel responsible," said Daniel.

"The staff in these hotels knows everything that goes on. Between the doorman, maids, and bellboys, we have stories that would make you blush. I think that your friend Nettie is in a lot of danger. The fact that Molinsky is having dinner, alone with her tonight, means the game is on."

"I don't understand. The *game*?" Daniel said, as he cocked his head to one side in an attempt to understand.

"This guy Molinsky preys upon new immigrants that don't know the language and are separated from their families. He likes to get the young girls and set them up here at the hotel as high-level prostitutes. They service the guests—usually wealthy men—that don't want to go down to the Lower East Side. It's too dangerous. When the girls are no longer getting top dollar, he sells them to one of the gangs down there. They work them till they are no use to anyone and then kick them out on the street. Before the deal goes down, he likes to sample the wares, and I think this is the night for your Nettie," said Asa.

"OK, I'll go get her now and take her home," Daniel blurted out.

"No, much too dangerous. She doesn't know what's going on and will resist you. Molinsky will know you think something is up and will have you arrested. With his connections, you will never get out of jail. Worse yet, he could get you deported. We need a plan. The way he works, the following night or whenever he invites her back to the hotel is when the final arrangements are made. After that, there is no getting her back. We have one chance to do this right. The management of the hotel is on his side, but many of the employees are disgusted with what is going on and would love to save someone. Give me the address where you're staying. I will send you a note when the time is right."

"Asa, I still have my revolver from the service. I smuggled it on the ship. I will bring it."

"Yeah, I've got mine too. Once you have a gun, it sure equalizes things. Hope we don't have to use them and I lose my job."

With that, they hugged again. Daniel walked back to the waiting carriage, his mind running through all the possible scenarios that he might face during the rescue of Nettie. He knew he could trust Asa. After all, that was his job in the army to outthink the enemy. The element of surprise would give them a big edge.

Dinner and the Proposal by Elliot

At dinner, Elliot was exceedingly charming. The dinner was five courses, each with a special wine. As they ordered dessert, Elliot ordered a port wine. Nettie's head was already spinning and her speech a little slurred. She seemed to remember Anna saying, "Be careful when he gives you that second glass of wine," but that was three glasses ago.

"Nettie, I would like to make you a proposal. I know it's a little soon, as we have only known each other for a month. I knew from the moment I set eyes on you at the temple that you were the woman in my life I could settle down with. We can solve this problem with your sister and brother-in-law if you move to the hotel. I will get you your own room. It'll give us time to plan the wedding."

With that said, he pulled from his pocket a purple velvet covered box and handed it to her. Nettie opened it, and inside was the largest diamond ring she had ever seen. Even in her drunken state, she knew what this meant.

"Yes!" she shrieked, so loudly that patrons several tables away heard and saw what was happening and started to clap. Nettie moved around the table and grabbed Elliot and gave him a long and loving kiss. Everyone in the restaurant cheered. Asa, hearing the noise, went to the dining room area and saw the scene. *Just the first step. I'd better work on the plan.*

Nettie Is Drugged

The couple left the dining room among cheers from the diners. Up the elevator they went to the top of the hotel, the sixth floor. Elliot was supporting Nettie, as she could barely keep her balance. He opened the door to Room 33, and they stumbled in.

Could it have been all that wine or something else I ate? Nettie wondered. The rooms were elegantly furnished with sofas, rich drapes on the windows, oriental carpets, and Tiffany lamps. She could see the bedroom off the main living area had a four-poster bed.

Elliot said, "If you want to freshen up, there is a bathroom through this door." He pointed to the left of the bedroom door.

I just want to lie down, Nettie thought, but then the room started spinning around. "Just give me a minute. I'll be all right."

She must have blacked out, for when she awoke she found Elliot unlacing her corset as she lay on the bed. She felt powerless to do anything, but then he was to be her future husband. *This must be all right*, she thought.

Next he removed her shoes, dress, pantaloons, and underwear. Barely conscious, she could feel herself being moved up in the bed and under the covers. She closed her eyes. *Maybe sleep will help clear my head.*

Time seemed to drift by. She could hear Elliot's voice saying, "Soon we will be man and wife, and we will sleep together every night."

She felt his naked body move next to hers in the bed, his hand touching her breasts, feeling the stiffness of her nipples and then following the curves of her body till his fingers were touching her *sheyd* (vagina). This wasn't how it was with Moshe, even though he was experienced. Elliot must have had more experience. Even in her half-conscious state, he was arousing her to climax. It had only been since August that she last slept with Moshe before his death. *Oh, how I love the feeling that sex brings to my body.* All she could do was moan, as words would form in her mouth but she could not speak.

Elliot was now on top of her, pinning her arms above her head as he inserted himself into her. It felt so good as he pressed his body against hers. She could not move but just lay there. Elliot didn't seem to mind as she could feel him ejaculate within her. As he lay back on his side of the bed, she had a feeling of nausea come over her. Then sleep overcame everything. Several hours later, she awoke and remembered the bathroom was right out the door. She slid off the bed and on unsteady legs wobbled to the bathroom. Once there, she promptly threw up.

Whatever came over me? As she left the bathroom, she still didn't feel right and got back into bed and quickly went to sleep.

The morning came with Elliot leaning over her with a breakfast tray. "Just had room service bring this up. You had quite a night last night. Maybe too much wine?"

"I don't know, Elliot. I have never felt that way before. You may be right; it could have been the wine."

Looking around the bedroom for the first time, she could see how elegant everything in the apartment was. This man could surely provide for me, even better than Moshe. She leaned back against the pillows he had put behind her head.

As Nettie sipped her coffee, Elliot said, "I'll have my driver take you home, and you can pack all your things and get ready to come back to the hotel. I will get you an apartment, and you can settle in."

Things were going fast, even too fast for Nettie. What a year this had been, from her wedding to Moshe, his death, her escape to America, and now a marriage proposal to a very important man. How lucky could she get?

"OK, Elliot, it will be good to get out from under my mother's and sister's watchful eyes." She found her clothes. After taking a relaxing bath, she dressed and Elliot's driver took her home.

Daniel Reports to Mama Mary

Mama Mary was all questions for Daniel at breakfast the next day: "What did you find out, Daniel?"

"I did meet an old army buddy of mine who is a doorman at the hotel. You were right, Mama. This Molinsky guy is not one to fool with. Asa, my friend, is working on a plan. He will get back in touch with me."

Just then, Anna, blurry-eyed, came into the kitchen. "Mama Mary, Nettie didn't come home last night."

Mama Mary's back stiffened, and her eyes turned black as coal. "I'll bet it has something to do with that Molinsky boy. If he's damaging my baby's reputation, I will kill him."

"Calm down," Rose and Daniel said at the same time. "She's a widowed woman and knows what life is all about. I'm sure she's OK." Before Daniel could finish the sentence, the door opened and in walked Nettie. She didn't say a word and went right to her room. The group sat in stunned silence.

"Go see what's going on, Anna," said Rose. Anna knew it was her job as Nettie's best friend to find out what was happening. As she entered the bedroom, she saw Nettie lying on the bed.

"It's this headache, Anna. I just can't seem to get rid of it. By the way, Elliot proposed to me last night. Here, look at this ring." Nettie was the master at using dramatic pauses.

"Nettie, I can't believe it. I'm sorry I was so wrong to doubt you yesterday. This is wonderful. Let's tell Mama."

"I don't think we should right now. I know she must be upset that I didn't come home last night. I got sick or maybe drugged. Let's just keep quiet about all of this."

"You know I can keep a secret, Nettie. My lips are sealed," Anna replied.

Anna came back to the breakfast table, where everyone was on the edges of their chairs. "What did she say?" asked Mama Mary.

"She has a headache and just wants to sleep. That's all she told me," said Anna.

"Well, she is going to tell me more when she wakes up," said Mama Mary in a tone that would make even the strongest man shake in his boots.

Nettie Waits for Elliot's Note

It took a whole day for Nettie to start to feel right again. When she did, she began to pack her things so she would be ready to go at a moment's notice. The atmosphere in the house was stifling. Both her sister and Mama Mary wanted more details of her "night out." Nettie would tell them nothing. Meanwhile, Daniel waited for a note from Asa but knew it wouldn't come till Nettie left the house. Two days passed, and not a word. Then, on the third day, a message came for Nettie and off she went with her bag. She also took her satchel that had the rest of the precious stones from Moshe's safe. It was about 3 o'clock in the afternoon. Daniel was now on edge. He checked his gun and secured it in the waistband of his pants. Then a messenger came.

The note read:

Daniel, the deal will go down tonight. Bring your gun. Come now. We have a plan.

Asa.

Daniel bolted down the stairs and around the back where the carriage was kept.

To the driver, he said, "Hitch up the team. We're off to the Windsor Hotel."

Within minutes, the team was hitched and they were off to the hotel. This time, he got off at the main entrance and told the driver to wait as long as he had to but to stay near the front entrance.

Asa was waiting for him and whisked him into the doorman's ready room. "Here's the plan, Daniel. We saw Nettie come in this afternoon and go directly to Room 33 on the sixth floor. A while later, two more men came in. One was Michael Nagle, and the other was Monk Eastman."

"I know Michael," said Daniel. "He had been dating my sister. I've heard about this Monk Eastman. He's a thug."

"Once we know they're all in the room, we're going to have room service give them a call and report back to us how many are in the room. We'll be waiting on the back stairs on the sixth floor. If the coast is clear, room service will knock again. This time, you burst into the room with your gun out and yell, 'I'm here to get my sister.' I'll have two house detectives behind you in disguises to look like Pinkerton[12] men. They will enter the room and back you up. Grab Nettie and get in the elevator. The detectives will pretend to take names and press charges. This will give you time to get away."

"I got it. Let's go up the stairs."

Nettie's Rescue

When Nettie got to the hotel, no one was waiting for her. She took the elevator to the sixth floor and knocked on the door to Room 33. "Come in" was the reply. "Good, Nettie. You are here," said Elliot.

Nettie felt it was strange that he didn't hug or kiss her, but then she really didn't know him that well.

"Did you have any trouble with your family when you told them where you were going?" asked Elliot.

"I didn't tell them anything. It's none of their business what I do. Is my apartment going to be close to yours?" Nettie asked.

"Close enough that we can see each other every day," Elliot said. "First, I want you to meet a few of my business associates. They should be right up." There was a knock on the door. When Elliot opened it, Nettie saw Michael Nagle. With him was a man about five-foot-six with a bullet-shaped head and bull neck wearing a derby hat that was too small, perched on the back of his head. He was in his middle 20s. She couldn't tell if he was smiling or it was part of a scar that started at the corner of his mouth and went up his cheek.

"This is Monk Eastman, Nettie." Nettie was confused. *Wasn't this the Monk Eastman that was part of a gang? Why was he here?*

---

12 The Pinkerton detective agency was founded before the Civil War. It concentrated on catching swindlers, cheats, confidence men, and other no-goods in the big cities. They were the first to develop the mug shot and relentlessly pursued famous outlaws, including Jesse James, Cole Younger, and Butch Cassidy and the Sundance Kid.

"Hey, Elliot, yous gots a perrty little boid here," said Monk, and with that he reached out and touched her hair.

Nettie pulled back.

"What's da matter, little boid, you afraid of your Uncle Monk?"

"Elliot, don't let him talk to me like that," Nettie said indignantly.

"I'm afraid, Nettie, that he can. You see, you are now part of our business. Isn't that right, Michael?"

"That's right, boss. Nettie, you're going to be one of our girls right here in the hotel. Uncle Monk will have one of his boys with you all the time—you know, for protection. We'll take care of the money end."

"Oh no, you won't," cried Nettie, as she made a break for the door. Before she could get there, Monk grabbed her from behind, spun her around, and with a knife—in one stroke—cut all the buttons off the front of her bodice, causing her breasts to be exposed from the tight-fitting bodice.

"I like them dem tings, boss. Gets a lots of money for dis one."

"She's not for sale yet, Monk," said Elliot.

Nettie was now on the floor clutching her bodice together trying to cover her breasts.

Just then, there was a knock on the door. "Room service for Mr. Molinsky."

They all looked at each other. "Who ordered room service?"

No one went for the door, but the service attendant had a key and everyone heard it in the lock. Just as the door opened, Nettie screamed, "Help me, help me!"

Monk went over to her and put his hand over her mouth.

"We didn't order room service," Elliot said, and pushed the door closed.

That's when Nettie bit down on Monk's hand. With the other hand, he lifted her up by her torn bodice and threw her across the room. She landed on a couch. With the back of his other hand, he hit her across the mouth. "Don't you ever bite me again, or you'll lose dem perrty teeth."

Nettie was in shock. How could she have gotten in this mess? Elliot was going to marry her.

Another knock on the door, and then the words "Room service."

"I thought I told you we don't want room service," Elliot bellowed, as he grabbed the door handle and jerked it open. There standing at his full height was Daniel with gun drawn.

"Give me my sister," Daniel said, in his most commanding voice.

"She's not your sister!" Elliot yelled back at him.

"She is now. Put your hands above your heads and turn around."

Behind him with guns also drawn were the phony Pinkerton men with their distinctive derby hats.

"Don't think I'll forget this, Daniel. This town is too small for you to hide from my boys. You're a dead man." This was Elliot's threat.

Nettie was never so happy to see Daniel in her life. With one hand holding her dress together, the other grabbing her satchel that had all her precious stones, she ran to Daniel's side. The phony Pinkerton men moved in front of Daniel and Nettie as the two of them ran for the elevator. It was the slowest trip down they ever had.

We could have gone faster down the stairs, thought Daniel. The elevator stopped at the third floor and another couple got on. The sight of Daniel and Nettie must have disturbed them, as nothing was said the rest of the way down. When the attendant opened the door, they made a dash for the carriage and off to the house. They passed Asa at the door. He had their carriage held right in front.

Nettie clung to Daniel all the way home, crying in his arms as she kept repeating, "They were going to make me a *hurve* (prostitute)." It was now November and winter was on the way in New York City. Daniel threw a blanket over her, as she had left her coat in the apartment.

Nettie Comes Home

The two of them got out of the carriage and walked up the stairs to the apartment. Mama Mary was there to meet them. She no longer had a stern look on her face. She embraced Nettie with her torn clothes and a large red welt growing on the side of her face.

"Mama, you were right. Elliot and Michael are bad men and I should have listened to you and Rose. Can you forgive me?"

"Of course we can. You are now home safe with us."

"I'm afraid he's going to try to hurt your business. He made a death threat against Daniel."

"Don't worry about me, Nettie. I plan to take a job offer in Pennsylvania and dig some coal," said Daniel. "He and his boys won't find me there. I leave tomorrow."

"Talk to Rabbi Rabinowitz, Mama. Get the information on the finishing school. I think it's time for Anna and me to really learn English and become proper ladies of New York."

This was music to Mama Mary's ears. *Finally, there will be a safe place for my adventurist daughter, at least for a while,* thought Mary.

That night, as Anna and Nettie lay in their beds, Nettie said, "Anna, in all the confusion, I still have the ring. Look." She held up her hand to show Anna. "I guess that means I'm still married to the mob." They both had a laugh and went off to sleep.

Becker's Institute

The next day, Mama Mary lost no time going to the temple to talk with Rabbi Rabinowitz about the details of the finishing school on Long Island. It was Becker's Institute in Glen Cove, New York. It was a coed boarding school that was patronized by the most intelligent class of the Hebrew community, so they were told. You could easily reach it using the railroad from Manhattan. Visits in both directions would not be out of the question.

Mama made the arrangements, as she and the rabbi planned to accompany the girls and help them settle in. The girls got the news almost as soon as Mama Mary. They had been accepted to the school. Nettie wanted to wait a few more days for the swelling to

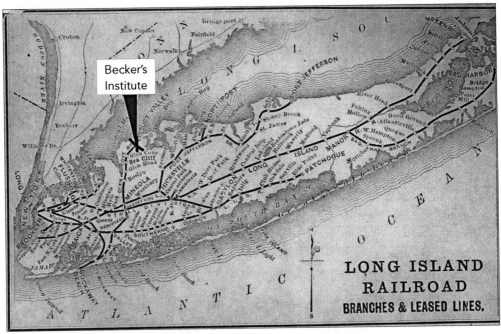

Map of Long Island Railroad Line, Route 1900. *Courtesy of Wikipedia*

go down and her black eye to look more normal. This was something she did not want to have to explain at the school. Besides, she and Anna had some shopping to do to get ready, since Nettie had left all her clothes at the hotel in her haste to escape. That was a minor inconvenience.

The Trip to Becker's Institute

It was Monday, November 8, when the five of them went to the train station for their trip to Glen Cove. It was an unusually warm fall day with the temperature in the middle 60s and a bright sun overhead. Many called this an Indian Summer day for being so warm at this time of the year. The warmth of the sun and gentle breeze gave everyone an optimistic feeling. This was their first trip outside the city since arriving in October.

The girls had a few suitcases and a trunk with everything they felt they would need. The Long Island Railroad had service to Glen Cove, but they would have to make a few transfers.

Four of them were still having trouble with English, so Rose came along to be their guide. The first leg of the journey took them across the East River using the Brooklyn Bridge connecting Manhattan to Brooklyn.

"Oh Nettie, I can't look down. We are up so high," Anna whispered in Nettie's ear.

"Hold your breath, Anna, and close your eyes. I'll tell you when we reach the other side," Nettie assured her.

What a view, Nettie thought. *I can see sailboats and ocean ships that look more like toys from up here.*

Built in 1883 as the first suspension bridge, it was over a mile long and 135 feet above the river. After crossing the bridge, it was time to make their first transfer at the Jamaica station. All hands took turns moving the trunk and suitcases.

"Are you OK, Anna?" asked Nettie.

"Yes, I'm fine, but I couldn't hold my breath that long. I have to admit I did peek once or twice, Nettie."

"I told you it would be OK," answered Nettie.

The next leg of the journey took them through sparsely developed sections of Long Island. They saw vast grasslands and marshes with a few homes or groups of houses scattered here and there. This area was very different from anything the girls had seen in America.

The next transfer was Mineola Station. It was the last stop before Glen Cove. This was a major hub station with tracks leading off in many different directions. They were to take the Oyster Bay Branch to Glen Cove. The scenery was now changing and getting a little hilly with more trees.

Anna said, "I like the way the land looks here, Nettie. Don't you?"

"Yes, it reminds me more of home now that we can see trees instead of buildings," agreed Nettie.

After unloading at the station, they all got in a carriage for the short ride to the institute. They passed along a bluff overlooking the Long Island Sound.

"Anna, can you smell the salt air?" asked Nettie as she took a deep breath.

A breeze was blowing in over the Sound as their carriage made the turn onto Hammond Road and went up the hill to Becker's.

"Oh yes, Nettie, it smells so sweet and clean, not like the air in the city."

There to greet them were the trustee, Louis Frohman, and the head mistress, Pauline Fechheimer.

"Hello, Rabbi Rabinowitz," Frohman called out as the group stepped out of the carriage.

"You must be Louis Frohman?" the Rabbi asked.

"Yes, here to greet you and the girls. This is Madam Fechheimer, our head mistress. She will show the girls to their room."

"Right this way, girls. The driver will bring your bags," she said.

Madam Fechheimer was a no-nonsense woman. Nettie thought she resembled Mama Mary with her stern manner, only a much larger woman. She had emigrated from Germany and projected a superior attitude, as many of the German Jews seemed to display. She was a tall woman with a very upright posture. Her hair was worn in a tight bun.

"This is going to be a serious place, Anna. I hope I can behave myself," Nettie whispered. Madam Fechheimer turned and gave Nettie a look that she had seen many times before from Mama Mary. That look confirmed Nettie's suspicions.

The boarding school had both boys and girls. They were housed in two large dormitories on opposite ends of the campus. There were three other buildings, all built with a red brick in a colonial style: a gymnasium, classroom building, and the administration building. The administration building also served as the living quarters for the staff and the dining hall for the students. The girls would share a room on the second floor of the ladies' dormitory.

Looking out the window, Anna remarked, "Nettie, come look. You can see the water from here." Nettie looked out the window. Again, the breeze from the Sound wafted up the bluff and into their open window.

"Smell that salt breeze, Anna, the smell of the country." The two girls stood for a moment enjoying the autumn breeze. They both unpacked and went downstairs. They walked over to the administrative building. Rabbi Rabinowitz, Mama Mary, and her sister Rose were served dinner with the girls. After dinner, the three of them were off to return to the city.

Mama Mary hugged Nettie and said, "You and Anna will be safe here and have a chance to learn English. Please don't find any trouble." Nettie knew what she meant. With a kiss on the cheek, they were off.

As they got in the carriage, Mama Mary put her head out the window. Looking back, she said, "We'll let you know when the wedding date is set."

Anna and Nettie looked at each other and together shouted at the departing carriage, "*Mazel tov*, Mama!"

The girls were given a tour of the campus by Anna Gould. She had been at the school for two years and seemed to be about their same age. "Don't cross Mistress Fechheimer," she warned them. "Don't ever be late for anything. She runs this place like an army barracks, and don't think you can go around her and talk to Mr. Frohman. We think they are more than just business associates," she said with a wink.

The girls were up early to start their first day. They both had attended the girls' school in Mariampole until they were 12. They had mastered several languages and domestic skills, embroidery, and needlework, but not much else. This was going to be a very different education. The philosophy of Becker's Institute was a good education in the liberal arts. This would make its students well rounded.

For the girls, its goal was to make them more interesting people, ready to be proper wives to influential men. Mistress Fechheimer patterned the school from the teachings of Catharine Beecher, who felt women should get a complete education. Learning proper English would be the first step. Their first day of school found them in the "learn English class," and their teacher was Mistress Fechheimer. There were about 12 students, three of whom were boys. Boys and girls in the same class would have been unheard of in Mari-ampole. It didn't take long for the boys to find Nettie.

Mistress Fechheimer began by saying, "You students will never amount to anything in this country if you can't speak proper English. For the boys, English is your way to enter the elite of American society. For the girls, may you find a suitable husband and not end up on the streets. It's my job to teach you society English. No one will mistake you as a greenhorn immigrant. There are certain principles that will help your speech. There is no *th* sound in your native language, Yiddish. 'Zank you so much for zis' is not correct. You are missing the *th* sound. I want all of you to practice the *th* sound until you're doing it in your sleep."

Nettie turned to Anna and said "th th th" and ended up spitting on her.

Anna let out a laugh. BANG! went Mistress Fechheimer's ruler on the desk in front of her. The whole class sprang to attention. "I will not have any talking in my class. The next time this happens, you will feel the sting of this ruler. If you think this is so funny, girls, here is a list of *th* words that I want you to repeat to the class tomorrow!" With that, she handed them a list of words. "The next sound will be *W*. Most of you use a *V* instead. 'Vhy is the voice like vine?' is not correct. Now, everyone together, 'Why is the voice like wine?'"

This went on day after day until magically they seemed to get it. They even worked on the disappearing *R* in the New York society accent. *Fourth floor* came out *fawth flaw*, *fear* was *feeah*, and *doctor* was *doctah*. They were both starting to understand the language. Having mastered other languages, their ears were in tune for these subtle changes. This was English with a bit of a British pronunciation. *Again* was *a-gain*, *been* was *bean*, *garage* was *ga-rage*, and *process* was *pro-ses*. They practiced pronouncing *T* as *T* and not *D*: *water* and *butter*. *Dance* was *dahns*, *perfect* was *puhfect*, and *together* was *togethaa*. The most frustrating part was the words that sounded alike but were not: *deer* and *dear*, *desert* and *dessert*, *fair* and *fare*, *flour* and *flower*, *hear* and *here*, and *pear* and *pair*.

There was also a course on how to dress and walk. They were taught about fashion and making the perfect hourglass figure. With a proper corset they could make the body into the exaggerated *S*. This was something the girls had seen when they came to New York and sister Rose helped them with their first dresses.

They received a letter from Mama Mary that her wedding to Rabbi Rabinowitz was going to be Sunday, December 19, just one day before *Chanukah*. They should get on the train Friday after school so they would be home before sunset. This would be their first trip by themselves. They could try out the English that they had learned.

Anna was afraid. "What if we get on the wrong train? What if we miss our stop?"

"Don't be like that, Anna. This will be another adventure for the two of us," Nettie assured her.

"That's what I was afraid of, you and your adventures," said Anna, with a worried look on her face.

Back to New York for the Wedding

The trip back to New York went without incident. They did meet several young men who were more than happy to "protect" these young women traveling alone. They promised to call on them at the school when they returned.

Nettie told Anna, "I bet they never get through the front door if Mistress Fechheimer is guarding it."

Sister Rose and her driver met them at the station and took them back to the apartment to prepare for the wedding. There was Mama Mary, looking quite frazzled and not herself.

"What's the matter, Mama?" Nettie inquired.

"I don't know Nettie. I never thought about marriage after your father died. I guess I'm the nervous bride."

"Don't worry, Mama. It will be a glorious day and we're all here to share it with you."

They would now get a chance to find some clothes for that perfect *S* figure fit for the wedding. Sister Rose was impressed with their knowledge of the current fashion, which they didn't have just one month ago.

"They have taught you well at Becker's Institute," said Rose.

"I'm saving my proper English for tonight," Nettie replied with a wink.

The Wedding

The temple that night was aglow with many electric lights. The whole congregation was invited. After all, this was their rabbi getting married. Nettie and Anna looked very sophisticated in their new clothes.

Anna was looking around the sanctuary. "There," she whispered to Nettie, "over on the other side two rows back, I see Elliot and Michael. No, Nettie, don't turn around. They'll see you looking at them," she pleaded.

With that, Nettie started to turn around. Anna stepped on her foot. "Ouch, what did you do that for?" Nettie said, giving Anna a stern look. "I've never seen you like this, Anna. Why are you so scared?"

"Those are dangerous men, Nettie. You must have the memory of a gnat. They almost turned you into a prostitute!"

"I'm not afraid of them. How can they hurt me now?" Nettie said, in a manner that sounded like an older sister. She then turned and saw both of the men across the aisle.

The Wedding Reception

The service was much shorter in the Reform temple than in the Orthodox tradition. The girls were eager to move to the reception area for the festivities. There they met Abraham, who was now the Rabbi's assistant. As they went through the line for their food, they got separated.

Before Anna knew it, a voice came from behind her. "Now where has my little butterfly been?" She turned and came face to face with Michael.

Not knowing what to say and scared to death, she said in her best English, "At Becker's Institute."

"Why, you and Nettie just dropped off the face of the earth. We were getting along so well," he said, with a sly grin.

In her best English, Anna said, "It has been a pleasure seeing you, Michael, but I have other people to meet. Good evening."

With that, she hurried off to the other side of the room, where Abraham and Nettie had found a table to set down their food and drinks. "Nettie, Michael just came up and talked to me. Why did you go and leave me?" she said, sounding very agitated.

"Oh don't be silly, Anna," Nettie said. "They can't hurt you here in public. I will protect you. Look, there's Elliot. I'm going right over there to talk to him."

"Please Nettie, stay here. Don't cause any trouble, not at your mother's wedding."

With that, Nettie got up and in her most regal posture moved toward Elliot and Michael near the center of the room. Elliot saw her approaching, and before Nettie could say anything, he said, "Ah, it's my little dove that flew the coop."

"Hello, Mr. Molinsky." Nettie used her best pronunciation.

"I see you have been learning English," he said.

"You noticed?" Nettie replied.

"You have something of mine that I need returned, my three-carat diamond ring." He said this like a man used to getting his way.

"I hardly think it would be proper of me to return such a ring that you gave me under false pretenses," Nettie said, with the air of a New York society matron.

"Look here, Nettie, I know where you've been hiding—at Becker's Institute. It's not too far for me or my men to retrieve my ring."

"You don't frighten me, Mr. Molinsky. I know who you are now—a liar, cheat, and crook. America is no place for a person like you."

"So now you're threatening me?" He raised one eyebrow. This man was not used to any woman telling him what to do. "Let me tell you what I can do to your brother-in-law's business. Our union movement can shut him down, and then you will all be out on the street. That's a threat and a promise if I don't get that ring back," Elliot demanded.

"Good evening, sir. I will take my leave, as I have nothing more to say to you. Consider the ring a donation to the temple." Nettie turned and the many layers of her gown brushed against the two men.

Getting back to her table, Anna's eyes were as big as saucers. "I heard what you said to them, Nettie. You'd better return the ring."

"Not on your life, Anna. Do you know what I went through after he gave it to me? That ring is mine. How did he know we're at Becker's?" Nettie asked.

"Oops, I guess I let it slip out when Michael came up behind me. I'm sorry, Nettie. I didn't mean to tell him," Anna replied, putting her head between her hands, wishing this night had never happened.

"That's OK, Anna. They don't scare me. Besides, I left it with my sister Rose. By the way, did you notice the ring that Rabbi Rabinowitz gave Mama? Yep, Mama now has that ring on her finger. That's one woman Elliot will never get the ring from." They both started to laugh so hard that the people around them turned to hear the joke, but this was a private moment of triumph.

"Tomorrow is the first day of *Chanukah*," Nettie said. "I'll bet I know what the rabbi is going to give Mama." They both started to laugh again. Abraham, still at the table, began to blush.

Christmas in New York

The school was closed for the next two weeks for the holidays. The girls could now get reacquainted with the city. This time, English would be their language, and they would use it everywhere.

Christmas decorations were going up all over town. There was a light dusting of snow on the ground. It gave the city a fairy-tale look. There was also going to be a big celebration for the New Year that would be special. New York's five counties, or boroughs—Manhattan, Kings (Brooklyn), Bronx, Queens, and Staten Island—would now be represented as one city, New York.

Everywhere they went, they played the game of English, trying their best to sound like the upper-class New York ladies. They went into the hotels on Park Avenue, ordered tea, and pretended they were American society ladies.

Back at Becker's Institute

Back at school, they redoubled their efforts at their studies. Winter had set in and a bone-chilling cold wind blew in over the Sound and slammed against their windows. Nettie remembered the winters in Mariampole, using her thick black hair to protect her face against the freezing wind. She again was thankful for her thick head of hair, which was a natural defense against the cold.

Mistress Fechheimer had them reading passages from writers with elegant styles. This was done to accustom their ears to the sound of sentences and peculiar turns of expression. This helped them get a ready command of the language.

There were also math, science, and a physical side of their education. The physical side was mostly calisthenics performed to music.

Each day, the class started with the reading of several newspapers. This kept them abreast of current affairs and was very important for intellectual conversation. It also taught them reading skills. Foremost in the news was the conflict with Spain. On February 15, the battleship USS *Maine* was sunk under suspicious circumstances in Havana Harbor in Cuba. All the newspapers keep repeating the phrase "Remember the *Maine*," where 260 sailors lost their lives. All this seemed so far away and something that would have little effect on their lives.

Mistress Fechheimer insisted they know what was happening in the world. "All educated men appreciate a woman who knows more than just fashion and house chores," she said.

Winter turned into spring. When the warm air hit the cold ocean waters, fog rolled in from the Sound. Some days it was so thick, they couldn't see the gate at the end of the driveway.

Anna couldn't believe how Nettie was absorbing her studies, like a sponge that had never seen water.

"This is what all the boys were learning back home where we couldn't go to school," Nettie said to Anna. "There's just so much to learn."

The Spanish-American War

The headlines in the newspaper: On April 22, "The USS *Nashville* Captures a Spanish Merchant Ship Off the Coast of Southern Florida." Then two days later, on April 24, in large letters across the top of the paper, "**Spain Declares War on America.**" This all seemed quite curious to Nettie and Anna, who always felt they were observers of the world, not participants. Now they were feeling more like Americans. Something inside of them said that no country must harm America! They were now looking for anything in the news about the war that was about to begin. On April 25, Congress made a formal declaration of war on Spain.[13]

The girls couldn't get enough information on the war and the battles that were taking place. Many of the men in town were volunteering to serve and local military groups were being formed. They read about Theodore Roosevelt who left his position as the Assistant Secretary of the Navy to become a lieutenant colonel in the First Volunteer Cavalry Regiment. His "Rough Riders" were men he had met when he went out west to live the life of a cowboy. It was his unit that stormed San Juan Hill on July 17.

Nettie Must Go to Houston

It was on that day that Nettie received a letter from Mama Mary.

Dear Nettie,

We just received word that your brother Edward in Houston, Texas, has lost his beloved wife, Carrie, to the Yellow Fever. This leaves him alone to take care of your 3-year-old niece, Carrie Rose. He is asking if anyone can help him care for her. He has sent money for passage to Houston. We are asking if you would be the one to go. It

---

13 America was far from ready for a war. At the time, the U.S. Navy consisted of 6 battleships, 2 armored cruisers, 13 protected cruisers, 6 steel monitors, 8 old iron monitors, 33 unprotected cruisers and gunboats, 6 torpedo boats, and 12 tugs. The Navy had no repair ships, transports, hospital ships, or colliers (coal ships for fuel). The government needed to purchase or lease scores of ships. By the end of the war, more than 103 additional ships were added to the fleet. Key West was the base of operations to blockade Cuba. At the same time, there was a need to protect the East Coast from Bar Harbor, Maine, to Key West. Commodore George Dewey destroyed the Spanish ships in the Philippines. When the war was over August 12, 1898, the United States had control of Cuba, Puerto Rico, the Philippines, and Guam.

Carrie Sacks, Edward Sacks's first wife.
From the Diane Sacks collection

will be difficult to find passage on a ship, as many of them are involved in the war, but it looks like the war will be over soon.

Please let me know if you will go.

Your Mother, Mary

"Anna, look at this letter." Nettie handed it to Anna to read.

"Nettie, does this mean you're leaving the school? I thought you loved learning here."

"I do, Anna, but this is my brother who needs me. I barely got to know him before he left for America. This will be a time for me to help him and get to see Texas. I have heard that Galveston[14] is the New York of the West."

"What about the war, Nettie?" asked Anna. "It will be dangerous to go now with all the fighting going on."

"I do know that we would have to go to Key West in order to get to Houston, and that's very close to the fighting," answered Nettie. "Let's see if there are any ships. We can take a trip to New York next week and see what's available. It will be good to take a break from all this studying."

"OK, Nettie, but a trip to Houston is not for me. Will you agree to let me stay here, Nettie?"

"I understand, Anna. I will miss you. It may be time for us to see life on our own. Besides, I'm not leaving tomorrow."

The Steamship Company

When they got back to New York, Nettie and Mama Mary went down to the steamship lines on Broadway. There they found the Mallory Steamship Company as the only

---

14　In 1898, the population of Galveston was 37,000 and the population of New York City was 1 million. Galveston was the fourth-largest city in Texas but a long way from the sophistication of New York City. Houston had a population of 44,000.

one with sailings to Galveston, with one stop in Key West. Unfortunately, the ship used for this trip was the SS *Concho*, and it was leased to the Navy. It would be released from service September 23. Then it was to be refitted from a troop carrier to suit commercial passengers. Nettie bought a ticket for sailing on Saturday, October 1. Edward would just have to make due until then. Nettie could continue her studies for a few more months.

Nettie Goes Shopping for Her Trip

The day had come to leave for Houston. Fall had already arrived in New York. There was a chill in the air as Nettie and the family loaded up the carriage to take her to the Mallory Wharf.

Anna had decided to end her studies at Becker's. Philip, Nettie's brother-in-law, hired her to do design work at his clothing factory. The prior week, the girls had a wonderful time picking out clothes and lingerie for Nettie to take. She had the very latest fashions, which included dresses for the warmer climate of Texas. Fashions were changing, and Nettie wanted only the most up-to-date wardrobe.

Skirts were now a trumpet shape, fitting more closely over the hip and flaring just above the knee. Corsets still helped define the hourglass figure. Undergarments, or "drawers," as they were called, fit each leg independently with a drawstring on top. These split drawers made the trip to the bathroom or outhouse much quicker and easier. Sportswear for women was now available for bicycling or playing tennis. Unfussy tailored clothes were more for sports and traveling. The cycling costume was a shorter skirt, or "bloomers," which were a Turkish trouser style. Afternoon dresses had high necks, wasp waists, puffed sleeves, and bell-shaped skirts. Evening gowns had a squared décolletage, wasp-waists, and skirts with long trains. Nettie had it all.

CHAPTER 4

Nettie Goes
to Houston

As they approached the wharf, they saw before them the SS *Concho*.

She was much smaller than the *Pretoria* that brought them to America. The *Concho* was 329 feet long and 47 feet wide, about half the size of the *Pretoria*. Built in 1891, she had both sails and a steam engine. The sails helped conserve fuel but also allowed her to sail should she have engine trouble. This was her first trip to Galveston since she was leased to the U.S. Navy in May. Cargo was being stored and passengers were arriving, some wearing cowboy hats and boots.

This is going to be a great adventure, thought Nettie. She had a first-class ticket and a stateroom. Her appearance said it all. Dressed in her traveling clothes with her upright posture, she stood out among the crowd. The family helped get her trunk aboard.

The **SS** *Concho* sailed the New York-to-Galveston, Texas, route. *Courtesy of davidharrisonwright.com*

As they walked up the gangplank, she saw the captain. He tipped his hat to her. Samuel Fisk was no more than 30 years old but had been at sea since he was 14. He grew up on a farm in Connecticut with his two older brothers. At 14, Samuel traveled to Mystic, Connecticut, to hire on a vessel bound for distant parts of the world. He even spent time on a whaling ship out of Nantucket.

Moving up the ranks, he was spotted by the Mallory brothers, who needed captains for their growing fleet of ships that traveled the East Coast and the Gulf of Mexico. His spotless record, being a man of high integrity, was just the ticket to command their ship. Standing six feet tall, he towered over everyone on deck. Clean-shaven, with piercing blue eyes, he was a commanding figure as he stood on deck in his tailored Captain's uniform.

Is this love at first sight, or has it been too long since I've been in the company of a man? The thoughts ran through Nettie's head. After getting settled, she gave Anna a tearful hug.

"This will be the first time we've been apart," said Anna, as she dabbed at her eyes with her hanky.

"You'll be just fine without me," said Nettie. "Just think of all the trouble you won't get into."

A grin came over Anna's face as Mama Mary gave Nettie a hug.

Before Mama could say anything, Nettie said, "I'll be careful and not get into any trouble." She winked at Anna over Mama Mary's shoulder, and then they were gone.

Out at Sea

The passage to Galveston was to take seven days, depending on the wind and weather. It wasn't long before the ship pulled away from its moorings at the dock. Nettie went out on the rail and waved to the family. She was reminded of her last sea voyage from Germany, when she and the others breathed a sigh of relief when the ship pulled out and no one had come to arrest them.

This trip would be fun. She was only one of several unescorted women. It didn't take long for the single men to find her. That first night, she was seated with another lady, who said she owned a hotel in Galveston. Based on her makeup and dress, Nettie guessed it was not just a hotel.

The gentlemen at the table introduced themselves as Bryan Stone, a cotton broker, and Duke Culpepper, a cattleman. All her training at Becker's Institute paid off, as she was the center of attention. She could converse on all the topics of the day.

During dinner, she could feel she was being watched from the captain's table. She occasionally looked his way, trying not to let the others at the table notice her glances.

On the second day out to sea, she received a note under her door:

Ms. Sachs,

Captain Fisk would like you to join him at his table this evening. I will escort you to the dining room at 7 p.m.

First Mate Christopher

She knew the magic was back. This time, she would be more careful.

Dinner with the Captain

That evening, she wore one of her new gowns and was escorted from her cabin by the first mate to the captain's table. He was waiting for her and politely rose as she was seated at the table.

"Good evening, Ms. Sachs. Thank you for joining me for dinner."

Nettie looked into those blue eyes and thought she saw the ocean. She felt for, the first time, a little speechless.

"How nice of you to invite me," she said, in her best New York accent. She wasn't really sure what they had for dinner, as the wine was flowing freely. The conversation was also so free-flowing, she felt like she had known him all her life. He talked about his adventures at sea, and she made up stories about growing up in New York City.

The feeling she had was new to her. She had never felt this way before. What was the problem with changing her life's story a bit? She told him that she was 19 years old and that her family had lived in New York since 1840.

His family roots went back to the Mayflower. He wasn't a puritan, but he was certainly very religious. Nettie had never met a man she was interested in who was not Jewish. Just exactly what was the difference?

After supper, he escorted her back to her cabin, said a polite "good night," and told her that he had to return to the bridge. Nettie spent the rest of the evening looking out her cabin porthole window at the waning moon, just dreaming and remembering the men in her life. *There must have been other women in Captain Fisk's life too*, she thought.

Second Night at the Captain's Table

The next night, there were four of them at the table. The captain had invited Greta Westmorland, the hotel owner, and Bryan Stone, the cotton broker, to dine with them. Bryan was interested in the part this ship had played in the Spanish-American War.

Captain Fisk said they had converted her to a troop carrier. Her first mission was to pick up Battery B, Pennsylvania Light Artillery, from Puerto Rico and bring them back to New York. That was 35 officers, 700 men, and 10 horses. "Have you ever cleaned up after a seasick horse?" he joked.

Once in New York, they picked up the 2nd Infantry, 2nd Massachusetts Volunteer Infantry, and the 4th and 25th Infantry. There were 71 officers and 1,256 enlisted men. In the lowest deck, the bunks were four tiers high and so tight together, a man could hardly pass. The ventilation was almost nonexistent down there. They could carry 800 on this deck, and the next deck would carry 460.

Most of their sailing was from Tampa Bay, where on one trip they picked up Roosevelt's Rough Riders and took them to Santiago de Cuba. They had only one water closet for the troops and a trough that could accommodate 10 men. This made for a very uncomfortable trip to Cuba.

"The men were really ready to get off this ship when we arrived," he said. "When we get to Key West to take on more coal, there will be many of our war ships still in port and you can get a better idea about our naval power."

After dinner, the group retired to the captain's quarters to have after-dinner drinks and play the board game The Checkered Game of Life.[1] They all knew the game and had great fun.

---

1   The game simulated a person's travels through his or her life—education, jobs, marriage, children, and retirement. It used a modified checkerboard and a teetotum, a six-sided top. The object was to land on the "good" spaces and collect 100 points. The player's goal was to make it to the upper right-hand corner, "Happy Old Age." It had a moral message, as it rewarded good behavior and punished bad choices in life. The players would laugh when someone landed on a bad square, such as gambling, and applaud when a good square was hit.

It was midnight before anybody knew it. The first mate knocked on the door and reminded the captain he was needed on the bridge. They all said good night. The captain escorted Nettie to her cabin. Nettie was not going to settle for a handshake this night. As they reached her cabin, she turned and faced him. Reaching up with one hand she pulled him to her and kissed him on the lips. She knew she startled him. He turned, said "Good night, Nettie," and was off to the bridge.

If I were to wait for him, Nettie thought, *the kiss would have never happened.*

On the bridge that night, Samuel Fisk had a lot on his mind. *I guess these New York society women are different,* he thought. He could still taste her kiss on his lips.

Fourth Day Out—The Gulf Stream

The fourth day out to sea, they could see a bank of fog in the distance. They were just off Cape Hatteras, and everyone was talking about the Gulf Stream.[2]

As they approached the fog bank, there was an announcement: "All passengers put on your life jackets and stay alert." This was the northern wall of the Gulf Stream. The fog was the result of the warm water and the cold air above it. The wind began to pick up as they entered the fog. Before long, the calm sea turned into large rolling waves that buffeted the *Concho* on both sides. It had the ship rolling from rail to rail.

What a great ride, Nettie thought. *I wish Anna were here to see this.* Retreating to the salon, she found her shipmates not feeling too well. Then a crash of thunder seemed to come out of nowhere, and torrents of rain hit the ship. This reminded Nettie of the hurricane she was in on her initial passage across the Atlantic, but the *Pretoria* was much bigger.

Several hours went by, and the sea became much smoother. The sun came out. They were through the Gulf Stream.

Captain Fisk came into the salon. "How did everyone enjoy the Gulf Stream?" he asked.

"Not so much," said Greta, looking a little seasick.

"Well, we won't have to do that again, or at least for a while," he said.

---

2   The Gulf Stream is an ocean current that loops up from the Gulf of Mexico around Key West and runs northward up the east coast of Florida. It is a vast river of warm water moving from 2 to 8 mph. At Cape Hatteras, it moves east out into the Atlantic Ocean. Because of its warm water, it makes its own weather and can be 30 to 80 miles wide.

"What do you mean for a while?" asked Nettie.

Bryan spoke up, "We hit it again outside of Key West, but it should be a lot warmer there."

"He's right," said the captain. "We'll stay off the Florida coast and away from the Gulf Stream until we come closer to Key West. That's where the current turns and flows north. The current can be quite strong. Until then, enjoy yourselves. That's a day's sail from now."

He turned and left the salon but not before acknowledging Nettie with a tip of his cap.

The Captain and Nettie

That evening after dinner, Nettie and Captain Fisk stood by the rail and felt the breeze in their faces. It was considerably warmer as the *Concho* moved down the coast.

"Nettie, sometimes I look out over the sea and wonder why am I here. What's my reason for being here? Did God give everyone a purpose in life? There's so much unhappiness in the world, and I have seen a lot of it," he said.

Nettie thought, *I can't tell him how much unhappiness I've seen. I can tell him about New York.* "Growing up in New York showed me just how lucky I am," she said. "Most women have no future unless they get married. You are lucky, Sam. It's a man's world. On the Lower East Side of New York, most of the immigrants have next to nothing. The women work in sweatshops or, worse, a life of prostitution is all some can look forward to. It's very sad."

"It's a man's world, Nettie. That just isn't right, is it?" he replied.

Nettie couldn't believe he was so sensitive to the plight of women. He was truly a special man. She moved closer to him, feeling a little chill from the night air. He did not move away but put his arm around her shoulders and drew her next to him. No words were spoken for a long time. They just stood there in their embrace. He escorted her back to her cabin, and this time he kissed Nettie. It was long and passionate, just like she had dreamed it would be.

"See you tomorrow, Nettie. Sleep tight," Sam said.

Now it was her turn to taste his kiss on her lips. She dreamed pleasant dreams as the hum of the ship's engine seemed to keep time with her breathing.

What is it about men named Sam? This was the first time in a long time she had thought about the other Sam. *I wonder how he's doing?*

Sailing Along the Florida Coast

The next morning, Nettie woke up to a bright sunny day. The ship was now along the coast of Florida, and the weather was quite mild. Today she would wear some of the clothes she brought for the weather in Houston. All her shipmates were full of spirit today, as the warm air seemed to breathe life into them. They were all on deck enjoying the warm weather. As the day wore on, they could see the beginning of the Florida Keys on their right.

They could hear the ship's engines straining to maximum horsepower as they moved against the current of the Gulf Stream. This is what Bryan and the captain referred to several days ago. The *Concho* could do 12 knots at full power, but against the current their speed was much less. Captain Fisk was keeping the vessel outside the shallow coral reefs that ran 200 miles parallel to the Keys.[3]

The *Concho* had a draft of 21 feet, and even though she was light on coal and riding higher in the water, he did not want to enter Key West at night or at sunset. The sun would be directly in front of them, and their vision would be impaired as they turned west. He needed the vision of the crew to read the water for depth. Blue was the deepest. Green was shallower, where they might go aground. Having done this passage many times, he preferred safety to speed. They dropped anchor that afternoon inside the shoal line just inside the Hawk Channel.

Key West 1898

In the morning, before Nettie woke, the ship was already on its way. They had moved from the shoals into deeper water and were now in the Main Ship Channel. They had to make two dogleg turns as they entered the harbor at Key West. It had been only a few months since the end of the Spanish-American War. Many Navy ships were still moored at the Naval base.

Nettie found a note under her door from Sam:

---

3   This stretch of reefs and shoals was known for its shipwrecks. During the 19th century, ships were wrecking on the Florida Reef at the rate of one a week. For a period of 100 years, wrecking captains and vessels had to hold a license issued by the federal court to retrieve cargo from these ships.

Nettie,

Wear your best summer clothes. We are going to tour one of our finest battleships today. Meet me in the salon.

Sam

Before she knew it, the *Concho* was docking in Key West across from the coal station. It was going to take half a day to load the coal. They had time to venture ashore. Their ship was taller than the tallest building in Key West. As she looked down, she saw palm trees between many of the houses. The houses were painted in the most beautiful pastel colors she had ever seen.

Look what Anna is missing, she thought. The houses looked like little gumdrops, all with tin roofs.

She decided to wear a summery dress with a pink parasol to match. Entering the salon, she found Bryan and Greta already waiting for the captain. It was obvious to Nettie that Greta did not understand fashion, or was she showing the fashions of Galveston?

In walked Captain Fisk, looking splendid in his uniform. "Is everyone ready?" he asked. "Follow me," he said, as he extended his arm to Nettie.

They left the salon and walked to the gangplank. There at the bottom was a brightly colored carriage with a fringed top. Two Navy seamen were standing alongside at attention. Over her shoulder, Nettie could hear the steam shovel picking up coal and placing it in large bags that were hoisted onto the ship and emptied into a chute that led to the coal bunker below deck.

When they got in the carriage, the captain announced, "We are going to tour the battleship USS *Oregon*. This is the ship that won the war for America.[4] She chased down a Spanish cruiser to end the battle of Santiago de Cuba."

---

4   The battleship USS *Oregon* had been stationed in San Francisco and had to steam around South America and up to Key West, a journey of 16,000 miles. She did this in 66 days—quite a feat at the time. This gave rise to the urgency to build the Panama Canal. On July 3, 1898, she caught up to the Spanish cruiser *Cristobal Colon* in the final battle of Santiago de Cuba. It was trying to break free, but because of the speed of the *Oregon*, 19.3 mph, she caught up to the cruiser, which was scuttled in the mouth of the Tarquino River to prevent capture. This ended the battle of Santiago de Cuba.

Nettie did remember the story that was in all the papers that they read at school. The USS *Oregon* was a famous ship, and now she was going to go aboard. She couldn't wait to write all about it to Anna.

Captain Fisk had met the captain of the *Oregon*, Charles E. Clark, during one of their stops in Key West. They had hit it off right away and became friends. He looked up to Captain Clark, who at 54 was more like a father figure. Now he was going to introduce Nettie to him.

Their carriage arrived at the USS *Oregon* in just a few minutes. Their group was escorted by the seamen to the gangplank, with Captain Fisk leading the way. Up they went with the captain, who saluted the ensign, then turned to the officer of the deck. "Request permission to come aboard," he said.

"Come aboard," was the reply.

As their group followed the captain, they did not see Captain Clark. Instead, they were greeted by Lieutenant Commander James K. Cogswell. "It's a pleasure to meet you, Captain Fisk. Captain Clark has taken ill with tropical fever and left for home aboard the *St. Louis*. He knew you were coming and asked me to give you and your guests a tour."

Samuel Fisk was disappointed. He wanted Nettie to meet the man he held in such high regard. Now it was just a tour.

Nettie couldn't believe the size of the 13-inch guns. The ship seemed top-heavy with all the heavy batteries and armament. The teak deck was spotless and devoid of handrails or anything to sit on. The commander explained that all wooden furniture and fixtures were thrown overboard on the trip to Key West. In battle, splinters from the wood were as lethal as bullets.

Below deck, there was little headroom, even for Nettie. It was all business and weapons. The mess room was also missing all its chairs. The men ate sitting on the floor. Around the hull of the ship was a band of steel 18 inches wide and 8.5 inches thick to protect against incoming fire.

Coming out onto the deck, they went to the aft of the ship, passing many more guns. The crew stood at attention as they passed, and Nettie could sense them looking at her, even though they were supposed to keep their eyes directed forward.

Before they knew it, they were back down the gangplank and into the carriage. On the way to the ship, they saw local merchants selling fruit, sponges, and cigars.

"Captain, can we stop and do some shopping?" Both Nettie and Greta seemed to say this at the same time.

"Good idea, ladies. We men need some cigars too," replied the captain.

They stopped, and Nettie bought sponges and some cigars for her brother. "I've never seen sponges this size," she remarked to Greta.

"I guess you've never been in this part of the world. You're going to see a whole different America than you've seen in New York City." Greta said this in a mocking tone, with a little nasal accent. Nettie caught the sarcasm in her tone. Could it be she was jealous of her relationship with Captain Fisk?

They were back on the *Concho*, and dinner was being served as they pulled away from the dock. They steamed out of Key West and into the Gulf of Mexico on the last leg of their journey. That afternoon, a steady breeze from the southeast was building, and the Captain ordered the sails to be raised and the engine shut down. This saved fuel. The *Concho* became very quiet, with just the sound of the waves hitting the ship.

It was dinner in the captain's quarters that night, and Nettie could feel the sexual tension building between them all day. The cabin walls were covered in a rich, dark wood. On one end of the cabin was a combination sitting/dining room. On the other end was the bedroom, separated from the main area by a semitransparent curtain. In the center was a roll-top desk and a chart, or map, table. The floor had an Oriental rug covering the center section of the cabin.

The orderly brought in their dinner, which they barely touched as they sipped the wine and talked about the tour of the *Oregon*.

"I really wanted you to meet Captain Clark," Sam said.

The orderly returned and cleared the dishes, and Samuel locked the door behind him. Nettie had moved to the couch that was next to the dining room table, and he joined her.

"Nettie," he said, in a tone she had never heard before. "Over these past few days, I have developed feelings for you that I have never had with any other woman."

Nettie stopped him before he could go on, as she leaned in to him and kissed him on the cheek. He returned the kiss but on her lips. She knew now that this was not going to be just a good-night kiss. While kissing, she started unbuttoning his top coat, vest, and shirt. He reached around her and loosened her corset, and her amble bosoms nearly exploded out the top of her gown.

Their hands were everywhere, feeling each other's bodies. It was only a few steps to the other side of the cabin and his bed. Samuel drew back the curtain as Nettie let her gown drop to the floor. He did the same with his trousers. As they lay on the bed Nettie, had the sensation that it was moving. There, overhead, she saw the bed was suspended on four chains. It would float or move as the ship rolled side to side.

Both were now down to their underwear. Nettie still had on her drawers and her chemise, but the corset was long gone. Her fingers reached into his drawers and then back out after touching his penis.

What am I feeling? she wondered. She reached in again and realized there was a flap of skin over the end of the penis. *Of course*, she thought, *he's not circumcised. That's the difference between Gentile and Jewish men.* Now she was distracted and just had to see what she was feeling. Using both hands, she removed his drawers and looked down at his uncircumcised penis, now very erect and hard.

"What's the matter?" he asked.

"Oh nothing, Sam. I was just admiring your manhood."

He then removed her chemise, and she was naked except her drawers, which extended up both her legs. As he rolled on top of her, she could taste the smell of his body next to hers. It had been so long since she felt this way about someone.

"Sam," she said, "now!"

He was fighting his puritan moral upbringing, but Nettie's sensual nature was just too much for him. She spread her legs in anticipation, but before he could enter her, he ejaculated onto her drawers. They lay there together both out of breath.

"I'm sorry, Nettie, but I just couldn't control myself."

"That's all right, Sam. I understand."

The name *Sam* came out of her mouth so easily. It brought back the memory of Sam, the future medical student she met on the voyage from the old country. She and Sam lay together most of the night. Later, he was able to enter her and withdraw in time. The gentle swaying of the ship under sail was hypnotic, and she slept soundly for hours.

Before daybreak, she awoke to the sound of the engines and found herself alone, but a note was on the pillow next to her:

Nettie,

Was called to the bridge. Will see you in the salon later today. Will be in Galveston this afternoon. Use the toilet to get yourself ready for the day. I have locked the door so you won't be disturbed.

Sam

She did just that and got back to her room without anyone noticing. At breakfast, she first saw Greta.

"Boy, are you looking chipper this morning," Greta said, with a little wink in her eye.

"I'm so glad to be finishing this trip and seeing my brother and niece," said Nettie.

She knew Greta could tell that was not the reason she looked so happy. Women know these things instinctively. She didn't see Sam again until the noontime meal. He joined the three of them at their table.

"We plan to be in Galveston late this afternoon," he announced.

"That's what I like to hear," said Bryan. "A Mallory ship is always on time."

Sam looked at Nettie in a way she had never seen before, at least not in front of other people.

Docking in Galveston

They entered the Port of Galveston[5] about 3 p.m. From the vantage point of the deck, Nettie thought she could see across the island. Along the dock were bales of cotton that would be going back to New York, headed for the clothing manufacturers.

She looked out onto the dock, and there in the crowd she thought she saw her brother, holding in his arms her niece Carrie Rose. The last time she had seen her brother, she was only 5 years old. Would he recognize her?

The gangplank was lowered, and the passengers began to disembark. Nettie stayed at the back of the line and let the others find their friends and relatives in the crowd. Almost last, Nettie made her entrance down the gangplank holding a parasol in front of her blocking the afternoon sun. Coming toward her was a man holding a little girl. It was Edward. She could not forget his round face and happy smile. He was wearing glasses that were also round and matched his face. Carrie Rose, her niece, was picture-perfect with her hair worn in long curls.

Carrie Rose was the first to speak. "Auntie Nettie," she called, and held open her arms as Edward put her down on the wharf.

---

5 Galveston Island is located just off the coast of Texas. It's 27 miles long and three miles wide at its widest point. In 1898, there was a seawall protecting part of the city, and the city's elevation was 7.2 feet. This all changed after the devastating hurricane of 1900, when the seawall was raised and lengthened to surround the entire city. The city was raised to an elevation of 17 feet by dredging sand from the nearby waterways and pumping it into the area within the seawall.

Nettie bent down and picked her up. "Yes, I'm your Auntie Nettie. We're going to have so much fun together."

It was Edward's turn now. He embraced the two of them in a bear hug only he could perform. Before she knew it, Sam was by her side. The captain and Edward were about the same age, both successful men at 30 years of age. Edward was a few inches shorter than Samuel. Both men had an air of confidence about them that Nettie loved.

"Let me make the introductions," Nettie said. "Captain Fisk, this is my brother Edward Sacks and my niece Carrie Rose."

"A pleasure to meet you, Mr. Sachs and Carrie Rose. You wouldn't be the Sachs of the Sachs Coal company that supplies our ships?" the captain asked.

Edward Sacks. *Courtesy of Shirley Furman*

"That I am, Captain, the best coal you can buy for your boilers. You know the jingle, *Get a sack of coal from Sacks.*[6]" He just beamed as he answered him. "Thank you for taking care of my little sister on her voyage from New York."

Nettie held her breath. *Would Edward say she was 13, her real age? I must change the conversation.* "Gentleman, it's time to find my trunk and see a little of Galveston, the New York of the West." She breathed a sigh of relief as they all started looking for her trunk.

"Found it," Edward said. He motioned for one of the stevedores to take the trunk to their waiting carriage.

"Do you mind if I tag along?" Captain Fisk asked.

"You are more than welcome, Captain," replied Edward.

He threw his bag in the back of the carriage. They all got in the carriage and proceeded along the main street paralleling the beach. Nettie saw bathhouses like the ones on Coney Island. These were bigger, and there were more of them. People were actually in the water, and it was October!

---

6   The local people in Houston started spelling the "Sachs" name "Sacks." It was easier just to keep the new spelling than to correct it.

There were many Victorian-style houses with multiple spheres and round projections. They reached the Grand Opera House and Hotel, which opened in 1895. The front wall of the building was made of red stone, brick, and terra cotta. Its large glass doors were framed by a carved Romanesque stone arch.

"This is where I get off," Sam said. "I usually stay the night here and take the *Concho* back to New York in the morning. Nettie, could I have your address in Houston?"

"Yes, Captain, I think it's 1720 Moore Street. Is that correct, Edward?"

"Yes," he replied.

Sam jumped effortlessly out of the carriage and swung his bag off the back and waved goodbye. Nettie blew him a kiss.

"What was that all about?" asked Edward.

"Oh, nothing. We just had a very good trip together," Nettie replied, and a smile came to her lips.

"We had better get going if we're to catch the last train to Houston," Edward said. "It's a four-hour ride, and you must already be tired."

Nettie did not feel tired at all. She was thinking about when she would hear from the captain again. Surely he would write.

The Train Ride to Houston

The train ride took them across Galveston Bay and through marshland. Few trees dotted the landscape. The train followed the course of Buffalo Bayou. Edward was the tour director as he pointed out landmarks along the way.

"See this bayou, Nettie? Someday, it will be deep enough to bring the big ships from Galveston Bay all the way to Houston. Whenever I get a chance, I buy property along its banks."

The thought was lost on Nettie, as all she saw was a weed-choked swampy creek. They arrived in Houston after dark. Nettie was surprised not to see streetlights so familiar to her in New York. They got into a carriage and proceeded down the dark, dusty, unpaved roads. No horseless carriages here, no crowds of people. It wasn't long until they reached a Victorian-style house with a large porch and two spires on either side of the house.

"We're home," Edward announced.

Carrie Rose had been sleeping. Nettie picked her up and carried her into the house. It was furnished with overstuffed couches and chairs. The windows had coverings of lace.

Buffalo Bayou 1898. *Courtesy of the Texas Historical Society*

The floor was a highly polished wood that you could slide on in stocking feet. The bedrooms were upstairs at the top of a staircase that had a landing midway up. That's where she took little Carrie Rose and put her to bed. Her room was next to Nettie's.

Edward had the driver bring her trunk upstairs. Tonight she would sleep well in the overstuffed feather bed and dream, maybe of Captain Sam or …

She awoke to the sound of little Carrie Rose running down the upstairs hallway. This little girl was so full of life. In some ways, she was like a little adult. She was a great comfort to Edward after the death of her mother in July. It was up to Nettie to be a mother to little Carrie Rose until such time as Edward remarried. That was the family tradition.

Houston 1898

Houston in 1898 was not New York. There were only a few paved streets, but they did have electric streetlights downtown and an electric streetcar line. Most transportation was by fancy horse-drawn rigs and bicycles. This is where Nettie first learned to ride one, much to the delight of little Carrie Rose. The two of them were inseparable, going to the parks and shopping in the downtown stores. Nothing was off limits as far as Edward was concerned. He was so happy Nettie was with him taking care of Carrie Rose. She did Carrie Rose's hair in the latest New York style and taught her many things she had learned at Becker's Institute. Her niece was going to be all American.

In November, she received a letter:

Dear Nettie,

Sorry it has taken me so long to contact you. Our line has been busy after the war with back shipments from Galveston. I have only been able to stay in town overnight. Later this month, I will get a few days over the Thanksgiving holiday, Friday the 25th and Saturday the 26th. I would love to see you. I will be staying at The Grand Opera House and will get you a room. Sarah Bernhardt is playing. It should be a grand time.

Yours truly,

Samuel
Captain Samuel Fisk
Mallory Line Office
Galveston, Texas

It didn't take Nettie long to reply. This was the letter she had been waiting for. This was her second Thanksgiving in America. With the captain, it would be wonderful.

When Edward got home, she had dinner on the table. After she cleared the table and put Carrie Rose to bed, she approached Edward in the den. "Edward, I just heard from Captain Fisk. He has invited me to spend Thanksgiving in Galveston."

Edward looked over his glasses and with a smile said, "I thought there was more to your relationship, the way the two of you looked at each other."

"Oh Edward," she blushed. "We are just friends. He's getting me my own room at the Grand Opera House."

"It's going to be lonely here without you for Thanksgiving, but we will manage."

"I'll have all the cooking done before I leave and will have the maid just heat it up for the two of you. You are such an understanding brother."

"No, Nettie, you have been a savior of late. Carrie Rose is really getting attached to her Aunt Nettie," he replied.

Thanksgiving Weekend with the Captain

The four-hour train ride to Galveston seemed to take forever. She took a carriage to the Grand Opera House. There in the lobby was Captain Fisk, looking elegant in his full dress uniform.

"My, you look wonderful. Houston hasn't changed you a bit," he said to Nettie.

He embraced her in the hug she remembered and had longed for the past month. He checked her in and waved off the bellboy as he took her to her room. Once in the room, they embraced again and kissed passionately.

"I'll leave you to freshen up. Then it's supper and the show in the Opera House." They kissed again. "Pick you up at seven."

Nettie could not remember the dinner as she looked into those blue eyes. Sarah Bernhardt was the headliner that night. She was making a tour of America after her success in France. Tonight's performance was *La Tosca*. As they approached the grand staircase, there was a large bronze statue of a woman holding a torch.

He took Nettie's arm. They circled the statue and climbed the stairs to the top floor and their opera box. There were eight boxes, four each on either side of the main stage. The chairs in the box were covered in blue velour. The stage curtain was red velvet. *I must be in a dream,* Nettie thought. *Everything is so beautiful.*

Sarah Bernhardt was the most famous dramatic actress in France at the time. She was making a tour of the United States, and the Grand Opera House in Galveston was one of the finest in America.

The play *La Tosca* is set in Rome in 1800 and has five acts, the last ending in the suicide of Tosca, who threw herself from the castle's parapet. A hush came over the audience as Act 1 began and the curtain rose. The house lights went dim. The setting was the church of Sant'Andrea in Rome.

Sam reached over and took her hand. Nettie's whole body felt energized by his touch. She turned to look at him as he leaned over to kiss her on the cheek. Acts I, II, and III were all a blur. After Act III, they just couldn't wait any longer, so they left, ending up at her room.

With the door closed behind them, they fell into each other's arms, eventually making it to the bed as they tore at each other's clothes.

"Oh Sam," she said. "I thought you would never write, but here we are together again."

"Forget you?" he teased. "That would be impossible."

That night was sheer bliss. They spent the night in each other's arms. In the morning, they awoke to the sound of rain hitting their window. They decided to sleep in and order room service.

"I guess we didn't need two rooms, Nettie," he joked. "Next trip, it will just be one."

They spent the rest of the two days together, even venturing out to do a little shopping. Nettie looked for a toy and found a precious little doll to take back to Carrie Rose. On Saturday, Sam took her to the train, as he had to get back to the ship for the return trip to New York.

"You will write?" Nettie asked.

"Of course I will," he replied.

The train ride back to Houston seemed much faster this time, as her thoughts were filled with Captain Sam. Carrie Rose was there to greet her as she got off the train. Brother Edward had that little twinkle in his eye that said he knew what was going on.

The months went by, and every three months, Nettie found herself in Galveston with Captain Sam. Carrie Rose was growing up and learning everything Nettie could teach her. Houston itself was growing with more paved streets and streetlights.

Life in Houston

This was Nettie's first summer in Texas. The heat seemed to go on forever. Carrie Rose was now 5 years old and going to school for the first time. Monday, September 3, was Labor Day. There would be marching bands and politicians making speeches in the park. Nettie wanted to go to Galveston, as the captain was bringing in the SS *Concho*. She just couldn't ask Edward to watch Carrie Rose. He had been so accommodating on her other trips to Galveston. Besides, he was very busy getting ready for his Labor Day sale. She would have to take Carrie Rose with her. This would be a good test of their relationship, as she would not be spending the night.

It was Sunday, September 2. Nettie knew the train would be full, as this was the last weekend before school started. They couldn't go on Saturday, the Sabbath. Edward didn't want to have Carrie Rose riding a train on the Sabbath.

"Rise and shine, Carrie Rose. You and I are off to the beach today, and we have to catch the early train."

Carrie Rose always liked the trips with Nettie, as she would let her do things her father wouldn't, like swimming in the surf by herself.

"I'm awake. Don't forget my bathing costume," Carrie Rose said. She was only 5 but wore the full-length swimming dress like the adults. Off they went to catch the train. Nettie had packed a picnic lunch. This would be the first time the captain would taste her cooking.

She loved going to Galveston. It was on its way to being the New York of the South. It was the third-richest city in America and had telephones, telegraph, trolleys, and streetlights.[7]

Arriving at the train station, they took a carriage to the Grand Opera House. Nettie went to the front desk and asked the clerk to deliver a note to Captain Fisk's room:

Dear Sam,

I am waiting in the lobby. Don't forget your bathing costume.

Love, Nettie

Nettie and Carrie Rose sat down in an overstuffed couch and waited for Sam. When he got the note, he thought, *This is strange. I wonder why she didn't come up to the room?*

He got his answer as he entered the lobby. "Hi Sam. Look who I brought with me today," as Nettie moved Carrie Rose in front of her.

"It's a pleasure to meet you again, young lady. I have heard so much about you." Sam said this as he reached out to shake her hand.

Carrie Rose, never at a loss for words, said, "I remember you when Auntie Nettie first came here. You are the captain."

"That I am, Miss Carrie Rose. Auntie Nettie says you're going to go swimming with us."

"Yes I am," said Carrie Rose, "and I brought my bathing costume too."

The captain now knew that Nettie would not be staying this weekend, but he loved her company. The addition of Carrie Rose would make it feel like a family outing. Out into the sunshine the trio went, with the captain carrying the picnic basket. The doorman hailed a carriage.

---

7   The population of Galveston in 1900 was 37,789. Some thought it should be higher, as it was taken in June when many of the residents were on vacation. After the hurricane in September of 1900, the population never recovered. Houston's population in 1900 was 44,633. By 1910, Houston had almost doubled to 78,800 and kept doubling every decade for the next 60 years.

"To Murdock's bathhouse," the captain ordered the driver, who cracked the whip over the heads of the horses.

The bathhouse was built right on the beach and just off the trolley line that hugged the coast. Murdock's extended out into the Gulf waters and was connected from the land by a bridge over the sand. The carriage driver had no trouble leaving the road and heading under the bridge that led to the bathhouse.

There they climbed the stairs directly under the bathhouse to enter. There were changing rooms and showers for both men and women. They took little time to change and set up their beach blanket. Nettie loved the feel of the warm sand between her toes. The water was still very warm from the hot summer, but it did cool them off. They started out under the building in the shade and then ventured out past the building into deeper water in the sunshine.

"This is so much fun," Carrie Rose said, as she paddled between the two of them in water over her head. "Papa would never let me go out this deep."

Nettie was lost in thought as she imagined them as a family and thought how nice this feels.

Before long, it was time for dinner. Nettie had a treat for Sam. "I want you to know, Sam, that I made everything in the basket myself."

"That's right," Carrie Rose said. "I helped too."

Nettie opened the basket and started to put out the food: *blintzes*,[8] bagels, lox, corned beef sandwiches with half sour pickles, chopped liver, and cabbage rolls. She even had baked macaroons for dessert.

"Oh my," Sam said. "This looks like Iceland Deli in New York."

"I wasn't sure if you would like this kind of food," Nettie said, with a smile that said *How could you not like it?*

"Iceland is my favorite. Every time I take the *Concho* back to New York, I make it a point to go to Iceland's Deli," Sam said.

The day just flew by. Nettie could feel the warm sand through the blanket. Sam held her hand and they would both doze off a bit as they watched Carrie Rose build sandcastles. *Sam is such a mensch*, Nettie thought.

The sun was going down. They all knew they must catch the last train back to Houston. They changed in the bathhouse and got back in the carriage. Sam went with them to the train station. As they got out of the carriage, Sam pulled Nettie to him and kissed her on the lips.

---

8   A *blintz* is a pancake filled with cream cheese.

"Be careful on the way back. Some of your fellow travelers may have had a bit too much to drink."

"We will, Sam, and you be careful on your trip back to New York."

Little did she know how prophetic that statement would be. Little Carrie Rose held up her arms, and the captain picked her up and carried her onto the train.

"Goodbye, you two," he said.

Nettie blew him a kiss, and then they were off. No sooner had they left the station, when Carrie Rose asked, "Auntie Nettie, why did you kiss the captain?'

"Carrie Rose, that's how good friends say hello and goodbye."

"I can't wait to get some good friends," giggled Carrie Rose. They both laughed.

On the train ride back to Houston, they both fell asleep to the sound of the click clack of the train on the track. Nettie found herself dreaming again. Sam was the star. As much as she wanted him to be the husband, she knew he could not. Jews just didn't marry Gentiles, no matter how much in love they may have been. It just wasn't permitted. The family would disown you, and family was very important.

Edward was at the station to pick up the two very tired travelers. It didn't take them long to get to bed and go to sleep.

The next day, Carrie Rose and Nettie were off to the park to take part in the Labor Day celebration.

"Two parties in two days. This is wonderful, Aunt Nettie" said Carrie Rose.

"Tonight you will go to bed early. The first day of school starts tomorrow."

Nettie thought, *How different things are here in America.* "In the old country, all that girls would learn in school was how to sew and speak multiple languages," explained Nettie.

"You went to a school that was all girls?"

"That's right, Carrie Rose. The boys went to a different school where girls were not allowed." Her thoughts raced back to the time she had impersonated a boy just to see what they were learning in school. "You get some sleep. Tomorrow will be here before you know it."

The Hurricane of 1900

The rest of the week, Carrie Rose would entertain the family with what she had learned at school. She could already read. Because she was so advanced, she became the star student and teacher's pet.

Galveston Hurricane, 1900. *Courtesy of the Texas Historical Society*

LEFT: Galveston Hurricane, 1900: Interior St. Patrick's church. *Library of Congress*
RIGHT: Galveston Hurricane, 1900: An opened passageway in the debris, looking north on 19th Street, Galveston, Texas. *Library of Congress*

On the morning of Saturday, September 8, Nettie was ready to take Carrie Rose out for the day. Unfortunately, it was very windy with periodic showers. They elected to stay in. By the afternoon, the winds became so strong that the rocking chairs on the porch were blown onto the lawn.

Edward wasn't working because it was the Sabbath, but he went by the lumberyard to see that it was OK. "If I didn't know better," he told Nettie, "I'd think we are having a hurricane."

"What's a hurricane?" Carrie Rose asked.

Nettie had firsthand experience on her crossing of the Atlantic. "I'll tell you, Carrie Rose, it's a lot of wind and rain that seems to go on forever. We went through one on the ship I was on when I came to America."

By 8:30 that evening, the gusts of wind increased but there were only a few episodes of wind-driven rain. The howling wind kept them all in the living room. No one wanted to go upstairs to bed. Just then a loud crack was heard. They watched in horror as a tree limb broke through the living room window, nearly hitting Carrie Rose.

"Come on, everyone to the kitchen," Edward shouted above the sound of the wind, as he scooped up Carrie Rose with one arm. There were windows in the kitchen but much smaller and higher up.

Nettie went upstairs and brought down pillows and comforters. "Let's pretend we are camping outside," she said, directing her message to Carrie Rose. "Let's get under the comforter and pretend it's a tent." This broke the tension a bit, but they could all hear the wind blowing into the living room through the broken window.

Carrie Rose cuddled up to Edward, and he put his arms around her. They had a kerosene lamp, but otherwise it was a dark night lighted only by the strikes of lightning and then a loud thunder clap. Nettie remembered that on the ship, the storm seemed to last forever, but this time there was only a steady breeze and no rain by morning.[9]

---

9 This was the 1900 hurricane that hit Galveston, Texas, on September 8. The eye of the storm did not go directly over Galveston but slightly to the west. It did bring a storm surge and tide of over 20 feet. Galveston's highest elevation was 8.7 feet, and the city had no seawall to protect it. The island is only three miles at its widest point, so the seawater washed over the island. It was all but wiped off the map. Over 3,000 homes had been swept out to sea. Those left were greatly damaged. Loss of life was estimated at 6,000 to 8,000 people. Some put the toll as high as 12,000. The 1900 Galveston hurricane is known as the deadliest natural disaster in the history of the United States. The city never fully recovered, as investors decided it was safer to go farther inland, and Houston was the beneficiary. In Houston, over half of the buildings sustained some wind damage, but they did not have flooding.

That morning, Edward surveyed the damage. "Looks like all we have is a broken window and a little water to mop up. I'm going over to the yard and see what has happened there. I will send some men over to get the tree out of the house."

Wow, what a night that was. I sure don't want to go through another hurricane, thought Nettie.

It was several days before the people in Houston knew the full extent of the damage in Galveston. All lines of communication were down. The railroad had been hit with the tidal surge, which knocked the train off the tracks. All telegraph and telephone lines were down.

Edward's wood and coal business was located on Buffalo Bayou at a spot where small boats could navigate all the way from Galveston Island. His business suffered only minor wind damage. He was up and running when the call came for building materials.

A thought came to Nettie. Captain Sam had left Galveston Wednesday, September 5, on the *Concho's* trip to New York. *Was he all right?* With no way to contact the steamship company or Sam, she could only wait for a letter.[10]

Overnight, Edward was overwhelmed with orders. He asked Nettie to work with him while Carrie Rose was at school. It seemed there was no end to the expansion of his business.

Houston Grows

On January 10, 1901, Texas celebrated the first oil well to strike pay dirt in the state; it occurred at the Spindletop oil field that sits atop a salt dome in Beaumont. This was the start of the oil boom in Texas and another increase in population for Houston.

That spring, a letter arrived that Edward shared with Nettie. "Nettie, I have a friend, David Cohen, in Springfield, Massachusetts, who is in the dry goods business. We grew up together in the same town in Lithuania. David has a son William who wants to find his own way in the world, and he's coming to Houston to help us. He has money from David to expand our business if I take him in as a partner. What do you think?"

---

10 The *Concho* left Galveston on September 5. Captain Fisk observed the barometer, and the pressure was falling at an alarming rate. He ordered a change of course, hoping to avoid the storm. He still caught the southwestern edge of the storm with gale-force winds and towering seas. For a day, he kept away from the worst of the storm, but the following day he was caught on the back side of the storm with a fury worse than the first encounter. The rain, however, seemed to keep the waves down. He got the *Concho* to Key West and then on to New York, getting into port on September 12 with seasick passengers ready to get off the ship.

It was not unusual for Edward to share business matters with Nettie. He respected her judgment. At this time, this was not the usual case between men and women.

"I know how heavy your workload has been, doing everything yourself. It will be good to have a partner, especially one with money," said Nettie.

"Good, we are in agreement. I will let David know. William will be coming by train, so we should see him in a few weeks," Edward said with an air of expectation of better days ahead.

William Cohen Arrives

The time went by quickly. Within two weeks, a carriage was pulling up in front of the house. It was about 2 p.m. and Carrie Rose had not yet come home from school. Getting out of the carriage was a very thin, tall young man. So thin, Nettie thought that a strong wind would blow him over. He had a thick head of black hair and the start of a beard that looked like it wasn't going to fill in. Wire-rim glasses drew attention to his face, which was thin, just like the rest of him.

"Hello," Nettie called from the porch. "You must be William."

Coal & Wood.
Prices and measurements are right. Prompt delivery
Try our big dollar dry wood and small chunks
SACKS & COHEN
Phone 1215

Edward Sacks and William Cohen ad in *Houston Post* January 21, 1908. *Newspapers.com*

"Yes, ma'am," he said, in a high-pitched voice. "William H. Cohen, here to see Edward Sacks."

"I'm afraid he's not home, but do come in and let's get you settled. I'm Nettie Sachs, his sister."

The carriage driver struggled with a large trunk. William and Nettie moved it into the foyer.

"You must be tired and hungry. Come into the kitchen and let's see what I can find for you to eat."

It had been a long trip, and there was no kosher food on the train. He ate everything Nettie put before him. Soon Carrie Rose came home, and she had to meet the new partner. As always, she was not shy. Before long, she had won him over.

When Edward came home, he gave William a bear hug. "Welcome to our home. Think of it as yours too. I see you have met Carrie Rose and Nettie. Your father told me so much about you and your ambition to be successful in America."

"That's true, Mr. Sacks."

"Call me Edward. After all, we are now partners," he directed him.

The two of them got along fabulously. They each complemented the other. Edward was the outgoing one, and William the shy partner who could read a customer like a book. Rarely did he make a mistake or let an account go into overdue status. The business just blossomed.

It wasn't long before William mentioned his older sister Dora. *Am I now acting like a matchmaker?* wondered William. "I think Dora would be perfect for Carrie Rose and Edward," he confided in Nettie. "Do you think Edward would object to having her come down for a visit?"

"I'll talk to him about it and let you know," answered Nettie.

That evening after dinner, she got Edward alone and approached the subject. "Did you know that William has an older sister?"

"I think he has mentioned it," Edward said.

"She's single and very good with children. He thinks she would do well with Carrie Rose. If it works out, I can go back to New York City."

"I thought you liked it here, Nettie?"

"I do, Edward, but I want to go back to school and do something else with my life. I know you understand."

"I do, Nettie. You have my OK to send for his sister."

Dora Cohen Sacks, Edward Sacks's second wife. *Courtesy of Ann Cohn Mitnick collection*

Dora Cohen Arrives in Houston

It was the first week of May 1901 when Dora Cohen arrived in Houston. When she arrived at the house, Nettie could see right away by her upright posture and determined stride that she was a woman who was not about any nonsense. As she mounted the stairs, though, Nettie knew her first impression was wrong. Dora gave Nettie a smile so warm that it could melt the winter snow in New York.

"Hello," she said. "I'm Dora, and you must be Nettie."

"Yes I am, Dora. Come right in and make yourself at home." Nettie filled her in on the details about Carrie Rose and the loss of Edward's wife to yellow fever.

The house was big enough for all of them. She showed Dora to her room upstairs. It wasn't long before Carrie Rose was home from school, and Nettie could see they would get along fine. When Edward came home, Nettie saw an immediate attraction between the two of them. Dora was almost as tall as Edward, and Nettie could see it in their eyes when first they shook hands.

"Hello," Edward said, in his typical outgoing manner. He held his hand out to Dora. "So you're Dora. I feel I know you already," he said. Dora took his hand in hers.

Dora said, "Nettie has told me so much about the family and has given me the tour. I feel at home already."

The weeks went by quickly. It was now June. Nettie could see that in time a marriage was certainly possible between Edward and Dora. She and William talked about the possibility. Dora had not been in the country long, arriving from Poland just one year ago. Nettie and William congratulated each other for performing the work of a *shadchan*.[11]

Nettie Leaves Houston for New York

In the mail, Edward received a letter from Mary, Edward and Nettie's mother:

Dear Son,

Hope all is well with you, Carrie Rose, and your partner's sister Dora. I know it's time for Nettie to return to New York, but we do not want her to take

---

11 At that time, it was common to have arranged marriages, especially after a wife had died. Usually it was arranged through a *shadchan* or matchmaker where the rabbi had knowledge of both families. The bride, of course, could refuse the match, as could the groom.

the ship. This relationship with the captain is not to our liking and has to be stopped. He's not Jewish, and we can't have Nettie marrying a Gentile. Please arrange rail transportation for her.

We have also found an opportunity for her to attend pharmacy school at New York University. The temple president knows a man on the board of directors who can get her into the school.

We hope school and a change in her life will help her forget about this captain fellow.

Your Mother, Mary

"What are you reading, Edward?" Nettie asked, as she fruitlessly looked through the mail for a letter from Capitan Fisk.

"Just a letter from our mother. She says they know a man who can get you into the College of Pharmacy at the City College of New York."

"Really?" Nettie said, with a surprised expression on her face. "I always wanted to do something in medicine, but I never thought about pharmacy."

"I'll tell you what, Nettie. If you get into the school, I will pay for it. You've been a great help to me with Carrie Rose during these past 18 months. I was wondering how I could help you, and now I know. When you get home, just send all the bills to me," volunteered Edward.

"Oh Edward, you're wonderful, and I won't let you down. Can I see the letter from Mama?"

"You may not like all she has to say," he said. Edward handed her the letter.

"I guess she knows about Captain Fisk. This time I have to agree with her; I can't marry a Gentile. I thought about this myself, and now with my new life in New York I will have to let him know our love is not meant to be." She said this as tears welled up in her eyes.

Edward knew how difficult this was for her, and he put a comforting arm around her. "Life is full of surprises, both good and bad, Nettie. I know you will survive."

CHAPTER 5

Nettie Returns to New York City

It was June and time for the trip to New York via the railroad. Edward had bought her a ticket for a sleeping car all the way to New York. It would be a long journey, but Nettie would see much of America. From Houston she would connect at Denison, Texas, with the Missouri, Kansas and Texas Railroad to St. Louis. From there, she would head east to New York.

Dora had just come on a similar journey, so she briefed Nettie on train travel. The sleeping car was a Pullman, which had a wide seat for travel during the day and a bed that pulled down from above the seat attached to the side of the coach at night. A ladder also came down, and there was a privacy curtain she could pull across the length of the bed. Some of the trains had dining and smoking cars. Others stopped in little towns and let the passengers off to dine in the local restaurants.

Nettie was more than ready to go back to New York, although she would miss everyone in Houston. The day arrived for her departure. Everyone accompanied her to the train station. Little Carrie Rose clung to her skirt, saying, "Please don't go, Auntie Nettie."

"I will send you the prettiest dress in New York, Carrie Rose." Nettie said.

"I don't want a dress. I want you to stay," was her answer.

There were hugs and kisses all around, and then she was on the train and off for her four-day journey to New York. The countryside flew by. She had never seen this part of Texas. It wasn't long before a tall man in his 20s with cowboy boots and hat passed down the aisle of her car. Nettie looked up as he passed and saw his rugged tanned face and deep blue eyes. She then thought of the captain, and her heart seemed to ache for what the future would not be.

It wasn't long until the tall cowboy was back. A woman traveling alone was a magnet for men. Dora had warned her about this, but nothing ever bothered Nettie when it came to men.

"Excuse me, ma'am, but I see you're traveling alone. I wondered if you would accompany me to the dining car? I hate eatin' alone," he said in the familiar Texas drawl.

Before Nettie could answer, he said, "Oh where are my manners, ma'am? My name is Walter Culpepper, son of Duke Culpepper of Austin, Texas." He then held out his hand to her. She could see it was not the hand of an office worker, as it was tan, calloused, and strong.

She reached out and took his hand. "It's indeed a pleasure to meet you, Mr. Culpepper." She placed her gloved hand in his and rose from her seat. "I'm Nettie Sachs, sister to Edward Sacks of Houston."

"Pleasure to meet you, ma'am. My, that's a mighty pretty dress you're wearin'. I can't remember seeing a lady with such a dress in these here parts."

"Why, it's from New York and that's where I'm heading," Nettie said.

"Right now, let's head on down to the dining car and we can chew the fat," the cowboy said. Nettie took his arm, and they headed down the aisle.

Nettie spoke in her best New York accent, which she was starting to lose since she came to Texas. When she stood up, she noticed Walter was much taller than she—even taller than the captain. As they walked through the car into the dining car, she noticed he had to bend his head to prevent hitting it on the car's doorway.

At last they were in the dining car and were seated by the porter. "When I came to Houston from New York, I met a man on the ship named Duke Culpepper. Could that have been your father?"

"I believe so, if it was before the hurricane."

"Such a small world," she said. She hardly remembered what she ate, as the conversation was so interesting. Walter was going to Kansas City to the cattle auction, and she found herself learning all about cattle. She almost thought he was more interested in cattle than in women. She found that was not the case. He was interested in her and what she had to say. She was on her way to study pharmacy in New York. *This indeed will be a pleasant trip after all*, she thought.

The countryside and the time moved faster than the train. Walter got off in St. Louis, where she changed trains. He helped her with her trunk. They exchanged addresses and promised one another they would keep in touch. It was then off to New York on the last leg of the journey.

Nettie Arrives in New York City

It was a warm day in New York when the train pulled into Grand Central Station. Standing on the platform was the whole family: Mother Mary, Rabbi Rabinowitz, Nettie's sister Rose and husband Philip, and Anna.

The first one to greet her was Anna. She ran to greet her with open arms. "Oh, Nettie, I missed you so much." They hugged each other like long-lost sisters.

"Look at you, Anna. You're no longer a string bean. You've filled out," observed Nettie.

"I guess I couldn't stay skinny forever," she answered.

They loaded everything into the carriage. It was decided Nettie would stay with her sister Rose until things got settled.

In preparation for school, Rabbi Rabinowitz had secured a job for her at Leon Solow's pharmacy on Lexington Avenue. "This job will give you an appreciation of the work a pharmacist does," he said.

Before starting her job, Anna and Nettie had a lot of catching up to do. Anna was living in a women's home. Nettie decided she would get a room there as well. It was best she was not under the supervision of her sister or mother.

After the first week with her sister and brother-in-law, Nettie moved into the same women's home as Anna. That night was the first time the girls were alone together. "Nettie, I've been dating a man named Barney Cohen—no relation to your family. He's working in a place that takes stuff no one wants and cleans it up and sells it again."

"You mean he's a junk dealer or a peddler?"

"I guess it's a little of both. At least he has a job, and that's a start."

"Are you serious about him, Anna?" Nettie was good at listening, but better at sizing up the situation.

"Yes, he treats me real nice and never hits me or talks bad to me. I'm not getting any younger, so getting married would be good for me. I'm doing design work for your brother-in-law, so between the two of us, we would be able to rent a flat and not have to stay with his family. Tell me everything that has happened to you."

Nettie had written Anna from Houston and told her of the captain, the hurricane, and little Carrie Rose. She had not shared with her many of the details. It was time to fill in

Grand Central Terminal, New York City, 1900. *Courtesy of Wikipedia*

the gaps. Maybe even tell her about Walter Culpepper. The two of them talked into the night. Then they fell asleep knowing that each of them had her best friend by her side.

In the morning, Anna said, "Nettie, tell me again about your decision about the captain. You said you couldn't marry him because he's a Gentile, but how will you tell him the relationship is over?"

Nettie was not quick to answer that question. "I've thought about it, Anna. I don't want to do it in a letter, but I'm afraid at this time, I can't do it face to face. This is the first time in my life I really feel like I love someone but know it can never be. Time may help. Maybe I will wait for him to send me a letter. Then I may know what to do."

Leon Solow's Pharmacy

Anna went with Nettie to Leon Solow's Pharmacy on Lexington Avenue. It was just on the other side of Central Park from the Garment District. Leon was a member of the temple, so it was easy for Rabbi Rabinowitz to arrange the job for Nettie. The next part, getting admission to the College of Pharmacy, would be more difficult.

As they approached the entrance, they noticed advertisements in the windows on each side of the door. Baby cough syrup for the little sufferers. Quick relief for whooping cough, colds, and hoarseness. Bromo Vichy, a speedy remedy for nervous headaches, neuralgia, and over brain work following alcoholic excesses. Worm cakes, a remedy for destroying worms from the system. An assortment of "electric rings" for curing rheumatism.

Opening the front door set off a little bell attached to the doorframe, signaling their arrival. In front of them was a polished stone counter with ice cream chairs in front of it.[1] The floor was a penny tile pattern. Above them was a tin ceiling laid out with a repeating square pattern. Behind the counter were the polished, curved pipes dispensing the carbonated water and seltzer.

They were greeted by a man not much older than themselves. He was about five-foot-seven, with black hair and a round hairless face. This was unusual. Most men had some type of facial hair. He wore the standard round metal frame glasses that gave the wearer the appearance of an owl.

"How can I help you, ladies?" was his opening remark.

Nettie didn't hesitate to answer, "I'm here to see Mr. Solow, and this is my friend Anna."

"You must be Nettie, the young lady who is going to work here. He told me all about you," he said, as a smile crossed his face.

"I hope not too much," was Nettie's reply. Flirting was second nature to Nettie.

"I'm Louis Zauderer. Nice to meet you." He reached his hand over the counter to shake hers, but Nettie noticed his gaze was not on her face as she leaned forward to shake his hand. Her white summer blouse had exposed much of her ample bosom.

"Come around the counter," he said. "I will take you to Mr. Solow's office."

Louis brought the girls to the back of the pharmacy. Off the hallway was a small office in which Leon Solow was sitting upright behind his desk. He was a little man, no more than five feet tall, with a receding hairline and a full beard. It looked to Nettie that all the hair on his head had come out onto his face.

"Sit down, girls. Which one of you would be Nettie?"

"I am," said Nettie, as she sat down in one of the chairs opposite his desk.

---

1   Soda fountains became so common in American pharmacies that even certain types of furniture are identified with them. These tables and chairs, once common in drugstores with soda fountains, are still referred to as "ice cream chairs" and "ice cream tables." The chairs were usually metal stools that would revolve.

"Well, young lady, you will not be the first woman who has tried to become a pharmacist. What interest do you have in pharmacy?"

Nettie thought of her time before she came to America. "Before coming to America, I worked for a doctor in my hometown. He gave his patients medicine, and it was all very interesting to me. I would like to learn more."

Leon looked at her over his glasses perched on the end of his nose. "So you shall, Nettie. First you will start at the soda counter and learn how to make an egg cream and other drinks. Then you will see what we do at the compound counter. I can't pay you now, but after you get accepted to school, you will be a preceptor and get paid like I pay Louis. Your experience here will go a long way in helping you get accepted into pharmacy school. They only want serious students, not women who will get married, have children, and never practice pharmacy."

"I can understand that," Nettie replied.

"Let's get started. Go up front, and Louis will give you an apron and your first lesson. Louis will be graduating from your school next year. He can tell you all about it."

The girls walked back down the hall and found Louis behind the counter.

"Here's your apron, Miss Nettie. Anna, you will be the customer, and I will have Nettie make you an egg cream."

They moved behind the counter, and the demonstration began. "First, get one of these cold soda glasses and add milk about a third of the way. Next, a few squirts of Fox's chocolate syrup. Now fill the glass to just overflowing with seltzer. With the back of this long spoon, mix the chocolate into the milk, keeping the spoon on the bottom. This will make a lot of bubbles. Add another squirt of chocolate to the top. Now that's an egg cream. Here, Anna, try Nettie's first egg cream."

"Mmm, yum. Very good, Nettie."

Nettie noticed throughout the demonstration, Louis was making a lot of body contact, reaching his arm around her and pressing his body against hers. She knew what was going on, and after the lecture by Mr. Solow, she also knew she would be needing his help to get through school. First she had to pass the entrance exam and get accepted. It would be almost a year before she would take the entrance exam in June of 1902. Louis would graduate then and have two more years of preceptor work before he could get his New York pharmacy license.

Nettie liked the work at the pharmacy. Leon was a quirky fellow still living at home with his parents. Louis had a room at the back of the pharmacy so he could study and work as well. Louis was the second of four children. He had a much older brother as well as a sister who was a few years younger than he. The last, another brother, was the youngest. Louis was born in America and was just a year older than Nettie. He was Romanian. She wondered if he knew Sam. She never asked.

Money was never a problem for Nettie, but she found an additional job working for a young couple that just had one child. Their little girl reminded her of her niece Carrie Rose. Her experience in Houston was helpful to her.

The husband worked in the financial district. Their apartment was big enough for Nettie to have her own room. This arrangement kept her expenses at a minimum. It would be easier on Edward, who never missed sending her money.

Louis helped her prepare for the entrance exam, as he knew what they would be asking. She never had much math in school. She knew this was important, and she appreciated his help. He was usually eager but sometimes he appeared drunk. She saw him drinking Bullard & Shedds coca wine. Its claim was that it would *cure* the "opium or alcohol habit."

Six Months Working in the Pharmacy

The next six months went by quickly. She learned all the counter drinks. People began to ask for Nettie's egg cream as well as her club sandwiches. She watched the pharmacist compound the prescriptions and learned about the latest drugs. The new drug, aspirin, was a great substitute pain reliever, not habit-forming like cocaine or opium.

She and Louis became an item, and would frequently double date with Anna and Barney. Her relationship with the captain continued through letters, and then the letters stopped. Nettie couldn't let this go unresolved. Even though she was relieved that he may have moved on, she wanted to see him in person. Knowing the *Concho*'s schedule, one day she left work early to go the Mallory pier where the ship docked.

As the passengers disembarked, she went aboard and entered the captain's cabin. His back was turned, as he was looking over the ship's manifest. "Sam," she whispered, as she quietly closed the door behind her.

He turned to face her, and expressions of surprise, relief, and joy flashed across his face. "I thought I would never see you again," he whispered into her ear as they held each other in a passionate embrace.

They both made it to the couch and sat down, still locked in each other's arms. Nettie said, "Why did you stop writing?"

"I had to, Nettie. Mr. Mallory told me I could never see you again or the city would pull our pier permit. If that would happen, I was to lose my job. Do you understand?"

"Whoever would do a thing like that?" Nettie raised her voice in an indignant manner.

"Mr. Mallory was visited by a man from Tammany Hall. That's all I know."

"I'm sorry Sam. It's all my fault. I think it has something to do with me getting into pharmacy school and my mother wanting to end our relationship. I know they only want the best for me, but they may have gone a little too far. I'm so sorry if you got hurt," apologized Nettie.

"That does explain some of what has been going on. I guess Jews have to marry Jews in this America. How could I be so naïve?" Sam said.

"I will always love you, Sam," Nettie confessed

"And I will always love you, Nettie. You will always be in my heart," Sam promised her.

They held each other again and kissed, each knowing it would be for the last time. They let go their embrace, and Nettie was out the door and down the gangplank. She had little to say that night when she entered the flat. She kept herself busy cooking dinner and taking care of the family. Then she went to bed and cried herself to sleep.

New York: The New Year 1902

The new year of 1902 was a gay time for both Nettie and Anna. Each had a steady boyfriend and they celebrated the New Year together. Neither couple had a lot of money, but they could do many things without money. Walking through Central Park and visiting friends, everyone was in the spirit of the season.

Nettie and Louis did not have to work at the drugstore, as New Year's Day was on a Wednesday and Mr. Solow closed the store. Louis was on call, but since he lived in the back of the pharmacy, he didn't have to go out in the weather to help a customer. The family that employed Nettie gave her the day off. She did not have to take care of their daughter or cook dinner for the family.

Louis was the first in his family to be born in New York. At times, he looked down on Nettie, Anna, and Barney as *greenhorns* from the old country. The group did a little drinking during the New Year's celebration. Anna and Nettie noticed that Louis had a bit of a mean streak when drunk. Barney tried to get him to stop, but he was no match for

Louis's habit. When Louis would go into one of his tirades, shouting obscenities, Nettie and Anna would pretend to put on airs with their sophisticated New York accents. They would pretend he was just a drunk on the street and not with them. This would calm him down, and the boys would have a good laugh when this happened.

Record Snowstorm Hits New York City

On February 17, 1902, the Monday after Valentine's Day, a massive snowstorm hit New York City with 15 inches of snow and 40 mph winds. Snow was pushed into drifts up to five feet high. The horses could barely get their footing, and streetcar wheels spun on the rails.

Nettie made it to the drugstore only to have Mr. Solow tell her she could go home. Everything was shutting down in the city.

New York was a mess, but soon the snow melted. Before they knew it, spring had come to New York.

Nettie's Interview for School

It was a week after Passover that Mama Mary told Nettie she would be hearing from a man from Tammany Hall, a Michael Murphy. He was the temple president's contact for the College of Pharmacy at the City College of New York. It seems that a deal was made with the garment industry through her brother-in-law to train Irish girls in the garment trade. This would help Mr. Murphy politically. In return, he would help Mama Mary and the rabbi.

Mama Mary had used him earlier to contact the Mallory ship line about Captain Fisk. Because of this, Nettie already disliked this man but agreed to meet him.

It wasn't long before a bicycle messenger arrived at the drugstore. "Is there a Miss Nettie Sachs here?" He said this in a tone loud enough for everyone in the store to hear.

Nettie was at the counter almost in front of the messenger. "Right here, I'm Nettie."

"Message for you, madam," he said, in a much lower tone.

Nettie reached into her apron pocket and handed him a coin. "Thank you," she said, as she tucked the note into her apron pocket.

At her next break, she opened the note. It was on Tammany Hall letterhead:

Ms. Nettie Sachs,

I understand you are interested in becoming a pharmacist. After talking to a friend of your mother's, I think I can be of some help.

On Friday, May 16, I would like to take you to the Iceland Deli to discuss this matter. I will pick you up at your place of work at 11 a.m.

If you are unable to make this, contact Michael Murphy's office in Tammany Hall so we can set up another time. If I do not hear from you, I will see you on Friday.

Michael Murphy, Alderman

On May 16, the temperature was in the low 60s and there was a smell of spring in the air. Nettie got off the trolley before her stop so she could walk through Central Park and see the tulips just ready to burst into bloom. She knew she had to get ready for a great performance today with Alderman Michael Murphy, a man she already disliked before meeting him. The walk through the park was just what she needed.

As she entered the drugstore, Louis was the first to greet her. "My, you look super today," he said. "Anything special going on?" The dress she was wearing was a sky blue color and very spring-like. Louis was just teasing, as he knew perfectly well what was about to transpire. Nettie had picked out this dress with her sister Rose. Rose insisted Nettie wear the latest spring fashion with matching hat. She looked like she had just come out of one of the fashion ads.

It was 8 a.m. She quickly removed her hat and donned her apron for the morning rush. Mr. Solow came out of his office to see her as she covered herself with the apron. "Don't want to spill anything on that nice dress today. Why don't you let Louis do the messy work? I can spare him from the compound counter."

"That's all right. I'll be careful, Mr. Solow. I want to do my part. Thank you for letting me off this afternoon."

"If it means you getting into school and you continue to work as hard behind the prescription counter as you do behind the soda fountain, you'll be a big help. Good luck."

In reality, even an independent man like Leon Solow knew the power rested in the hands of the politicians from Tammany Hall. This Michael Murphy was one man you wanted on your side.

Lunch with Michael Murphy

At 11 a.m. almost on the dot, a machine stopped in front of the store. Louis spotted it right away and said, "Nettie, that's a 1902 Locomobile. They say it's the best-built machine on the road."

Nettie lifted her head to see a rather large man get out of the right side of the machine. The bell rang on the drugstore door, and in walked a rotund man about 40 years of age. He had a reddish complexion and a very large head that seemed to sprout directly from his torso, without a neck in between.

Locomobile 1900. *Courtesy of Wikipedia*

It was May, and he wore a seersucker suit. The suit made him look like some of the candy in the apothecary jars. He removed his hat, showing a full head of brownish-red hair parted in the center. He maneuvered his body onto one of the ice cream stools and said, "I'm looking for a Nettie Sachs. Could you tell her Michael Murphy is here?"

"I'm the Nettie you're looking for," Nettie said. "It's a pleasure to meet you." Even for Nettie, this lie was difficult to say. All she could think about was the captain and what may have transpired with Mr. Mallory.

"Why, you are much prettier than what your mother described." The compliment landed flat on Nettie, and she showed no emotion. His voice seemed to come from deep inside him and came forth more as a growl.

"I'll be with you in a minute," Nettie said, as she turned and exited from behind the counter. She took off her apron, adjusted her hair, and put on her feathered hat and shawl.

She met Mr. Murphy on the other side of the counter. He rose and opened the door for her. Nettie turned and said, "Goodbye," to both Louis and Mr. Solow. They were both standing together at attention, looking at Nettie like she was a dignitary.

Mr. Murphy took her around to the left side of the machine and helped her in. It had no windshield like the electric taxies. She was prepared for the chill with her shawl. He got in the right seat as the machine leaned to his side. She could feel his body next to hers as his bulk overflowed the seat.

The pharmacy was on 74th Street, so they had a bit of a drive to the Lower East Side and the deli. It was time for some small talk before they arrived. "Your mother told me you have an interest in becoming a pharmacist."

"That's true Mr. Murphy."

"Call me Michael, Nettie. None of that Mr. Murphy stuff. It sounds too stiff."

"Yes, Michael," she said dutifully. "I had some exposure to medicine in the old country when I worked for a doctor."

"You're living with a family here and not at home?" he asked. It seemed to Nettie he was not really interested in the answers to his questions about pharmacy, but more about her personal life. "A pretty girl like you should have lots of boyfriends," Murphy said, fishing for an answer.

Nettie now knew what may be on his mind, and she was ready. "I'm too busy for boyfriends, Michael. I've been studying for the entrance exam next month. With the pharmacy and the family I work for, there is just no time for boyfriends."

Murphy was not new at this game. He now had a feeling this would be more difficult than he first thought. "You're not being truthful with me, Nettie. I saw how that fellow behind the counter looked at you."

"You must mean Louis," Nettie answered. "He's much too young for me. He just graduated from pharmacy school. He has been helping me get ready for my exam."

"Here we are at the deli," Michael announced. When they stopped in front, there seemed to be a parking spot just for him. A man from the deli saw him drive up. He came out to escort them in, although there was a line outside the door. "You see, Nettie, it's important to have friends in this world."

"That I do, Mr. Murphy. I mean Michael," replied Nettie, looking straight at him, trying not to show contempt.

"Your usual table, Mr. Murphy?" the waiter asked.

Michael nodded. The owner of the deli ushered them to a private booth on the other side of a privacy wall. It was clear Murphy was a regular here. "Nettie, I brought you here because I know Jewish girls like you like this food."

Nettie was furious inside to be talked to like this. *I am now an American first. What does religion have to do with it?* She bit her tongue and did not reply.

The waiter was at the table to take their order. Nettie wasn't hungry but did order a pastrami sandwich. Mr. Murphy ordered a corned beef sandwich with a bowl of *matzo* ball soup.

"You really have to try their egg cream," he said.

After all the egg creams she had made, the thought of another one was one too many. "I'll just have a glass of milk."

The waiter turned and went to the kitchen.

"You gotta love these Jews," Murphy said. "The best damn cooks in town. This restaurant will probably be here for 100 years.[2] Let's get to the point, Nettie."

The waiter was back and put the food in front of them. Nettie couldn't help but notice Mr. Murphy's red cheeks. When he would talk, the smell of his breath was overpowering.

He continued speaking as he filled his mouth with food. "I got all the big shots over at the college in my pocket. The dean, Henry Rusby; the registrar, Rudolf Tombo; and even the

---

2   He was right. The deli is still in operation and at the same location. It changed its name to Katz's Delicatessen when Mr. Iceland sold out his interest to Mr. Katz. It's still in the same location today on the Lower East Side of Manhattan.

chairman of the state board, Clarence Bigelow. They all owe me somethin', so if I say you are in, that's all it will take. Understand, Nettie, Michael Murphy don't do dese things for nuthin."

Nettie had heard this talk before, and an image of Elliot Molinsky and Monk Eastman flashed before her eyes. She had sensed this from the time he first spoke to her in the drugstore. *Did Mama Mary know what she was doing when she decided to pull some strings?* Nettie was ready this time and knew the game. "I understand, Michael. There's always a price to pay for a favor."

This girl is no beginner to this game, he thought. *This will be much easier than I first thought.* "Your mother said you were married once in the old country. I guess this won't be the first time you'll be with a man?" Murphy asked, with a smile forming on his face.

Just thinking about having sex with him turns my stomach, thought Nettie. *I think the pastrami is coming up.* Nettie was ready. "I sure hope your heart is up to it, Michael. I've heard older men like yourself take a risk with someone as young as me."

He was getting excited, as he felt the hard part was over.

"We Jewish women know how to treat our men. If I were you, I would cut back a little on this Jewish cooking," Nettie warned him.

Michael let out a laugh and, with it, some of the corned beef. It hit Nettie on the cheek, and some landed on her $8 ($215 in 2017 dollars) blue dress. Michael then ordered some blueberry blintzes and cheesecake. Nettie just nursed her milk and her half-eaten sandwich.

As they drove back to the flat that Nettie shared with the family, she was searching her mind as to how she could solve this problem. *Next month is the entrance exam. Surely I can hold him off until it's final that I'm enrolled in the school. Ah,* she thought, *if I was married, I would be off limits. Mr. Solow says that the school does not allow married women. If I get married, it will have to be kept quiet. If the public and rival politicians knew Murphy was having an affair with a 17-year-old married woman, it would hurt his political ambitions.* A smile crossed her face.

Michael said, "I see by your smile that you had a good time, and many more to come, my chickadee."

"Oh yes," she replied. *Men are so easy to read. He has no idea that my smile was the thought that it was time for Louis to get a wife.*

This was a world where men had all the power, but women could have the upper hand if they played their cards right. She had learned that from Mistress Fechheimer at Becker's Institute. "We've arrived, Nettie." He turned off the machine and walked around to her side and extended his hand to help her out. In an instant, he grabbed her about the waist and pulled her to him. "How about a little kiss to seal the deal?"

His breath was so foul, she almost passed out. With a free arm, she pushed him away. "Michael, there's plenty of time for that. Besides, I'm not enrolled yet." She extended her gloved hand. "A kiss on the hand will do for now."

He took her hand. She turned her head away, not wanting to see his lips on her hand. *These gloves will have to be discarded*, she thought. She turned and instantly vanished into the flat. She could hear him start his machine and drive away.

A Marriage Is Planned

The next day was Saturday, the Sabbath. The drugstore was closed, as most of its customers were Jewish. They would not conduct any business on the Sabbath. This day was almost always the day she and Anna got together. Today was very special, as she had to get marriage plans in the works.

Nettie went over to the women's boarding house where Anna was living. It was a nice spring day, and they went for a walk in the park. "Anna, don't you think it's time for you and Barney to get married?"

"He hasn't asked yet, Nettie, but I know he's the man for me."

"How long do you plan to wait, Anna?" asked Nettie.

"I don't know. I guess until he asks."

"What if that doesn't happen? At 17 in the old country, you would be getting too old to be a wife."

"Nettie, what plan are you cooking up now?" inquired Anna. "Are you planning something for me or for you?"

"For both of us, Anna. We both need to get married."

"Need?" Anna asked with raised eyebrows. She was now getting that scared puppy dog look on her face when Nettie included her in her plans. "Why do *you* have to get married, Nettie?"

"Mama Mary decided to pull some strings with a politician who wants sex for getting me into school. This man is so disgusting, I would give up pharmacy school just to have him stay away. I think being married would stop any advances. I would let him know that I would tell others he was having an affair with a married woman. Given a choice, politicians want power more than sex. Now, do you want to marry Barney or not?"

"I thought we were talking about you getting married, not me, but I do want to marry Barney. I think I should wait until he asks me."

"How long do you plan to wait?" Nettie asked again.

"I don't know, Nettie," Anna said.

"If you want Barney to ask you, tell him you don't want to see him anymore. When he asks why, tell him it's time to get married or you will find someone else," Nettie explained.

"I don't want to find someone else, Nettie. I love Barney."

"You're *Gornisht helfn* (beyond help), Anna. This is how you get him to ask you."

"I'm confused, Nettie. I tell him to go away so he will ask me to marry him?"

"That's right, Anna. I know how men's minds work. *Fershtay* (do you understand)?" Nettie said, with an exasperated look on her face.

"No, but if you say it will work, I'll try it. Who are you going to marry? Louis?" Anna asked.

"Yes."

"Does he know he is getting married, Nettie?"

"Not yet, but he will soon," she answered, with a smile on her face.

The Proposal

The next few weeks, both Nettie and Louis were busy studying, she for the entrance exam, he for his final exams to get his certificate of examination. He would be able to exchange it for a diploma—after two more years working under Mr. Solow.

Louis finished his exams before Nettie. He now had more time to help her with math, chemistry, and botany, subjects she had little knowledge of or hadn't studied at Becker's Institute. Louis told her that pharmacy school was more interested in these subjects than her command of the English language.

Nettie also took this time to let Louis get a bit more intimate with her. Louis was very awkward when this happened, and Nettie wasn't sure if it was lack of experience or something else that she knew nothing about. She did notice whenever this happened that Louis had been drinking or taking throat lozenges or toothache drops, medicine that had cocaine in them. Louis tried to get her to drink more Coca-Cola.[3] Nettie wouldn't. She

---

3   Coca-Cola was initially dispensed from the soda fountain as a syrup poured over ice, just like the other fruit flavors, to make sodas. It had many claims, including increasing sexual desire. The syrup also contained cocaine, but in 1903 the company started to reduce the amount of cocaine, and by 1929, nearly all traces of cocaine were gone from the syrup.

didn't like the sugary taste or its effects. Louis told her that his plan was to go to medical school after he got his pharmacy license. He had picked a school in St. Louis.

"That's wonderful, Louis. When I become a pharmacist, we can work together." Nettie felt this idea of a partnership should have a chance to grow in his mind until it became his idea.

"That would be a while from now," Louis said, without missing a beat. "I have two more years before I get my pharmacy license, then two years or more in medical school. Do you think you can wait that long?"

She didn't answer, just kissed him on the forehead. *He has taken the bait*, thought Nettie. "Why do we have to wait that long, Louis? If it's the money, I have enough to support both of us until we finish school," she offered.

"I didn't know you were independently wealthy, Nettie."

"My brother in Houston is paying my way through school, and I have other assets from the old country that I can use if we need more money. Aren't you saving your money from what Mr. Solow pays you?"

"I am Nettie, but not enough for a wife."

There, he said it. Now I have to respond. "Oh, Louis, I thought you would never ask." She hugged him, pressing her body against him, making sure he felt every curve of her body. "I can't wait to tell Mama and Anna. We can set the date later. Let's get back to this biology book."

Louis didn't know what just happened, or how, but he seemed pleased. "Are you sure you don't want a Coca-Cola, Nettie? I'm going up front to make myself a double."

Pharmacy School

Nettie took her entrance exam the first week of June. The results showed that all her studying paid off, as she passed easily. Next was the interview, which was tougher. She was one of only five women applicants in a class of 144. She felt it went well, as the interviewer was an older fellow who couldn't seem to look her in the eye the entire interview.

Later that month, she received the letter that made it official. She was to start school October 6. She wrote Edward in Houston and told him the news, and also told him that tuition was $100/year ($2,750 in 2017 dollars), with a $25 ($615 in 2017 dollars) textbook fee.

She continued getting messages from Michael Murphy that he wanted to see her. Now that she was formally accepted, she told him about her upcoming marriage and said it just wouldn't be right to see him. He did not take the news well. He had to laugh that the little Jew girl had beaten him at his own game. *There are others,* he thought, *who are not so smart.*

Anna and Nettie Get Married

Anna had gotten her answer from Barney. It worked just like Nettie said it would. She was a nervous wreck the whole time. "I didn't think I had the *chutzpah* (a person with nerve or gall) to tell Barney I wouldn't see him anymore," Anna confessed.

They both were to get married at the same time. "Nettie, do you love Louis?" Anna asked, as they were planning their double wedding.

"Not yet, Anna, but I think in time I will. I know what it takes to be a good wife, and that is what I will be. We both have a few more years of school before we can really settle down and call ourselves husband and wife. I can't let the school know that we're married and Louis is saving for medical school."

The weddings were planned for September 15, just three weeks before Nettie was to start school. The wedding day was nothing like Nettie's first wedding in the old country. This time, it had to be very low-key, as neither of them had money to spend on a wedding. They married in the temple on a Monday, and her stepfather, Rabbi Rabinowitz, went through all the proper steps, including having the grooms step on and break the wine glasses.[4]

In attendance at the wedding were Mama Mary, Nettie's sister Rose, and Rose's husband Philip and baby William Morris. Abraham, Anna's brother, was now working for Rabbi Rabinowitz. Anna's older brother Daniel made the trip from the coal mines of Pennsylvania to walk his sister down the aisle. Philip did the same for Nettie.

This was the first time Nettie had seen Daniel since the night he rescued her from Elliot Molinsky. Nettie ran toward him in her wedding gown. "Daniel, it's so wonderful to see you." She threw her arms about his neck and gave him a hug.

Daniel, a little embarrassed, hugged her back, and said, "These are much better times, Nettie. I am so happy for you."

---

4   This Jewish wedding tradition usually marked the end of the ceremony. Its meaning is varied, ranging from being a symbol of the destruction of the temple in Jerusalem to the glass representing the fragile nature of love and that life will bring both sadness and joy.

"I never got to thank you for rescuing me from that *gonif* (thief, swindler). I can never repay you, Daniel. You know that." Daniel nodded his head in agreement.

Louis had both his mother and father in attendance; his younger sister Lena, 18; and two younger brothers, Tobias, 15, and Samuel, 12. This was the first time Nettie had been in the presence of the entire Zauderer family. She could sense tension between Lena and Louis. He was one year older, but she seemed to have more power than him. *Maybe this is the same problem that Louis has in dealing with me. Could this be his issue with all women?*

Barney had his family there too. There were seven of them, all in rather threadbare clothes. Rose had offered them the opportunity to get new clothes from the store, but they were too proud to take the offer.

After the ceremony, all the guests, including Mr. Solow from the drugstore, had a luncheon in the adjoining assembly hall. Everyone made toasts to the newly married couples. Mama Mary liked the idea that her new son-in-law was going to be a doctor. Philip had arranged an open carriage for them and had made reservations for two rooms at the Waldorf Astoria. Nettie and Anna felt like queens for a day.

After they arrived and the brides changed out of their wedding gowns, the two couples had a light dinner in the Peacock Alley restaurant, located in the corridor that connected the two hotels. "Do try their Waldorf salad," Nettie said. "It's the specialty of the house."[5]

"There she goes again," said Anna, "telling people what to eat. You would think she was a Jewish mother."

After their meal, with a wink and a nod from Nettie to Anna, the two couples retired to their rooms. The rooms in the Waldorf were known to be "fit for a king." There were bathrooms in every room and telephones as well, and fully electric lamps, not gaslights. This would be the first time Nettie was to have sex with Louis. She wondered how it would be this first time.

"Louis, I'm going in the toilet to get into my night clothes."

"OK. I'll just dress out here," Louis said.

Nettie brought a beautiful silk nightgown from Philip's store. Rose said. "Think of it as your wedding present." The fabric was so light and airy that it clung to every curve of her body. With her upright posture, she looked ethereal when she exited the bathroom.

---

5   The Waldorf salad is made with apples, walnuts, celery, grapes, and mayonnaise. It was invented by Oscar Tschirky, better known as Oscar of the Waldorf, who was from Switzerland and became the maître d'hôtel from the hotel's opening in 1893 until his retirement in 1943. He is also credited with creating Eggs Benedict and Thousand Island dressing.

"Oh my God," Louis gasped, "you look like an angel, Nettie."

Louis was dressed in a muslin nightshirt that was buttoned from the waist to the neck. It had long sleeves, and the bottom of the shirt fell just above his ankles. The two of them dimmed the lights, and each got into bed. At first the kissing began, but nothing more.

"Are you all right, Louis?" she asked.

"Just a little tired. It's been a long day."

Nettie placed her hand lower on his nightshirt to feel for some sign of arousal. Louis pulled away from her. Nettie became more aggressive and rolled on top of him, unbuttoning his nightshirt with her free hand. "I'm your wife, Louis. It's OK to touch me anywhere you want."

Louis did reach for her breast but didn't seem to know what to do. Nettie lifted up his nightshirt and reached for his penis. She expected an erection, but nothing was there. His little solider wasn't even at half-staff.

"What's wrong, Louis?" she asked. "I'm your wife, and this is our wedding night."

"I'm sorry, Nettie. Maybe I'm just not like all the other men in your life," he said, in a somewhat sarcastic tone.

Anna must have told him about the captain or maybe Molinsky, thought Nettie. *Does Louis think I'm damaged goods? What could be wrong? He's only 19.*

"I'm sorry, Nettie. I think I need some wine or maybe a little cocaine."

"That's OK, Louis. Let's *gay shlafen* (go to sleep). We're both tired. There is plenty of time for this." She rolled over to her side of the bed but couldn't sleep. The walls were well constructed at the Waldorf, but she could hear Anna and Barney in the adjoining room consummating their marriage. She would have to wait.

Married Life

Early that next morning, Nettie awoke to the caresses of Louis. He seemed more than ready to consummate their marriage. Before she knew it, he was on top of her with his nightshirt up around his waist and the same for her nightgown. The act was over before she could enjoy the pleasure of the moment, but at least Louis would not be in a bad mood today.

After they dressed, they met Anna and Barney for breakfast. Anna couldn't wait to get Nettie alone and tell her all about her first night with Barney. Nettie listened to her explain how wonderful it was and ask why she waited so long. This is what Nettie had experienced years earlier with Moshe. The two couples had the Waldorf's signature Eggs Benedict. During breakfast, Barney asked, "Did you know they just started direct train service from New York City to Chicago? I'm thinking there is more opportunity for Anna and me in Chicago. There's a large community of Jews from Russia already there. It will be easy to make friends. I hate to break up you girls, but there is always the mail and phone."

"I think that's wonderful, Barney—a new life for the two of you," agreed Nettie.

Louis had no comment. He was deep in thought about work and the future with a wife.

"Well, ladies," Barney said, "let's *mach shnell* (hurry up) and check out of the hotel. We have families to raise in this new country of ours, America." They all held up their water glasses and clicked them together with a *mazel tov* (good luck) for America.

Pharmacy School

School would start in two weeks. Nettie tried her best to be a wife to Louis and spent more time at the drugstore. She made Louis his midday meal before she had to go back to the family whose daughter she was caring for. They tried to make a honeymoon out of the little time they had when the drugstore was closed. Nettie could arrange only a few nights off from taking care of her little charge. School started, and it didn't take long for her to feel like she was in over her head. She was so happy she had Louis to help her.

As a first-year pharmacy student, her work at the drugstore was now Tuesdays, Thursdays, and a half day on Sunday. She was now getting paid a small sum. Several of the male students in the class tried to get close to her, but Nettie held them off. They must never know she was married. Some offered to help with her class work, but the library was as far as it would go. When it came to difficult classes, Louis had warned her about George A. Ferguseon, the professor of analytical chemistry and mathematics. *If I get through this course, the rest will be easy,* thought Nettie.

It was 1903 before anyone knew it. Nettie got a letter from her brother Edward in Houston:

My Dearest Nettie,

I know you and Louis are busy with work and school, but I have great news for you. I've asked Dora for her hand in marriage, and she said yes. We have it planned for March 1 in Springfield, Massachusetts. I do hope you and Louis can make the trip. We are so sorry we could not make it to your wedding.

Enclosed is a money order for your tickets and other expenses. If you can come on Friday, February 28, we will have the weekend together with the whole family. Our ceremony is on Sunday, the first.

Dora sends her love. Carrie Rose can't wait to see her Auntie Nettie.

Love, Edward

"Look, Louis, I got a letter from my brother in Houston," Nettie said, with an air of excitement. "He's asking us to come to his wedding in Springfield, Massachusetts, in March. This could be the honeymoon we never had."

Louis squinted his eyes behind his wire-rim glasses. "Who has money for a trip like that? I sure don't," he announced.

"Edward sent us a money order. See?" Nettie held it out for him to see.

Louis let out a big whoop. "$25! ($685 in 2017 dollars). I guess now we have to go," said Louis, with a sound of resignation in his voice.

"It's just for the weekend, and I'm sure Mr. Solow will let us off. He'll only be short-handed Friday and Sunday," Nettie calculated, knowing how important they had become to the operation of the drugstore.

Mr. Solow overheard them talking in the hallway and came out of his office. "What's this about time off?"

"It's my brother, Mr. Solow. He's getting married on March 1 in Springfield, Massachusetts. Will you let us go?"

"You kids never did have a honeymoon, and I have time to get some other help in here that weekend. Go ahead and plan your trip," he said.

Edward's Wedding in Springfield, Massachusetts

This was the first real trip Nettie had been on accompanied by a husband. Louis had not done much traveling. It was up to Nettie to show him the ropes. The train trip was less than 100 miles. They were in Springfield by noon on Friday. Edward was there to greet them.

"Hello, Auntie Nettie." She heard her name called as she exited the train. Running across the platform was Carrie Rose, now 8 years old and too big for Nettie to pick up.

She bent down and put an arm around Carrie Rose and kissed her. "How's my big girl?" Nettie asked.

"Getting bigger every day," Carrie Rose said.

Coming up from behind was Edward. He gave her a bear hug and then looked over at Louis. "You must be Louis, the young man I've heard so much about?"

"That's right, Mr. Sacks. Nettie is now a Zauderer."

"Pleased to meet you, Louis. I'm sure we'll have a lot to talk about without my sister hearing." They both laughed, gathered up their luggage, and headed for the house.

Mama Mary and her sister Rose had been there all week preparing for the wedding. This was Mama Mary's oldest son. In the tradition of the old country, he was the head of the family in America. The whole *mishpocha* (family) was coming for the wedding. This was the first real reunion of the family in America.

Rose and Philip now had three boys, William, Theodore, and Ellis. Nettie's other older sister Fannie and her husband Julius had two children, Rose and Gussie. Older brother Nathan and his wife Jennie brought their first child, Ruth.

The wedding was held in the Cohens' house, which had been expanded over the years and was big enough to hold the entire wedding party. David Cohen was doing quite well in the dry goods business. He had expanded the business and was now supplying stores all the way to Boston.

The wedding was a beautiful family affair. Everyone got a chance to tell their stories of their assimilation in America. This country gave them opportunities that they never had in Lithuania.

On the train ride back to New York, Louis told Nettie that Edward had told him to look into the requirements for a pharmacist license in Missouri. "Edward said that each state would have different certification requirements. You know, I plan to go there for medical school."

"You still have another year here with Mr. Solow, Louis," Nettie said, reminding him of his obligation.

"Maybe not, if one year of experience is all I need for a license in Missouri. I need to find out. I would make more money as a pharmacist than an assistant," reasoned Louis.

"I agree, Louis. We can write some letters when we get back." *Is he going to leave me here and go to St. Louis without me?* wondered Nettie.

News from Europe

News from Europe was in all the papers April 7. On April 6, there was a pogrom in Kishinev, Moldova, and 49 Jews were killed.

"Did you see the paper this morning, Louis?" Nettie asked, as she came into the drugstore. "It's a good thing we left the old country when we did. Things are really getting bad. They killed 49 Jews yesterday." Nettie had not told Louis about her experience with a pogrom in her town, as she still felt she might be on someone's wanted list.

"That's so far away, Nettie. You greenhorns are always looking over your shoulder, like the old country is coming over here."

"No, Louis, this is serious and I'll bet it gets worse," Nettie predicted. Louis was born in America of Romanian immigrants. He had no appreciation for how bad things were in Russia for the Jews. To him, it was just stories told by his father, the tailor, from long ago. Not so for Nettie. She didn't sleep well that night and woke up with a headache.

Nettie and Louis Rent a Flat

When in Springfield, Edward told Nettie that he would pay for a flat for her and Louis until she finished school. "A married couple should not sleep in separate beds," he said. Nettie couldn't tell Louis of the offer, so just said she had some money saved to afford an apartment. They found one midway between Nettie's school and the drugstore. It was in an older mansion that had been divided into four separate apartments. Nettie insisted on finding one where they did not have to share a toilet down the hall.

Life was now much easier for Nettie. She had one less family to take care of, as well as Louis and her schoolwork. Life was not so easy with Louis. She never knew what mood he was going to be in when he came home. Sometimes he wouldn't speak to her for hours. She could smell liquor on his breath and knew that he had been drinking. Rarely was he as sweet and attentive as he had been before their marriage. *It's probably just the pressure at work, and things will get better*, thought Nettie. She did everything she could to please him. She cooked the foods he liked and tried every sexual position and idea that came to her. Sometimes she used sex to calm him down when he became violent. He would call her names, and one time he hit her.

"I'm sorry, Nettie, if my family has not done as well in America as yours. My father is still a trimmer in the garment district. I got into school on my own. I didn't have to pull strings like you," Louis complained. Nettie had heard all this before, especially on Friday nights after they had their Sabbath dinner, usually at Rose's house. He seemed to resent her family's success. Nettie knew he felt less than a man when she was paying the rent. After these violent outbursts, he would apologize in the morning and promise never to do it again. It did happen again—all too frequently.

She talked to Mama Mary about Louis. Mama told her that a wife must please her husband no matter what happens in the marriage.

Louis Goes to Missouri

In the mail, a letter arrived from the Missouri Department of Pharmacy. It looked very official. When Louis got home, Nettie couldn't wait to show him the letter. She hoped it would put him in a good mood. "Look what came in the mail, Louis. It's from the Missouri Department of Pharmacy."

Louis took the letter and tore open the envelope. "It's my license application, Nettie. Just like I thought, I only need a one-year apprenticeship to apply for a license. By the end of April, I will have finished my first year. That is just three weeks away. I'll tell Mr. Solow tomorrow and get him to sign it showing I did one year. Three weeks is enough notice; don't you think?" Louis said, now excited by the thought of going to St. Louis.

"Mr. Solow has always been good to us. I think you should ask for his advice first, not tell him you are leaving," Nettie suggested.

"There you go again, telling me how to act," replied Louis.

Nettie saw that he was getting angry and didn't want this to escalate into an argument. "Let's celebrate, Louis. I have a special bottle of wine we can have with dinner." That changed the tone, and after a few glasses of wine Louis was mellow. Nettie learned just how much wine was enough. Too much, and he became an angry drunk. They celebrated the good news both at dinner and in the bedroom. Nettie felt she had done her duty as a wife. Mama Mary would be pleased.

Louis Resigns

It didn't go well the next day at the drugstore. Louis didn't ask for advice but told Mr. Solow he would be leaving in three weeks for Missouri. That hurt Mr. Solow's feelings, but there was little he could do. He signed the form stating that Louis had completed one year with him. Nettie tried to smooth things over when she came in to work the next day. "Is he going to leave you and go to St. Louis?" Mr. Solow asked.

"He wants to go to medical school and needs the money. Maybe he will find us a flat in St. Louis when I finish school."

"Do you really think that *zhlub* (an insensitive, ill-mannered person) will be looking for a place for the two of you?

New York City College, 1898. *Courtesy of Wikipedia*

I think he only cares about Louis, but I could be wrong. We will see."

The three weeks sped by. Louis had been sending letters to all the drugstores in St. Louis. One, the Economy Drugstore run by Andrew H. Coussens, replied and said they had a position for him as soon as he could get there.

"Nettie, looks like I'm on my way to St. Louis."

"You're really going, Louis? I thought maybe you would wait this one last year." Nettie was hoping he would reconsider but didn't push the issue.

"Don't be silly. Once I get enough money, I'm going to start medical school and you can come and join me when you graduate." Nettie didn't want to start a fight on their last week together. "I do need some money for my ticket and a little more to get me started before my first paycheck," Louis said.

Nettie went to her purse and gave him $30 ($800 in 2017 dollars), more than enough to get him started. She did not want to ask him what he had been doing with his paycheck from Mr. Solow. That would just start a fight. She also didn't tell him that she had missed her last period. Schoolwork and the drugstore were Nettie's life.

One day while she was studying in the school library, out of the corner of her eye she saw a man who looked like Sam Herskovitz,[6] the boy she sailed with on the *Preto-*

---

6   Sam was getting his college education at New York City College, the same school where Nettie was getting her pharmacy training. Sam had seen her that day in the library. Around her were several men helping her with her studies. Sam was too shy to say hello. Besides, he was late for his job as a watchman (security guard).

ria. It was just instant, but he would be hard to miss with that reddish hair. It seemed so long ago. Besides, she was now a married woman. With Louis in St. Louis, she now had more time to study. She needed it, as he was not there to help her. She missed her next two periods and knew she was pregnant. This was not good for school or for their shaky marriage.

Nettie Is Pregnant

Louis arrived in St. Louis, and Mr. Coussens let him live in the back of one of the drugstores along with another clerk on Thirteenth Street and Franklin Avenue. This allowed Louis to save as much money as possible. He was hoping he would have enough money to enter the College of Physicians and Surgeons in the fall.

Nettie's pregnancy was not going well. She was having bleeding and lower back pain, and the cramps were awful. Worse, she really had no one to talk to. She had to hide the pregnancy from her classmates at school and even Mr. Solow.

Was this normal? She didn't know. Before she knew it, the nausea stopped. So did her vomiting but not the cramps. Rose had three children. She had to talk to her about her symptoms. She would see her Friday at Sabbath dinner. That's when she would ask her. Friday couldn't come soon enough. As they prepared the meal, Nettie cornered Rose and said, "Rose, I'm pregnant."

"That's wonderful, Nettie. Does Louis know?" Rose asked, excited that there would be another baby in the family.

"No," Nettie said. "I'm afraid if he knew he would be angry."

"What's the problem?" Rose asked.

"At first I got all the usual symptoms—cravings, nausea—and then they stopped, but the cramps haven't. I'm having some bleeding and some cramps double me over," said Nettie, with a worried look on her face.

Rose knew the symptoms of a miscarriage and felt she had to take care of her sister. As the family sat at the table, Rose announced, "Nettie and I will not be going to temple with all of you after supper. We have some things to take care of, and Nettie isn't feeling well."

The rest of the family finished supper and left for the temple and services. Nettie and Rose moved to the bathroom where Nettie collapsed on the floor. "Oh the cramps," she cried. Rose helped her onto the toilet and used a cold towel on her forehead. It was two hours before Nettie passed the fetus.

SEEK MISSING DRUG CLERK WHO DISAPPEARS FROM HOME

Louis Zauderer Last Seen by His Friends Friday When He Was in Despondent Mood.

Friends of Louis J. Zauderer, a drug clerk, recently employed at the Economy Drug Store, corner of Thirteenth street and Franklin avenue, are uneasy about his whereabouts, and have reported his disappearance to the police.

Zauderer, who is about 24 years old, was last seen by his employer, Andrew H. Coussens, Friday night. Coussens had paid Zauderer his salary and the latter said he would be at work in the morning. He did not go to his room, situated back of the Crescent Drug Store at Ninth and Carr streets that night, however, and when he was not heard of by his roommate, Joseph Lasersohn, on Saturday and Sunday, inquiries were begun.

No one has been found, however, who could explain his disappearance. He had been heard to say that he had received a telegram from New York, saying that his brother was in trouble, but it is not believed he would start for New York without at first informing some of his friends of his intention.

Zauderer came to St. Louis about three months ago from New York City, where his relatives live. He had intended to attend the College of Physicians here this winter, and had about $165 saved to further his education.

He is described as being 5 feet 7 inches tall, with dark eyes and hair. His face was smooth shaven, and he wore glasses.

St. Louis Republic, August 26, 1903.
Newspapers.com

"Nettie, you're going to stay here tonight. I'm going to call the doctor to come in the morning. I've sent the maid to the telegraph office to notify Louis in St. Louis."

To Louis Zauderer stop Need to come home stop Nettie ill stop Rose Cohn

Louis found the message on the door to the drugstore that evening when he came home from a little drinking at the local saloon. This is what I get for getting married. Medical school will have to be put on hold again. His roommate asked him about the telegram. "It's about my brother in New York," Louis lied. For some reason, he didn't want them to know he was married. Louis packed his bags and was off to the train station, telling no one—not even his employer—where he was going.

Several days later, a missing person report was in the newspaper asking if anyone had seen a man about five-foot-seven, dark hair, smooth-shaven, wearing glasses. He had been in St. Louis only three months but had been able to save $165 ($4,025 in 2017 dollars).

The Miscarriage Confrontation

In the morning, the doctor came and gave Nettie a clean bill of health. He said she must not leave her apartment for the next two weeks. Rose told the family that Nettie had come down with the flu and that as soon as Louis got there, they would move back to their apartment. Nettie sent a message to Mr. Solow. She told him she would not be able to come to work until she was over the flu.

Louis arrived the next day. "Rose, I'm here. What has happened to the love of my life?" Louis asked, with an air of concern.

"She's a little under the weather, Louis. When you get her home, I'm sure she will tell you all about it," Rose replied.

Louis entered the bedroom where Nettie was propped up on a pillow. He moved quickly to her and planted a kiss on her forehead. "You had me so worried. I got here as fast as I could," he said.

Rose took note of the show of affection and concern that Louis had for her sister. They bundled Nettie up, and the two of them went back to their apartment. As soon as Nettie got into bed, she saw a different Louis. "What's going on with you? It's time to tell me." His voice was loud, coarse, and demanding.

"Oh, Louis, I couldn't tell you when you left that I had missed my period. I didn't want you to worry about me. Then after three months, I knew I was pregnant," Nettie sobbed.

Nettie was now frightened by his tone. "So you had a miscarriage at Rose's house?" Louis surmised.

"Yes, I'm so sorry I lost our baby," Nettie cried.

"Don't be sorry. That baby was not going to be good for us now," Louis concluded.

"Don't say that, Louis. We would have found a way to have a baby in our lives. Don't you want a son someday?" Nettie was making her case for a future family.

"I don't know, but right now you have cost me a spot in the freshman medical class that was supposed to start in two weeks. Why did I ever get married?" Louis threw his hands up in the air, left the room, and slammed the door behind him.

Nettie didn't know what to feel, but the loss of the baby was something she was not prepared to face alone. Rose would be the one to help her get through this. In the other room, she could hear Louis opening a bottle of wine. She feared the worst; Louis was getting drunk. For the first time, Nettie really feared Louis, and she was in no condition to defend herself.

It was good she was not going back to school or work, for later that night, Louis took out his anger on her. The bruises on her face would heal, but the ache in her heart would be a different matter.

Louis Returns to Mr. Solow's Pharmacy

Mr. Solow didn't welcome Louis back with open arms. Louis couldn't say why he had come home, just that things didn't work out as planned in St. Louis. He would wait until

Nettie had finished school before he went back to St. Louis. Mr. Solow thought he must have gotten into trouble. He knew Louis was a drinker and liked cocaine. He would hire him back for Nettie's sake. He knew Nettie would try to keep him in line. "How about $60 a month, Louis?"

"I was getting more in St. Louis," he said.

"How much was that?"

"$80," said Louis.

Mr. Solow knew he was lying, and Louis knew it too.

"OK, I pay you $75 a month, but I take $5 out of your paycheck for every day you miss or are too drunk to work." This was $5 a month more than he was getting in St. Louis. The penalty for not coming to work was something he wasn't expecting.

"I'll take it, Mr. Solow, and thank you." The thank-you was hard for him to get out.

Nettie Goes Back to School

Nettie's second year at school seemed to fly by. As a senior, she spent three days a week at the drugstore and only two days in school. Work at the compounding counter was more interesting than the soda counter. She learned all about the new drugs coming on the market as well as the old ones. Her school was to merge with Columbia University

LEFT: Nettie Sachs, graduation from Columbia School of Pharmacy, 1904. *Courtesy of the Diane Sacks collection*
RIGHT: Louis J. Zauderer, passport photo, 1917. *Courtesy of U.S. passport photos*

at the end of her session. She was so glad she got into school before this happened. She didn't have the requirements that were needed by Columbia.

In the spring, Louis's younger sister Lena got married. She married William Caldwell, a successful attorney. Shortly after the wedding, the entire Zauderer family moved into Caldwell's house. The family saw Lena as the golden girl, and Louis was definitely on the outside.

"You see how money talks, Nettie? You can never have enough," Louis reasoned.

Nettie wondered why he couldn't just congratulate his sister on her fortunate choice of husbands. She guessed it was a sibling thing.

Graduation

April 13, 1904, was the date that Nettie graduated. She received a certificate of examination. She was the first person in the family to go to college. The whole family was there to see her walk on stage and accept her certificate. After the ceremony, it was off to the deli for the celebration. This was where she had her first meal in this country, so it was only fitting that they should celebrate here. Of course, she was not a pharmacist yet. She would need two years as an apprentice before she could get her diploma.

Louis finished his second year as an apprentice and exchanged his certificate for his diploma. It was now time to pack and move to St. Louis.

On April 30, the Louisiana Purchase Exposition[7]—commonly known as the Saint Louis World's Fair of 1904—opened in St. Louis, Missouri. St. Louis was the gateway to the West, and Nettie and Louis would be a part of it. They didn't leave New York until May.

7　St. Louis was the fourth-largest city in America, with over 575,000 people, 40,000 of whom were Jews. When the St. Louis territory was under the control of Spain, Jews were forbidden to enter the territory. That all changed with the Louisiana Purchase in 1803. The Louisiana Purchase Exposition took place in Forest Park, which was bigger than Central Park in New York. The Exposition opened April 30 and closed December 1. More than 187,000 people went through its gates on opening day. John Philip Sousa's band performed. President Theodore Roosevelt opened the fair via telegraph from the White House. The Expo was circled by a train that ran over 14 miles of track and took 40 minutes to make the complete trip around. In September, the third modern-day Olympics were held in conjunction with the Exposition, the first time the Olympics were held in the United States.

CHAPTER 6

Nettie and Louis Move to St. Louis

It was going to be a two-night trip to Chicago. They got tickets on a Pullman sleeping car. They would change trains in Chicago and meet Anna and Barney. The four of them would travel together to St. Louis. Nettie had been writing to Anna in Chicago. It was planned that they would meet at the train station. Anna and Barney would make the hotel reservations, which would be difficult. There was a huge interest in Chicago in the St. Louis fair, which celebrated the centennial of the 1803 Louisiana Purchase. When the school term ended, the Exposition was the place families would take their summer vacations. The Exposition was both entertainment and an educational experience.

It had been over two years since the girls had seen each other. "Over here, Nettie." She heard Anna's voice above the hissing sound of the steam engine.

"Look, Louis, over there." She waved at Anna and Barney.

Through the steam cloud let loose by the engine, he saw them. "Hello, old man," Barney said to Louis, as the couples found each other.

"Look who's calling who an old man," Louis answered. "I understand you're now a father."

"Anna, let's see a picture of your son, Cecil." Nettie said. Anna opened her purse and took out a handful of pictures. "Look, Louis. Isn't he precious?" Nettie asked, while showing him the pictures. Louis didn't seem too interested.

"Barney," Louis said, "let's find our trunks and get a porter to get them onto the other train." The men went off, and Nettie and Anna found a bench to sit down on to look at the pictures.

"Everything is going so well for us, Nettie. I think I told you we're living in a little town just outside Chicago called Whiting, Indiana. Barney has opened a saloon there. It's a much better business than the junk business. There's a very active Jewish community in our area."

"I'm so happy for you, Anna. We still have a few years before Louis finishes school and we can start a family," said Nettie, but the thought of a family brought back memories of her miscarriage last year.

The train was packed with people on their way to the Louisiana Purchase Exposition. They were lucky to get seats. The people were talking about the elevated price of hotel rooms and everything else in the city because of the Expo. On the way, Louis talked about getting his old job back and Nettie doing her apprenticeship at the same pharmacy. She needed one year before she could get her license in Missouri. With both their salaries, they should be able to get a nice flat and Louis could save enough money for medical school. *When Nettie gets her license as a pharmacist*, thought Louis, *she can earn the family income while I'm in school. This is a much better plan than the one I had when I was in this town last year.*

They knew St. Louis would be busy with all the visitors to the Exposition, but they were used to New York. That was busy. When they pulled into Union Station, Nettie remembered it from her trip from Houston a few years earlier, when she met Walter Culpepper. This is where they parted company and he went on to Kansas City. *I wonder what he's doing now*, she thought.

The station was massive, even bigger than Grand Central Terminal in New York. Trains seemed to be coming from everywhere to the Exposition. It was good they planned ahead for a hotel room. They had reservations at the Laclede Hotel on Market Street, six blocks from Union Station, on the direct trolley line to the Exposition.

"I'll be happy when we get all this baggage to the hotel and I can get a good night's sleep," said Louis.

"We have a big day tomorrow, Louis. Get ready to be amazed at what we'll see," said Barney.

"The first thing I'm going to do in the morning is contact Mr. Coussens to see when Nettie and I have to report to work," Louis answered.

Sam Herskovitz Comes to St. Louis

Sam Herskovitz was on a mission when he stepped off the ship in New York City. He wanted to become a physician, and nothing was going to stop him. The next four years, he studied at New York University, not far from his mother's boarding house. Most of the family was living there—his older sister Ettie, and brother Marcus. Sam worked as a watchman to make tuition money. It was a perfect job, as he could study at the same time.

His sister Ettie married Newman Hillel, a watchmaker. In 1901, their first child Pearl was born. They moved to Connecticut where their second child Sarah was born in 1903. The lure of the West had them moving to St. Louis in January 1904. This was fortunate for Sam. Newman was very involved in the Russian Jewish community by the time Sam came to St. Louis for medical school. Newman was a Harmony Club member with Isaac Schwab and Elias Michaels. These two men were on the board of directors of the St. Louis Exposition Company, and he could ask them for a favor.

As coincidence would have it, Sam boarded the same train out of New York as Nettie and Louis. He saved money by not getting a seat in a Pullman sleeping car. Nettie and Sam were in different parts of the train and never crossed paths. When Sam got to Union Station in St. Louis, his sister Ettie Hillel and his baby nieces Pearl and Sarah were there to greet him.

Through his connections, Newman had secured Sam a job as a Jefferson security guard at the Expo. His experience as a security guard in New York was a help. He was to earn $50 a month. It would go a long way toward his $100 ($2,450 in 2017 dollars) medical school tuition. He just met the physical requirements to be a Jefferson guard at five-foot-eight and 145 pounds. Medical school was not to start until September. The guards were provided with sleeping quarters. This allowed him to save more of his earnings for tuition.

Louis Gets a Job

The next morning, it didn't take Louis long to contact Mr. Coussens about their jobs. "Hello, Louis," Mr. Coussens said. "We all wondered what happened to you last year when you didn't come back to work. We even put out a missing person report in the newspaper."

"I'm sorry, Mr. Coussens. Family problems I couldn't discuss, but all is better now."

"I know about family problems, Louis. You remember my son Joshua?"

"Yes I do, sir, a very bright boy," Louis answered.

"He died two months ago from typhoid fever. We had a bout of it in the city, and he caught it."

"I'm so sorry to hear that, sir. My condolences to you and the family," Louis said with real concern in his voice.

"Why thank you, Louis. You told me you were bringing your wife. I can't wait to meet her."

"That you will, sir. When do you want us to start?" Louis wanted to appear eager.

"You can start today. We are very shorthanded with all the visitors in town," answered Mr. Coussens.

"I do need a little time to find a place to live. We are staying at the Laclede Hotel. We came to town with friends from Chicago who want to see the Expo," Louis explained.

"You understand, Louis, that I have a business to run. I can give you a few days, and your wife a week, before reporting to work. Otherwise, I'll have to look elsewhere," Mr. Coussens said, with an air of authority in his voice.

"OK, sir, I'll be at work in two days." Louis knew Mr. Coussens meant what he said, and he didn't want to lose this job before he had it.

"That's what I wanted to hear. See you then."

Louis hung up the phone with a look of disgust on his face. Turning to the group, he said, "The old bastard won't give me a week off. I have to start in two days. Nettie, you get a week. Guess you are on your own after I go to work."

"That won't be so bad, Louis. We will help Nettie find a flat as well as see the Expo," answered Anna. With that, they went to breakfast and then took the trolley to the Exposition.

The St. Louis Exposition

The main gates were on Lindell Boulevard and DeBaliviere Avenue. The Expo had been open for a few weeks, but the crowds were enormous. On the first day, almost 200,000 people attended. Today didn't seem much different. The admission cost was 80 cents per day; monthly or season tickets were also available. They chose the daily rate and entered the Expo through the main gates at the Plaza of St. Louis. There in the middle of the plaza was the statue of St. Louis of France.[1] From there, they entered what was known

---

1   The 1,576 buildings were made of yellow pine and ivory-colored "staff," a mixture of plaster and hemp that could be easily molded, sliced, sanded, and sawed. Most of these buildings were air-conditioned, a technology only a few years old. There were 73,000 exhibits from 53 foreign countries and 43 states. The fair could feed 36,650 people at one time. Five restaurants could seat more than 2,000 people each. The fair claimed many firsts: the debut of Dr. Pepper, the ice-cream cone, iced tea, hotdogs, hamburgers, peanut butter, cotton candy, and puffed rice cereal. The Quaker Oats company shot its cereal out of eight cannons every 50 minutes.

Louisiana Purchase Exposition 1904, St. Louis, The Pike. *Courtesy of the Missouri History Museum*

LEFT: Louisiana Purchase Exposition 1904, The Cascades. *Library of Congress*
RIGHT: World's largest Ferris wheel, Louisiana Purchase Exposition 1904. *Library of Congress*

as "The Pike." It ran for about a mile and a half from the plaza of St. Louis to the Grand Basin. Along the Pike were 50 shows, restaurants, and amusement attractions. There were hoochie coochie girls, ragtime rhythms, and food. Troupes of entertainers beckoned visitors to come enjoy their shows. There were water chutes, a fun house, animal shows, and firefighting demonstrations. The Grand Basin was at the bottom of the Cascades. The Cascades started 90 feet above the basin with the water flowing down three terraces, 45 feet wide at the top and 150 feet wide at the base. Ninety thousand gallons of water a minute poured from the bowl above. Four fountains at the base threw water 75 feet into the air. At night, the water and buildings were illuminated by 120,000 electric lights until closing time at 11 p.m.

The group looked at their programs as they wandered down the Pike. "Look at all the different palaces," Anna said to Barney. "We can't see them all in just one day. It says here it would take weeks."

"Let's just pick a few today. Let me list them," Nettie said, as she read the program. "Transportation, Machinery, Electricity, Varied Industries, Education, Mines, Liberal Arts, Manufacturers, and Agriculture."

"I vote for Electricity," Barney said.

"I want to see the largest pipe organ in the world. It's at Festival Hall," said Anna.

"I see they have an exact replica of the town of Jerusalem. Hey guys, that's our heritage. We have to see that," reminded Louis.

The sounds of Scott Joplin's ragtime music filled the air as they moved on down the Pike. Barney pointed to the giant Ferris wheel, the biggest ever built, which loomed over the fair. "I want to take a ride on that and see the whole fair from the sky," he said, craning his neck to see the top of the Ferris wheel.

As they approached the Palace of Electricity, Anna pointed to a man walking in front of the building. "Look at that man wearing earpieces that sprout from a wheel he's holding in his hand."

"I think that's called an hPhone. It works without wires," explained Louis.

The day went by quickly. With so many things to see and do, they did only half of the items on their list. "We need to get an early start tomorrow," Louis suggested. "It's my last day with you before I have to start work."

They didn't waste any time the next day and got an early start. The gates opened at 8 a.m. When they got there, a crowd was already at the gate. As they passed through the gate, Barney said, "Look up there on top of the Electricity building—the Zionist flag. I didn't see it yesterday." Barney pointed to the northeast corner of the building. There in all its blue and white glory, with the Star of David in the middle, was the Zionist flag.[2] It was alongside the American flag and others displayed above the Hall of Nations. They all looked up in amazement.

"How can that be?" asked Anna. "There's no Jewish nation."

"Maybe it's a wish for the future," said Louis. "After all, this fair is supposed to give us a glimpse of what is to come. Let's go to the Town of Jerusalem first. It's the farthest away," said Louis. "If we take the train, we can see a lot of the fair and get off at Station 10 and walk over to the exhibit."

The Jerusalem exhibit was gigantic and stretched over more than 10 acres. There were 300 structures, an exact replica of the city of Jerusalem. They saw the Dome of the Rock, the Wailing Wall, the Church of the Holy Sepulcher, and the Tower of David.

"I feel like I'm in Jerusalem," said Anna. "Everything looks and feels so real."

"Someday I plan to see the real thing," echoed Louis.

I've never seen Louis as calm as he has been while at the fair, Nettie thought. Maybe things will be different now that we're in St. Louis.

Sam and Nettie Meet Again

Their two days at the fair ended with everyone wanting a rest, especially their feet. Louis was off to his first day of work. The three others were scouring the paper for flats to rent. As luck would have it, they found a group of buildings on Blair Street and without too much trouble rented a flat on the second floor at 1506 Blair St. They couldn't move in until the end of the week. That was perfect for all of them.

The next day, they were off to the fair again, just the three of them. This time, they concentrated on the larger pavilions, taking the train and then walking from the stations. They had just come out of the Liberal Arts Pavilion and were walking through the Sunken Garden when a voice came from behind them. "Excuse me, but can I see your fair passes?"

---

2   When the fair was being organized, Michael Stiffelman, a local Zionist leader, won support from Jules Aubere, a non-Jewish newspaperman. He persuaded the fair's board of directors to approve the request to fly the Zionist flag. It's interesting to note that it was under President Harry Truman from Missouri that the United States was the first nation to grant diplomatic recognition to the new state of Israel, on May 14, 1948, 44 years after the fair.

Nettie stopped and turned to look straight into Sam's blue eyes. He was in the uniform of the Jefferson Guard. *He looks so handsome,* thought Nettie.

Sam had seen them go into the Liberal Arts Pavilion. He was waiting for them when they came out. Nettie couldn't control herself and put her arms around him for a big hug. "Oh Sam, it's so good to see you again. You do remember Anna? This is her husband Barney Cohen."

"It's been a long journey since we were shipmates."

"Tell me, Sam, is that dream of medical school still alive?" asked Nettie.

"It sure is. I apply this August at the Medical School of Washington University. If accepted, I will start in September. What about you, Nettie? I see Anna got married."

"I finished the pharmacy program at New York University and came down here with my husband, who is also a pharmacist. His name is Louis Zauderer."

"Where is he today?" Sam asked.

"He had to start work."

"Is Louis from New York?" Sam asked.

"Yes, he is. He was two years ahead of me in school," Nettie explained.

"I think I know him or maybe someone in his family. The name sounds very familiar." Sam was squinting his eyes as he tried to remember the name.

"Barney and Anna live in the Chicago area and are down for the week."

"What do you do, Barney?" asked Sam.

"I have a saloon in Indiana, and I'm planning on expanding. People just can't get enough of the good liquor."

"You'll probably be interested in the bourbon judging here at the fair. I hear Jack Daniels[3] is the one to beat," offered Sam.

"Well, folks, I have to walk my beat. Don't want to get fired. Nettie, what pharmacy are you working at?"

"I think it is called the Crescent City Pharmacy," Nettie said.

"If I need anything, I'll be sure to look you and your husband up."

That said, Sam hugged Nettie and Anna and shook Barney's hand, and they went their separate ways. On the way back to the hotel, Nettie told Barney and Anna, "Please don't

---

3   Jack Daniels did win the competition for the best whiskey. This honor gave his company the start it needed. The rest is history.

say anything to Louis about Sam. No sense in getting him jealous. He has been in such a good mood of late." They both agreed.

The three of them had a few more days at the fair. On the last day, they helped Nettie move into their new apartment. It was a tearful goodbye at the train station. They promised to see each other soon.

Nettie started her apprenticeship at the pharmacy. From time to time, she and Louis would go to the fair. Sometimes at night when all the lights were on, it seemed like a fairy land. Everyone was in good spirits.

Louis and Nettie Enjoy the Fair

October 31, Halloween, was on a Monday night and a perfect time to go to the fair. Nettie and Louis got some masks from the drugstore to fit in with the crowd. As they walked through the gate, Louis said, "They're playing my song, 'Meet Me in St. Louis, Louie.'" He took Nettie in his arms and danced her around in a circle.

"Oh, Louis, you are so gay tonight," she said.

"Let's go down the Pike and see Princess Raja dance the cooch." Princess Raja would dance and whirl around like a belly dancer. She would end her routine by picking up a chair with just her teeth and then dance with it high over her head.

Along the Pike, Louis bought them the newest craze, hot dogs in buns. They had such a good time that when they got home, they were both in good spirits. They had a nightcap and then went to bed. That night in bed was a special one: Louis was like an eager and energetic bridegroom. Afterward, they both slept soundly.

Sam Starts Medical School

September 26, 1904, was Sam's first day at medical school. He paid his $100 tuition and additional lab fees. This didn't leave him much left after his few months as a Jefferson Guard at the Exposition. His sister introduced him to a distant relative, Ian Abrams, who had an extra room for him in his apartment at 817 N. Ninth St. Ian also agreed to be his official guardian, a requirement of the school.

Sam had Dr. M.W. Sharpe of 3505 Franklin Ave. give him a certificate of moral standing and make the official recommendation to attend medical school. Sam was almost broke but arranged to continue to work after school at the fair as a guard and night watchman.

He could always study at night, just like he did in New York when he was attending college. The other guards teased him, calling him "Dr. Sam."

The fair ended in December. As luck would have it, he got a night job in one of St. Louis's many slaughterhouses. He was studying anatomy, so cutting up cows was like surgery. Money was always a problem. He had to pay for his room, and he was always hungry and sleepy. The only good meal he had was at his sister's house at Friday Sabbath dinner.

Ettie was a great cook. It was roasted chicken or braised brisket. *Gefilte* fish, chopped liver, matzo ball soup or borscht (a cabbage and beet soup), stuffed cabbage, and *schmaltz* for his bread and potatoes. He missed his mother's *schmaltz*, a rendered chicken fat that she used instead of butter. He would always feel full on his walk back to his flat. The pain in his stomach was much reduced after these Sabbath dinners. Sam made sure he always had some milk on hand when the pain returned. That helped. *Maybe I will visit the pharmacy where Nettie works for some medicine*, thought Sam, but then he ruled that out. *I have no money. I will just suffer.*

Because of his hours at the slaughterhouse, Sam found himself falling asleep during lectures. He thought to himself, *Can I do this for four years?*

Nettie Is Pregnant, Again

It was the end of January 1905, and both Nettie and Louis were working in Mr. Coussens' pharmacies. Sometimes they were together, many times in different locations. Nettie had to work until May before she could apply for her state license.

It was on one of those cold winter evenings after she had made sure Louis had a good meal and a little wine that she told him. "Louis, remember Halloween night when we went to the fair?"

"Yes, I do remember. We had a grand old time."

"That we did, Louis. Well, I have great news for you. You are going to be a father!"

"What?" asked a surprised Louis.

"I said I'm pregnant. I've missed my last three periods." There was a long pause in the conversation. It was so silent that you could hear a pin drop.

Louis had a scowl on his face. "I thought we decided you wouldn't get pregnant until after I finished medical school. That's at least three years from now."

"I know, Louis. I guess we made a mistake."

"We made a mistake? It's you that made the mistake. Not me."

Nettie knew she was in for it now. He was not happy about the news. She wanted to say that it takes two to make a baby or ask why he didn't pull out in time, but she didn't.

"Do you know what a baby is going to cost?" he asked, in an even louder voice.

"Please don't shout, Louis. The walls are thin in these apartments. We don't want the neighbors to hear."

"I don't give a damn about the neighbors!" he yelled. "I ought to give you the back of my hand, woman. You have messed up my life again with your damn babies."

"I thought you would like the idea. Didn't you see how happy Anna and Barney were with their baby?"

"That's Anna and Barney. He isn't planning to go to medical school. I am. We have been living on your salary and saving mine for the tuition. This baby will wipe us out."

"Don't worry, Louis, I'll pay for everything."

"How do you plan to do that?"

"I'll take a second job and work nights as well as days."

"Yes, but you won't be working at all by your sixth month, and I don't know how many months after that. Who will take care of the baby? It costs money, you know," he said.

"It's always about the money, money, money. That's all you care about." Nettie just couldn't be silent; she had to state her case.

Louis flew out of his chair with his arm raised and slapped her across her face.

"You're *meshugga* (crazy), Louis," Nettie yelled at him.

"Don't you ever talk back to me like that again, or you'll get more of that. Women are supposed to keep their mouths shut, and you haven't learned that lesson yet," he scowled.

Nettie held back the tears. She wasn't going to give him the pleasure of seeing her cry. What was supposed to be such a happy announcement turned into disaster. Just then, they heard the sound of a broom handle hitting the floor of their apartment from below. "Keep it down up there. Other people live here too." The voice came from the apartment beneath them.

Louis stomped on the floor. "Oh go to hell yourself," he roared back at them. Then there was a period of calm.

"You'll see, Louis. I'll ask my mother to come down from New York to help with the baby. She's a wonderful cook, even better than me. You'll see. It will all work out."

Louis grumbled, "We'll see. Another mouth to feed."

Sam Meets a Pregnant Nettie

In July, and just by chance, Sam passed Nettie while he was walking to school and she was going to her job. "Oh my, Nettie, look how pregnant you are. How many months?"

"Hi, Sam. I'm eight months and due at the end of July."

"Well, *mazel tov* to you and Louis. Was that your husband's name?"

"Yes, that's correct." Nettie answered. "What are you doing in the neighborhood?"

"I have a room just around the corner at 817 Ninth St."

"That's great, Sam. My mother is arriving this week from New York to help me with the baby. After she gets settled, you should come over for supper and meet Louis."

"OK, I will. What's your address?" Sam asked.

"See the building over there?" Nettie pointed at a building behind them. "We are on the second floor. It's 1506 Blair."

Sam scribbled the address on the front of his notebook. "I'll drop by soon, maybe after the baby is born, and we can all get acquainted."

"Wonderful. So good to see you again," Nettie said. They had an awkward hug, as the baby bump was all too prominent. They walked another block together, and then they went their separate ways.

Baby Edward Noah Sachs Zauderer Is Born

"Waaaaaa," was the cry heard from 1506 Blair St.

"It's a boy," said Dr. Kean, who delivered baby Edward. Immediately, they all noticed something was wrong with the baby's left arm. It was very short, and the fingers on the hand were malformed. He was a very small baby, just over five pounds. He seemed to have a smaller than normal head, which was covered with black hair. His eyebrows were connected across his forehead in an almost straight line.

"Something is very wrong with this kid," said Louis.

"Oh don't be silly," said Dr. Kean. "All babies look a little funny when they're born. He just has a malformed hand."

"I don't want to disagree with you, doctor, but I think it's more than a withered arm and malformed hand," said Louis.

"I don't care what you say, Louis. He's a beautiful baby and your son," added Mama Mary.

During the next few days, Nettie and Mary found other problems with the new baby, who was named Edward, after Nettie's brother in Houston. Louis wanted Noah to be Edward's middle name, to remind him he was a Jew.

Little Edward had difficulty nursing and was constantly throwing up. There was also a partial joining of the second and third toes. Nettie brought this to the attention of Dr. Kean, but all he would say was, "All babies are different, and it's an easy thing to fix."

It was almost eight days since Edward's birth and, by Jewish law, time for his circumcision. Nettie would invite Sam for the *brit milah* (circumcision) and ask him what he thought about all the abnormal things they had found with the baby. She still had Sam's address and would send Mama Mary over to his house with a note:

Dear Sam,

The baby has arrived and my invitation for dinner is still good. If you can come by next Sunday, we are having a *brit milah* for Edward, my son, and you can meet the family.

Nettie

When Sam came home, Ian handed him the note. "It's an invitation to a *brit milah*. My friend had a baby boy. They have invited me to supper and to meet the family," said Sam.

"Good for you," Ian said. "Another good meal."

Sam Meets Louis and Baby Edward

Sam knocked on the door at 1506 Blair, and Nettie opened it. Sam could smell the wonderful odors of food cooking on the stove. There in the living room was the baby in his crib. Louis, a balding man without facial hair, was sitting on the couch. The round glasses he was wearing on his rounded face made him look owl-like. Next to him was the rabbi, who was also a *mohel* (Jewish person trained in circumcision).

Louis rose to greet him, and Sam found him to be almost his same height. "Hello, Sam. I'm Louis. I've heard so much about you from Nettie. Your trip across the Atlantic was quite an adventure, Nettie tells me."

"It seems so long ago, Louis, but you're right, and I wouldn't want to do that again."

"Can I get you a drink, Sam?"

"Sorry, I have a touchy stomach and alcohol does it no good. Milk would be fine." Nettie got him a glass of milk.

"Can I see the new baby?" Sam asked.

"Over here, Sam." Nettie picked up little Edward, and right away Sam saw something was wrong. "Sam, we're worried about the baby. He seems to have a number of problems—his arm, toes, and hairy eyebrows, just to name a few. Doctor Kean doesn't think anything is wrong, but we do."

"Let's take a look." Sam lifted the baby from her arms and placed him in his lap. "What you're describing sounds like what we have been taught is a syndrome, a number of features that together give you a picture of a certain type of problem. I'll write everything down that you have found and ask my professors if they can put a name to the syndrome."

"He also has a hard time keeping any food down. He throws up a lot. We're concerned he's not gaining much weight," said Nettie, with a look of concern on her face, hoping there would be an answer for little Edward.

"This is all good information I can take back to find an answer," Sam said.

"It's time for the *bris*," said the mohel. "It's tradition for the oldest member of the family to hold the baby."

"That's me," said Mama Mary. She picked little Edward up and cradled him in her lap covered with a soft towel. The rabbi/*mohel* said a few words in Yiddish and a prayer for the future of Edward and the Jewish people. Then in a quick movement of his special knife, the foreskin was removed. Mama Mary and the others thought it odd that Edward made no sound, but in unison everyone said *mazel tov*.

The rabbi placed a dressing on the incision, and Mary placed Edward back in his bassinet. *Shlof mayn kird* (sleep my child), she said, in Yiddish.

It was time to sit down for dinner. Mary had been cooking all day, as this was to be a very special dinner in honor of her grandson. Sam was the first to make a toast. "*Le'chayim*, to life," he said. "May Edward be the first of your many sons."

Louis mumbled something under his breath. "*Az a yor ahf mir*" (I should have such good luck). They all touched glasses—Sam with his milk, the others with their wine.

After dinner, they had a chance to relive their trip across the ocean and how they had adjusted to life in America. Louis, having been born in America, made the comment that they were all still *greenhorns*.

After Sam bid them good night, Mama Mary took Nettie aside as they were doing the dishes. "That Sam, Nettie, he's a real *mensch* (a good person). Some woman is going to hit the jackpot with him."

For an instant, Nettie remembered her feelings for Sam when she was posing as boy on the ship. She knew that she had a special feeling for Sam. *Why didn't I try to see him in New York,* she thought?

What Is Wrong with Baby Edward?

The problems with Edward were the focus of much discussion at home. Accusations flew between Nettie and Louis. Had it not been for Mama Mary, blows would have taken place.

"It was all your drinking and cocaine that caused the problem with Edward," accused Nettie.

"I'm sure it was all those other men in your life. That's the root of the problem. There has never been an imbecile on my side of the family," Louis said. He continued, "I hear they're thinking about sterilizing women who give birth to these idiots."

"Don't you talk that way about our son," Nettie admonished him. "He's not speaking yet, and you make him out to be an idiot. Sam said the doctors at the medical school are interested in seeing Edward, so I'm going to take him there."

"Go ahead. Maybe they'll put him on display somewhere. At least he would be out of my life," said Louis, in a sarcastic tone. "Expenses for all the doctor visits are just starting, so tell me, when are you going to go to back to work now that you have your pharmacy license? We need the money."

Nettie had finished her one-year apprenticeship and had gotten her license in May. She was feeling pulled from all directions. At least Mama Mary was here to help with Edward and keep Louis from hitting her.

Edward Is Examined

Sam arranged a visit to the pediatric unit at the medical school. Nettie told the doctors, "He's almost three months old, and he still can't raise his head or make a fist with his good hand. He's not gaining a lot of weight or growing much since he was born. Feeding is always a problem, and he doesn't seem to respond to sounds or toys."

The doctors all examined Edward and felt that he was having some sort of developmental problem, as he was not hitting the normal milestones for development. They gave Nettie the name of a specialist in child development whom she was to see on a regular basis to monitor Edward and help with his feeding and other problems.

Thank goodness, Mama Mary was there to help. Nettie had to get back to work, as the bills were piling up. She was hired back as a registered pharmacist, so her pay increased. Louis had an idea that if he opened his own pharmacy, he could make more money and still be able to start medical school in the fall, letting Nettie run the pharmacy.

Sam Moves in with Ettie and Newman

With money always a problem, holding down a night job and going to school, it seemed like the right thing to do when Sam's sister offered to find a place for him in her house. He would now have regular meals and would not have to earn rent money. All his money could go toward his next year's tuition. It was during this second year of medical school that Sam became interested in the writings of Emma Goldman.[4] She was an anarchist who believed in changing existing institutions and codes of behavior. He brought her literature home and shared it with his sister, who now had two children and had never had an opportunity for an education. She had an arranged marriage to Newman Hillel at age 19 shortly after she arrived in America. Newman was 17 years her senior and did not want to change his ideas about how women and a wife should be treated.

Ettie Embraces New Ideas

Ettie and Sam seemed to be talking about Emma Goldman all the time in the house. The idea of free love, and being able to choose your husband through love and not an

---

4   Emma Goldman, born to Jewish parents in Kovno, Lithuania, in 1869, came to America in 1885. She was an advocate of a new social order and limited government. Sexual freedom, birth control, and independence and education for women were some of her messages. She published the journal *Mother Earth* from 1906 to 1917. An anarchist who felt any government was oppressive, she opposed WWI and was imprisoned for 18 months. In 1919, she and others were deported to Russia under the 1918 Alien Act. Disillusioned by the Bolshevik regime, she spent the rest of her life wandering through Europe. She died in Canada in 1940. Her body was allowed to be buried in Chicago near Haymarket Square next to anarchists whose actions were the inspiration for her lifelong crusade.

T. LOUIS, FRIDAY EVENING, SEPTEMBER 28, 1906   PRICE (In St. Lou Outside St.

FAMILY BROKEN UP WHEN WIFE DESERTS HUSBAND TO FOLLOW ANARCHY TEACHINGS

Newman and Ettie Hillel, 1906. *Courtesy of St. Louis Post Dispatch, newspapers.com.*

arrangement, made sense to Ettie. Sher also embraced the idea of getting an education to make her more independent of her husband for room and board. By July of 1906, she felt she could no longer be a wife to Newman. She and Sam moved to 2827 Gamble with her two girls. This made the front page of the St. Louis Dispatch in September: "Family Broken Up When Wife Deserts Husband to Follow Anarchy Teachings."

Sam Becomes Agent for Emma Goldman

Sam supported his sister in her beliefs at her trial for separation from her husband and custody of the children. He used the money he had saved for his next year's tuition to pay for their

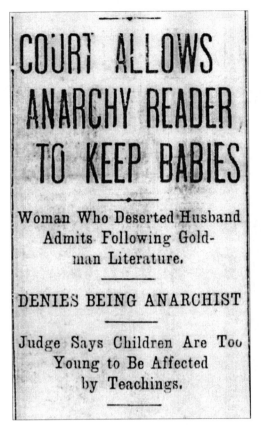

COURT ALLOWS ANARCHY READER TO KEEP BABIES

Woman Who Deserted Husband Admits Following Goldman Literature.

DENIES BEING ANARCHIST

Judge Says Children Are Too Young to Be Affected by Teachings.

St. Louis Post Dispatch September 28, 1906
Newspapers.com

living expenses. Newman withdrew any financial support in an effort to get Ettie back. Ettie now believed in free love, not arranged marriages where she had to love the man picked for her. These were the teachings of Emma Goldman. Sam was now a lieutenant in Emma Goldman's organization. He was distributing her journal *Mother Earth*. The family home was a meeting place for Goldman's followers. The judge gave child custody to Ettie, but Newman could visit on Wednesdays and Sundays.

Ettie and Newman Reconciled

It was just four months later, January 1907, that Ettie and Newman reconciled and the suit for divorce was dismissed. It was said that relatives from both sides agreed that it was Sam who had caused the split and that he must leave the house. This he did, but not before Newman agreed to let Ettie further her education and study to become a midwife. Sam moved back to live with Ian on Ninth Street.

Sam Meets Dora Shultz

Spring was just around the corner. It couldn't come too soon for Sam. He was used to the winters in New York, but this winter was so cold that the Mississippi River froze solid. When this happened, they called it an "ice gorge." People could walk across from the Missouri side to the Illinois side. The newspaper warned people not to cross the ice, as "air holes" were waiting to suck them down, where the last thing they would see was the distorted transparency of an ice sheet over their heads. This warning went unheeded by many, and they came across on bicycles, driving mule-drawn wagons, and pushing baby carriages. As the ice moved, the river would groan and make noises like a steel cable being stretched, *zzzzeeeppps* and *squurrrrrrs*. The people thought it was great fun.

By the spring thaw, the river was still very high from all the melting snow upriver, but March 21 was *Purim*.[5] This celebration meant a special dinner at the local synagogue. Sam would go to Bais Abraham Congregation on Seventh Street. They were having a special *Purim* dinner for newly arrived Jewish students.

Sam had just turned 23 on February 14. *This will be my birthday celebration. One night off work will be OK*, he thought. He still had his Jefferson Guard uniform. It was his best piece of clothing. He would wear that and hope to fit in. When he arrived, he recognized many students in his class he had never talked to. Now was the time to make some friends.

Before long, the hostess, Phyllis Lieberman, introduced him to a petite lady, maybe in her 40s, with thick brown hair and flashing black eyes. "Sam, I would like to introduce you to Mrs. Dora Shultz," Phyllis said.

"It's a pleasure to meet you, Mrs. Shultz." When she heard him speak, his words enveloped her like a blanket covering a shivering person. He was the most beautiful man she had ever seen. Maybe it was his uniform or his upright posture. Who knows what triggers an attraction? She had been attracted to him since he entered the room, and now she could barely speak.

"Oh, please call me Dora, Sam."

Phyllis saw Dora was having trouble speaking, so she said, "Sam, Dora is one of our benefactors who want to help struggling new immigrants adjust to the area."

"Well, that sure describes me," Sam said.

Dora finally found her voice. "What are you doing in St. Louis, Sam?"

"I'm studying medicine at the Medical College of Washington University. I came here from New York City."

---

5   *Purim* is a Jewish celebration that commemorates the deliverance of the Jews from their enemies, told in the book of Esther, where Esther, a Jewish-Persian queen, prevents a massacre of the Jewish people. In the story Mordechai, Esther's cousin, is a hero and Haman, the king's prime minister, is the villain who plots against both the king and the Jewish people; when the plot is foiled, Haman is put to death. *Purim* is a joyous celebration, and a time when Jews are expected to be very charitable, especially to the poor.

"You look like you could use a good meal, Sam. Why don't we sit over at the end table to have our meal and get acquainted?"

"Sounds good to me, Dora. I never turn down a good meal."

They picked up their plates at the end table and went to a long table that held all manner of food. Sam filled his plate. When they sat back down, Dora started her questions. "Where are you living, Sam?"

"Not far from here, on Ninth Street."

"Do you pay rent?" she asked.

"Yes I do."

Dora saw her opening. She was remembering what her astrologer had told her, that she would meet her "*soul mate,*" and here he was. "Sam, why don't you come stay at my house? We have a spare bedroom, and you won't have to pay any rent," she offered.

"I can't believe my ears. Did you just say I could stay at your house without paying rent?" He almost choked on a piece of brisket.

"That's right, Sam. I want to do something good for the immigrants, and this is what I want to do for you."

Sam couldn't believe it. *Just when things look the darkest, here comes an angel, maybe heaven sent, to help me.* Sam didn't have much experience with women, but they were always there to help him along. Both his mother and older sister saw him as the baby in the family, so this offer didn't seem so unusual. He was thinking of the teachings of Emma Goldman about rules of society should be turned upside down. Here it was in front of him.

"Do you have any relatives in St. Louis?" she asked.

"Yes, Dora. My sister and her husband live here."

"Why aren't you living with them?" questioned Dora.

"They have a very small house and two children. There's just no room. I'm now living with another family relative just a few blocks away." Sam didn't dare tell her of the real reason. He hoped she hadn't seen the newspaper article where he gave his opinions about free love and anarchy.

"What's the address?" Dora took out a notepad and pencil.

"817 Ninth St.," Sam said.

"What do you think about my offer, Sam?" Dora was trying to pretend this was a philanthropic offer and not appear to be too excited.

Mississippi River frozen solid, St. Louis, Missouri, February 1905. *Courtesy of the Missouri History Museum*

"Well, it's very generous, Mrs. Shultz—I mean Dora—but why me?" Even in the desperate state he was in, Sam was a little cautious about the offer.

"Do you know what a *soul mate* is, Sam?" asked Dora.

"I've heard the term. I think it means a relationship made in heaven."

"That's right, Sam. From the minute I saw you come into the room, I knew you were my *soul mate*. Even my astrologer said it was to happen tonight."

"We have Gypsies in my country who try to predict the same thing," Sam said.

"Don't you feel the attraction we have for each other, Sam?" She looked at him from across the table and reached out to touch his arm. She could feel the electricity course through her body at the mere touch of his arm. "Do you feel that?" Dora asked, as she squeezed his arm.

"Uh, I guess I do." He was feeling fuller from his meal and maybe a little gas from the cabbage rolls than from any electricity from Dora. Maybe it was the satisfied feeling of a good meal that caught him off guard, but no woman had ever spoken to him like this. The words *peculiar* and *strange* came into his mind. *This is what Emma has been lecturing about*, he thought. *We must break all norms of society.*

"Now don't worry, Sam. I'm a married woman and our relationship can only be platonic. I don't plan on getting a divorce." Sam thought, *How did we get to this stage in our conversation? I just met this woman an hour ago.*

"You don't have to make up your mind right now. Think it over. Then come by the house, or I'll stop by yours. I'm at 1338 Blair St." *This is only two blocks from Nettie's flat,* thought Sam.

The Yiddish phrase *Ven dos mazel kumt, shtel im a shtul* came to his mind. (If fortune calls, offer him a seat.) "OK, Dora, I'll think about it. The school term is almost over, and I have a lot of studying to do. I must also tell my cousin that I would be moving out. Give me a few months."

"I don't think I can wait that long. My heart is burning for you, I just can't help myself." Dora was now showing her true feelings.

A burning heart? What's that all about, he wondered? *Maybe it was the food. Now I'm not feeling so well myself. I can wait two months and make sure this is real before I move.*

They had just announced that the worship service was about to begin. Being an Orthodox synagogue, the women were separated from the men. *Thank God,* Sam thought. *This is really getting very uncomfortable.*

When the service was over, Dora insisted he walk her home, which was the only gentlemanly thing to do. She invited him in, but he said he must get home. He had to study. Dora reached under his coat and gave him a full body hug, pressing herself against him. Sam, not sure what to do, hugged her back. "Now do you feel the electricity?" Dora asked.

Sam wasn't sure it was electricity but he sure felt something. "Yes, I do," he replied, hoping she would let him go. She released her grip, and Sam headed home.

It was an uncomfortable night's sleep. He kept rerunning what had happened and was not sure whether it was a dream or reality. He didn't have to wait long to find out. There was a note on the door in the morning from Dora and a pan of fresh cheese *blintzes* on the doorstep. "What have you got there?" asked Ian, who was just waking up and saw the platter of cheese *blintzes* in Sam's hand.

"A little gift from a lady I met last night at the synagogue," Sam answered.

"It must have been quite a meeting, college boy," said cousin Ian.

"You can say that again," replied Sam. "This lady wants to give me free room and board with nothing in exchange."

Ian was quick with a few sayings: "*Nit als vos glanst iz gold*" (all that glitters is not gold) and "*vi me bet zikh ois, azoi darf men shlofen*" (as you make your bed, so will you sleep in it.)

"All this is true, Ian. Here, take a bite of this *blintz*. It's heaven to the tongue."

The note said:

> Dearest Sam,
>
> I hope you like the *blintzes*. They came from my heart. I will come to your house tonight.
>
> Your Soul Mate.
> Love, Dora

Ian read the note over Sam's shoulder. "OK, college boy, the ball is in your court now. It looks like you don't have a chance."

Sam laughed, took another *blintz*, and went to his room to get dressed. "I'm going to ask some of the guys at school about this. I might ask one of the doctors that works at the St. Louis Insane Asylum." Sam said this in a loud voice, as Ian had his door closed.

"In your financial situation, I think this is an opportunity you can't pass up, *soul mate*. You have my OK to move out if you want." Sam heard this from Ian through the closed door.

Sam Learns about "Soul Mates"

At school, he asked his lab partner, Garfield Hertel, if he knew anything about *soul mates* and women who claimed they'd found one. "Where have you been hiding out, Herskovitz? Across the river in East St. Louis?" (East St. Louis was across the river in Illinois and known for its saloons and dives.)

"I wish I had been. No, right here, and at the synagogue no less."

"I say you talk to Dr. Bliss at the St. Louis Insane Asylum. I see him on the lecture schedule for the seniors this week. It will save you a trip."

"Thanks. I'll look him up."

Dora Shultz Makes Her Move

That evening when Sam got home, waiting for him on the stoop was Mrs. Shultz. *That lady just won't give up,* he thought. "Good evening, Mrs. Shultz. Would you like to come in?" he asked.

"Yes, Sam, I would. I've brought you dinner, stuffed cabbage rolls."

Sam could smell them in the basket she had over her arm. "I hate to eat and run, Dora, but I have to work at the drugstore tonight."

"That's OK, Sam. Have you made a decision about coming to live with me and my husband?" she asked.

"The answer is yes, Dora, as soon as I finish my exams at the end of May," Sam answered.

Ian was already eating one of the cabbage rolls and nodded his head in agreement. He couldn't talk because his mouth was full. Sam went into his room to change into work clothes. When he came out, Dora had made a plate of food wrapped up for him to take to work.

"Thank you, Dora. I'm not used to such treatment, especially from Ian." They all laughed.

Sam thought she was going to follow him to work. Instead, she settled for another hug and left for her house.

"What did you find out today at the school about this crazy lady?" Ian asked.

"The doctor from the insane asylum said she may be a little delusional and suffering from an unfulfilled marriage. He doubts she is harmful to anyone. He said I should watch out for the husband, if he doesn't know how she feels."

"OK, college boy. You're on your own, but could you bring me a *blintz* from time to time?" Ian asked.

"Sure, Ian, maybe more than one." They both got a good laugh on that one.

Sam Moves in with Dora Shultz

Sam's new address was 1338 Blair St., just two blocks from Louis and Nettie Zauderer. This area of town was also known as the Jewish quarter. Dora had given him the guest room and attended to all his needs. She even paid for his yearly tuition, books, and lab fees. Dinner was always on the table whenever he arrived home. After finishing his second year of medical school, Sam had a job as a pharmacy clerk. It was the same pharmacy where Nettie worked. At times, they worked the same shift. It was much less taxing than the job at the slaughterhouse, and it fit right in with his studies.

After a few months in Mrs. Shultz's house, he told her they must tell her husband about the "*soul mate*" stuff. This was on the advice of his professor to protect him from any violence. They did this together.

"Joseph, I want you to know my relationship with Sam is purely platonic. I want to keep our marriage too, but I felt the stars have guided me to Sam, and I must obey."

Joseph knew Dora was into the occult and learned to let her indulge in her fantasies. She also made Sam pledge to her that he would not see any other women. If she couldn't have him, then no other woman could either. Sam mumbled in agreement. He felt he had no choice. He would work things out later. There was only one thing that bothered him. Some nights he would wake up and find Dora lying next to him in his bed. He pretended to be asleep, but it was difficult as she was completely naked. He tried locking the door, but she had the key. He didn't want to risk getting thrown out on the street. He would suffer in silence.

Louis Opens a Pharmacy

The next year went by quickly. Before they knew it, Edward was a 1-year-old. He had the development of a 6-month-old, according to the doctor. He was starting to babble and reach for objects that he held, for as long as 30 seconds.

Despite their two incomes, the medical expenses kept mounting. They needed more space and a larger apartment. They found one at 1721 Carr St., not far from where they were living. It was obvious that Mama Mary was going to have to stay to take care of Edward while Nettie worked. The tension in the house that you could cut with a knife usually centered on Edward and money.

"It doesn't look like we're going to have enough money for me to enter medical school this year," said Louis. "I have an idea. We can take the money that we've saved and open our own drugstore. This way, we can make more money."

"That seems like a good idea, Louis," Nettie agreed.

"I'm glad you like the idea, because I just put a deposit on the store next to our apartment. The current tenant is moving out. We have a month to get it ready."

"That's wonderful, Louis, our very own pharmacy. Let's name it The New Era Pharmacy."

"Sounds good to me," Louis said. "I'll get it started. Then when it can support both of us, you can quit your job and we can work together. Wasn't that what you said years ago in New York?" he reminded her.

Nettie replied, "Maybe it's what we need to bring us closer together, Louis."

Sam Comes to Supper

Sam was a welcome guest at their apartment and took the edge off the family troubles. He had such a happy manner about him when he was not studying. For Sam, it was a good excuse to get away from Dora, his *soul mate*. Supper would usually be on Friday night for Sabbath. Sam would never turn down a home-cooked meal and a chance to see Nettie. For some reason, he was getting very fond of her.

"I wish Nettie would give me the attention that she gives you, Sam," Louis said. "She waits on your every need. You would think you're a guest or something," joked Louis. Sam and Louis had gotten to be good friends. Louis asked Sam questions about medical school, which he had hoped to start in the fall.

What disturbed Sam were the bruises he noticed on Nettie's arms and sometimes her face. He was learning to notice these things when he examined patients. He asked Nettie what had happened. "Oh clumsy me," she would say. "I'm always bumping into something."

Sam suspected another reason: Louis. This just didn't add up. Louis was always so cordial to him. Why should he suspect him? He didn't know, but something in his gut told him all was not right. Sam, working at the same pharmacy as Nettie, had time to introduce Nettie to the teachings of Emma Goldman. The freedom of a woman to make choices in her life appealed to Nettie.

Louis had Nettie keep her job as he started The New Era Pharmacy. Maybe now they could get ahead. They were always going into debt and then trying to work their way out. Just when they were starting to save again, Edward would need another operation, usually on his hand or toes, and then they were broke again.

That year, clerking at the same drugstore, Nettie confessed to Sam. "Sam, I know you have asked me about my bruises. I have to tell you that sometimes Louis takes his frustrations out on me."

This upset Sam, as he wanted to protect Nettie, but he couldn't see how. There was also the problem of Dora Shultz. She would show up at the drugstore and see Sam and Nettie together. When he got home, she would make him pledge that they were still *soul mates* and no other woman was in his life. Sam went along with her. He just had one more year of school. None of this was good for the pain in his stomach. *This abuse of women was the injustice that women had to endure in our society*, he thought.

Edward Is Two Years Old

Little Edward was celebrating his second birthday today, and Sam was invited to the party. At 2 years old, Edward's lack of development was obvious. He was still crawling on his hands and knees and was saying just two or three words. Everyone knew he would never be normal. Nettie and Mama Mary would not give up, as they saw improvement, however slow.

The rift between Nettie and Louis was getting worse. Louis decided to open another drugstore about four blocks away, at 21st and Carr Street. It had an apartment in the back where he could stay. Nettie would run The New Era Pharmacy and use the money she made to pay the doctor bills for Edward and the rent on the apartment and store. Louis would use the money from the new pharmacy to save for medical school.

After Louis moved out, Sam was a more frequent visitor. Mama Mary liked Sam almost as much as Nettie did. They kept their relationship platonic, but they both knew it was growing into something permanent.

St. Louis Insane Asylum

During his senior year, Sam did a rotation at the insane asylum.[6] In 1907, during Sam's junior year, construction began on new wings and annexes to the building. It went from accommodating 150 patients to 2,000 patients and employees. The philosophy was to get the patients integrated into society and out of the hospital. Sam saw this as a perfect place for Edward to get specialized care in the many areas that he needed, all paid for by the state.

---

6 The St. Louis Insane Asylum, formally the St. Louis County Lunatic Asylum and now the St. Louis Psychiatric Rehabilitation Center, accepted patients with all types of mental problems. Children were accepted and able to get an education as well as get help with their developmental problems.

"Sam, I don't think I could ever put little Edward in a place like that," Nettie said, with concern written all over her face.

"Hear him out," said Mama Mary. "Maybe they have people that can help Edward where we can't."

"All right, I'll take a trip over there with Edward and see what they say," relented Nettie.

The doctors at the asylum were quite helpful. They told Nettie that they would accept Edward after his third birthday in July. They had never seen a problem quite like Edward's and were eager to help. Nettie still had six months to think it over.

Emma Goldman Comes to Town

On February 28, 1908, Emma Goldman came through St. Louis to give a series of four lectures. Sam was part of the welcoming committee that met her at Union Station. She was staying at 1331 Franklin Ave. Chief of Police Creecy told reporters that he would not permit her to speak. He and his men tried to identify as many of her supporters as they could. Sam was easy to spot with his reddish hair. The police didn't stop her from speaking to the press or holding receptions in her small chilly apartment. Sam brought Nettie to meet her. Emma talked about labor unions charging large fees to increase their treasuries, which prevented workers from joining. Churches, she said, were monopolies that were enslaving the masses. On marriage, she called the laws absurd. A contract should not be needed. A relationship should be voluntary and based on love. Sam had talked to Nettie about all of this, but hearing it directly from Emma Goldman was electrifying. Goldman's next stop was Chicago, where authorities announced that if she returned there, they would have her deported as an undesirable immigrant.

Graduation Day for Sam

On May 15, 1908, Sam realized his dream. He graduated as a doctor of medicine. Dora Shultz, Nettie, and Mama Mary were all at the graduation ceremony. Louis was absent, sick in bed.

"I'm so happy for you, Sam," said Nettie, as she gave him a hug that knocked off his graduation mortar board hat. As he picked it up, there was Dora, also giving him a hug of congratulations. Sam could feel the tension between the two women.

Mama Mary turned to Nettie and whispered in her ear, "What's wrong with that woman? Look how she touches Sam." Nettie looked the other way and then back at Dora. Nettie and Dora didn't speak to each other, but if looks could kill, one of them would have been dead. This time, Dora got her way and took Sam by the hand and led him off to her own celebration. Sam did look back at Nettie and mouthed the words "help me" with a smile only Sam could give.

Dr. Samuel Herskovitz Opens His Practice

It wasn't long before Sam was in Nettie's drug-store. On the walls Sam couldn't help but notice in big letters that Nettie was the only woman drug-gist in St. Louis. She also had posted her diploma awarded by the New York College of Pharmacy. She talked to Sam while she flitted hither and thither, selling a child a penny stick of candy, then filling a prescription while answering the tele-phone. Not once did she lose her composure or appear flustered. Louis had his pharmacy four blocks down the street. There was spirited rivalry to see whose pharmacy would do better. Nettie had won the competition, and at only 21 years old, she had a snug bank account after having grown her business to large proportions.

Samuel Herskovitz medical school graduation, 1908. *Courtesy of the Hatchet Washington Medical School Yearbook. Researched by Jeff with American Ancestors.*

Nettie suggested that Sam open an office in the back two rooms. The obvious large customer base of women clientele was not lost on Sam. She would help him with a loan for some equipment that he could pay back later. Just then, Louis showed up. He had his pharmacy coat on, but it looked like he had just woken up. What little hair he still had was in disarray on his head. His lab coat had lost its starch and looked like Louis had slept in it.

"Hello, Dr. Sam. Sorry I couldn't make it to the graduation, but I haven't been too well of late. How would you like me to be your first paying patient?" Louis asked.

"You're my friend, Louis. I can't take money from you, but I will be your doctor. If you're going back to your pharmacy, I'll come over later and examine you."

"OK, Dr. Sam. I just need to pick up a few things here that I'm out of." Louis went behind the counter, and Sam could hear the sound of bottles clicking together as Louis picked up what he needed.

"See you later, Sam. Maybe this afternoon?"

"That will be perfect, Louis," Sam replied.

There was just one customer in the drugstore. When she was gone, Nettie asked, "Did you see that, Sam? Louis is always taking my supply of lozenges and Stickney & Poor's Paregoric[7]—and anything else with cocaine in it. I think he has a real addiction problem."

"Thanks for telling me, Nettie. I'll be sure to ask him about it this afternoon."

Sam Examines Louis

That afternoon, Sam arrived at Louis's pharmacy, just four blocks down the street from The New Era Pharmacy. Louis was behind the counter and waved to Sam, as he was helping a customer. After he finished, Louis asked a clerk to cover for him, and he and Sam went into his office.

Sam had his little black doctor bag with him and was ready to give Louis an exam. "Are you ready for this, Louis?"

"Go ahead, doc. Let's see what you find."

Sam had Louis take off his shirt, and Sam placed the stethoscope on his back and had him take a few deep breaths in and out. He then placed the stethoscope on his chest and had him do the same thing. Next, he checked his pulse and blood pressure with a sphygmomanometer.

"What's that contraption?" asked Louis.

"It's the latest thing to check the pressure of your blood. It was invented a few years ago by a Russian doctor. Louis, can you lie down on the couch? I want to check your internal organs." Sam pushed his hand around Louis's rib cage and around his stomach. "OK, Louis. You can put your shirt back on now," Sam directed.

"What did you find, Sam?"

---

7   Stickney & Poor's Paregoric was a mixture of opium and alcohol. At 46 percent, or 92 proof, it was very potent.

"I need to ask you a few questions, and be honest with me. Are you taking any medicine?"

"Maybe a few cocaine lozenges from time to time," Louis volunteered.

"I said the whole truth, Louis. Otherwise, I can't help you." Sam sounded very direct in his "doctor" voice.

"OK, Sam, cocaine and alcohol most of the time. I just can't seem to stop myself. I've tried several times to stop. I got real sick—nausea, vomiting, and a feeling like bugs were crawling under my skin.[8] I just couldn't take that feeling and had to start again. This habit is ruining my marriage to Nettie. I get crazy sometimes. Then I get these panic attacks. You've got to help me, Sam. I'll never get into medical school if I don't kick the habit." Louis sounded desperate.

"Let me be straight with you, Louis. You could die if you don't stop. I noticed your blood pressure is higher than it should be, and your heart is racing and making some strange sounds. None of this is good. I recommend you cut back on the cocaine a little each day and stop all alcohol. The only way proven to stop drinking is cold turkey. We will get through this together, Louis."

"All right, Sam. I'll start today. I really will. You'll see the change," Louis promised.

"I'll check with you tomorrow and see how you're doing." Sam knew he could not tell Nettie about this, as it was doctor-patient confidentiality. She already suspected the problem. This was a real conflict for Sam, treating Louis, for he knew he was in love with Nettie. He would have to stay out of any decisions that Nettie made and take no sides in the marital problems.

His other problem was Dora. Now that he was spending more time at Nettie's and using her pharmacy as his office, Dora was getting very controlling. "Sam, you must tell me again we are *soul mates* and no other woman will come between us," she demanded. This confrontation happened at her house about three weeks after Sam started his practice.

He couldn't take it any longer and said, "Dora, I'm moving out. This relationship is just not right. I'm a young man that wants to have a family, and that will never happen with you."

"I've given you everything, Sam. I paid your tuition, cooked your meals, and darned your socks. Doesn't that mean something to you? Please, you can't just leave me. I love you," Dora pleaded.

---

8 Cocaine is a powerful stimulant and makes users feel happy. In large doses, it causes mood swings, paranoia, insomnia, psychosis, high blood pressure, and drastic changes in personality. Sudden deaths from strokes or heart attacks occur. Withdrawal symptoms cause a "crash" and depression, paranoia, exhaustion, nausea, and vomiting. The feeling of something crawling under the skin, or "coke bugs," is common.

Sam, without saying another word, packed his bags and left the house, going to his office in the back of the pharmacy.

The next morning when Nettie opened up, she found Sam. "Did you sleep here last night, Sam?" she asked, with a quizzical expression on her face.

"I just couldn't take it any more at the Shultzs's house."

"Sam, you can't live down here. You have to come upstairs to the apartment. Mama and I will make a space for you."

"Thanks, Nettie. I don't want to intrude. If you have a spot for me on the couch until I find a place of my own, that would be perfect."

"Don't be silly, Sam. You're going to stay right here. Think of this house as your house too," said Nettie, as she helped him upstairs with his suitcases.

"You're too kind, Nettie," said Sam.

Dora Confronts Sam and Nettie

It was only a few days before Dora showed up at Sam's office at The New Era Pharmacy. She came at lunchtime. She brought with her a plate of cabbage rolls, Sam's favorite. Sam ushered her into the back office. Nettie was behind the counter but the walls were thin, so she heard everything.

"Oh, Sam, the house has been so empty without you. I can't sleep a wink at night now that you're gone. The past two years have been heaven for me with you in the house. Would you please come back? I'm so sorry I was cross with you. I will be better; you will see. If you don't come home, I think I will kill myself. I'll do it in your room. I'll slit my wrists and bleed to death on your bed. That is where you'll find me, dead in a pool of blood."

"Calm down, Dora. Maybe you need a pill to help you sleep," Sam said, trying to calm her.

"It's not a pill I need. It's you, Sam. I can't live without you. You owe it to me to give it another try. Please." Dora broke down crying. Dora knew this was his soft spot. Sam put his arm around her to console her. With that, she threw her arms around him in a bear hug. "You'll come back, then?" Dora said through her tears.

"OK, Dora, I'll come back, just to give it another try."

"I'll see you tonight?" she asked.

"No, tomorrow I'll come back," Sam said.

After Dora went out the door, Nettie asked Sam, "What was that all about?"

"I think I have to go back, Nettie. The woman is very unstable and says she's going to kill herself. I just can't have that on my conscience. I have to give it another try. After all, she did pay for my last two years of medical school."

"You're such a good man, Sam. She doesn't deserve you. Remember, Mama and I will always have a place for you here."

What a mess I have myself in, thought Sam. *I'm treating the husband of the woman I love, who is also my friend. The lady that paid for my education thinks I'm her "soul mate" and is about to kill herself. Tsulib ton kost tomid tei'er (trying to please is always costly).*

Ettie Is Going to Have a Baby

Sam had graduated from medical school in May. His sister, Ettie Hillel, was pregnant with her third child. The bad feelings between Sam and Ettie's husband Newman had been resolved now that the marriage was back together. Ettie had decided that Sam should be the doctor for the birth of her baby. After all, there was now a doctor in the family. Ettie had been learning to be a midwife. She was prepared.

While there was a lull at the pharmacy, Sam took advantage of it to talk to Nettie. "Nettie, you know my sister Ettie is pregnant."

"How could I not notice, Sam? This is wonderful. I know Newman is hoping for a boy this time."

"The problem," Sam said, "is that she wants me to be her doctor. She will have a midwife, but she wants me standing by for any complications."

"How do you plan to do that when they live all the way across town?" Nettie asked.

"I thought maybe I could use my office if it's OK with you?"

"Don't be silly, Sam. We'll make room for her upstairs in the apartment. That way, whenever it happens, you will only be steps away. Besides, having a baby in the house will be wonderful, and Mama is here to help."

Sam relayed this information to Ettie. She would let them know when she was close to delivery.

Edward's Third Birthday, July 4, 1908

It was July, and Edward's third birthday was at the end of the month. That was the time to take him to the asylum. Before taking him, they would have another birthday party. Nettie wanted him to remember happy times with his mother. What better than to celebrate his birthday on July 4, the birthday of America? Edward was the first generation that was born in America. He should have an American birthday.[9] He now knew his name and could ask for food or a drink. He was walking without help, more like a 2-year-old than a 3-year-old. He was still wearing a diaper. July 4 was on a Saturday, and the whole family was going to the bank of the Mississippi River to watch the fireworks. First they would have the birthday party at the house.

Louis came over for the celebration, but Sam could see he had no love for Edward. They sang happy birthday and had a cake that Edward tried to eat with his one good hand, without much success. Nettie and Mama Mary took turns feeding him the cake. As the sun began to set, they packed up to go watch the fireworks. Louis said he had to go back to the pharmacy. Everyone knew it was a lie.

They sat on the levee watching the fireworks burst in the air with brilliant colors. The crowd would ooh and aah as they burst in the sky. The stroller was between Nettie and Sam, and little Edward had dozed off. Sam felt Nettie's hand on his as it supported him as he leaned back. He didn't move it.

Then came the finale, with red, white, and blue colors. The band started playing patriotic songs: *Stars and Stripes Forever*, the John Philip Sousa march (it always sent chills up one's spine), followed by *The Star Spangled Banner* and *My Country Tis of Thee*. The last song was *Hail Columbia*, the official national anthem of America. Everyone tried to sing along with all the songs. When they ended, a cheer went up from the crowd. It was thought that over half the people celebrating the Fourth were immigrants. They couldn't wait to show their love for their adopted country. Sam was having second thoughts about the views of Emma Goldman about his new adopted country, a country that had given him so much already, including an education and a profession. *Could she be wrong about some of her views*, he wondered?

On the walk back home, Sam and Nettie held hands as Mama Mary pushed Edward's stroller.

Edward Goes to the Asylum

It was Friday, the 31st of July, one day after Edward's official birthday. This was the day to pack his things and take him to the asylum. The staff was waiting for them and promised Nettie she could see him whenever she wanted. They checked him in as Edward

---

9   This became a tradition for Nettie as she celebrated all her children's birthdays on the closest American holiday. She loved her adopted country and all its holidays.

Druggist Is Sued by Wife, Also a Druggist Who Wed at 15.

HER STORE HIS GIFT

Offered $100 to Leave Her, He Refuses and Begs Reconciliation.

When he learned Wednesday that his young wife, who married him when she was 15 years old, and to whom he recently deeded one of his two drug stores, had filed suit for divorce, Louis J. Zauderer arose from a sick bed, hastened to her store at 1701 Carr street and pleaded with her for a reconciliation.

Mrs. Zauderer, before his visit, declared that she and her husband could never agree, and said that she intended to press her suit for her freedom and the custody of her 3-year-old boy, Edward.

Zauderer owns a drug store at Twenty-first and Carr streets. He says his wife's store, four blocks east, was his gift to her. It was made over to her, he says, one year ago, just before the time which she names in her divorce petition as the date of their separation.

Studied Pharmacy Together.

Mrs. Zauderer is 21 years old, and her husband is three years older. They are living in the same house at 1721 Carr street, and her mother, Mrs. Sachs, lives there also.

They were married in New York City in 1902, and studied pharmacy together after their marriage, both becoming qualified druggists.

Zauderer has been in poor health for some time, and has been in the care of Dr. Herkovitz, who is known in the neighborhood as a friend of both the Zauderers.

"I love my wife," said Zauderer Wednesday, "and it is not true that I ever struck her or that I drank to excess, as her petition says.

"Yesterday she offered to give me $100 if I would leave her, but I refused. I shall try to persuade her to forget her grievances and drop the suit."

Noah Sachs. He was going into one of the new wings that were built last year, reserved for children his age with developmental difficulties. Louis did not go with them, saying he had to work at the pharmacy. Sam, Nettie, and Mama Mary said goodbye to Edward. He waved goodbye with his good arm. Nettie ran to him, picked him up, and gave him a kiss with tears running down her face.

They were back on the trolley. Sam put his arm around Nettie. "Did I do the right thing for Edward, Sam?"

"I think he has a better chance at a normal life growing up there," answered Sam. Sam held her all the way back to their stop. Sam walked them back to their apartment. Then he walked to the Schultzs's house.

Ettie Has a Baby

When Nettie and Mama Mary got home, they got a call from Ettie. She was ready and wanted to know if she could come over. Nettie had little time to get things ready, let alone worry about little Edward Noah at the sanitarium.

Before she knew it, Ettie and Newman were at the apartment. "My water hasn't broken yet, but I'm really dilated," she said to Nettie. Within minutes, her midwife, J. C. Fluschummer, was there.

St. Louis Post Dispatch Newspaper Archives, September 2, 1908. *Reproduced with permission of the copyright owner. Further reproduction prohibited without permission.*

I don't have to notify Sam, Nettie thought. *He'll know tomorrow when he comes in.* She really didn't want a confrontation with Dora Schultz tonight. Ettie and Nettie talked through the night, especially about the teachings of Emma Goldman. They were kindred spirts on the issue of the independence of women. From that day on, they knew each other's heart and let their lives live the dream. Nettie now knew what she had to do with her marriage.

The next day when Sam got to the pharmacy and his office, he was surprised by the news. After consulting with the midwife and examining Ettie, he knew birth was close, so he decided to stay overnight in the office. Two days later, on August 3, 1908, Jacques Hillel was born. Newman would have an heir to the Hillel family, and Sam a new nephew as well as his first delivery as a doctor. "*Mazel tov*," Sam said to Newman. "You now have a son." They both embraced. The hard feelings were now in the past.

Nettie Files for a Divorce from Louis

It had been two months since Sam moved back with Dora. Sam could see it was not going to work out, even with Dora being less controlling and not suicidal. His practice was growing, and he thought Louis had stopped drinking and was cutting down on the cocaine. Now was the time for Louis to go "cold turkey" and kick the habit. As it turned out, this was not a good time, for Nettie had filed for a divorce from Louis on August 31, 1908, only two days after Louis stopped all drugs.

Louis got up from his bed and walked over to The New Era Pharmacy to protest the divorce. "Nettie, how can you say I hit you and abused alcohol and drugs as you said in the divorce petition?" Louis had the petition in his hand and was waving it in the air. "Let's forget all about this, Nettie, and go back to the way things were before," pleaded Louis. "Nettie, I gave you this pharmacy. This is the thanks I get?"

Louis was suffering withdrawal symptoms, and it was difficult for him to think straight or even argue.

"I'll give you $100, Louis, if you won't contest the divorce," Nettie responded.

Sam had never seen her quite like this. She was standing her ground, looking unafraid of Louis. Sam was torn. *Whose side would I be on?* Both Louis and Nettie looked to him to show support for their side. He decided he would not take sides and just let things work themselves out. He retreated to his office and closed the door. *This is far from over*, he thought. During this time, he made sure he was never very far from a glass of milk. *Emma Goldman sure has a way of making a woman stronger*, he thought.

Sam and Nettie Leave St. Louis

The divorce was finalized on September 18. Nettie would give Louis The New Era Pharmacy, and she would have custody of Edward. Louis would not give Nettie a *get*,[10] just to make a point. Sam moved back in with Nettie and her mother, but not before Dora came by the pharmacy and called Nettie a homewrecker, a *farshitinkener* (awful person), and a *nafka* (whore). "I'm going to have the Gypsies put a curse on you. A *brokh tsu dayn lefn* (your life should be a disaster)." These were her final words as she slammed the pharmacy door behind her.

"Don't give the curse a second thought," said Sam. "Dora is *gornisht helfn* (beyond help) and *meshuggina* (crazy)." Sam thought Dora's anger was a much more normal response. Now he didn't fear she would commit suicide.

After all the commotion died down, Sam asked Nettie to come into his office. "Nettie, I always knew I loved you," said Sam. "It started the first day I met you on the ship, a feeling I couldn't understand, but it wasn't until I found out you were a girl that I could let my heart soar. So many times after that, I saw you from afar and was too shy to talk to you. That's all in the past now. Will you marry me?"

"Of course, Sam. I knew you were the one I've been waiting for all my life. I hate to bring Dora into this, but I think we really are *soul mates*," confessed Nettie. This was what free love was all about, they both confessed.

The term *soul mate* didn't make Sam cringe at all, despite its former association with Dora, as he felt the connection too. "What next, Nettie?" Sam asked.

"I think we need to get away from this place. Let's go up to Chicago. Anna says Barney is really doing well, opening new saloons. He and his brother Myer have just finished an

---

10 A *get* is a writ of Jewish divorce that terminates a Jewish marriage and allows the couple to be free to remarry, according to Jewish law. The *get* is presented by a husband to his wife, releasing her from her vows, annulling the marriage. The *get* makes no reference to responsibility or fault and has no effect on a civil settlement. If a woman does not receive a *get*, she is still considered married under Jewish law. Many rabbis will not perform another marriage if a woman does not have a *get*, a stigma that is passed down to future children for 10 generations.

office building with apartments. It might be a good place to start your practice. The Block brothers are expanding their Inland Steel Mill in East Chicago. The immigrant population is exploding, as they need workers in the mill. Anna says the Jewish community is growing too, and they need doctors. The whole area should be friendly to us, we'll fit right in," Nettie explained, as the plan seemed to develop spontaneously in her head.

"Before we leave St. Louis, Sam, why don't you apply for your citizenship?" suggested Nettie.

"You're right, Nettie. I'm now an American doctor and should be a citizen," agreed Sam.

Sam applied but was turned down. *Could it have been my association with Emma Goldman, the anarchist,* he wondered?

CHAPTER 7

Nettie and Sam Move to Chicago

"A fresh start it is. Leave the memories of Louis[1] behind you. And I will leave behind all my memories of Dora," said Sam.

"We can stay with Barney and Anna," said Nettie.

"I wanted to go to Chicago to do postgraduate work at The Rush Hospital. I didn't know how I would do it, but now I know. They have a three-month course in the diseases of the ear, nose, and throat," explained Sam.

"We need to take Mama back to New York. These trips back and forth to St. Louis have been hard on her and Rabbi Benjamin. We can get married in New York with the family. This way, your mother, Pepe, won't have to travel. We can come back and get a place in Chicago near the hospital while you do that three-month study program. While you're doing that, I can figure out where you will open your practice."

---

1 Louis left St. Louis for Kansas City in 1909, where he opened a pharmacy. He returned in 1910 to enter The St. Louis College of Physicians & Surgeons, where he graduated in 1912. The school, known as a diploma mill, was closed in 1920. In September of 1912, he opened the Drug Department in Albuquerque's largest department store. On September 8, 1917, Louis enlisted in the Army Medical Corps. He was discharged only five months later, on February 28, 1918. In May of 1918, he got a passport to go to Palestine to do relief work. He married three more times and had more divorces. He never had more children. On May 17, 1937, when he was 54 years old and living in Los Angeles, California, he joined the Abraham Lincoln Brigade to fight in the Spanish Civil War, which was illegal under U.S. law. The brigade fought against General Francisco Franco and fascism—on the side of the communists, joining forces with the communist left and the Socialist Workers party. Those who returned to the United States were labeled subversives and hounded by the FBI, and some were prosecuted under the Smith Act and state sedition laws. Louis died April 7, 1944, in Los Angeles.

Sam was amazed at how Nettie had worked out everything so quickly. *That must be one of her special talents. I will remember.* "That works for me," Sam agreed. "I'm ready for another adventure in America with the woman I love." Sam and Nettie kissed, and the deal was sealed.

The trio packed what they could and boarded a train for Chicago. Barney and Anna were there to greet them. "What a surprise," Anna said to Nettie, as they embraced. "I guess it was Sam all along?"

"I think I've finally made the right decision. He's such a wonderful man, Anna. I'm so lucky." It appeared to Anna she had never seen Nettie so happy.

Barney was busy greeting Sam and Mama Mary and getting their bags off the train. "You'll stay with us in Whiting before going off to New York?" Barney asked.

"Just a night or two, Barney. We really have to get to New York and get married," said Nettie, with a smile from ear to ear.

In a few days, the trio was off again on their trip to New York. Upon arrival, Rose and Philip were there to greet them. Nettie looked up at all the new skyscrapers and the changes that had happened since she left New York four years ago. "I didn't think they could build buildings so fast," she exclaimed.

"This city is just exploding with new development," Philip said. "You can't hold back progress."

Nettie and Sam Get Married

They took a few days to get things ready for the wedding. Nettie had not received a *get* from Louis, but she filed her divorce papers with the Supreme Court of New York on Thursday, October 1. This allowed her and Sam to get a marriage license. The wedding would be a low-key affair in her stepfather's office on October 8, 1908. Rabbi Benjamin was so happy to have Mama Mary home, and he couldn't wait to conduct the marriage. Only the immediate family was there: Rose, Philip, and their six children; sister Fannie, her husband Julius, and their five children; brother Nathan, his wife Jennie, and their two children; and Sam's mother Pepe and his older brother Marcus, who was still in New York. His other brother David and sister Ettie were now living in the Midwest. Marcus was his best man. Nettie's sister Rose and Sam's sister Fannie were bridesmaids.

After the ceremony, Nettie and Sam went to the Waldorf Astoria to spend their wedding night. This was Nettie's choice, as she wanted to feel like she was starting her life over. She wanted to replace the memory of Louis with that of Sam. She didn't tell Sam that this was the same hotel she spent her wedding night with Louis. As the bellboy escorted them to their room and opened the door, without warning Sam lifted Nettie and carried her over the threshold. "This is how we do it in the old country," he said. He tipped the bellboy, and they both lay exhausted on the bed. There was no hesitation for them to consummate the marriage. The sexual tension had been building for months, with all the drama of little Edward, the divorce, the move from St. Louis, and Sam's separation from Dora Schultz.

They grabbed at each other's clothes until they were both naked on the bed. They kissed passionately as Sam's hands and fingers massaged her, reaching her clitoris, where he expertly touched her like no other man had done before. She could feel her body move in rhythm with his, and soon she was touching his rigid penis with expectation and anticipation. *When is he going to put it in,* she wondered? No other man had waited this long, and she was burning up with waves of heat coursing up through her body.

Just when she was about to mount Sam, he mounted her and she lost all control. She felt a gush of fluid fill her vagina, and then Sam ejaculated. The sheets under her were soaking wet. *This is what sex is all about,* she thought. *Did Sam learn all this in medical school, or is this what love is really all about?* "Oh Sam," she cried out, "I love you so much."

They lay locked together for what seemed an eternity, both breathing heavily. "I love you too," he replied.

In the morning, they made love again. This time, Nettie knew what was about to happen with her true love. Now the thoughts of Louis were erased and replaced with those of Sam.

Starting a New Life in Chicago—the Move from St. Louis

On the train back to Chicago, they made their plans. Sam would start his three-month residency in Chicago while she went back to St. Louis to pack up the household goods and send them to Chicago. Nettie also wanted to see how Edward was doing at the hospital. This would be the first of Nettie's many visits to see Edward and check on his progress.

When Nettie arrived in St. Louis, it felt so empty without Sam. Her first stop was the hospital and Edward. "How's my little man?" she asked, as Edward started running toward her from across the room. She picked him up and held him in her arms. The nurse told her how well he had adjusted, and they all just loved him. This was what Nettie wanted to hear. She now knew she and Sam had made the right decision.

Her former husband Louis seemed to be adjusting. He said he was going to sell the pharmacies and move to Kansas City to start a new life. She wished him well. On her last day in town, she picked up a copy of the *St. Louis Dispatch*. There on page 2 was a column titled "Wife Sues Her Soul Mate when He Weds Rival."

There in black and white was the story of Sam and Dora Schultz. It told how they met and their life together while Sam was in medical school. Now that Sam had married Nettie, Dora was suing Sam for years of room and board and tuition for medical school. The suit was for $900 ($23,000 in 2017 dollars).

Nettie couldn't believe that Dora would send this to the newspaper. Should she show it to Sam? She decided not to. He didn't need any more things to upset his stomach.

WIFE SUES HER SOULMATE WHEN HE WEDS RIVAL

Mrs. Dora Shultz Wants $900 for Board and Money Given to Affinity.

PROMISED TO BE TRUE

Says Husband Knew of Attachment and Made No Objections to Comradeship.

Dora Schultz sues Sam Herskovitz, St. Louis, September 14, 1909. *Courtesy of Newspapers.com.*

Dora and the Gypsy

Nettie wasn't the only one to see the article in the paper. The Gypsy that Dora used to put a curse on both Sam and Nettie saw it too. She made a beeline to Dora's house. "Dora, what are you trying to do? Ruin my business?" she said to a very surprised Dora Schultz.

"What do you mean?" Dora asked, quite surprised by the question.

"The article in the paper about Sam," the Gypsy said.

"I plan to get my money back. He left me for that pharmacist. I heard she was in town. I wanted to let her know she stole my *soul mate* and I don't forget," Dora said, with a crazed look in her eyes.

"You're a crazy woman, Dora. If you go ahead and sue them for the money, you cancel the curse. My curses work, and I won't have you making me look like an amateur. Curse or the money—which is it?" she demanded.

"I didn't know. The curse is worth more than the money," answered Dora. "I'll have my attorney stop the filing in Crown Point. I never would have sent that to the paper had I known. Let the curse stand," said Dora.

"If you want to really cause them a problem, I have a friend from New Orleans that makes voodoo dolls. She will show you how to use them. Are you interested? They ain't cheap," offered the Gypsy.

"I'll do anything to get back at the two of them. Money is no problem." Money for the occult was never a problem for Dora. She was deep into all facets of the occult, from astrology to tarot cards, numerology, and psychics.

"I'll send her over today," the Gypsy said, and then she was gone.

Northern Indiana 1908, Boom Town

The Indiana state line is just 16 miles south of Chicago. At the turn of the century, this area was just marshland bordering the southern shore of Lake Michigan. In 1888, the Chicago & Calumet Terminal Beltline linked the settlement of East Chicago, Indiana, to Chicago's trunk rail system.

East Chicago incorporated as a city in 1893. In 1900, it had a population of 3,411; by 1910, it had swelled to 19,098. This increase in population was due to the development of the Inland Steel Company and its need for workers. Most were from Eastern and Southern Europe. In 1910, over 50 percent of the population was not native born. East Chicago is known as the Twin City of Indiana Harbor. The two cities are divided by the Indiana Harbor Ship Canal that runs from the Grand Calumet River to Lake Michigan.

East Chicago borders Whiting, Indiana, to its northwest, the first town over the Illinois state line. Whiting, the home of the Standard Oil Company Refinery, was incorporated as a city in 1903, much smaller in land area than East Chicago, with a population in 1910 of 6,587.

To the east was the city of Gary, founded in 1906, the home of United States Steel Corporation.

Together, these cities made up a vast industrial complex of companies supplying freighters, railcars, pipelines, coal, iron ore, limestone, oil, and other materials from around the nation for processing. This area, called the Calumet Region, was a booming place when Sam and Nettie arrived back from New York as newlyweds in the fall of 1908.

Sam Opens His Practice

Sam finished his three-month residency in the diseases of the eye, ear, nose, and throat, and was now ready to start his practice. In September of 1907, Anna's husband Barney and his brother had finished building the Auditorium Building in Indiana Harbor, a three-story structure with a tavern, grocery store, and pharmacy on the ground floor. Offices were

One of Sam's drugstores, The Auditorium Drug Store. *Courtesy of Stephen G. McShane, archivist, Calumet Regional Archives, Indiana University Northwest*

on the second floor, with apartments in the back half of the building. On the third floor was an auditorium big enough to seat 800 people, with the latest in gasoline lighting.

In March of 1909, Sam opened his office on the second floor of the Auditorium Building. Nettie found an apartment just around the corner for them and their anticipated baby, as Nettie was three months' pregnant.

"Anna, I'm so worried about the baby. You know about the problems we have with Edward. I hope it won't happen again."

Auditorium Building, Indiana Harbor. *Courtesy of Stephen McShane, archivist, Calumet Regional Archives, Indiana University Northwest*

"Don't be silly, Nettie. Something like that can happen to anyone. I'm already five months' pregnant with my second child. We can go through all this together."

This is very strange, Nettie thought. *Here Anna is helping me through this instead of me helping her. What a nice feeling. Too bad my older sister Rose wasn't around when I was growing up in Lithuania. Having a big sister to talk to would have been so nice.*

The Family Grows

The lease on the drugstore in the Auditorium Building had just run out, and Sam took the lease on Barney's advice and opened the Auditorium Pharmacy. The practice took off. At $1 an office visit ($26 in 2017 dollars) and $2 for a house call, it wasn't long before Sam could afford his first car. Sam did his research and found that the Buick was one of the most dependable machines made, alongside Ford and Cadillac. It had a four-cylinder engine and was engineered by Walter L. Marr. The basic model was $900 ($23,000 in 2017). Sam went for the upscale version with the Surrey seat for $1,050 ($27,000 in 2017). He got a 1909 EMF 30 Studebaker

Dr. Samuel Herskovitz in his 1909 Buick Model 10 Surrey. *Family photo collection*

Touring Car, which was made in South Bend, Indiana. The 30 stood for its horsepower. This really helped, as Sam didn't have to rely on drivers to go on house calls.

"Waaaa" was the sound they heard as Sam delivered Pearle, his and Nettie's first child, on September 16, 1909.

"What a beautiful baby," said Anna, as she cradled her youngest, Lloyd, only 8 months old.

"How's the baby, Sam?" asked Nettie nervously.

"The baby is just fine. She has all her fingers and toes, if that's what you mean," answered Sam.

"Yes, that's exactly what I mean, and you know why." Sam and Anna cleaned off the baby, wrapped her in a blanket, and placed her next to Nettie on the bed. Nettie looked down and started to cry. "Oh, she's so perfect. I knew it wasn't me, and I'm not cursed."

"Don't be silly, Nettie. Curses only happen in the old country, and we're too far away for any to reach us here," Sam said, with a smile on his face. They all saw the humor in this, although it was dark humor.

Just two days before the baby arrived, Nettie sold two lots she had bought the year before, on Barney's advice, for $1,500. She made $1,000 ($24,500 in 2017 dollars) in just a six-month period. As the town boomed, so did land prices.

"Oh, Nettie, I almost forgot to tell you. While I was studying at the Rush Hospital, I made a visit to the Romanian section of Chicago. I needed a haircut, and guess who I found? It was Sol Goldenstein from the ship. You know, my friend that needed his appendix removed? Seems he followed his uncle into the barber business. We had a long talk, and I think he's going to go to medical school here in Indiana, at Valparaiso University. It's a two-year program to become an allopath."

"I would love to see him again and catch up. Is he married?" asked Nettie.

"No, not yet. I think he wants to finish school first."

"Let's not lose touch with him. We should get him out here for dinner. He can meet the family."

"By the looks of him, I'm sure he would accept. He's just as skinny as he was when you last saw him."

Barney Gives Sam Advice

Barney became the vice president of the Indiana Harbor Trust and Saving Bank in East Chicago. He was also involved in the Tolleston real estate development in Gary as a

Calumet Drugstore, 1910. Sam, Nettie, and children lived upstairs. Doctor office in back behind pharmacy. *Courtesy of the Calumet Regional Archives Anderson Library, Indian University Northwest*

director. "Sam, I think it's time to think about building your own office and pharmacy. I predict Pearle is just the first of a growing family for you. I think the Calumet area of town has a real need for a doctor just like you." This area of town was growing with eastern European emigrants.

"I agree, Barney. Just as soon as I have time, we can find a lot and I'll come down to the bank for a loan."

In the fall of 1910, Nettie, Sam, and Pearle moved into their new home at 724 Chicago Ave. The lot was on the corner of Melville and Chicago Avenue. The building was two stories and measured 30 by 80 feet. Nettie decided it should be all brick. She had seen too many fires with wooden buildings. They used Chicago red brick.

The pharmacy was downstairs. Its door, set at an angle, faced the corner of both streets. The door was set back into the corner of the building, which provided a natural awning for the front door. Sam's office was at the back of the pharmacy.

On the second floor was their 10-room apartment, entered from the front of the building on the Chicago Avenue side and up one flight of stairs. Everything was just the way Nettie wanted it. Along the west side of the building about two-thirds of the way back, she had a 20-by-20-foot area without a roof. This area was accessible from the master bedroom as well as the kitchen and laundry area. It could serve several functions. The primary one was to dry clothes.

Nettie didn't want to go downstairs to the backyard to hang clothes and then have to quickly bring them back inside if it started to rain. This upstairs patio would be especially useful in the winter when the weather was less predictable. The apartment also had space for a servant's room.

On the back side of the building was a set of wooden stairs that allowed Sam to enter his office from the apartment by just going downstairs. The stairs went all the way up to the roof. Around the top of the roof was a 3-foot parapet made of bricks. This area turned out to be another play area for the children as they got older. Throwing things down on unsuspecting customers was a frequent cause for discipline and a spanking.

Last was the basement. It had a very low ceiling and a coal bin. They had the latest central heating system, which used a boiler to heat water that ran to radiators in each room throughout the building.

"This is one of the most wonderful days in my life, Sam," Nettie exclaimed. "I now feel like I have a real home and family."

The move was none too soon, for on November 27, 1910, Nettie and Sam's first son, Justin Lloyd Herskovitz, was born. Anna Cohen had just given birth in August to Irving Cohen, her fourth child.

"Now that our family is increasing, Mama Mary is coming to help me with the new baby. Everyone is so happy. I only wish we could spend more time together, Sam. Your patients are so demanding."

"That's what I signed up for, Nettie. It's the life of a doctor and a doctor's wife."

"I know, Sam. I wasn't complaining, but you never seem to sleep, all that tossing and turning. I worry about you."

"I guess I have a lot on my mind. Let's put an ad in the paper for a servant to help you around here. This is a big place to take care of by yourself."

Mama Mary came into town just in time to help Nettie hire a servant. Her name was Anie Baranchick, 20 years old, who had emigrated from Hungary just two years earlier. She was a sweet girl—very clean and willing to work, which pleased everyone.

Dora and Her Voodoo Dolls

"Do you have to bring dem dolls to bed with you?"

"They're important to me, Joseph, and they aren't just dolls."

"What are they then if they ain't dolls?"

"They are spirit dolls. Sister Marie told me they represent Sam and Nettie. See, here's a lock of Sam's hair that I sewed to this doll, and this one is Nettie. I got one of her pharmacy coats from her ex-husband Louis, cut it up, and sewed a piece to this doll. Louis was glad to give it to me when I told him what I was about to do."

Joseph knew better than to quiz Dora about using voodoo dolls. He thought it was a bunch of nonsense. He just let her ramble on. When Dora believed in something like this, there was no use trying to change her mind. "Just keep dem dolls on your side of the bed," he said, as he moved over on his side as far as he could, with his back facing Dora and her dolls.

Dora was about to push another needle into Sam's head, and maybe one to the heart. As she felt the heartache of losing Sam, so he should feel it too. "That should keep him awake tonight," she muttered under her breath. She had taken a subscription to the *Hammond Times* newspaper that had all the announcements and town news. She knew about Sam, Nettie's baby, and the new office. *When will I know if any of this voodoo is working? Sister Marie said it takes time and money.*

Sam Becomes City Health Officer

In January of 1911, Sam took the position of city health officer for the city of East Chicago. This, in addition to his two offices and two pharmacies, kept him super busy. He was always looking for a pharmacist. It was difficult, as they had to be able to speak many languages, especially Polish and Hungarian.

Sam's two brothers, Marcus the attorney and oldest brother David the tinsmith, moved to East Chicago in 1911. David was the only one who spent time in the Romanian army and never had a chance to go to school.

Their mother Pearl, nicknamed Pepe, stayed in New York.

Newman Hillel Dies

It was Friday August 30, 1912, and the shop was especially busy today. Newman ate his dinner, a corned beef sandwich, by his workbench as he struggled with an especially difficult watch mechanism. Yesterday, the temperature was 93 and the forecast for today was the same with the threat of thundershowers this evening. The overhead fans did little to cool the store even with the back door open to create a breeze. It was then he had another attack of indigestion. These attacks had been happening with somewhat regularity after Ettie had filed for divorce. In the reconciliation agreement he had allowed Ettie to study to become a midwife.

Now, more of the household tasks went to him as she attended her patients. It was hard for Newman to adjust to this but if it meant keeping his marriage and his children he would do it. This attack of indigestion was worse than the others. He had a pain in his left arm and felt nauseous. Before he knew it he was vomiting in the waste container by his workbench. He called out to his partner. "Hershel, you're going to have to finish this watch for Mr. Schwab. I need to go home and recover from this indigestion."

"Alright Newman, it's Friday, and you have the whole weekend to recover." Newman gathered up his coat but did not put it on. He was already sweating and the pain in his chest was not going away. He slowly left the store and faced the afternoon heat and humidity as he waited at the streetcar stop. He barely made it into the streetcar; it was a struggle, as he was short of breath. "If I can just get home, a glass of bicarbonate of soda will relieve this gas," he thought.

The streetcar ride seemed to take forever. His stop was just one block from the house where the family now lived at 2517 N. Prairie Ave. The walk to the house was agonizing.

Ettie was home getting ready for the Sabbath meal, which meant cooking most of the day. Jacob was also at home; he had just turned four. "Get me a bicarbonate," Newman said, his voice just a whisper. Ettie knew the drill as this had happened too many times to count. She handed him the drink. This time she knew things were different. His color was very pale and with his right hand he seemed to be clutching his chest.

She called the doctor over his objections. "We can't afford a doctor's visit," he said. "This indigestion will pass—just give me a little time." The doctor came and gave Newman some camphor as he lay almost motionless on the sofa. The electric fan pointed in his direction gave little relief from the heat. The girls, Pearl, now 11, and Sarah, age 9, came home from school but kept quiet as directed by their mother. There would be no Sabbath dinner tonight.

Ettie stayed by Newman's side after the children went to bed. It then started to rain with occasional claps of thunder. Around 11:00 pm Newman said, "Ettie, I think the pain is letting up a bit."

"Thank goodness," she said, but before she could finish her sentence she saw Newman take one more breath and then lay silent. She called the doctor, who came to the house and pronounced Newman dead.[2] That's when Ettie called her brother Sam.

It was late Friday night when the phone rang, at almost midnight. Nettie thought, another emergency call for Sam, but she was wrong. Sam answered the phone and Nettie could tell by his tone that it was not a patient. He hung up the phone and turned to Nettie. "Newman Hillel died tonight. Ettie said the doctor said it was acute indigestion, but after hearing his symptoms from Ettie, I think it was something else." Thoughts of Ettie, the birth of Jacob in her apartment, and the teachings of Emma Goldman all came flooding back to Nettie's memory. "We need to have her move here from St. Louis. It would be good to have her here, Sam. As a midwife she could help you with the practice, and the children will get to know their cousins." Sam nodded in agreement. He was still thinking about Newman and his diagnosis.

Ettie moved the family—Pearl, Sarah, and Jacob—to East Chicago to be with her brothers. She started working as a midwife for Sam's growing practice of pregnant patients. Sam's sister and both his brothers were now in the same city.

In the fall of 1912, a typhoid epidemic erupted in East Chicago. As the city health officer, Sam had to track down the problem. He issued an order for everyone to boil their milk. Sam finally found the problem, a typhoid carrier who worked on a farm that was supplying the milk.

On December 12, Barney came into Sam's office. "Sam, I've got this splitting headache that just won't go away. It seemed to come on after I got a cold a few weeks ago. Can you check me out?"

"Sure, Barney, come on in the exam room." Sam did a thorough exam and found nothing wrong with Barney. "Barney, let me prescribe some aspirin for that headache and let me know what happens," Sam said.

That was a Thursday. By Monday morning, Barney was back in the office. "Sam, the headache is getting worse. I feel nauseous and want to vomit."

---

2   In 1912 heart attacks were not diagnosed. Instead, acute indigestion was named as the cause of death. It was in 1912 that Dr. James B. Herrick documented the first case of death by heart attack in Chicago. The medical profession took years to accept this diagnosis. Doctors in 1912 were kept preoccupied with infectious diseases, which were the leading killers. It would be 20 years before heart attacks were routinely diagnosed. Still today, many heart attacks masquerade as symptoms of indigestion.

Sam took his temperature along with his exam. "Looks like you're running a low-grade fever. Maybe that flu is coming back. Let's get you on something stronger. Maybe a little codeine syrup will help. Let me see you tomorrow and see if you're any better."

Barney left the office and went downstairs to the tavern to do some paperwork.

That evening, Sam called him. Things just didn't feel right. "Barney, old boy, how are you feeling?"

"Not much better, Sam. Now I'm really vomiting. I can't hold anything down. I feel a spot on the side of my head that is really sore."

"That's not good, Barney. We need to get you to the North Chicago Hospital. They can really find out what's wrong."

"Can it wait a few days? I have so much going on here I have to finish up."

"That's up to you, Barney, but I wouldn't wait. I'll call the hospital tomorrow and tell them we'll be bringing you in tomorrow or the next day."

When Sam got off the phone, he turned to Nettie. "I'm really worried about Barney. Tell Anna to encourage him to let me get him to the hospital tomorrow."

"What do you think he has, Sam?"

"Don't know, but if it's something in his brain, I'm not equipped to handle it here."

Dora Works with Her Dolls

"What's the matter with my dolls?" Dora asked Sister Marie, her voodoo practitioner. "I've done everything you taught me, and still I don't see any results. I put the needles in the heart, like you said, but no deaths from indigestion in the newspaper. All you want is my money. I'm beginning to believe my husband that you're a fraud."

"Don't you be talkin' to Sister Marie like that, or she be workin' her magic on you." Sister's eyes got as dark as coal, and she seemed to radiate some sort of energy that made Dora's hair stand up on end.

"I'm sorry, Sister, how could I doubt you? Please forgive me." Dora clasped her hands together as if in prayer and fell to her knees at Sister Marie's feet.

"Don't you be questioning my power. Get up, and I gives you your next lesson."

Dora rose from the floor, relieved that that she had not brought the power of Sister Marie down upon herself and her family.

"Problem is, you is not focusin' clear on your target. If you be scatterin' your mojo, it be hittin' other peoples close to the one you is aimin' to hurt. Your voodoo is like a loaded gun. It keeps firin' off with nobody aimin' it. You need to be goin' into the deep concentration, or voodoo don't work."

"I'm pushing pins into Sam's doll to give him headaches and keep him awake at night. I put one little one in his heart to give him the pain that I feel after losing him. Is that good?"

"That be a minor effect. Does you wants to just hurt des peoples or kill dem? Makes up your mind."

This was the first time Sister Marie mentioned killing, and it took Dora a minute to process the answer. She knew the dolls could cause pain, but she wasn't sure about causing death. *What if I've been using the dolls wrong?* "I don't want to kill them now. Just hurt them."

"Well, den, just be a focusin' on dem. Otherwise, you is gonna get the wrong peoples."

She paid Sister a little extra this time to make sure she didn't cast any spell on her.

Barney Has a Brain Abscess

The year 1913 didn't start out well. Sam heard from the hospital the day after he admitted Barney. He had a brain abscess.[3] The only treatment was to drain it and hope Barney's body could kill the bacterial or fungal infection. Two days later, they told Sam they had drained it again.

"What going on with Barney?" Nettie asked, with more than a little concern on her face. "I've never seen you look so intense, Sam."

"I can't help but think that I didn't get him to the hospital soon enough."

"Yes you did, Sam. It was Barney that wanted to wait."

"I know, but they teach you not let your patients make treatment decisions, even if it's your best friend."

They drained Barney's abscess a third time, but the infection must have traveled to his heart. During the night of January 11, 1913, Barney died of a heart attack. He was the closest friend Sam and Nettie had. He was only 38 and died in his sleep.

"There's so much about medicine that we don't know," sighed Sam.

---

3   Today, brain abscesses are treated with antifungals or antibiotics. The cause of the infection can be from a sinus or dental infection, ear or heart infection, or trauma. These are the most common problems. In 1913, antibiotics did not exist. The only treatment was to drain the abscess, clean and sterilize the area, and allow the body to heal itself. Rarely did this happen. Most brain abscesses were fatal.

The whole community was in shock. Barney was such a force for good in East Chicago. Anna, now a widow with four children, decided to move from their house in Whiting to one of the apartments in the Auditorium Building. She would now be closer to manage the property and tavern, leaving her brother-in-law Myer to run the taverns in Whiting and Hammond.

Dora Sees the Announcement

Dora saw the announcement in the *Hammond Times* and knew that this was Sam and Nettie's best friend. She had been experimenting with pins to the heart, as she was heartbroken about losing Sam and wanted him to feel the same. She decided not to tell Sister Marie about the article in the paper.

The Family Grows and Sam Gets Sick

Diphtheria, smallpox, and scarlet fever cases were found in East Chicago only three days after Barney died. Sam, the city health officer, had to see the patients and quarantine their houses. This was dangerous for both him and the community. He did not want to bring the diseases back home to his family. Rarely did Nettie see him, but he made it to Barney's funeral and then was back out on calls.

Nettie gave birth to their third child, Bernard, on January 31, 1913. Anie their servant resigned, as she got married and started a family of her own. They now were running an ad for a new servant.

Sam opened his third pharmacy, The Red Cross Pharmacy, on Cedar Street in Indiana Harbor.

It was April, a beautiful spring day in 1913, when Nettie came into the bedroom after feeding Bernard, her youngest child. Sam was still in bed. Good, she thought, I'll let him sleep. He was exhausted when he came to bed last night.

A few hours later, she returned to the bedroom. Sam was awake but could not get out of bed. "Nettie, call Eli to come over. I don't know what's the matter."

Nettie dialed Eli Levin's number. They were one of the few houses with a telephone. "Operator, I want to reach number 89, Dr. Eli Levin."

Eli was related to Anna Cohen. He had recently graduated from medical school.

"Eli? This is Nettie. Please come over. Sam needs you." She didn't want to say too much, as the operators were the town's source of information as well as its source of gossip.

Within minutes, Eli was at Sam's bedside examining him. "Sam, I think what you have is complete exhaustion. I know you have been burning the candle at both ends, and it has now caught up to you."

"He also has trouble sleeping at night, Eli," Nettie chimed in.

"When this happens, the body shuts down. It's a kind of paralysis that keeps you in bed until you get rest. I think we should get Sam to a hospital in Chicago for a few weeks, away from all his duties here."

Looking on with great interest was their new servant, Mamie Jackson. She had just come from her home in Georgia for a better life in the North. She was the seventh of nine children and a wonderful cook and housekeeper. She was a large woman in her 20s, and always had a smile on her face. The family had never eaten so well. She was learning about the foods both Sam and Nettie loved from the old country, and she put her Southern touch to them. She had been with the family for only four months, but the children all loved her.

After Sam was moved to Chicago and Nettie was back home, Mamie couldn't keep quiet any longer. "Ms. Nettie, now don't you be thinkin' I's a fool, but I thinks Dr. Sam is under some type of black magic. One of my older sisters lives in New Orleans. She works for some peoples that say voodoo magic is very powerful. It can work from miles away. I thinks that may be what's keepin' Dr. Sam awakes at night."

"Oh Mamie, I know you want what is best for our family, but I think Sam is just overworked. He has too many responsibilities. I am going to see that he gets help or cuts back when he comes home."

"Would it be OK if I asks my sister what we can do to stop this magic? It won't hurt none to try, Ms. Nettie."

Hammond Lake County Times

April 15, 1913

DOCTOR BACK FROM HOSPITAL

Dr. S. Herskovitz secretary of the East Chicago Health department has returned from Chicago where he had been for several weeks in a hospital taking treatment for what seemed to be a species of nervous break-down and this morning was trying to get in touch with the smallpox situation in Indiana Harbor. When seen this morning however, he had been unable to get a hold of anyone who could give him definite information regarding conditions, Dr. Herskovitz until a few days ago did not know that there was any smallpox in this region. When he heard he could not rest until he came out and got a line on the conditions. As soon as he was able therefore, he left the hospital, and this morning he announced that he was prepared to take personal charge of the situation. Dr. Herskovitz is still far from being a well man. His voice is weak and he shows the effect of his illness in many ways. "I will soon be myself again" said the physician. "My breakdown was due to overwork. I have not only had no vacation for four or five years, but I have been up night and day much of the time, and have suffered from the lack of sufficient sleep.

Courtesy of Newspapers.com

"You have my blessing. If you think it will help, you just ask your sister in New Orleans."

Two weeks later, Sam was back home. A newspaper article was published telling all he'd had a nervous breakdown. Sam said in the article that he blamed it on overwork and no vacations since he came to America.

Dora Sees Article about Sam's Nervous Breakdown

None of this went unnoticed by Dora, as the article was published in the *Hammond Times*. She showed the article to Sister Marie. "I tell you my magic gonna work. You give it some time, it work," she said, as she opened her hand, a gesture for more money from Dora, who paid.

Sam Comes Home

Sam was recovering at home after a few weeks of rest in the hospital in Chicago. "Nettie, guess who came and visited me in the hospital? Sol Goldenstein. He has changed his name to Golden. He was doing rounds in the hospital as part of his last year. Seems his school has merged with the Chicago College of Medicine. He graduates in May. We should go to his graduation."

"That would be nice, Sam. We could spend a weekend in Chicago. It would do you some good to get away again."

Dr. Samuel Herskovitz. *Family photo*

No sooner did Sam get out of the hospital than he had to convince the new immigrants in town that they needed smallpox vaccinations. He seemed to be pulled in all directions, as he still could not say no to anyone for anything.

"This has got to stop," Nettie begged Sam. "All this work is killing you. You get no sleep, and I know your ulcer is always giving you pain. Promise me you will give up the job as city health officer after this year."

"You're right, Nettie. I just can't do it all. This will be my last year, I promise. My children are growing up without me. I really need time with them too. Today, when I was going to a house call, I had Sergeant Mike

Gorman riding with me. We were held up by a train for 30 minutes. He was all upset and gave the engineer a ticket for blocking the Roadway, but I have to say, I enjoyed the 30-minute rest in the car."

Mamie Gets the Gris-Gris[4]

Mamie got a letter from her sister in New Orleans. She told her to get some coarse salt and a teaspoon of garlic powder, and mix them together. Mamie then put the mixture on every windowsill and doorway in the apartment. She even put some in the fireplace hearth, targeting any opening that the voodoo spirit could use to get in.

"What's all this white powder around the house?" Sam asked, as he came upstairs from his office for a quick lunch.

"Oh dat's to keep dem spirits away from you, Dr. Sam. It will let you sleep at night. My sister from New Orleans tell me so."

Sam couldn't believe it. The next morning he awoke and felt more rested than he had in the past year. *Was Mamie right? Did her powder protect the house?*

The Auditorium Building Burns

The year ended with a fire that burned down the Auditorium Building on December 22, 1913. Sam had closed both his office and pharmacy in the building as an attempt to slow down. The building was completely destroyed.

Anna and her four children were living in the apartment on the second floor when they smelled smoke. They escaped with just their bedclothes into the frigid winter night and stayed with neighbors across the street.

The fire was blamed on mice playing with matches in the grocery store basement. The gasoline that fed the lights in the upstairs auditorium fed the flames with an explosion that rocked the neighborhood.

---

4   Gris-gris is a voodoo amulet originating in Africa. It can supposedly protect the wearer from evil. It came to the United States with enslaved Africans in Louisiana, and it was quickly adopted by practitioners of voodoo. The ingredients can be reduced to powder, which can be used for both good and evil.

Dora Practices Her Voodoo

Dora was through with Sam for a while and decided to set her Nettie doll's hair on fire. She saw the article in the *Hammond Times* about the fire destroying the Auditorium Building. This voodoo was working, but as Sister Marie said, she had to focus. Reaching her intended victim was always a problem. Dora always had trouble concentrating.

Anna's Family Moves in with Sam and Nettie

Until they could find another place to live, Anna and her children moved in with Nettie and Sam, who were living in a 10-room apartment above the drugstore in Calumet. Luckily, the Auditorium Building had been insured for $100,000 ($2.4 million in 2017 dollars), more than enough for Anna to rebuild. She used the rest of the money to build a boarding house next door.

Nettie and Anna loved the time together. It felt just like they were schoolgirls together again in Lithuania.

War Is on the Horizon

In 1914, it didn't look to Nettie like Sam was slowing down. He was a member of the Independent Order of Odd Fellows, The Knights of Pythias, the Independent Order of B'nith Abraham, the Fraternal Order of Eagles, and the Indiana Harbor Commercial Club, and he was a director of the *Twin City Sentinel* newspaper.

"Nettie, I got a call today from Sol. He told me he has volunteered for the army. He said that with only one year of practice, he was ready to do something for the country that has offered him so much."

"How do you feel about that, Sam?"

"I feel the same way, but how could I leave you and the children? I'll find some way to do my part for the country. I'm going to first do something about my ulcer. I haven't told you, but I've been having bouts of nausea. Only vomiting seems to ease the pain. I heard of a doctor in Chicago who is doing surgery for my problem. If we are going to war and I have to do my part for the country, I need to be healthy."

Nettie agreed. "I hope you can wait until this baby is born, Sam."

"I'll do my best," Sam said. Nettie was always reading the newspapers, recalling something that she had learned at Becker's Institute from Mistress Fechheimer. She could hear her words, "Women must know the news of the world, as men respect a woman who has knowledge and can enter into the conversation."

On June 28, 1914, she read that the Archduke Franz Ferdinand and his wife were assassinated by a Serbian nationalist in Sarajevo. As Nettie was pregnant with their fourth child, she was resting more and had time to read.

Cecil Herskovitz was born July 4, 1914, amid the Fourth of July fireworks. Sam and Nettie remembered the time in St. Louis when they sat on the Mississippi Levee with little Edward and Mama Mary, and she was reminded that it was almost time to return to St. Louis for Edward's ninth birthday.

WWI Begins

By August, France, Great Britain, Russia, and Serbia were all in the war against Germany and Austria-Hungary.

"What do you think, Sam? Should America get in the war?" asked Nettie on one of those rare evenings when Sam was home.

"You know what it was like in the old country. The people have no say in their government, especially the Jews. I'm afraid those that are left in Europe will be slaughtered. I think we should come to their aid, but President Woodrow Wilson says we will remain neutral. That's why I think it's time for me to become a citizen. I want to vote in the next election for a Republican."

"Wonderful, Sam," said Nettie, who had become a naturalized citizen while she was living in Houston with her brother. "You really need to get naturalized, although it is not as easy as it used to be. A little book work other than medicine will be good for your mind."

Sam Gets an Operation

September 1914 was the month Sam had set for his operation. He had Dr. Eli cover his office. Baby Cecil was now 2 months old.

Mamie was worried that her gris-gris would leave Sam unprotected in the hospital. "Now, Mamie, don't you worry about me. I'll be home before you know it and be able to eat your wonderful cooking," Sam said, in a consoling tone.

The operation was devised by W.J. Mayo. The excision of the ulcer meant the separation of the posterior adhesions and pushing the ulcer-bearing portion forward through an opening made in the anterior wall of the stomach. There the ulcer would be safely excised.

It was hoped that after the surgery, there would be better evacuation of the stomach and the reflux of alkaline duodenal juices would neutralize the acid in the stomach.

Sam was in the hospital for a week and came home much improved. He was even able to eat Mamie's cornbread when he came home.

The Family Grows and the Country Goes to War

As the older sister to her three younger brothers, Pearle was always telling them all what to do. Sam was as busy as always, but the war was always in the headlines. In May 1915, the RMS *Lusitania* was sunk by a German U-boat, and 123 Americans died. Survivors said the U-boat fired on them in their lifeboats. Still, President Wilson would not go to war.

In September, Tsar Nicholas II took charge of the Russian armies. This was the same tsar who had made life so difficult for Nettie's family.

Sam was now an appraiser for the City Savings and Loan. On August 15, 1915, he became a naturalized citizen. His days of supporting Emma Goldman were in his past and had not followed him from St. Louis. He still believed in equal rights for women but not the overthrow of the government. Nettie arranged a surprise party for him with lots of flags and red, white, and blue bunting.

Sam's Ulcer Problem Returns

In December 1915, Sam noticed that his ulcer was back. It started with just a little bleeding. As the new year started, the bleeding episodes became more frequent. Then pain and vomiting started, and then a swelling of his stomach. Sam knew this meant the opening from his stomach to his small intestine was constricted. There must be scaring of the duodenum. He would need another operation. He explained all of this to Nettie and said he had to talk to the surgeon again.

The doctor who did his first operation, Dr. William Michel, was still at the South Shore Hospital in Chicago. This operation would be more extensive than the last one, as he planned on tying off the ulcer-bearing area from the stomach with a fascial ligature. The doctor felt it was a pyloric or duodenal ulcer. He had done a number of these operations, with more successes than failures. Surgery was always risky, as there was very little they could do for infection, and only saline through the rectum for hydration. Blood transfusions were not available. Loss of blood was the fatal complication to this surgery.

Sam Has Second Operation

There was never a good time for Sam to get his operation. He finally decided he would do it after the wedding of Valerie Popescu, his clerk at the Red Cross Pharmacy; she was having her ceremony at the newly rebuilt Auditorium Building on February 18, 1916. He didn't eat a thing at the reception because he didn't want to vomit. Nettie was worried, as Sam was getting thinner every day. After the wedding when they were back home, Sam said, "Nettie, I'm calling the hospital on Monday and setting up my surgery."

March 21, 1916, was the date he went to the hospital. Nettie was very worried. She confided in Anna that she couldn't see herself living without Sam.

"You're really going to go through with this, Sam?" Nettie asked, on the day he was leaving for the hospital.

"I can't live like this any longer, Nettie. If I'm to be the man you married, I must get this corrected. I promise I will come home." They hugged each other for what seemed to be an eternity, and then he was gone.

When he entered the hospital on March 21, he called Nettie to tell her that they wanted to observe him for the week and that he would call her every day.

"How is Dr. Sam doing, Ms. Nettie?" asked Mamie.

"We'll know more after the surgery on Friday."

"I dis wants you to knows that I be worried. He ain't protected from da spirits in da hospital."

"I'm sure they can't find him there," Nettie said, as she tried to calm Mamie.

The surgery went as planned. The doctor widened the base of the stomach and tied off the ulcer portion. He noted that the ulcer was on the verge of complete perforation. Sam came out of the anesthetic, and there at his bedside was Nettie. As he opened his eyes, she was the first person he saw. "I told you I wouldn't leave you," he said, with a slight smile on his lips. She kissed him. "No hugging," he said. "We don't want anything to come loose."

"Is the pain gone, Sam?"

"The ulcer pain is gone, but now I have a few other pains from the surgery."

They talked through the afternoon about how he was going to cut back at the office and about the plans for the children. Later that afternoon, Nettie left. She had to go home to the children.

"I should be here a few more days, and then I will be home. I have to be able to get up the stairs to the apartment. I want to take my time to heal."

"Take all the time you need. Just come home. I love you, Sam," were her parting words.

"I love you too, Nettie." With that, she was out the door.

That evening, Dr. Eli Levin came to visit. He and Sam were talking. Then, with no warning, something popped. They both heard it.

"Eli, a suture popped. I'm bleeding inside." Sam was terrified. He knew there was nothing anyone could do. He was going into shock from loss of blood. He slumped back in the bed, his head fell to one side, and he was dead. It was 7 p.m.

Dora Sees the News—Sam Is Dead

It had been almost three years since Dora had seen anything negative in the *Hammond Times* about Sam or Nettie. Nettie had given birth to a few more babies, but nothing since Sam had his nervous breakdown and one ulcer operation. Dora had taken to having a drink after dinner. On March 31, she was not in a good mood.

"You playing with dem dolls again?" asked Joseph. Dora had put the dolls on the kitchen table while she was cleaning up after dinner.

"Don't talk to me about those dolls. I told you they ain't dolls." Dora was not a sweet drunk. Joseph knew it, but he couldn't help himself. Life with her was getting more difficult every day.

"What if I take dem dolls and threw dem in the trash? What would you do?"

Dora picked up a kitchen knife and appeared to threaten Joseph. Then, without realizing it, she stabbed it into the table, unaware that Sam's doll was lying directly in its path. She plunged the knife into the belly of Sam's doll. Pulling it out brought the stuffing with it. The time was 7 p.m.

"Look what you made me do. That's what you will get too, so don't tempt me." She tried her best to put the stuffing back in Sam's doll, but it just kept coming out again and again.

Two days later, the article appeared in the *Hammond Times* about Sam's death. That night, Dora couldn't sleep. She heard voices and kept waking up Joseph to ask if he was hearing them too. He said yes, just to shut her up.

"I killed my *soul mate*, and it was your fault, Joseph. Please forgive me, Sam." She kept repeating that all night. Nothing was going to be the same between her and Joseph again.

Dr. Samuel Herskovitz.
Family photo collection

Sam's Funeral

The funeral was a sad affair. All of Sam's family was there, and many of his patients. They all told Nettie what a wonderful doctor Sam had been. He always took the time to listen to his patients, and that was half the cure. Many of East Chicago's elected officials were also there, as were the men in the fraternal organizations that Sam belonged to.

Men from the Independent Order of B'nith Abraham gave Nettie money, the death benefit provided to the widows of its members; the death benefit would give the family money over the next year.

Sol Golden came and looked handsome in his military uniform. He promised Nettie that he would be there for her and would look in on her and the children for as long as he could. He, like everyone else, felt the United States would enter the war and he would be shipped overseas.

WIDOW OF HARBOR DOCTOR HIT BY CAR

Mrs. Samuel Hershcovitz, widow of the late Dr. Hershcovitz, narrowly escaped death this noon when she ran into a moving South Shore interurban at the corner of Michigan and Guthrie streets, Indiana Harbor. She fortunately escaped with slight bruises. The car, a new Dodge, was badly wrecked. She was taken to her home in Indiana Harbor.

Nettie's Dodge runs into interurban train. *Hammond Lake County Times*, August 23, 1917 *Newspaper Archives*

"I will always be here for you, Nettie. You know that." Nettie nodded her head in agreement. He put his arm around her in an effort to console her. Nettie embraced him as well and she thought she felt more than just a consoling embrace.

Nettie Adjusts to Life as a Widow

"We is gonna be all right, Ms. Nettie. Mamie take care of you and the chilins."

Nettie just couldn't stop crying. The love of her life was gone. How could she go on? Anna had lost Barney three years ago, and she was now there for Nettie. "Now, Nettie, you have to take charge of the pharmacies just like I did at the saloon. You know about drugstores. Just make sure you have honest people managing them. The work will help you through the pain. It worked for me."

Nettie now knew that Sam's dream of a chain of Calumet Drugstores would just be that, a dream. Sam, Nettie, and Louis Steimer, a grocer from Franklin, Ohio, had formed the Calumet Drug Company on June 30, 1913. It was capitalized at $7,500 ($184,000 in 2017 dollars). The goal was to "own and operate" multiple drugstores. The company was disbanded in 1946.

Nettie received Sam's insurance benefit of $100,000 ($2.296 million in 2017 dollars), some of which she used for new clothes, lingerie, and a 1917 Dodge. She and Anna would go on shopping sprees to Chicago. She also got a stockbroker, or did he find her? Anyway, she was investing in stocks and buying vacant land in Gary, which was just starting to grow.

One day, she was in Indiana Harbor and had stopped to let the South Shore Interurban train pass, when her Dodge car jumped forward and slammed into the side of the moving train. She escaped with only minor injuries. Explaining it to Anna, she said, "I had my foot on the brake and the machine was in neutral when the car just jumped forward, completely out of my control, like an unseen hand pushed me into that train."

Nettie had only slight bruises, but the Dodge was badly wrecked. Reading the newspaper and keeping up with the war was also a way to distract herself. Today, the headline was "Secret Zimmerman Telegram Sent to Mexico by Germany Decoded." This telegram from Germany promised Mexico it could have the states that bordered it with the United States—Arizona, Texas, and New Mexico—if Mexico entered the war and Germany won.

President Wilson made this telegram public to the American people. Still the United States stayed out of the war. Making the telegram public was Wilson's way of swaying public opinion. It worked. The public demanded that the U.S. go to war. It was official on April 6, 1917. The United States declared war on Germany.

On November 7, 1917, the Bolsheviks overthrew the Russian government and Tsar Nicholas II abdicated the throne. Nettie showed Anna the paper. "It couldn't happen to a nicer family," she said sarcastically, "for all the pain that tsar put the Jewish people through and all the lives lost. *Vi me bet zikh ois, azoi darf men shlofen*" (as you make your bed, so will you sleep in it). He should receive the same fate." In July of 1918, Tsar Nicholas II and his entire family were executed by the Bolsheviks.

Prohibition Becomes the Law

The United States passed the 18th Amendment in December of 1917. It now needed 75 percent of the states to ratify it. "This really worries me, Nettie. What am I going to do with the saloon if Prohibition becomes the law?"

"We'll think of something, Anna. I've heard some counties in Indiana are already dry and have converted their saloons to have paid entertainment. Then you just give the drinks away free."

"I think we'll be one of the first states to go dry. I remember how hard it was for Barney to get his first license in 1902. It took two years, and it had to be voted on in an election by the whole county." In April 1918, Indiana passed statewide Prohibition; it ratified the 18th Amendment on January 14, 1919. Prohibition became the law nationwide on January 16, 1920.

Sixty-fifth Congress of the United States of America;

At the Second Session,

Begun and held at the City of Washington on Monday, the third day of December, one thousand nine hundred and seventeen.

JOINT RESOLUTION

Proposing an amendment to the Constitution of the United States.

Resolved by the Senate and House of Representatives of the United States of America in Congress assembled (two-thirds of each House concurring therein), That the following amendment to the Constitution be, and hereby is, proposed to the States, to become valid as a part of the Constitution when ratified by the legislatures of the several States as provided by the Constitution:

"ARTICLE —.

"SECTION 1. After one year from the ratification of this article the manufacture, sale, or transportation of intoxicating liquors within, the importation thereof into, or the exportation thereof from the United States and all territory subject to the jurisdiction thereof for beverage purposes is hereby prohibited.

"SEC. 2. The Congress and the several States shall have concurrent power to enforce this article by appropriate legislation.

"SEC. 3. This article shall be inoperative unless it shall have been ratified as an amendment to the Constitution by the legislatures of the several States, as provided in the Constitution, within seven years from the date of the submission hereof to the States by the Congress."

Champ Clark,

Speaker of the House of Representatives.

Thos. R. Marshall

Vice President of the United States and
President of the Senate.

18th Amendment to the Constitution, Prohibition. *Courtesy of Wikipedia*

CHAPTER 8

A New Man in Nettie's Life

After Sam's death, Sol was a regular at the house. Regular meant every other weekend, as he was working hard doing physicals for the men enlisting for the war.

"Nettie, it looks like my number is going to come up to go overseas. If I don't come back, I want you and the children to get my government benefits."

"What are you saying, Sol?" Nettie wasn't sure what Sol meant.

"If I die and we're married, the government will give you and the children widows benefits. I would want that," Sol explained.

"Sol, don't think like that. You'll come back. I know you will."

"I don't want to take any chances, Nettie. We can get married in Cook County by the justice of the peace before I leave. The next group of guys will go to Camp Greenleaf in Georgia in August. Will you marry me, Nettie?"

"Sol, are you doing this because you think Sam would want you to?"

"Maybe, Nettie. I know you will never love me like you did Sam, but that's OK. Maybe things will change when I come back from the war. Please let me do this for you and the children."

It was two years since Sam died, a respectable interval. Sol was right. She didn't love him like she did Sam, but he was kind and good with the children. "Yes, I will marry you, Sol."

They were married June 15, 1918. Anna came with them. Sol was mobilized on August 23, 1918.

Sol Enters the War

Sol's first stop was Camp Greenleaf in Georgia. This was the location where the United States started building its ambulance service.[1] Sol made many friends during the three weeks he was here. Many would be with him during his service in France.

Word War I ambulance. *Courtesy of Wikipedia*

On September 23, he was aboard the SS *President Lincoln*, which took Sol and the other soldiers to France. The ship was crowded with more men than it should hold. Many slept on the deck, which was a lot cooler than below deck. Sol remembered his last trip across this ocean. It was slower, but the anxiety of what was on the other side was just as great. On this trip, there was no chance of an appendicitis attack. Everyone was wondering if an enemy sub would try to sink the ship. All on board were wearing their life vests, but that would do little good in the middle of the ocean. There were practice drills in case they had to abandon ship as well as drills on the use of their gas masks.

When they landed in France on October 7, Sol's medical unit got a 10-day crash course in setting up a mobile field hospital. Their unit was assigned to the First Corps Sanitary Train, then switched to the 116th Sanitary Train attached to the 41st Division. It was composed of the 81st and 82nd Infantry Brigade and the 66th Field Artillery Brigade. They traveled together to the Meuse-Argonne offensive, which had started September 26.

They arrived October 24, three days before the third and final phase of the offensive. It was 2 o'clock in the morning when they arrived. Everyone knew they had to get the tents set up as quickly as possible. Their best guess was that they were between five and eight miles behind the front lines. They knew guns could fire up to 20 miles. They were within range.

---

1   Before the United States entered the war, all ambulance drivers were volunteers who went to Europe on their own and donated their services. They were not part of the AEF (American Expeditionary Force). Later, when the United States entered the war, they were inducted into the AEF. In 1917, the U.S. Army developed its own Ambulance and Sanitary (medical) Corps. The Army sent 3,070 GMC and 3,805 Ford ambulances shipped in two sections, chassis and body, to France. There they were put together. The men especially liked the Ford ambulances. They could go through high water and climb steep hills. If they got stuck, they were light enough for three or four men to lift out of the mud. The song of the volunteer ambulance officers: *Put on your old gray bonnet with the strap ahangin' on it, and we'll go through shrapnel and through shell, then the roads of desolation. We will cure your constipation with a wild night ride in hell.*

The morning of October 26 and again on October 27, starting at 2:30 a.m., thousands of gas and high-explosive shells were coming their way from the Boche.[2] The nighttime sky was lighting up like a mono-color July 4, with white puffs of smoke. It was deadly gas. Sol was assigned to Field Hospital 163, designated to receive the wounded and gassed soldiers. It really wasn't much of a hospital—just a large tent set up for emergency medical care. A section of the tent was partitioned off for the doctors' sleeping quarters. It was fall. The ground was wet and muddy. *How can we treat infections in such a filthy place?* Sol thought.

The smell of war was all around him. The gunpowder of exploded shells and the lingering acrid odor of chlorine and mustard gas from previous attacks was in the air. It was 4 o'clock on the morning of October 27. He and some of the other doctors couldn't sleep because of the shelling. Just then, he heard someone yell "incoming," and then the sound of the gas whistle. Sol didn't know what to expect, but he knew enough to grab his helmet and gas mask. He and the other doctors dove under their cots.

Kaboom, kaboom! He felt the ground shake as one shell hit and then another even closer. Through the fog in his gas mask, he saw what looked like water hitting the side of the tent and then shrapnel tearing holes in the canvas as it flew over his head. It wasn't water, but mustard gas. He smelled it, even though he wore his mask. Thank goodness no patients were in the hospital. Sol remembered seeing soldiers who had returned to the states who had suffered from mustard gas attacks.[3] *This is what they*

---

2   Boche was a term used as a disparaging offensive term for the German soldiers. The French used it first, and then it was copied by the Americans.

3   Up to 20 different gases were used by both sides during WWI. Phosgene, chlorine, and mustard were the most well-known. Chorine caused death quickly by asphyxiation, as the bronchial muscles would go into spasm and block the airway. Phosgene also caused death by suffocation but had a delayed effect, as much as 24 hours. It affected the blood-air barrier in the lungs. When mixed together, the two gases were called White Star, as they were labeled on the shells with a white cross. Mustard gas was different. It was a blistering agent that could remain active for many weeks in the trenches and on the ground. Using powdered bleach helped decontaminate an area. Mustard gas affected the lungs and eyes. Touching it would cause blisters and sores, some down to the bone. It could soak through clothing, where it was absorbed by the skin. If inhaled, lung damage would occur. Eyes were easily affected, causing swelling and temporary blindness, forcing the eyes closed. It could be ingested in the food and water, causing internal problems. Washing the body with hot soap and water, and airing out or steam cleaning clothes was effective. Showering within 30 minutes of exposure was the ideal but almost impossible. Drinking bicarbonate of soda would help if the gas was ingested. Many would not show the effects of the gas until years later, with scarring of the lungs. Mustard gas was related to many lung problems, fibrosis and constriction of the tissue, chronic bronchitis, and cancer.

smelled, he thought. Their problems seemed to multiply with time instead of getting better. Both their eyesight and lung problems were the main issues. There was little the doctors could do.

Sol lay on the ground under his cot keeping his gas mask on the rest of the night. It was difficult to breathe, but the thought of the mustard gas convinced him to keep it on. In the early-morning light, he and the others saw the craters of last night's shelling. The mustard gas was still visible on the ground and the side of the tent. One of the men was spreading bleach powder over the area to neutralize the gas.

"That was a close call, Doc," one of the men said. "I hope those Boche were not aiming at us."

"They say it's the one you don't hear that kills ya," said one of the orderlies.

Sol didn't have time to think about it. He and the others were heading for the showers and a change of uniform. He knew he'd had some exposure to the gas, and a hot shower was the best medicine. No sooner had he gotten dressed than he saw a line of ambulances heading for his field hospital. He had to marvel at the drivers. They must have been in the thick of the shelling and were carrying the wounded his way.

The stretcher bearers started taking the men out of the ambulances. This was the first time Sol had seen the injuries of war as they were happening. Men with broken arms and legs, some burned from head to toe with gas burns. Men without limbs and barely alive. Those who could walk had bandages covering their eyes, blinded by the gas, holding onto the soldiers in front of them as they walked to the station.

This was the time for Sol and the other doctors to render emergency care and make the decisions about who should be sent back to the base hospitals for extended care and who could stay in the field station for a few days, recover, and return to the front lines.

Dysentery, flu, gas gangrene, trench foot,[4] shell shock, and gas shock were other problems they were seeing.

The stretcher bearers were the second to see the wounded at the aid stations. They were then put in the ambulances. At the field hospital, it was up to Sol and his men to treat the gassed victims.

"Get his clothes off," Sol ordered for a soldier who could not walk. "Wash him down and put his clothes in the decontamination area."

---

4   Clean water and clean dry feet were a must to prevent dysentery and trench foot. The boys were given clean socks to change on the buddy system, so each man would look out for the other. This seemed to work. Shell shock and gas victims were another matter.

"Yes, sir" was the reply.

The wounded kept coming out of the ambulances, victims of the last two nights of bombing. The men who had bandages on their eyes now needed bicarbonate of soda sprayed in their eyes, noses, and throats to mitigate the corrosion of the gas on the mucous membranes.[5]

"Put him over here." Sol motioned to the soldiers carrying the stretcher. He quickly examined the soldier who was moaning in pain. Another victim of mustard gas. Sol helped remove his uniform. The doctors could not help but be contaminated by the wounded soldiers. Sol tried to remember to keep washing his hands but could do little to stop inhaling the lingering gas. His gas mask gave him limited vision. He could not work with it on. "Get his clothes off, and use these sponges to clean every sign of the gas." Blisters would appear on the skin where the gas would settle. Broken bones, shrapnel, and bullet wounds were nothing compared with the effects of the gas. If the field hospital couldn't treat them, soldiers were evacuated to the base hospital many miles from the front lines. As the battle lines moved, so did the field hospital.[6]

One week at the field hospital, and Sol was ready for anything, or so he thought. The work was mind-numbing as the casualties just kept coming in. The ambulances would stop coming when the shelling started, and they couldn't bring in the casualties. During the offensive, it would take only two to three hours to get a soldier from the trenches to the field hospital, a record they were proud of. By November 11, the battle was over and so was WWI. The 17 days in Field Hospital 163 seemed like an

---

5   Medicine had not changed much since the Civil War. They had saltwater to clean the wounds but no antibiotics. Olive and castor oil were used to coat the stomach if food was eaten that had been contaminated by mustard gas. This was the first time blood transfusions were tried and the first time x-rays were used to locate bullets.

6   WWI began July 28, 1914, and ended November 11, 1918. The United States entered the war April 6, 1917. They thought they knew what they were getting into, but they were unprepared for the casualties brought on by gas warfare. Sanitary (medical) trains accompanied the battalions. When a soldier was injured, he was first treated by the battalion aid station 250 to 500 yards to the rear of the front line. Then the stretcher bearers or litter squads would take him to the ambulances no more than 1,000 yards away. Many ambulances were modified Model T Fords with the drivers in open cockpits. Some had weatherized canvas enclosures but were not gas-proof. They would then go to the dressing stations 3,000 to 6,000 feet from the front line. The next stop for the wounded was the field hospital five to eight miles back. Each sanitary train had four field hospitals that moved as the solders advanced. Each had 108 beds. Although they were several miles behind the front lines, they were still within artillery range. Each field hospital had a different function—one for the sick, another for skin or venereal diseases, another for the wounded and gassed, and the fourth reserved for convalescents. From the field hospital, casualties would be taken by train to base hospitals many miles behind the front, and, if necessary, on to a hospital ship and back to America.

eternity to Sol. His next move was Luxemburg and the Army of Occupation and the 3rd Corps Sanitary Train.

On April 18, he was en route to the United States, arriving May 8, 1919, at Camp Dix in New Jersey. Discharged May 10, 1919, Sol felt like the seven months he was gone was more like seven years. He had lost weight. That was not good, as he already was thin. He had a persistent cough and always seemed short of breath. He couldn't stop coughing up mucus. He knew he had signs of emphysema. Some called it "mustard lung." He knew there was no cure.

Real Estate Deal Gone Bad

Anna could sense that something was wrong when she and Nettie were on a shopping trip to Chicago. "Tell me what's going on, Nettie. You know you can't keep anything from me," Anna said.

"I made a decision right after Sol went overseas that it was time for me to leave East Chicago," Nettie answered. "There's really nothing here for me except you, and we can always get together. This town knows that I have the insurance money, and I feel everyone is out to get a piece of it. I can get lost in Chicago. Besides, that's where Sol has his medical practice. I've bought a lot of land here in East Chicago, and I thought I could trade it for some property in Chicago and get everything in place before Sol comes back from the War. I went to L.W. Saric and asked him to find me some property, and he did. It was a great apartment building on the South Side of Chicago owned by John Borowski. I put $500 ($6,500 in 2017 dollars) down and we both agreed on a $5,000 ($65,000 in 2017 dollars) damage clause if either of us backed out of the deal. The attorneys got involved and broke the deal for both of us. Luckily, I only lost the $500. Anna, it feels like something is keeping me here. Mamie says the drugstore building is possessed with spirits, and I'm starting to believe her."

Leon W. Saric, Realtor. *Courtesy of Calumet Regional Archives, Anderson Library, Indiana University Northwest*

"Well, I'm glad you're not leaving me. What would I do without you as my partner in the saloon? We work so well together, and things are going to go crazy with this Prohibition," Anna said.

"Yes, I guess everything works out for the best," said Nettie, with an air of resignation. "I'll see what Sol has in mind when he comes back from the war."

Sol Comes Home from the War

Nettie was waiting for Sol at the train station in Chicago. She was unprepared for what she was about to see. Getting off the train was Sol in an ill-fitting uniform with his duffle bag over his shoulder. His uniform looked two sizes too big for him.

"Nettie," he cried out, as he saw her among the crowd waiting for other soldiers coming off the train.

"Over here, Sol," was her reply as she waved her hand in the air. They found each other, he dropped his duffle bag, and they embraced. Nettie could feel something was wrong; he was skin and bones and very pale.

"Nettie, let's go into the station where we can sit down," Sol said.

"I have a better idea," she suggested. "Let's go around the corner to the café and get you something to eat. You are skin and bones." She pointed in the direction of the café.

"Good idea. I haven't eaten all day," he said. They walked around the corner, during which Sol had a coughing attack.

"Are you all right, Sol?"

"No, I don't think so. I'll tell you all about it when we sit down," he explained.

They entered the café. He put down his duffle bag and slid into the booth across from Nettie. The waiter came over and they ordered.

"I received your letters, Sol. They came in bundles of 10 at a time. I guess it was difficult mailing from the front?" Nettie tried to start the conversation.

"I didn't tell you everything in the letters. Nettie, I'll get right to the point. I'm sick. I was stationed in an area that got a lot of mustard gas. I tried to use my mask, but with so many wounded I couldn't see what I was doing. I guess I got a low dose of it. I get these coughing attacks, and I just feel run down. They say it affects everyone differently. I guess I was very sensitive to the gas. What I'm saying is, I'm not the man that left here seven months ago. Now that I'm home, there is no need for us to stay married. You're still young. You and the kids have a whole life ahead of you. I don't. Please understand, this is a gift I'm giving you. I'll give you a divorce and you can use whatever grounds you want."

"Don't say that, Sol." Nettie started to tear up. Soon tears were running down her cheeks. "Didn't we say *Tsum glik, tsum schlimazel* (for better or for worse) when we got married?"

"This is not appendicitis, Nettie. I know you saved me once. This time you can't."

"You will get better. I know it. Please say you'll stay. Let me nurse you back to health," begged Nettie.

Their food came, but neither of them had much interest in eating. They picked at the food.

"I know too much about my condition, Nettie. I will not get better, only worse. I've seen too much that I didn't tell you in my letters." He summoned the waiter for the check. When he came to the table, he said, "No check for you, sir. You saved our country from dem Germans. This is how I thank you." Sol left a large tip instead.

"Nettie, I know I'm dying. I just don't know when."

Nettie started to sob uncontrollably. *Az dos hartz iz ful, gai'en di oigen iber* (when the heart is full, the eyes overflow).

Sol moved to her side of the booth and put his arm around her. "You'll be all right. You'll find another man that can be a real husband to you and father to the kids. I'm going to check myself into Michael Reese Hospital and see what they can do for me there. I'll then get my office up and running again. I may even have a few patients that have waited for me to get back from the war. Let's get you back on the train to East Chicago. We can talk and plan our reasons for the divorce. It's not so easy with all the new laws."[7]

He escorted her out to the station where they waited for her train. They stayed huddled together in an embrace, not talking until it was time for her to board. They both knew he was right, but Nettie still felt she could somehow save him if only he would let her try. With tears streaming down both their faces, they said goodbye. Nettie didn't stop crying

---

7   Section 1a of the Revised Statutes of Illinois provided that in every case in which a divorce had been granted for any of several causes contained in Section 1 of the act, neither party shall marry again within one year from the time the decree was granted. When the cause was adultery, the person decreed guilty of adultery shall not marry for a term of two years from the granting of the decree. Imprisonment in the penitentiary for not less than one year or more than three years was the punishment if the person violated this provision, and the resulting marriage shall be held absolutely void.

until the train was at her station in East Chicago. She now knew why the real estate deal was not meant to happen.

Sol and Nettie Get Divorced

Sol checked into Michael Reese Hospital. He got the news he already knew, "mustard lung." The doctors felt that going to a better climate might be good for him and suggested California. He and Nettie talked about the story they would use to get their divorce. They decided Sol would be accused of not supporting Nettie. She would say she tried to kill him—first with a knife, then with a pistol. He would have two different patients say they witnessed the act in his home office. Everyone knew the problem with divorces in Illinois: The witnesses could use a little extra money.

Nettie got her summons and went into Chicago to the court. This was the first time she had seen Sol since the train station. Sol looked worse now than when she saw him getting off the train. "Sol, do you still want to go through with the divorce?"

"It's for the best, Nettie. I have two of my patients willing to testify. Now get your mean face on. Remember, you want to kill me." They both had a laugh.

Two months later, Nettie got the papers that the divorce was official. Sol stayed in Chicago for the next year. He heard that Nettie had gotten married again. It was time to try California, where he got his license to practice in 1921. By September of 1921, Sol was back in Chicago at Walter Reed Hospital for his lung condition. He had surgery on September 14 and died November 2, 1921.

CHAPTER 9

Joseph Finkelstein, Mariampole 1897

The day before the mob attacked Nettie and Moshe's house, Joseph had met with some of the local people who were bent on causing some kind of trouble for the Jews. The local government officials were being pressured by the Tsar to show their support for the laws that were meant to keep the Jews in line. Joseph had dressed in peasant clothing. He could pass for a peasant if he wanted. There was a reward waiting for him if he could get the mob to do some damage to a Jewish merchant. Joseph couldn't forget that Nettie turned him down for Moshe. He thought that it was all about money and that he didn't have any. Moshe's business would be the target. The mob was easy to convince. If the money lender was gone, so would be their debts to him. In his twisted logic, Joseph thought if Moshe was out of the way, then Nettie would be his. He was given a gun by the official, who said, "Use this if you want. No one will be upset if some Jews are killed."

The Night of the Attack

That night, the mob gathered outside of Moshe's house and started throwing rocks at the windows. It quickly escalated. Joseph made sure they had plenty of liquor before this began. When they pushed in the front door, they didn't expect Moshe would have a gun. Joseph had given his gun to one of the peasants he knew would use it. Joseph wasn't about to be in harm's way. He moved to the side of the building to let the mob do its work. After the gunfire was over, Moshe and the peasant were lying dead on the floor. Joseph entered with the mob to ransack the house. He looked everywhere for money and precious stones. He knew they were there but couldn't find a thing.

"Set the house on fire!" he shouted to the mob in his frustration. They did just that.

Joseph Goes to Collect His Reward

The next morning when the smoke cleared, he reported to the government official to get his reward. He got less than a cordial welcome. "Where's that money you said was in the house?"

"I didn't find any, sir. I looked, and then the mob burned down the house."

"Are you sure you didn't find anything, you little Jew weasel? If you're holding out on me, you will regret it," he said.

"Honest, I didn't find nothing,'" Joseph replied.

"What about his wife, mother, and mother-in-law? Where are they?" the official asked.

"Don't know, sir. Maybe left town?"

"You can bet they have the money with them. You won't get a ruble from me until they are back here to pay the price for killing one of our citizens. You know that man had a wife and six children. What will become of them?"

Joseph kept his head down and didn't say a word. Inside, he was burning up with anger at having been cheated out of his reward money.

"I'm sending the police and some army officers to get those Jews back. Find out who helped them and what Jews are missing in this town."

"Yes, sir." Joseph was angry at the official but dared not show it. He went back on his word. He could do nothing about it.

It wasn't long before Joseph tracked down the missing people. He knew Nettie's friends. Neche, Anna's father, was taken into custody to answer questions. Luckily he had the money Nettie gave him to bribe the officials and was soon back home. The Okhama, the Russian secret police, were now on the trail to find them.

The Escape from Mariampole

The head start the group had leaving in the middle of the night was enough to make it difficult for them to be found. Daniel, using all his skills from his time in the army, helped keep them safe. Using the back roads gave them plenty of places to hide, and they would be seen by fewer people. With just two people visible in the wagon, they were less conspicuous, as the police were looking for six people.

The police called upon a unit of Cossacks from the army. They were much faster and better at a chase than any army unit. When they passed the group, Daniel knew they were hot on their trail. His hope was that they would not double back but look for them on another road. His instinct to not move but hide in the woods worked this time. Their next stop was to be Bialystok. Here they would take the train to Hamburg. The police staked out the train station. With their change of clothes and splitting into three different groups, the fugitives managed to avoid being caught. Hamburg was the last hurdle.

By staying inside their rented rooms and taking on other identities, they again slipped by the authorities. Nettie, posing as a boy, confused the police, as they were looking for a woman, not a boy.

Joseph the Traitor

It didn't take long for the Jews in Mariampole to identify Joseph as the traitor in their midst. This time he had gone too far, and every door was closed to him and his family. The community shunned them and stopped all the sources of charity. They had no choice but to leave town. This wasn't the first time the family was run out of a town. This time would be different. Joseph convinced his father, Reuben, that it was time to go to America. A part of him was still longing for Nettie. That's where she had to have been headed. He would go too.

They bought steerage tickets for the nine of them. The children all thought this would be a great adventure, going to America. They passed through Immigration at The Battery in New York City. There was a German interpreter to help them change their name to Diamond. Yiddish was very close to German, and *Finkelstein* in Old German is *diamond* in English.[1]

The family got to New York shortly after Nettie and her group of "fugitives" had arrived. It didn't take long for Joseph and his father to find the Monk Eastman Gang on the Lower East Side. Joseph was too young for the gang but worked the juvenile gangs stealing from pushcarts, extorting money from store owners, and practicing *schlamming*

---

1 Finkelstein is the Yiddish word *funk*, meaning sparkle stone, or diamond.

(using an iron pipe wrapped in newspaper against striking workers or scabs). He quickly learned the words pimp (*simcha*), detective (*shamus*), and loafer (*trombenik*). His father, Reuben, learned about racketeering, prostitution, and narcotics. His specialties were arson, burglaries, and fencing stolen goods.

Defrauding the insurance companies was an easy way for the mob to make money. Joseph also acted as a lookout and shill for the three-card Monte game.[2]

After several years, Reuben and Joseph had saved enough money for the family to leave New York and try their newfound skills in a different town. Louisville, Kentucky, was their next stop. They knew of an extended family member already in the town. He would help them. The established Jewish population in Louisville had come from Germany and looked down on these new immigrants from Eastern Europe. Most of them settled around the Preston Street area. Here, Joseph and his dad set up a pawn shop on Preston Street.

Within a year, Joseph married Esther Brown. Their first child, a boy, was born on Christmas Day 1898. They named him Harry. In April of 1901, Joseph was charged with stealing eggs and a chicken from John Willard's store. The case was dropped due to lack of evidence—the family had eaten it. Things were tough for the family. With Esther and now baby Harry, there were more mouths to feed. The family applied to The National Council of Jewish Women for help. They also asked for help from a social service agency called the Neighborhood House.

In 1902, they were living at 535 E. Madison, just a few blocks from their pawn shop on the corner of Preston and Billy Goat Strut Alley. The pawn shop was a great front for fencing stolen goods. Reuben and Joseph's apprenticeships in New York came in handy. Many of the tricks they used in New York were foreign to these new immigrants in Louisville.

Joseph's family quickly grew, with a baby every other year: Rebecca, Lena, Fannie, and David. In 1909, Joseph was sued by four companies: Brinkhaus & Block, J.M. Robinson, Norton & Company, and Falls City Clothing Company. The suits were for over $180 ($4,853 in 2017 dollars). The courts seized their house to pay off the debts.

In 1911, now without their house, the growing family had to move back in with Reuben and Joseph's mother Leah and his brothers and sisters. They all needed larger quarters,

---

2   A shell game using cards. The victim thinks he can find a specific face-down card. The dealer knows he can't. The dealer uses confederates in the crowd. Sleight of hand is always employed.

and everyone moved to 936 Jefferson, about five blocks away. This same year, their sixth child, a son Julius, was born.

Joseph felt his run here in Louisville was over. It was time to move on. Reuben had kept in touch with a fellow Monk Eastman Gang member, Abe Rosen. Abe had a furniture store in Gary, Indiana, which he used as a front for a number of illegal activities. Abe had told Reuben that if he ever wanted to join forces, they would make a good team. There was a growing Jewish community in Gary, where a large steel mill had just been built. The area was exploding with an increase in population to work in the steel mills and the oil refineries in the area. A place where there were a lot of new immigrants was just the spot for Reuben and Joseph to make some money. Teaming up with Abe would be a winning combination.

The Diamond Family Moves to Gary

Abe—a man about five-foot-six with a medium build, blue eyes, and dark hair—was there to greet them as they got off the train. He had found them a rental house at 630 Broadway. It was the main boulevard running through the center of town in Gary.

Harry was 14 and was enrolled as a student at Froebel High School, which had just opened in 1909. It had special courses for immigrants. He also took classes at Emerson High.

Joseph took a job at a men's clothing store, and Reuben went to work with Abe at the furniture store. This would give them time together to plot their various scams. Joseph would be part of the team when needed.

Harry got a job after school at Goodman's Department Store. He soon lost the job after he was caught stealing clothes. He argued that he was just trying them on for size and forgot he had them on, but he couldn't explain why he was wearing them under his current clothes.

By 1915, Joseph's debtors had found him. On February 3, on Abe's advice, he filed for bankruptcy. In April of 1916, Joseph noticed an article in the local paper, "Prominent physician dies after ulcer operation." This doctor was from East Chicago, the next neighboring town to the west. It said his widow had an insurance policy worth $100,000 ($2.6 million in 2017 dollars).

"Boy, would I like to get my hands on some of that money," he remarked at the dinner table that night. "It says the widow's name is Nettie." *I wonder if that's the same Nettie I knew in Lithuania?* he thought to himself.

Harry Diamond high school graduation, 1917 yearbook. *Courtesy of Calumet Regional Archives, Indiana University Northwest*

Harry Graduates and Looks for a Job

Harry graduated from both Emerson High (May 1916) and Frobel High (January 1917). In the Emerson yearbook, it showed he was in the senior play, oratorical and commercial clubs, and chorus. It said his favorite work was dodging Miss Lynch. (Miss Lynch was Louise Elinor Lynch, head of the Department of Expression.) He was surely skipping class. In the Frobel yearbook, he was in similar activities. Under future, it said "Undecided." It also said Harry had a very high opinion of himself.

When Harry graduated, he was 18 years old, five-foot-ten, 160 pounds, with hazel eyes and jet black hair. He looked nothing like his father, who was just over five feet tall and very stout. Harry decided to try law school. At that time, you could enter with a high school diploma. He entered Valparaiso University for two months. He quit because he said there wasn't enough money in law. Besides, he thought he was smarter than most of his professors.

Instead, he got a job at Inland Steel, like so many of his fellow graduates. He was working in the tin plating plant. On one occasion, he inhaled sulfuric acid fumes from the plating process and had to be hospitalized. It was then that he was treated for epileptic seizures at the Mayo Clinic in Minnesota. That was the last time he worked at the mill.

On September 12, 1918, all able-bodied men had to register for the draft for WWI. Harry was rejected because of his accident at the plant. He had a doctor's note that said the accident had affected his lungs.

CHAPTER 10

Joseph Meets Anna and Nettie

The start of Prohibition was an opening for organized crime to have another opportunity to make money. Abe and Reuben saw this as another business that they would add to their growing list of illegal activities. They opened "The Standard Bottling Company" in 1919. They had a permit for 573 gallons of alcohol each year, and they knew just how to use it. They would use the alcohol to dilute the branded whiskeys to stretch them farther and make a bigger profit.

Abe and Reuben called a meeting with Joseph to get him to be part of their new endeavor. "Joseph, we want you to go to all the saloons and drugstores in the area and introduce them to our new bottling company," said Reuben. "Tell them we will supply them with ice and anything else they need in the way of beverages. Abe and I have the mayor and police chief in our pocket. You can tell them so that they know they will be safe only if they buy from us. You can get Harry to help with the deliveries."

Joseph's first stop in Indiana Harbor was the Auditorium Saloon, now a speakeasy. They gave the liquor away for the price of their entertainment. The new law banned the manufacture, sale, and transportation of alcoholic beverages but not the consumption of alcohol. They got around the sale issue by giving it away for the price of the entertainment.

Anna also had a drawer installed in the wall for blind tiger sales.[1]

Joseph and his bottling company were breaking the law when they transported their alcoholic beverages. Joseph entered the speakeasy. It was about 11 a.m., and no customers were present—just Hal, behind the bar.

"I'm looking for the owner," Joseph said. "I represent a new bottling company here in town, and I vould like to get your business."

"Just a minute," Hal said. "I'll get her from the office."

Get "her" from the office? Could this owner be a voman? Joseph wondered.

Hal went the length of the bar and entered a room behind it. The office had a one-way glass mirror, so Anna could see everything happening in the bar. "There's a guy out here that wants to see you. He said he's from The Standard Bottling Company here in the Harbor."

Anna came out of the office. Even in the dim light, she recognized Joseph as the same Joseph Finkelstein from her hometown in Lithuania. He didn't recognize her, as she had changed from that little skinny girl in Lithuania. As the owner-operator of the speakeasy, she was no longer the shy young girl from Mariampole.

"What's your name?" she asked, with a tone of authority.

"Joseph Diamond," he replied.

She was a head taller than him and now felt she towered over this little man. "Nice to meet you, Joseph. I understand you have just started The Standard Bottling Company here in the Harbor."

"That's right, madam. Ve have all the latest equipment for making da ice and beverages."

"Who's the owner?" she asked.

"My father, Reuben Diamond, and Abe Rosen."

---

1   Speakeasies (usually identified with green doors) were places where you could buy alcoholic beverages. The blind tiger or blind pig was a method of paying for your drink without seeing the seller. The customer would put his money in a drawer, close it, and ask "the wall" for his drink. The drawer would reopen, and there would be his drink. This bootleg alcohol could be dangerous, as it often contained creosote, lead toxins, and even embalming fluid. This could cause paralysis, blindness, and death. The speakeasy was also the place you would find "flappers." Six months after the passage of Prohibition, the 19th Amendment was passed, giving women the right to vote. This also "liberated" women to some extent. The flappers were women who smoked cigarettes, drank cocktails, wore short skirts and no corsets, and had bobbed hair. They could dance the night away doing the Charleston, Tango, Quick Step, and Black Bottom dances.

Anna knew anything connected with Abe Rosen was not on the up and up. She was used to working with the people just on the edge of the legal system now that Prohibition was in force. Maybe a local dealer would be safer than the guys out of Chicago, she thought.

Joseph had a feeling that he knew this lady from somewhere but could not connect the dots. Anna sensed this and decided to end his puzzled look. "Your real name was Joseph Finkelstein," she said. "You lived in Mariampole, Lithuania."

Something clicked in Joseph's head. Anna could see it in his eyes. "You're Anna Kalish, aren't you?"

"I was, but now I'm Anna Cohen. I can say I'm really *not* glad to see you."

"*Vos ret ir epes* (what are you talking about)?" said Joseph, as he slipped into Yiddish. "I've left all my old life in the old country and started a new life here. I'm married and have seven children. I'm just trying to make an honest living. Can't ve let bygones ve bygones?" Joseph asked.

"A leopard doesn't change his spots, but I'm willing to give your company a try," said Anna.

"I can tell you," Joseph said, "that you von't ve having any trouble vith de police if you buy from us. Ve've got Mayor Frank Callahan and Police Chief O'Donnell on our payroll." Joseph knew this would seal the deal.

"Will you be doing all the deliveries?" Anna asked.

"No, my son Harry vill take over once I develop da route. Vhatever happened to that friend of yours, Nettie Sachs?" asked Joseph.

"Funny you should ask. She owns a drugstore in Calumet that I'm sure is on your list. I don't think she will give you a very warm welcome."

"Is she the Nettie Herskovitz vet lost her doctor husband a few years ago? I think I saw an article in the *Twin City Sentinel*."

"Yes, that's her." *Good luck with that visit*, she thought, as Joseph turned to leave.

"Ve vill set you up for Monday deliveries. Ice, beverages, and any hooch you vant. You vill get to meet my son Harry."

Anna Tells Nettie about Joseph

That afternoon when Nettie came by the saloon, Anna gave her the news. "Guess who I saw today, Nettie? Someone out of our past."

"I haven't a clue, Anna. Who is it?" Nettie asked.

"Joseph Finkelstein. He was setting up a route for The Standard Bottling Company. He's now Joseph Diamond, is married, and has seven children. He'll be coming by your drugstore any day now to sell his liquor and ice. I thought you should be ready for him."

"I hope he doesn't think there is a price on our heads for what happened the night we left town. Knowing that *farbrecher* (con man), he would turn us in to the authorities if he thought there was any money in it," Nettie warned.

Joseph Thinks about Nettie and Her Money

Joseph didn't know how, but he smelled the money and wanted a piece of it, if not all of it. He knew Nettie was a widow. *Maybe this is my opportunity*, he thought. *For the money, I would divorce Esther in a New York minute.*

Joseph Meets Nettie

Nettie didn't have to wait long. Two days later, she got a message from the drugstore downstairs that there was a man from The Standard Bottling Company who wanted to see her. Nettie had a provision in the lease that gave her control of the vendors used in the drugstore. She and Anna tried to use the same ones when it came to alcohol. It was legal to buy it for the drugstore, and sometimes she shared her supply with Anna's saloon.

Nettie was ready for her meeting with Joseph. She entered the drugstore through the back door from Sam's old office. She saw Joseph at the counter before he saw her. Memories of their time in Mariampole flashed through her head. She could hear the crowd yelling outside their house and see the last image of Joseph handing off a gun to a rioter. She could not forget those narrow-set eyes with the eyebrows that almost touched each other.

Like Anna, she was a full head taller than him. It gave her a sense of power over him. She quickly regained her composure.

"Hello, Nettie," he said, as he extended his hand over the counter. She didn't take it. "I understand," he said. "I apologize for everything in da past, Nettie. I'm a changed man here in America. *A nei'er bezim kert gut* (a new broom sweeps clean)."

"*Tsu vos men iz gevoint in der yugend, azoi tut men oif der elter* (that which is practiced in youth will be pursued in old age)," Nettie answered. She continued, "*Gai feifen ahfen yam* (Go peddle your fish elsewhere)!"

"Von't you give me a chance to make dings right, Nettie?" Joseph was almost begging for forgiveness, but he didn't know she saw him hand off the gun that killed her husband.

"*Ven dos harts iz bitter, helft nit kain tusker* (when the heart is bitter, sugar won't help)," she replied.

"Look, I'll make vou a deal. Let me deliver just ice to start, and maybe soft drinks. Den ve can talk about da alcohol. Anna Cohen is letting me make deliveries to her place. Vhat do vou say?"

She saw he wasn't going to go away. *Just maybe America had changed him some*, she thought. "OK, we'll put in an order for ice and soft drinks and see how that goes."

"Oh, tank vou so much, Nettie. You von't regret it. You vill see a changed Joseph." With that, he exited the drugstore backward, bowing toward Nettie as he left.

"What was that all about?" R.H. Canan, the druggist, asked.

"Just someone from my hometown wanting a helping hand. Keep an eye on him, R.H. He was a thief in the old country. Can't see how he would change," Nettie warned him.

CHAPTER 11

Harry Courts Nettie

That night after dinner, Joseph took Harry into the bedroom to have a private talk. "What's this all about, Pop?"

"Listen to me, and listen close, Harry. Dis caper could set us all up for life. You're going to be 21 dis December. I tink it's time for you to get married."

"Married?" *Why is my father trying to dictate my life?* thought Harry.

"You may not know it, Harry, but you have da looks veman love. You've got 'it' (sex appeal), so you got to use it. I'm not talkin' 'bout the vemans at Buconich's place in South Chicago. Dose are flappers. Dey easy. I'm talkin' 'bout a real classy vomen vit money."

Pop always had plans for him, and Harry never let him down. He had this strange power over Harry all his life, or maybe Harry just wanted to please his father.

"I met me a vidow today that I knew in da old country. She owns a drugstore over in da Calumet Region of East Chicago. Her old man left her with 100,000 smackers. It's going to be your job to get her to marry you."

"So I have to marry an old dame?" Harry asked.

"That's right, an old dame with 100,000 bucks. Besides, she's a looker. I tink she's only 34."

"Does she have nice gams?" Harry asked, trying to act like he was buying merchandise.

"I don't know nothin' about her legs, but she's a real *Sheba* (a woman with sex appeal). She's no flapper. She's a ritzy dame and not a pushover. Here's da plan. First, I vill go vith you on our first delivery and I vill introduce you. After that I vant you to take her flowers every time you go and try to get her to go out vith you. Tell her how young she looks. That's what dem dames vant to hear, how beautiful dey are."

"But, Pop, all I have is an old Tin Lizzie."

"I vill get Abe to let you use his Hudson, and you can take her to Chicago to one of dem cabarets. Don't you have some connections with 'Diamond Louie' Cowan?"

"Yeah, he's the guy I fence diamonds for. I meet him at the Morrison Hotel."

"Vell next time you're dere, ask him about the classiest place to take a dame in Chicago. If you run short of jack (money), we can hit up Rosen for a loan. I don't vant her to think you're a piker (cheapskate). Once ve get control of the drugstore, ve vill have an easy outlet for our hooch."

"OK, Pop, the game is on." Harry was ready.

Harry Meets Nettie

"Ms. Nettie, dey says dey's be needin' you to come downstairs. Da beverage man and his son be there."

"OK, Mamie. Just let me put something nice on." Nettie went to her armoire and picked out a spring dress to wear downstairs. This first week in June, the spring-like weather was perfect for the dress.

When she got downstairs, she entered through the back office. She could see at the front of the store a young man with Joseph. As she came closer, she saw a dashing young man, five-foot-ten with jet black hair and hazel eyes. She was mesmerized.

"Hello, Nettie," Joseph said. She barely heard him and didn't look his way. "Dis is my son, Harry. He vill be making your deliveries." Harry extended his hand toward Nettie. This time, Nettie reached her arm and hand over the counter.

Harry accepted it and cradled her hand in both of his. "So pleased to meet you, Ms. Nettie. Pop has told me so much about you, but he didn't tell me how beautiful you were."

Nettie could feel the warmth of the blood rushing to her face, the blush giving a natural color to her cheeks. "Why, thank you, Harry. Such a nice compliment."

Nettie was feeling something she hadn't felt since Sam died. She thought all those emotions had died with him, but they hadn't. She was still alive. She had never gotten these feelings with Sol Golden. This Harry fellow was almost the same age as Sam was when she married him in 1908.

"I got your order right here. Where shall I put it?" Harry asked.

"You can take the ice down to the basement and put it in the ice box at the bottom of the stairs. You can leave the beverages up here behind the counter." She watched as he lifted the block of ice with the tongs and could imagine the muscles on his arms and back flexing with the load. He was back up the stairs from the basement in a flash.

"All done, Ms. Nettie. See you again next week," he said, as he turned to leave. She thought he winked at her but wasn't sure.

Nettie couldn't wait to compare notes with Anna. That afternoon, she went over to the saloon on the Indiana Harbor side of town and discussed this Harry fellow over a cocktail in Anna's back office. "Have you seen Harry, Joseph's son?" Nettie asked.

"Yes, he made their first delivery today," said Anna.

"What did you think of him, Anna? Did you get a look at those hazel eyes?" Nettie asked.

"You're sounding like a schoolgirl, Nettie. I think he put a spell or something on you. You're acting like you're 20 years old with a crush on a boy. Do you even know how old he is?" asked Anna.

"I think in his 20s," answered Nettie.

"You turned 34 this year. That makes you almost old enough to be his mother," Anna said.

"That may be true, Anna. Maybe I've been without a man too long to take me places and show me a good time. Raising four kids, even with Mamie's help, is a full-time job and takes all my energy," Nettie said, looking exhausted.

"I'd be a little cautious, Nettie. You know me, always looking for problems, and you're always jumping in without knowing how deep the water is. You know the saying 'the apple falls not far from the tree,' and you know about his father," cautioned Anna.

"Maybe I should be careful, but if he asks me out I'm going to go," said Nettie.

"What if we go on a double date? That would be safer," suggested Anna. "It'll be like old times when we were in New York. Did I tell you that one of my boarders, Morris Fishman, asked me out? He was a union organizer in New York before he came to town. He's been one of my boarders for the past year."

"I suppose he's your age?" Nettie asked, with a quizzical look on her face.

"OK, he's 10 years younger. I guess I can't say anything about Harry," said Anna.

"I'll let you know what happens with Harry. Hope it's soon," Nettie replied, with an air of anticipation. With that, Nettie left with an almost skip in her step.

Anna watched her go and shook her head. *The old Nettie is back, getting into trouble without knowing it*, thought Anna.

Nettie was right. It wasn't long before Harry asked her to go out with him. Harry thought the flowers each week and the candy were the reason. They weren't. Nettie had a crush. She called Anna, even though she knew the operator was listening in. Nettie said, "Anna, he asked me out. I told him you and Morris would have to come too. We're going to Jim Colosimo's on South Wabash Avenue in Chicago. Let's take a shopping trip first."

Nettie knew the message would be all over town, but she didn't care. Fun was coming back into her life. The girls went shopping and got the latest clothes in fashion. They even had their hair cut a little shorter, but not bobbed. While in Chicago, she visited with her stockbroker at Redmand & Massey. She had been buying stock since September of 1917 after Sam had died. The insurance money was being put to good use. She didn't trust the banks and had many accounts in Chicago as well as East Chicago.

It was almost time for Harry to pick up Nettie and go across town to pick up Anna and Morris. "My, Ms. Nettie, you is lookin' like da cat's meow," Mamie exclaimed. "Now you be careful out there. Tings be different now dan when Dr. Sam was alive. You knows Ms. Mamie gets da feelings, so you bes' be careful."

"My first really big night out in three years. You're right, lots has changed but I'll be careful."

Harry came up the stairs on the Chicago Avenue side of the building and knocked on the inside door. Mamie opened it, and a chill went down her spine. She knew evil when she felt it. She would not say anything to Nettie. "Yous must be Mr. Harry. Ms. Nettie be right out."

Nettie came around the corner, and Harry let out a whistle. "You're *farpitza* (all dressed up). You look like a doll," Harry said.

Nettie, always one for fashion, had a dress that almost showed her knees, with a feather boa around her neck. She truly looked like the bee's knees. She took his arm, and they were off to pick up Anna and Morris and then on to Chicago. Abe Rosen had lent Harry his Hudson, so they were riding in style.

First Date: A Night on the Town

They pulled up to Colosimo's restaurant at 2126 S. Wabash, and Harry gave the attendant $2 ($28 in 2017 dollars). The whole group piled out of the car and into the restaurant. When they entered, the maître d' said, "Right this way, Mr. Diamond. Mr. Colosimo has a special table reserved just for you."

Harry felt like a big shot. His mentor, Diamond Louie, said he would set things up for him, and he did. In the corner was a small band with a stage less than a foot above the dance floor. Before they finished eating, the band began to play and people got up to dance. They had a bottle of wine at their table. This loosened everyone up a bit till they were all on the dance floor. The girls were new at these dances, so Harry became the instructor. Soon they were doing the fox trot to the tune "Dardanella." They even tried the Charleston and the Black Bottom dances. The band played the "St. Louis Blues," which held so many memories for Nettie. It brought back the thought of little Edward Noah, who turned 14 this year. The sentimental tune "After You've Gone" led to some slow dancing. She could feel Harry's lean body press into hers. *This is going too fast*, she thought. *Oh, what the hell.*

They danced and drank until midnight. Then there was the ride home. Before she knew it, they had dropped off Anna and Morris and were upstairs at the door to the apartment. "I'd ask you in Harry, but everyone's asleep."

"That's OK, doll. I gotta hit the road. How about a *cash* (kiss) before I go?" He leaned down and Nettie kissed him on the lips, first quickly. Then she kissed him back a second time, only longer. Then he was off. Nettie went to bed with many dreams to sort through.

The morning found Nettie in very good spirits. Mamie noticed it right away. She didn't want to say anything. After all, Nettie was her employer. What right did she have talking about her man?

Harry was a frequent visitor. Each week they always seemed to have something to do together. Nettie tried to slow things down, but Harry was persistent. Nettie and Anna got to see the Green Mill Jazz Club and meet Jack "Machine Gun" McGurn, the owner. Club Lucky had a hardware store front to disguise the speakeasy downstairs. Anna was a bit worried. *How does Harry know all these thugs?* she wondered. They were nice enough when they met them, but she knew their business was not about being nice.

Dora and Her Dolls

"You playin' wit dem dolls again?" Joseph asked, with some trepidation. He knew how sensitive Dora was about this subject. This time she wasn't.

"I have a new doll now." She held it out to him. It was a doll fashioned in the likeness of a young crooner. "This is the next man in Nettie's life. She has been without Sam for almost three years now, so it's time. I want her to find a man that will steal her heart and then lose him, just like she stole Sam from me. I want to break her heart for the rest of her life."

Joseph knew she was serious, as she had never given up on this fixation with Sam and Nettie. He had gotten used to the candles and knew there would be no peace until she got her wish.

Unrest in the City and Nation

July 27, 1919, a race riot started in Chicago. A black swimmer, 17-year-old Eugene Williams, floated into the white section of the beach on Lake Michigan and was stoned to death by the white mob. They would not allow his friends to come to his aid. The riot continued into the Negro district of Chicago by white gangs. It didn't end until August 3, when the governor called up the state militia. In the end, 23 African-Americans and 15 whites were killed and 525 people were injured.

Labor Unrest in America

At almost the same time as the riot, the streetcar and elevated-train workers went out on strike. Some tied the country's labor unrest to the success of the Bolshevik communists in Russia, led by Vladimir Lenin. This movement gave voice to many sympathizers in the labor movement, and the U.S. government was worried. The country had let so many immigrants in over the last 30 years that they were outnumbering Americans. The labor movement seemed to be an attraction for these immigrants. They worked long hours in dismal conditions. All this made a time ripe for revolution, and the government knew it.

On September 11, 1919, the steel workers went on strike around the country as well as in East Chicago and Gary. Working seven days a week for 12-hour shifts alone was enough to incite unrest. The unions did the rest. The steel mills were determined to stop the strike and kill the union movement. They used everything in their power to do so.

On October 4, the mills brought in Mexican and black workers to try to break the strike. This is the same day a strikebreaker was shot and killed. Violence was in the air. The mayor of East Chicago was sympathetic to the workers and held off asking the governor to send in the state militia, but in two days he did.

On October 6, the militia and some regular Army troops descended on both East Chicago and Gary. The towns were now under martial law, with curfews in place. Many people in militant groups were picked up and jailed.

The Courtship Continues

None of these events slowed down the courtship of Harry and Nettie. The influx of Mexicans to work in the steel mills provided Harry's father another means of income. He would frequent the bars in Gary on Pennsylvania Avenue by the railroad tracks. When meeting many of the Mexican workers, he would get them drunk and then find out if they were citizens. If illegal aliens, he would blackmail them by threatening to turn them over to the authorities for deportation back to Mexico. This turned into a steady source of income for the family.

The World Series of 1919

October 9 was the last game of the World Series, between the Cincinnati Reds and the Chicago White Socks. The two couples went to the game at Comiskey Park. "I've got a lot of money riding on this game, Nettie, and I really want to see it," said Harry.

Nettie knew Harry was into gambling. Although it was illegal, he always found a way to place a bet.

"Not many times does a 'sure thing' happen, and this is one time Harry is in on it," he said.

"What do you mean?" asked Nettie.

"My grandfather knows some guys in New York who know Arnold Rothstein, a big shot with the Jewish mob.[1] They say he's paid some Chicago players to throw the game. If I win, you'll see me with a new Hudson."

Cincinnati was ahead in the series, four games to three.[2] Chicago could tie the series or give it to Cincinnati if they lost. Game eight started with Cincinnati getting four runs in the first inning. Chicago got one in the third. Cincinnati got one in the fifth and three in the sixth. The score was now 9-1. In the eighth inning, Chicago came alive and scored four runs, but Cincinnati scored one more, making the score 10-5. That's how it ended. Cincinnati won the series, five games to three.

---

1   It was true. In September of 1920, the feds found out the game was fixed by Arnold Rothstein. He was the son of a rich man, and he was able to consolidate organized crime in New York by getting the Italians, Irish, and Jews together to form a larger organization. Eight players for the White Sox were indicted, but all were found not guilty. They were, however, banned from baseball for life. For a while, the team was referred to as the Black Sox.

2   Although almost all World Series competitions have been played in a best-of-seven format, the 1919 World Series was a best-of-nine format (as were the Series in 1903, 1920, and 1921).

"You did it, Harry!" Nettie said. "You won!"

"Ab-so-lute-ly! Whoopee, finally my luck has changed!" said Harry. "I'm going to be living on easy street. You're looking at the owner of a new 1920 Hudson!"

Late in 1919, Johnny "The Brain" Torrio, cousin of Al Capone, asked Al to come to Chicago. He was to help in the business, as Frank Yale was having trouble with a murder charge. Capone was to organize his criminal gang to take over all the illegal liquor sales in the Chicago area. Joseph and his father knew of Capone in New York City. They were not pleased that they would have to deal with him in East Chicago. Abe Rosen and his group did not have the muscle to stand up to Capone, so they were pleased that Capone was staying on the Illinois side and not coming over to Indiana, at least for now.

December 25 was Harry's 21st birthday. He said it was his 23rd. Nettie was going to take him out for a change, but most places were closed on Christmas Day. The exception was West Hammond, just over the Indiana state line in Illinois.[3] The four of them hit the speakeasies and gambling tables. They all had a swell time.

After 10 weeks, the strike ended on January 8, 1920, without a clear winner. It did, however, set back the union movement until the 1930s.

A week before the strike ended, there was a nationwide crackdown on Bolsheviks and communists in America. Several groups were found, and hundreds of people were arrested. In northwest Indiana, the "Calumet raid" found 17 people who were picked up for subversive activity.

Harry Proposes to Nettie

January 16, 1920: The Volstead Act was now law, and the states and federal government had the means to enforce the 18th Amendment and Prohibition. The roaring '20s were just beginning, and the consumption of alcohol increased in spite of Prohibition.

It was New Year's Eve when Harry proposed to Nettie. "Nettie, I can't tell you how much you mean to me. These past six months have just flown by. I want it to last the rest of my life. Will you marry me?"

---

3   West Hammond was in Illinois just over the state line from Indiana, only 30 minutes from downtown Chicago. It gained the reputation as a "Sin City," where gambling, prostitution, and illegal booze were available. When Capone came to town, he further developed this area for his illegal operations. The people in West Hammond were so affected by its reputation that they changed the city name to Calumet City in 1923.

"Harry," Nettie said, "I've had a wonderful time. You've shown me things in Chicago that I never knew existed. I need to think about marrying again. I don't seem to have much luck in that department, and I don't want another disappointment. Give me a week. We can talk about it again next weekend."

"OK, doll. I don't want to rush you," replied Harry.

Anna and Nettie Discuss the Proposal

"Anna, Harry asked me to marry him the other night. I don't know if it was the booze talking or if he really meant it, but he says he's serious."

"You had better think about this long and hard, Nettie. He's more than 10 years younger than you, and you have four children. You know his family background and all his connections with shady figures, and still you want to spend the rest of your life with him? Are you sure he's not a forty-niner (a male gold digger)?"

"If it was the money, don't you think he would have had me pick up all the checks? No, I think he really loves me. He would be good with the kids, I know it," reasoned Nettie.

"Far be it for me to ever tell you what NOT to do, Nettie. Just remember things are not always what they appear. Nettie, before you do anything you may regret, why don't you see a lawyer and get something in writing that Harry can't get at your money even though you two are married," Anna cautioned her.

Nettie had made up her mind. She was tired of living without a husband. It was a man's world, and she couldn't participate without a husband. This younger guy really brought out the girl in her, and she liked it. *Next weekend, I will say yes,* thought Nettie, *but first, I will see my lawyer.*

The Wedding

The wedding was held by the justice of the peace in Waukegan, Illinois, January 29, 1920. Harry picked Waukegan because there was no waiting period and he didn't want Nettie to get cold feet and not go through with the wedding. His mother's sister and brother-in-law lived in Waukegan, and they would witness the wedding. It was one of those cold days during a Chicago winter. Nettie wore her full-length fur coat.

Before the ceremony started, Nettie had a paper for Harry to sign and the justice of the peace to notarize. "What's this paper all about, Nettie?" Harry asked.

Marriage license, Harry and Nettie, January 29, 1920. *Courtesy of ancestry.com.*

"It's called an antenuptial agreement. It's a lot like a *ketubah*.[4] For the sake of the children, my lawyer said you need to sign it before we get married."

Harry had heard of a *ketubah*, but he wasn't ready to stop the marriage. He had gotten her this close. He wasn't going to blow it. "OK, Nettie, where do I sign?"

She could tell he was a little upset but eager to get on with the marriage. "Right on this line, Harry, and the notary signs here." She pointed to the lines for both men to sign and the notary to sign and stamp. This was easier than she thought, but then Anna and the

---

4 A Hebrew marriage contract dating back 2,000 years. Most reflect on a couple's commitment to love and honor each other. Some *ketubahs* discuss the trousseau and other financial aspects of the marriage.

lawyer had Nettie's and the children's interests at heart. *What if I were to die? Would I want Harry to be in charge of my children and all of my estate?* The answer in her head was no.

The marriage license showed Harry listing his age as 23. (He was really 21.) Nettie listed herself as 24. (She was really 34.) Taking years off her age was nothing new to Nettie. She knew it would be difficult to explain her age since Pearle, her eldest child with Sam, was now 10 years old. Harry didn't seem too interested in the subject, so she just let it drop.

The wedding was on a Thursday, so the weekend crowd was not around when they drove south back to Chicago from Waukegan. They checked into the Morrison Hotel and celebrated with dinner at the Terrace Garden Restaurant.[5] The hotel reminded her of the Astor Hotel in New York City.

They checked in as Mr. and Mrs. Diamond, something Nettie would have to get used to. The bellman took their luggage to their deluxe bedroom suite at the top of the hotel, the 21st floor. They had a magnificent view of both the city and Lake Michigan. They quickly dressed for dinner. The Terrace Garden Restaurant was on the first floor. It offered patrons live music and dancing with their lavish meals. The restaurant was built in a semicircle.

There were seven levels. The lowest level was the dance floor. Each level was defined by a white pillared railing. The chandeliers above the diners were adorned with flowers that hung luxuriously down over their edges, looking like grapes from a Roman orgy. Harry slipped the doorman a clam ($1, equal to $13 in 2017 dollars), and they got a table on the dance floor. The restaurant had one of the best jazz bands in Chicago. After dinner, they danced the night away.

When they returned to their room, Nettie could see out the window that the moon was half full. Its light sparkled off the nearly 6 inches of snow that had fallen the week before. It was a cold night, only 10 degrees, and Nettie could see both the waves and pieces of ice on the shore of a cold Lake Michigan. The Morrison was one of the first hotels in the

---

5   The Morrison Hotel was first built as a four-story structure in the late 1800s and was the center of social life in the city. It next expanded to eight floors. Harry C. Moir purchased the Morrison in 1903 and completed an expansion to 519 rooms in 1913. Every room in the hotel included a private bath. Additions were made in 1916 and 1925 that expanded its capacity. In 1927 its signature 46-story tower was completed, and it became the world's tallest hotel. (The hotel was razed in the summer of 1965 and is now the site of the Chase Bank Building.) The entrance was grand, with a high atrium and marble columns. At street level, the Morrison had two lobbies—one opening on Madison Street, the other on Clark Street. It was designed in the Georgian style with a gray marble floor, wood-paneled walls, and a 28-foot-high ceiling. The front desk was all marble.

Morrison Hotel, 1920. *Courtesy of wikipedia.com*

LEFT: Terrace Garden Restaurant, Morrison Hotel. *Courtesy of wikipedia.com*
RIGHT: Morrison Hotel Grill Room. *Courtesy of wikipedia.com*

country to have bathrooms in each room. Nettie took advantage of this luxury and took a hot bath as Harry left the room. He said he had a little business to take care of. This was the hotel where he would meet "Diamond Louie" and pick up hot diamonds to fence. Nettie tried to overlook this "business" of Harry's.

By the time he came back, Nettie was already in bed. She had purchased some very expensive silk lingerie for this, her wedding night. She had just dozed off when Harry got into the bed beside her.

"You awake, doll?" Nettie knew better than to ask where he had been. She could smell a combination of cigar smoke and liquor on his breath. This would be the first time they would be more intimate than just kissing and some heavy petting.

"I'm awake, Harry. How could I sleep? It's our wedding night," she said.

Harry took no time to embrace her and pull up her silk lingerie. Before she knew it, he was on top of her. She could feel his hard body and erect penis against her body searching for her *pot* (Yiddish for vagina). She had forgotten how hard a *shvantz* (Yiddish for penis) could become, but then he was only in his 20s. She reached down and guided it into her. His breath became quicker, and he thrust himself into her, and then he was done.

As he lay over on his side of the bed, he asked, "How was that, doll? Harry always leaves them satisfied."

"It was wonderful Harry." She knew better than to disagree with her husband. That was not what a Jewish wife was supposed to do. Maybe things would get better with time. The morning was a repeat of the night before. *Young men really do have more energy*, Nettie thought, *but it was just as fast as last night.*

They had breakfast in the Grill Room. While they were eating, Diamond Louie came over to their table. Harry made the introductions. "Diamond Louie, this is my wife of only one day, Nettie Diamond."

"Pleased to make your acquaintance, Nettie. Mind if I pull up a chair?"

"Go ahead," Harry said, with a fork full of eggs in his mouth. Nettie wondered if the chair would hold a man of Diamond Louie's size. It did.

"Harry, I got that package we talked about last night. I just need two grand ($26,000 in 2017 dollars) to seal the deal."

"I'm a little short on cash, Louie, but I could get it to you next week. You know I'm good for it," Harry said.

"Ya kid, I knows you're good for it, and you knows Diamond Louie always collects." With that, he slipped Harry an envelope and was gone.

"Hey, doll, could you loan me two grand so I can pay this guy off?" Harry said to Nettie over the table. "I have a bunch of ice (diamonds) in this envelope. When I sell them, I'll pay you back."

"All right, Harry. I think I can help you out. We can stop by my bank today. I'll draw out the cash." Nettie looked at the diamond on her finger and wondered if it was one from Diamond Louie.

"You're a doll, Nettie. You'll see your money back in no time."

On the way home to Nettie's drugstore, they stopped at the First National Bank and Trust. Nettie went in and asked to talk to James G. Allen. He was her personal banker. This was the bank where she had deposited most of Sam's life insurance money.

"Hello, Nettie." She turned, and there was James Allen. "What can I do for you this cold winter's day?"

"Can we go into your office?" Nettie didn't want the word of her withdrawal to get circulated around town. "I need to withdraw $2,000."

"My, that's a very large amount. As your personal banker, can I ask about the investment?"

"Well, it's not really an investment. My new husband needs a loan for his business, and I said I would loan him the money."

"I didn't know you had remarried, Nettie. Congratulations are in order," James said.

"I got married yesterday to Harry Diamond." A strange expression of recognition seemed to come across his face, like he knew the name.

"Will you be changing the name on all your accounts?"

"Hmm, I don't think I'll do that quite yet," Nettie said.

"Wait right here and I'll get your withdrawal." James disappeared behind the counter. He was back in barely five minutes with an envelope with her money.

"Thanks so much, James. We'll be talking later."

You can bet on that if it's the same Harry Diamond that I know, thought James. "Good day, Nettie, and stay warm." That was his parting remark.

As she got into the passenger seat and closed the door, she handed the envelope with the money to Harry. There was something about it that seemed unclean to her. "Here it is Harry, all $2,000 ($26,000 in 2017 dollars)."

"Thanks, doll. You'll see it back in no time."

Back at Nettie's apartment, Harry carried her bag up the stairs. They met Mamie at the door. "Meet the new Mrs. Diamond," Harry said.

Mamie wasn't impressed. She just took Nettie's bag from him and put it in her bedroom. *This man is no good, I'm believin',* she thought.

Nettie kissed him goodbye and said, "Are you coming to Sabbath dinner tonight? It's been a long time since we had a man to lead the prayers."

"Don't think so, Nettie. Got plans," he said.

"When will you be moving in, Harry?" asked Nettie.

"I don't know, Nettie. Got to finish up some stuff before I can move."

"Just let me know. *Dhr dsif sd zhstty lrgy* (I love you)," she said, as Harry left. She could hear him go down the stairs and the door close behind him. She looked out the window and saw the Hudson making tire tracks through the snow.

The Plot Thickens

"OK, Pop. I'm now a married man, just like you wanted. What's the next step?"

"You did good, *boychick* (affectionate term for a young boy). I knew you could do it," said Joseph.

"Ya, I even got a cool two grand out of her to buy some diamonds," Harry boasted.

"You da devil, Harry. Guess your old pop could learn a dhing or two from you."

"She did make me sign a paper before we got married. It says what is hers before the marriage is always hers, and I can't get at it," Harry explained.

"Ya, it's like a *ketubah*. Your mom and me have one too. Dere is otter vays to get her money. Ve also need to get her out of dat apartment above da drugstore. Ve got to get her away from all dem Herskovitz brothers. One of dem is a mouthpiece (lawyer) and he vould be on to us. Vit all her money, get her to buy a house in Gary. Don't move into her place until she gets that Gary house," said Joseph. "Dat vould be da time to gets rid of her maid. Da vord is, she is one smart nigger. I think Al knows some guys in the KKK[6] that could do

---

6   The Ku Klux Klan was revived in the 1920s and spread to the North. The NAACP was helpless against the mob violence and race hatred. It seemed impossible that a black person would ever be considered equal in white America. It was the nationalistic movement of the time. Marcus Garvey preached black pride and racial separation and a return to Africa, which appeared to be the only hope for racial unity and survival. His movement did not make much headway against the white-supremacy feeling in this postwar decade.

a number on her if ve want. Ve den need to get control of dose drugstores—I think she got two or tree. Den ve can sell all the booze ve vants with illegal prescriptions. You also needs to get her pregnant as soon as you can." This was Joseph's plan.

"I don't know, Pop. I don't think she wants to have another baby. She already has four, maybe five. With them all runnin' around, I can hardly count em," Harry complained.

"Vell, it's your job to convince her dat you vants de baby. She vill give it to you if she loves you."

"OK, Pop. I'll give it a try," answered Harry.

"Now dat you is married, get a life insurance policy on her for as much as you can."

CHAPTER 12

Married Life for Nettie and Harry

February turned into March, and still Harry had not moved into the apartment over the drugstore. He was always complaining to Nettie about "all them damn kids" making noise and being underfoot. Nettie could tell he didn't have those fatherly instincts that she was hoping for.

"If you want me to stay here, Nettie, you've got to get rid of your maid. I don't think she likes me. I'm afraid she's going to put somethin' in my food," complained Harry.

"Don't be a silly goose, Harry. Mamie loves this family and wouldn't do anything to hurt anyone."

"I'm not so sure she thinks I'm part of the family," Harry said.

"She would, Harry, if you would move in."

"I'll make you a deal, Nettie," Harry said. "I'll try living here, but if Mamie doesn't change her attitude about me, you'll fire her. We'll find a new maid and look for a house in Gary. If we moved to Gary, you could rent out this apartment and my sisters would be a big help with the kids."

Nettie didn't have a choice. This would be the only way she would get Harry to be the real husband and father that she wanted. "It's a deal, Harry." The next day, Harry moved in.

Family Time

Gone were those weekends in Chicago with Anna and Morris. Harry seemed to have his own plans on the weekends that did not include Nettie. Today was different. They were going to go to Chicago to the Morrison Hotel. Harry would meet Diamond Louie. Nettie would take Pearle to start violin lessons at a music school just around the corner from the hotel. It would be a family outing. This trip became a ritual every Saturday. It seemed to Nettie that Harry liked the trips. In truth, Harry liked that the music lessons and the family appearance provided a cover for his illicit diamond dealing. He had stopped doing deliveries for the bottling company since they got married. Fencing the diamonds and getting checks from Nettie were his sources of income.

"Nettie, look here at my drawers." Harry held up a pair of underwear so heavily starched that they stood up by themselves. "What's your nigger trying to do to me? If you want me to be a husband to you tonight, you'll get her to loosen up my shorts," Harry said. "I swear she's puttin' somethin' in my morning coffee."

Nettie found it hard to keep from laughing. "OK, Harry I'll have a talk with her."

The apartment wasn't so big that Mamie didn't hear what Harry said. "Mamie," Nettie said, "can you do anything to loosen up Mr. Harry's shorts?" She held them up in front of Mamie like a piece of cardboard. Nettie couldn't keep the smile from her face. "He thinks they're a little too stiff."

"Mamie sees what she can do to loosen dem up," she replied with a smile.

"Mamie, are you putting something in Mr. Harry's coffee?"

"Mamie can't lie to yous, Ms. Nettie. I tell my sister about your Mr. Harry, and she send me a powder to help make him better, to gets the devil out of him. He's not like Dr. Sam, Ms. Nettie. I feels something bad gonna happens, and I be fearful of him."

"You know he wants me to let you go, but I don't want to," explained Nettie.

"Mamie can finds anuder family to takes care of, but I be prayin' for you and the chil-ins." She gathered up her things. After the noon meal, she was gone.

Harry had one of his sisters come over to help with the kids and meals. Pop knew the plan was working, and he didn't even have to get the KKK.

I'll find another maid, Harry thought. *Maybe one of those flappers would like a daytime job.*

Women Get the Right to Vote

August 18, 1920: The 19th Amendment to the Constitution was now law and women had the right to vote. "Nettie, are you going to register to vote?" Anna asked her over one of their girls' day out shopping trips.

"I don't know, Anna. Harry told me the other day that women voting was against the teaching in the Talmud. I think he was just saying that because he can't get it through his head that women are as much a part of this country as men. You remember back in the old country that they thought a woman's place was only in the home? It was not that long ago. I didn't believe the Talmud was right then, and I don't think it's right now."

Anna had a flashback of when she cut Nettie's hair and Nettie wore Anna's brother's clothes to the *yeshiva*. "Barney was a Republican, and I know Sam was too. I'm going to register as a Republican. Want to come with me?"

"I'd better not. Don't want Harry to get mad. He really has a short fuse and thinks he's in control of the house. He has me looking for a house in Gary so we can be closer to his family. I don't know how the kids are going to like it. They have their friends here, and they really like the school."

"I know you, Nettie, and this doesn't sound like you. Do you have to walk like you're on eggshells around Harry?" Anna asked.

"You know, I didn't see it that way, but I guess I am," Nettie agreed. "He seems to be pushing me away from you and everyone I know here in East Chicago. Should I be worried about him getting an insurance policy on me?" asked Nettie.

"Now that's a real alarm bell, Nettie," Anna said.

"Don't worry, Anna. He was turned down on that one. Guess I'm not worth as much as he thought." They both had a laugh on that one.

A Night on the Town

Just when Nettie was feeling that the happiness was leaving their marriage, Harry decided the two couples should go out on the town. This time it would be the Hotel Sherman in downtown Chicago. It had a famous restaurant, The College Inn. It was frequented by local celebrities and members of high society.

"Anna, do you remember when we would visit the hotels in New York City and use our new accents pretending to be socialites?"

"How could I forget? You had me as nervous as a cat trying to get out of the rain," answered Anna.

The lobby of the Sherman Hotel had marble columns, giving it a regal look. The Sherman was known for its band leader Isham Jones and his orchestra. He broke with tradition and eliminated the violins and waltzes for a jazz venue. He had an all-white jazz orchestra. The two couples danced the night away and then had a nightcap at The College Inn.

"This is so much fun. I could dance all night," said Nettie, slightly out of breath as she sat down at their table.

Morris commented, "You can, but you'll pay for it in the morning."

How Not to Break a Lease—Harry and Nettie Arrested

"Look here, Nettie," Harry said, as he showed Nettie the last month's order from the drugstore. "We've got to get a new tenant for the drugstore downstairs. They're not buying my booze."

"Why, Harry, buying your booze is not the only thing important with a tenant," replied Nettie. "Gavalis pays his rent on time, and sometimes he's early. Besides, he has a lease."

"He's not buying our booze. Says he gets a better deal with some guys out of Chicago. I know we can break his lease. There's a line in every lease that says if the renter breaks the law, then the lease is *kaput* (broken). I got an idea. If he's arrested for selling illegal whiskey, we can get him out," said Harry.

"He's an honest man, Harry. I know he wouldn't break the law," replied Nettie.

"Yeah, yeah, I know, honest as the day is long. We can get around that. I know two guys that live next to the bottling plant that would like to pick up some extra dough. They're real suckers. They work at Inland Steel, a father and son. We can pay them off and have them testify that they bought whiskey at the drugstore, and then Gavalis is out."

"I can't do that, Harry. It's dishonest, and I like Mr. Gavalis and his manager, Herschel Canan." Nettie didn't like this idea, but she didn't want to get Harry angry.

"You goin' soft on me, Nettie? Remember who the man is in this house. Besides, they can get another drugstore. You put up the cash, and I'll handle everything," Harry assured her.

Later that day, Harry met with Nicholas Tumbry and his son Frank. "You guys interested in making a little change?"

Always interested in some extra money, they knew what was going on at The Standard Bottling Company, but they both had good jobs at the mill. "What's the deal?" Frank asked.

"All you got to do is say you bought whiskey at the Calumet Drugstore. You will have to go before a grand jury and say you did. Then say the same thing at the trial. My wife and I will pay you for any wages you lose and give you each another $15 ($180 in 2017 dollars)."

"Sounds easy, Harry. My boy and I will do it. Just tell us when," Nicholas said.

The Setup

"Look what came in the mail today." Herschel Canan, manager of the Calumet Drugstore, showed a summons to the owner, Algerd J. Gavalis. "It says here we have a court date over in Crown Point to explain why we sold whiskey to two guys named Tumbry. Do you know anyone named Tumbry?" he asked Algerd.

"Never heard the name before, but I have a feeling Harry Diamond is behind this. You know he wants us to buy his rotgut whiskey. I think he dilutes it with formaldehyde or something worse. I can't let my customers buy that junk. It's not enough we buy his ice and soft drinks. I draw the line at the whiskey," said Algerd.

"I think he wants to break our lease," offered Herschel. "Dr. Sam would be rolling over in his grave if he knew this *gonif* (thief) was trying to get us out. I know Nettie wouldn't do this, but I don't think she can control Harry."

The Trial

At the trial, the Tumbrys testified that they bought whiskey on the morning of May 31, a Monday. All was going well until the attorneys for Gavalis found that the Tumbrys had been working at Inland Steel on that day and their time cards proved they were lying. They were both charged with perjury. Nettie and Harry were accused of serious offenses as well. Nettie had given Harry $50 ($600 in 2017 dollars) to pay the Tumbrys. Only Nicholas got paid $10 for his testimony at the Grand Jury and $5 for the trial. His son was never paid, and they didn't get paid for the time they missed work. Harry chiseled them out of their money. Nettie didn't find out about it until their trial for perjury. Nettie swore to herself never to do this again. She knew it was wrong, but she was now afraid of Harry.

Nettie's Apology

The day before the Tumbrys' trial, Nettie went downstairs to the drugstore to talk with Algerd Gavalis and Herschel Canan. "I'm so embarrassed, Herschel, for what happened with the Tumbrys. I couldn't stop Harry from doing this. How can I make it right?" she asked.

"We suspected it was Harry's doing, Nettie. I've know you for such a long time, and I know Dr. Sam would never do anything like this," Algerd said. Algerd had come from Suvalki, Lithuania, the same region where Nettie's parents, Sam and Mary Sachs, grew up. "Just promise us you'll tell us if Harry has any other harebrained schemes to break our lease."

"Thanks, Algerd. What if I extend your lease for another three years at no increase in rent?" Nettie offered.

"That would be great, Nettie." They all shook hands, and the matter was settled.

After the Tumbrys' trial for perjury, the judge asked Gavalis and Canan if they wanted to press charges against Nettie and Harry Diamond for plotting with the Tumbrys to try to break the drugstore's lease. Nettie's talk with them the day before worked, and they told the judge they would not press charges.[1] Harry looked very surprised. He suspected Nettie had something to do with Canan's change of heart, but then he really didn't care.

Anna and Nettie Talk

The whole affair came up when Nettie was talking to Anna about Anna's upcoming marriage to Morris. "Anna, I think I've made a terrible mistake. Harry is not acting like the man I married. You were right. Harry is a *shtunk* (a stinker, a nasty person). I should have known better," said Nettie. Then, to change the subject, she said, "Tell me about your wedding with Morris."

"I'm sorry for your trouble, Nettie. Maybe in time you can reason with him," Anna offered, but in her heart, knowing Harry, she didn't think he would change.

---

1   R. Herschel Canan had a different view of life after an industrial accident—perhaps the reason he did not press charges against Nettie in the Tambry case. In May of 1918 he was working in the Aetna Chemical Plant, thinking it was a better opportunity than being a chemist in a drugstore. He was helping the war effort, as the plant was making explosives with TNT. On Saturday, May 15, there was a terrific explosion at the plant. Two hundred people were killed, and many more were injured. Herschel was blown through the roof of the building and surprised everyone by being only slightly injured. After he recovered, he went back to work as a drugstore chemist, returning to a more tranquil existence.

"I don't know, Anna. I thought I would have a little control now that I have the insurance money, but that doesn't seem to be the case. He's always asking for 'loans' that he never pays back," complained Nettie.

"I hope my marriage to Morris doesn't wind up the same as yours. I guess when women have money, they attract the wrong kind of men. I'll know more after we get married October 19. I just found out that Morris is only six years younger than me. Wish me luck."

Dora Sees the Headline

It had been a long time since Dora had seen anything in the paper about Nettie. This time, she knew her voodoo had found the "perfect" husband for Nettie. "Here, Joseph, read this about Nettie and her new husband."

Joseph read the article about Harry and Nettie and the Tumbrys. He had to show he was interested, or there would be an argument. Dora looked positively gleeful. "Looks like my voodoo is working again. We got her tied up with a two-bit hoodlum. I bet she didn't know what hit her. Let's see her try to get out of this marriage. I sure hope he doesn't land in jail before he takes all her money." Dora grabbed her dolls and started dancing around the room.

Joseph knew Dora was unstable and thought maybe her voodoo adviser Sister Marie was somehow involved. Dora slept well that night, with the voodoo dolls between them in the bed.

Drugstore Robbery

Less than a week after Anna and Morris were married and two months after the attempt by Harry to break the lease, the drugstore was robbed. Harry and his dad had talked about other ways to get Canan and Gavalis to leave the drugstore, and they knew a holdup would be easy. Abe Rosen had some boys perfect for the job. Harry knew the drugstore also served as an American Express office, so there would be plenty of cash on Monday. The robbers came at closing time and backed Canan and Gavalis into the rear office. They got $2,774 ($25,000 in 2017 dollars) of American Express funds and $172 ($2,000 in 2017 dollars) from the cash register.

Herschel Canan had his unique way of looking at things. "At least we're not dead," he said to Gavalis. "I'm sure The American Express Company can stand the loss. If it was Harry Diamond and his friends behind this, they don't know us very well. We're not moving."

DARING HOLD-UP IN E. CHICAGO

Bandits Get $3,000 in Drug Store This Afternoon and Make Their Escape

Three thousand dollars in cash was the loot secured this afternoon by two audacious bandits who entered the Calumet Drug Store in East Chicago, on Chicago and Melville ave., which is also the American Express Agency, while Mgr. R. H. Canan was counting up his cash preparatory to taking it to the bank. The bandits backed Canan and A. J. Gavolis, the owner, into the rear office while they turned their attention to the cash register. They got $2,774 of American Express funds and $172 from the cash register. Both bandits made an easy escape. The one who was most active was a man about 35, wearing a red sweater and a rain coat.

Holdup of the Calumet Drugstore, *Hammond Lake County Times*, October 25, 1920. *Newspaper Archives*

Nick Slade and the Buconich Brothers

When you marry someone, their friends are part of the package. Along with Harry came Nick Slade. Nick was about nine years older than Harry and was born in Croatia. He was the second of six children but moved up to be the oldest after the death of his older brother Mato when Nick was 2 years old. Nick was a little shorter than Harry at five-foot-eight but had the same build. He had brown eyes and dark hair. He had an attitude like Harry's, that laws were not meant to be followed. He immigrated to America in 1907 from Austria and just happened to be on the same boat as the Buconich family.

Nick started work as a laborer at a cement plant, but it wasn't long before he had a "café" in Gary, Indiana, that was really a saloon. To say he was a little reckless would be an understatement. On November 23, his Dodge truck was struck by a Michigan Central train at the Clark Street crossing just in front of his West Gary café. He said he didn't notice the train until it was too late to stop. The truck was completely demolished.

It was always all about Nick, and to be his friend was a little like keeping company with a venomous snake. You just never knew when he would turn on you. In many ways, he was like Harry, only older.

Nick was friends with the Buconich brothers, Matt, Steve, and Mike. The brothers were all about 10 years older than Nick and much bigger physically. Nick met them on the boat when they emigrated from Austria in 1907. Their friendship continued in America, each supplying something the other didn't have. The brothers looked more like triplets, as they were all well over six feet tall and had stocky builds. There was an air of danger about them, with mops of brown hair on their heads and muscular builds thacould only come from hard work.

Matt had been a laborer in a quarry, and Mike and Steve were both stock men working at the stables. None of them could read or write when they came to America. They needed their new friend, Nick Slade, to help them out. Nick could read and write in several languages. The brothers needed him, and Nick knew it. He took advantage of this skill. It didn't take the brothers long to figure things out in their newly adopted country. They readily participated in the wild, anything goes, South Chicago at the time. It wasn't long before the Buconichs had a "resort" (house of prostitution) in South Chicago. They also operated gambling houses and any other illegal operation they could find.

Nick and Harry

Nettie knew that Harry would be palling around with Nick when he left the house late at night. Harry would be the driver in his new Buick Roadster, one of several cars he owned. Nick was a crazy driver and most of his cars and trucks were damaged, so Harry was the driver.

Harry saw Nick shortly after he married Nettie. "Hey, Harry. Heard you got hitched to some old lady."

"That's right, Nick, and she ain't some old lady. She's a dame with a $100 large." (A "large" was $1,000).

"How did she get that dough, Harry?" asked Nick.

"She was married to a *croaker* (doctor). He died and left her the insurance money," answered Harry.

"Looks like you're sitting pretty, Harry. Maybe sometime we can hit Chi town together with our wives."

"Might be more fun without our wives, Nick," Harry answered. Nick nodded his head in the affirmative. "By the way, you haven't seen my motor meter,[2] have you?" asked Harry.

---

2 A motor meter was a type of thermometer made up as a radiator cap. It allowed the driver to view the coolant vapor temperature through the windscreen. Coolant water temperatures had to stay just below 212 degrees for engines to function properly. 170 to 180 degrees was ideal. This was before the use of antifreeze or pressurized cooling systems.

"I think someone snatched it off my Buick last night. Not sure if they wanted the meter or the radiator ornament. Those things ain't cheap."

Nick shook his head no but wondered if it was one of the Tumbrys after what Harry had put them through, getting charged with committing perjury.

Insurance Policy

"Nettie, look what I have here." Harry was waving a paper in his right hand. "This should show you how much I love you, Nettie. It's an insurance policy for $5,000 ($70,000 in 2017 dollars), and you're the beneficiary."

"Are you planning to die, Harry?" Nettie asked.

"No, but just in case. A lot of guys I know pack heat (carry a gun), and one never knows what can happen. Don't you think you should do the same for me?" suggested Harry.

"You mean take out an insurance policy and make you the beneficiary? Now, why would I do that?" replied Nettie. Nettie had learned to be cautious whenever it came to insurance and Harry. He had a history of filing false claims to insurance companies, just like his father.

"To show you care for me as much as I care for you," Harry said.

"That's a lie, Harry, and you know it," Nettie replied sarcastically.

"The way it stands now, Nettie, if you die, I get nothing and the kids get everything. I don't think that's fair. I'm your husband." Harry thought this line of reasoning might get Nettie to act.

"OK, I'll take out a policy, but I want the children to be the beneficiaries. You can use the money to take care of them."

"That's OK with me," Harry said.

"Harry, give me your policy and I'll put it in the safe." Nettie took the policy out of his hand and left the room to put it in the safe.

Stolen Purse

Living with Harry was one scam after another. Was it Harry's bad luck, or was it his way to scam the insurance companies? In March of 1921, Harry reported that Nettie's purse was stolen from Nettie's handbag by a black man. It had $5,000 ($70,000 in 2017

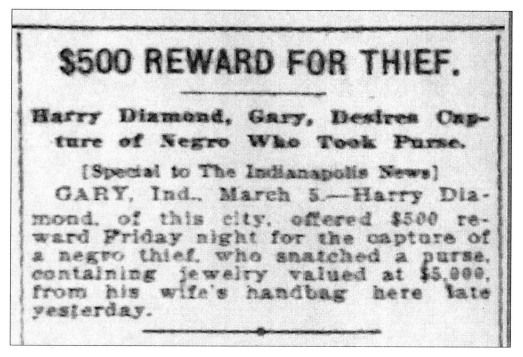

$500 REWARD FOR THIEF.

Harry Diamond, Gary, Desires Capture of Negro Who Took Purse.

[Special to The Indianapolis News]
GARY, Ind., March 5.—Harry Diamond, of this city, offered $500 reward Friday night for the capture of a negro thief, who snatched a purse, containing jewelry valued at $5,000, from his wife's handbag here late yesterday.

Harry places bogus ad for missing diamonds, *The Indianapolis Times*, March 5, 1921. *Courtesy of* The Hammond Times *and Newspapers.com*

dollars) worth of diamonds in it. He offered a reward in the newspaper for $500. There were no takers. Nettie knew the story was a lie, but Harry had insurance and they paid him 50 percent of the estimated value. Harry and his father were careful not to use the same insurance company twice. In May, Harry had to ask Nettie for money to bail Nick Slade out of jail. He was put in jail for the desecration of the Sabbath, keeping his saloon in Gary open past 1 a.m.

Nettie said, "Harry, I know Nick is from Austria and he hasn't become an American citizen. Isn't he afraid of being deported for breaking the law?"

"Nick isn't worried about nutin," Harry said. "He thinks breaking the law is just the price of doin' business."

"It says here in the paper that the Emergency Immigration Act was just passed." Nettie showed the paper to Harry. "The U.S. doesn't want any more immigrants. The law says now only 3 percent of the population of existing immigrants from each country will be allowed to enter the country. I've heard if the government has a case, they'll send any alien back to their country, especially if they feel they're not contributing to the U.S. Nick should be worried."

Harry did show some interest in what Nettie just read. *Maybe a little blackmail would get some money out of Nick*, he thought… There is no honor among thieves.

CHAPTER 13

Nettie Buys Houses, Moves to Gary

Nettie had promised Harry that she would buy a house in Gary nearer to his parents. They lived on Monroe Street. She wanted to wait until school was out before she moved the children. Pearle was 12, Lloyd 10, Bernard 9, and Cecil 7. She found the Tolleston section of Gary had the best schools and found several houses for sale on Pierce Street and bought three of them—one to live in at 521 Pierce St., and the others for rental. She also had purchased some lots a few years earlier and now took an option to buy a house on Buchanan Street that she really liked. It would be available next year.

This was the first move since Nettie and the family moved above the drugstore in 1910. She knew the kids would miss playing on the roof and with their friends just down the street. If it meant her marriage, she would do it. Harry felt it would be best if her safe was moved to the bottling company. In it were her bearer bonds, insurance papers, and some stock certificates. She could come over anytime and clip her coupons, or he would bring them to her. It was so very heavy, and they really didn't have room at the new house. Harry reassured her she would have access to it anytime.

They moved in July, giving the kids enough time to make new friends before school started. No sooner had they moved in than Nick Slade was arrested for assault and battery on his wife. Nettie had to "loan" Harry more money to bail Nick out of jail.

Night on the Town

It took them several months to move in and get settled. To celebrate their move to Gary, Harry decided they should have a night on the town with Anna and Morris. They decided to go to Chicago and try out some of the new clubs: the Club Lucky, The Drifter, and Vito Giacomo's restaurant. They danced to the new tunes: "Wang Wang Blues," "My Blue Heaven," "April Showers," "Bye Bye Blackbird," and "Avalon." They ended the night with the song "The Sheik of Araby."

There was something magical that came alive again in the marriage, and Nettie felt it that night. Harry was extremely attentive, and Nettie knew that was the night that baby Fay was conceived, October 21, 1921.

Maybe the new baby will change Harry, she thought. *This will be his first child, and now he will be a real father.* His gesture of bringing the kids Oreo cookies to win them over was never very sincere, and everyone knew it. All the times he had Nettie make the kids go into the basement below the drugstore so he could have peace and quiet in the apartment would be forgotten, or would they? *Maybe now the family would be different.*

The Berghoff Inn & Cabaret

It was November 1921, and Harry was having lunch with Nick Slade. "Harry, you want to get in on a good deal?"

"You know me, Nick. Always lookin' for a deal if it's gonna make me some cabbage."

"Do you know the Buconich brothers?"

"Oh yeah, I've been to their resort (house of prostitution) in South Chicago."

"The boys are planning to add a cabaret to the restaurant they're building over in Hobart, just off Ridge Road. They're calling it the Berghoff Inn. It used to be a gambling house until the Hobart marshal closed it down. I've been living in the old gambling house behind the place ever since my wife threw me out. They're adding a cabaret and will be needing booze. It's a sure deal. The boys have bought off the police. All they need now are the dancers and booze. We can ride out there this afternoon, and you can talk to them."

"I don't have to think about this one. Let's take a ride out there. I'm driving," said Harry.

This wasn't the first time Harry had met Matt Buconich. He knew him from his South Chicago resort. This would be the first time he had any business dealings with him, though. Matt was a good six to eight inches taller than Harry and 20 years older.

They pulled into a spot in front of the building that was still under construction. The two of them walked inside. There sitting at a table was Matt Buconich. Nick had called ahead and told him he was bringing a pigeon. Nick would get a cut if he got Harry to invest.

Matt stood up as the two of them entered. "You must be Harry Diamond?" His voice was like a megaphone as he directed his question at Harry.

"That's right, and you're Matt?" Harry replied.

"In the flesh. Nick told me yous may wants a piece of dis action. It's gonna cost ya."

"How much?" Harry asked.

"Two grand six now." ($2,600 was $31,385 in 2017 dollars.)

"OK," Harry said. "If I put up the dough, I want to be the one to write all the checks and keep da books. You'll have to buy all your hooch from us."

"Fair enough, Harry. You drive a hard bargain," said Matt. He saw Harry as a kid trying to act like a big shot. He didn't care what deal Harry asked for. He wouldn't honor it. He just wanted his cash. They shook hands, and the deal was done.

Nettie to Finance the Deal

"Nettie, doll," Harry said. Nettie knew it was about money because he used the word *doll.* "I've got a sure thing, a great opportunity to get in on the ground floor of a cabaret in Hobart. Nick told me about it, and I need two grand six hundred to get in. Can you give me a loan?" Nettie knew the word *loan* meant nothing to Harry. It would be a gift. "I'm going to be the one to keep the books and write all the checks. They're also going to buy all their whiskey and beer from us. Like I said, it's a sure thing."

"OK," said Nettie, "if it means you're actually going to work a job, I'll write you a check for the money." This would not be the last check Nettie would write on this endeavor. Before two weeks had passed, Harry was asking for another $2,000 ($24,000 in 2017 dollars). Matt was using Harry like his own piggy bank. He knew all he had to do was make Harry feel like he was a big shot. It worked.

Nick Borrows Harry's Hudson

Nick was without a vehicle after his run-in with the train. "Harry, I need to borrow your machine (car). Trying to get back with my old lady and want to take her to dinner on Thanksgiving. What do you say?"

"OK, Nick, but you have to promise me you'll not speed. I already have my share of tickets for speeding." The Hudson was more a family car; his Buick roadster was for picking up women.

"Don't worry, Harry, I'll treat your Hudson like it was my baby," Nick promised.

All Thanksgiving Day, it rained—not hard, just a steady drizzle. It wasn't cold enough for snow, but later that evening it was cold enough for the rain to turn into sleet. At 9 p.m., Nick was driving with his wife from Gary to Hammond for a late Thanksgiving dinner. He hoped to repair their marriage. He may have been in a hurry or was just not aware of his speed, as the heavy Hudson touring car had a more powerful engine than his old truck. He was going 40 mph, catching up to a Flivver (Model T) in front of him when he entered the intersection at Gostlin and Sheffield. Right in front of him was the "North Western Bus," driven by Joseph Hanrahan. Nick slammed on the brakes and swerved to the right, but the heavy Hudson was more than a match for the brakes and the slick road. Blam, it hit the rear end of the bus, then fishtailed around and hit the bus again on its side, tipping the bus over. The 15 passengers inside were tossed into a heap, and every window in the bus was broken.

Later, an inspection found every joint in the passenger section of the bus was broken. The men on the bus were going to a party at the K&P Hall (Knights of Pythias) and were cut by the flying glass. One man, Raymond Cliffton, was thrown through a window and suffered both a broken collar bone and shoulder. He sued for $2,000 ($24,000 in 2017 dollars). Nettie paid the damages to the bus, the car, and Cliffton.

1921 Mack Bus. *Private Collection*

"Harry, if you ever let that *schlemiel* (clumsy, inept person) use your machine again, you are on your own for the damages," said Nettie.

"Well, at least no one was killed," answered Harry.

"It's not over yet, so don't be so sure, Harry," she said in jest, but from the look in her eyes, Harry wasn't sure.

The Berghoff Inn in Trouble

Winter is not the best time to start a cabaret business, and it wasn't long before the business was losing $50 ($666 in 2017 dollars) a day. Harry wanted Matt to release some of the cabaret girls who didn't just *dance* for a living. Matt refused. Matt then took charge, and Harry was looking in from the outside. The Buconich boys failed to contribute their share or fire any of the dancers. Matt was also writing checks on the account, something that was not in the original agreement. Seeing he was going nowhere by talking to Matt, Harry went to his attorneys, Shuravsky, Peters and Morthland, to file for receivership. This was done December 29, 1921.

Nettie had just lost more money—$4,600 ($62,000 in 2017 dollars)—on another one of Harry's schemes. *Another waste of money*, Nettie said to herself.

The end of 1921 couldn't have been worse for Harry. His investment in the cabaret was a bust. His ace in the hole, the East Chicago Police Chief Edward P. O'Donnell, along with his Captain Thomas Downey, was convicted of taking bribes and sent to Leavenworth Penitentiary for two years. Now his group at the bottling company had to cozy up to the new chief. *This new chief is going to be very careful, seeing what happened to O'Donnell,* Harry thought.

Harry Robs the Excel Company

Nettie was still reminding Harry of his last "sure deal" that ended in disaster. Harry was working with his attorneys to try to get back something on the receivership of the cabaret. He didn't dare cross the Buconich brothers. They had too much muscle in the area, and even Harry was afraid of them. He wouldn't admit it. He called it respect.

Harry had another deal. The Excel Company in Hammond had bought some of Harry's alcohol. They wouldn't pay him, as they thought he had watered it down and it was no good to them. They were right. Harry, however, felt they were wrong for not paying him. He reasoned that they did check the shipment, so he was going to get the money or the alcohol. Harry was getting nowhere talking to them. He had another plan. He decided he would take some of Abe Rosen's boys and get his alcohol back. On the night of February 6, he had his trucks drive to the warehouse of the Excel Company at 131 Sibley St. They took back what Harry said was his, 290 gallons of grain alcohol valued at $3,000 ($42,700 in 2017 dollars). They were careful not to take the barrels that came from Harry's Standard Bottling Company. Witnesses identified Harry but he didn't care; he thought he was just getting back his goods. Harry was arrested on February 16 and taken to the Hammond police station. There he called Nettie and she came by with the $2,500 ($35,600 in 2017 dollars) bond money.

Nettie Asks for a Divorce

It was just a few days after Valentine's Day 1922, and Harry wasn't around to celebrate it with Nettie. This day had a special significance for Nettie, as it was the day they celebrated Sam's birthday, even though it was really on February 2. She never shared this information with Harry. It was just another piece of her life that kept Sam's memory alive. She knew Harry had been out with one of the flappers and his buddy Nick. She was four months pregnant with their first baby. Maybe it was the hormones. She was now physically afraid of Harry, but her frustration with him had come to a boiling point. They had been married two years, and it was one problem after another. It always involved bond money or paying off a fine.

"Listen here, Harry. I've had about enough of you loafing around here. It's about time to get a real job and support your family. It won't be long before we have another mouth to feed."

"Hey, I'm always working on ideas to make more money, and the bottling company brings in a lot."

"If it does, this family hasn't seen it," said Nettie, trying not to raise her voice. She didn't want to provoke Harry to violence. Pearle was in her bedroom at the time, and the boys were outside playing in the snow making a snowman. Pearle heard everything. "If you were a good husband, you wouldn't be going out with other women. Is that why you're always asking for money?" Nettie was starting to raise her voice.

"I was just a little short and needed a loan," Harry explained.

"A loan, my foot. You've never paid me back a penny on any loan, including the one I gave you the day after we were married. Harry, you think you're a *gantseh macher* (big shot), but you're really a *ligner* (liar) and a *gonif* (crook, thief, swindler), just like your father. *In drerd mein gelt* (my money went down the drain). You've been *lebst a chazerishen tog* (living high off the hog) on my *gelt* (money)."

Harry had never seen Nettie like this, but he knew he had her in a corner. Getting a divorce would be very difficult if both parties didn't agree. "*Ich hob dir lieb* (I love you), Nettie. *Host du bi emir an avleh* (so I made a mistake; so what)! I've tried to be a *mensch* (a man who can be respected) to you and the kids, and this is what I get?"

Nettie wasn't done. She had made up her mind she wanted out. "I want a *get* (divorce)."

"OK," Harry said. "I'll crawl out of this marriage for $10,000 ($142,000 in 2017 dollars)."

Nettie was in shock. Anna was right. It had always had been about the money. *How could I have been so blind?* Or was it this force that she just couldn't explain, like a spell or power she couldn't resist?

Just then, Harry doubled over in pain clutching his right side.

"What now, Harry?" she asked.

Harry had a history of the dramatic when he wanted to change the subject. "Oh, it's only a little pain that comes and goes. I'll be all right."

Nettie knew that Harry liked to pretend to have an epileptic seizure to get sympathy. Nettie had never seen one since they were married. The seizures started shortly after he graduated from high school. He had worked at the tin mill. On one occasion, he inhaled sulfuric acid fumes and then started getting seizures. He went to the Mayo Clinic in Minnesota for treatment. This got him out of the Army and a settlement from the mill.

This pain was different, and it just may be real, she thought. Nettie called the doctor. Dr. Levin came by the house and diagnosed it as appendicitis.

Appendicitis

Nettie now felt bad about the way she had talked to Harry. That's not how a good Jewish wife would talk to her husband. She knew she hurt his feelings, but she had to vent her frustration. Maybe now he would change.

Two weeks later when Harry doubled up in pain, she found herself in the hospital after Harry had his appendix removed. *Another bill*, she thought. *He's more expensive than all my children combined.*

Nettie and Pearle Go to New York

When the school year ended, Nettie was seven months pregnant with Harry's child. She felt it was time to take Pearle to New York. This would give Nettie a chance to catch up with her sister Rose (sister Fannie had died during childbirth) and brother Nathan. Pearle would now get to meet her cousins. Seeing New York would be good for Pearle's education, and Nettie needed some space from Harry. She had heard from Rose that the family was planning a move to Los Angeles, California, so now was the time to visit. They were no longer living in Manhattan but in Bensonhurst in Kings County. (Kings County is now Brooklyn.)

The two of them arrived at Grand Central in New York. "Oh, Mama," Pearle said. "The buildings are so tall, and there're so many of them." She turned in a 360-degree circle, looking up the whole time.

"The buildings aren't the only things to see here, Pearle. Wait until you ride in the subway and cross the Brooklyn Bridge. Your 'Aunt' Anna couldn't look down when we first crossed it."

They then took the train to Kings County to meet Philip and Rose at the train station. They loaded everything into the car for the short trip to the house. Rose and Philip had more than enough room for them in their house in the country. Philip had had enough of the city with all its crime and congestion. He wanted space.

"Come meet your cousins, Pearle," Rose said. "This is Albert; he's 12. George is 14, Flora 16, Louis 18, and Moe is 19. You'll meet the others later when we have dinner."

Rose had never been the older sister that Nettie would have liked, someone to grow up with and confide in. On this trip, she would have to do. Mama Mary was getting up in age and was ill and frail. She couldn't withstand the stress that Nettie was now experiencing in her life.

After they got unpacked, Nettie cornered Rose in the kitchen. "Rose, I need to talk with you. Everything is not rosy with me and Harry. I think I made a mistake, but I don't know how to make things right."

"What's the problem, Nettie? Is it his age? I know he's younger than you," said Rose.

"No, it's not the age. Or maybe it is. I don't know. He's a gambler and bootlegger and has connections with the lowlife in Chicago. He buys stolen diamonds and tries to resell them, and he doesn't take his family duties seriously. I'm always bailing him out of trouble. Frankly, if this keeps up, I'll be out of money."

"My, this doesn't sound good, Nettie, but I've never known a Jewish man not to take care of his family. Maybe when the baby is born, everything will be different."

Nettie could see that Rose was not understanding her problem, or did she just not want to be involved? "One thing I didn't tell you, Rose. Remember the story of me leaving Mariampole in the dead of night after our house was broken into by the mob?"

"Yes, I remember. That was when your husband was shot by the mob and you escaped."

"That's right, but what I didn't tell you was that the man in the mob that gave his gun to the man that shot

Nettie Diamond pregnant, summer 1922.
Courtesy of Ann Cohn Mitnick Collection

Moshe was the father of Harry, my husband."

"Oy vey!" Rose said. "This is serious. Mama always said your middle name was *Trouble*. Now it's not funny. Have you asked for a *get*?"

"Yes, and he says it will cost me $10,000 ($142,000 in 2017 dollars)."

"All I can say, Nettie, is be patient and hope the baby will turn him around."

Nettie was hoping for an idea that she had not already heard, but then Rose was never the strong older sister. Later that evening, she met her nephew William, the oldest son who served in the Navy in WWI, and his wife Anita and their son Seymour. Theodore, the second son, was quite ill with kidney problems. He had been abused by a nanny when he was 3 and never really recovered. The third son, Ellis, seemed to be Nettie's favorite, but she liked them all.

Pearle was taken under the wing of cousins Flora and Louis, who wanted to show her everything. Bensonhurst was not far from Coney Island, where the family took several trips. Before they knew it, the visit was over and they were back on the train to Chicago.

On the way back, Pearle was telling Nettie all that she had seen with her cousins being her guide. Nettie was refreshed and determined to turn her marriage around. The baby would help.

The Family Moves and Grows

The first week in July 1922, they were ready to move into the house on Buchanan. The option to buy came up, and Nettie thought this house was perfect for them. It was a two-story brick with basement. There were three bedrooms on the second floor. Pearle would now have her own room, and the boys would share a room. Three weeks after the move, Gertrude Fay Diamond, Harry's first child, was born July 21, 1922. Would the family be different now? Would Harry be different?

The one thing that didn't change was Harry asking Nettie for money. He would send Pearle to Nettie with Nettie's checkbook and ask for a check. When she would bring it to him and the amount was too small, he would say, "Nettie, what can I buy with this small amount? You know I need clothes and other stuff." He would then tear it up in little pieces and throw them in her face.

Nettie would say, "I know what you want it for. A flapper girl that you keep company with when you don't come home till 3 o'clock in the morning. That's no way to treat your family and your baby."

Nettie liked to remind him of Mabel, the dancer from the failed cabaret that he brought home to be the family maid. She was 21 years old, and cooking and cleaning was not her chosen line of work. It was not a stretch to say she was a lousy cook and housekeeper. Nettie suspected she was having an affair with Harry when she was not home. They were not careful, as Nettie found some of Mabel's clothing in their bed. When Mabel bragged to Nettie that Mr. Harry had bought her a dress for $40 ($570 in 2017 dollars), she fired her on the spot. Nettie hired the next maid without asking Harry.

The family finally had fallen into a routine. The children were taken to school and then picked up at the end of the day. Nettie was nursing Fay. When she had to go to Chicago, she left Fay with the maid or Esther, her mother-in-law. They no longer had a full-time maid but had help three days a week for the housework. On Fridays, they would go to the Diamonds' house for Sabbath dinner with both families. Nettie could feel something odd like jealousy or envy toward her children from the Diamonds; she let it pass.

647 Buchanan, Nettie's last home in Gary, Indiana. *Personal photo collection*

Harry Meets with His Father

"Pop, I've done everything you said, and I still don't have a way to get at all her money. She even asked for a divorce, but I told her it was gonna cost her 10 big ones ($142,000 in 2017 dollars)."

"Vy don't you show her a little attention? Be sweet to her and get her to change her vill for da kids. Den she is wort more to you dead."

"I was thinkin', Pop, maybe take her and the babe to Europe. She could have an 'accident' there, but only if I can get her to change her will."

"I heard that yous been seein' anudder voman, Harry?"

"Well, Pop, there's this little flapper girl I'm really swell on."

"You're a *schlemiel* (dopey person), Harry. Vell, don't let Nettie catch you vit that *shikseh* (non-Jewish girl), or she vill have grounds for divorce."

"Nah, she's too busy with dem kids to notice."

"You vant I have Rosen's boys bump her off for you?"

"No, too risky. Let me think about it. I'll come up with my own plan."

Joseph thought, *Can I trust Harry not to screw this up?*

Passports, Wills, Insurance, and the Anniversary

December 25 was Harry's birthday. He took Pop's advice and thought about giving himself and Nettie matching $25,000 ($350,000 in 2017 dollars) insurance policies. He had the agent, H.J. Gillman, come over to the house to write them up. The company denied coverage.

Their three-year anniversary was coming up January 29, 1923. Harry thought the passports and a future trip to Europe would serve a dual purpose. He tried being the good, attentive husband and didn't ask for any money. Nettie noticed. *Maybe things are getting better*, she thought.

He went to the passport office. They thought it strange that he had the photos for the passports. This was going to be a surprise for Nettie. The problem was she had to sign the passport papers.

"Nettie, I was thinking it's time for us to take a trip. Maybe Europe? We could visit Germany, Italy, France, and Poland," Harry suggested.

"Now, why would I want to do that, Harry? I escaped Europe with my life and lost my last husband because of the war. I certainly don't want to go there."

That ended Harry's plan for Europe. He must think of another. Nettie had her own plans for their three-year anniversary. They needed a new seven-passenger auto. Nick had run into the bus with their current Hudson, and it never ran well after the accident. Nettie picked out a new 1923 seven-passenger Hudson.

There were two seats that unfolded from the floor in front of the backseat, giving them seven seats, enough for the whole family. The body was India blue, the bonnet (hood) was black enamel, and the interior had blue broadcloth upholstering throughout. It was a beautiful machine for $2,272 ($29,000 in 2017 dollars). She put $1,500 down and planned to pay it off in two more payments—one each in March and April. She had discussed all this with Anna, saying giving him the car and changing her will would bring Harry around. The new will gave Harry everything if she should die. Dinner was going to be his favorite. Just like Sam, Harry loved cabbage rolls. After dinner was when she would present him with the new will. Surely this would make everything right, following the advice of her sister Rose, who said, "Give it time, treat your man well, and all things will work out."

Anniversary Dinner

They decided to have their anniversary dinner on Saturday, the 27th, only two days before the actual date. Harry made some excuse to Nick as to why he couldn't meet up with him. The notion of an anniversary dinner would not give Harry any stature with the boys.

Nettie had farmed out all the kids for a sleepover at various relatives, so they had the house to themselves. The evening started with Mr. Shafer, owner of the car dealership, delivering the Hudson that Nettie had purchased on the 23rd.

Original ad for 1923 seven-passenger Hudson. *From original Hudson literature*

After dinner, she also made Harry a present of the new will. "Here, Harry, I have a few papers for you to read," she said, as she handed him the will across the table.

Harry couldn't believe his eyes. It had all come true, just like Pop had told him. Being nice and attentive was the ticket. "Oh, Nettie, you've made me a very happy man." Harry was actually smiling, but more sinister than happy.

"I'm so glad, Harry. Now we can be a real family and make memories together."

That night was another special one for Nettie, as Harry showed his appreciation. For Harry, he had to keep from exposing his real objective, cashing in on the will.

CHAPTER 14

The Check;
New Will;
Harry Panics

Anna and Nettie took a trip into Chicago the next Friday, and Nettie sold her Durant Motor stock. The brokerage house gave her a check for $17,000 ($250,000 in 2017 dollars). With her newfound trust in Harry, she endorsed the check and asked him to deposit it in her account at the Indiana Harbor National Bank. He did not. Instead, he deposited it in his account at Abe Ottenheimer's American State Bank in East Chicago. (Abe was also Harry's lawyer.)

The next day, February 6, Nettie checked her account and didn't see her deposited check. "Harry, did you deposit the Durant Motor check at the Indiana Harbor Bank?" she asked.

"I'm not sure, Nettie. I had so many checks with me yesterday, I may have made a mistake."

Leave it to Harry to let his greed screw up his own plan. "You bet you made a mistake, Harry." He could swear Nettie's eyes were flashing red. Harry knew he had been caught. "You *shmendrik* (stupid person). I thought I could trust you, and now you have shown your hand. *Hots mikh un zayts mikh* (the hell with you). You're going to make this right, Harry. After the check clears, you will write me a check and get the money back into my account. I was a fool to change my will and give you everything. First thing tomorrow, I'm making a new will."

Harry was in panic mode. Everything was falling apart, and fast. He had to get a plan before she had time to finish and file the new will. There was no talking to Nettie tonight.

Without saying a word, he was out the door. He went over and picked up his father. The two of them went over to Nick's Café to hatch a plan.

When they got there, Steve Buconich was there too. "Look boys, I got a problem. The old lady is about to write me out of the will, so it's now or never."

"So's you wants to get rid of the manacle (wedding ring), or you wants to give her a Chicago overcoat (coffin)? Which is it?" asked Steve.

"You want she should have an accident?" Nick asked.

"No, she might survive. She's like a cat that has nine lives. Remember the story when her Dodge hit the train back in 1917? I say an accident is too risky," Harry said. "What about somethin' like the Wanderer case up in Chicago in '20? Remember, Wanderer wanted to knock off his wife, so he paid a sucker to act like he was holding them up, and he killed the guy and his wife and said the guy done it."

"Yeah, I remembers the story, but the guy swung for it (was hung), didn't he?" asked Steve.

"Yeah, we need a better plan. I need to get something in writing so that I can frame my stool pigeon," Harry replied.

"Vhat about gettin a chauffeur for da new machine of yours and let him take the rap? You gots to kill dem both, or you vill get the electric cure (electrocution) for sure," Joseph said.

"Now that sounds like a plan, Pop."

"Hey, get yourself one of dem niggers down at the Majestic Garage. They should be dumb enough to frame, and no jury would convict you and let a nigger go free," Steve chimed in.

"Good idea, Steve. I've taken the Hudson there a time or two. I think I know just the nigger to hire. The kid just dropped out of high school."

Harry Tries to Adopt

The next day, Harry saw that Nettie had cooled down a bit, so he tried another tactic. "Nettie, to show you my heart's in the right place, I want to adopt the kids. No strings attached. I really screwed up with the check business. I'm sorry. Will you forgive me, Nettie?"

Nettie wasn't sure. He had done so many things like this, she was sure she was being conned again. "I'll have to think about it, Harry. I'll ask my attorney today and see what he thinks."

"OK, Nettie. I'll be waiting for the answer." Harry felt he had bought a little time. She had not rewritten the will yet, and this idea of adoption should slow her down while the old will giving him everything was still in effect.

Harry Finds a Chauffeur, February 9, 1923

Harry took the Hudson into the Majestic Garage in Gary for a wash, as the salt and snow on the streets would damage the finish. He looked around for the kid he wanted for a chauffeur. He found him in William Armstrong, a mulatto colored boy who was a recent high school dropout. William looked more white than black, with white features and medium-length curly hair. He was only five-foot-four and 135 pounds—no match in size for Harry if there would be a scuffle.

He called out to him as he was washing the Hudson. "Hey, boy, what's your name?"

"William Armstrong, sir."

"Can you drive a machine?"

"Yes, sir. Been practicin' with all these cars for two months."

"Are you looking for a job?"

"Sure am, sir."

"How old are you, boy, and how much schooling have you had?"

"I'm 17, sir, and I've gone to the 11th grade at Froebel High. I left school last December to get a job." (The truth was that he didn't have enough credits to stay in the 11th grade. School was over for him.) "Trying to get me a job at the steel mill, but my friend Louis got me a part-time job here at the garage. I really love cars."

"That's good, William. I'm a fan of cars too. I'm looking for a chauffeur that can drive this Hudson Super 6. Think you can do it?"

"I sures can, mister."

"My name's Harry Diamond, William."

William finished washing the car. Harry paid him. As he got into the Hudson, he said, "I'll ask my wife first. If she likes the idea, then I'll come back to pick you up so you can meet her."

It wasn't long before Harry was back at the garage to pick up William to meet Nettie. "She likes to feel import-

William Armstrong *Courtesy of the Hammond Times and Newspaper Archives*

ant, William, so we'll let her offer you the job." Harry didn't want William to know that Nettie held the purse strings.

"I'll check with my boss Mr. Harry. I'm sure it's OK, but I needs to check first."

"OK, kid, you ask your boss."

It was almost 1 p.m. when Harry and William arrived at the house. Nettie was nursing the baby, so they waited in the kitchen until she was done. "Nettie, this is William Armstrong. He's looking for a job as a chauffeur," Harry said.

William extended his hand toward Nettie. She followed suit and shook his hand. "How old are you, William?"

"I'm 17, ma'am."

"Where do you live?"

"Live at home with my folks an' three older brothers on Broadway."

"Did you finish high school?"

"No, ma'am. Just finished 10th grade."

"How long have you been driving?"

"Well, officially two months. Gets lots of experience at the garage."

"I can offer you a job and give you room and board if you like," offered Nettie.

"No, ma'am, I'd rather stay on my own, but dinner would be good if I'm here," answered William.

"I can offer you $8 a week," Nettie said.

"If I'm not too out of line, ma'am, I would like $10 'cause I was making $8 a week at the pool hall."

"I thought you were working at the Majestic Garage?"

"I am now, but really only for tips. When I was making $8, it wasn't enough." William needed the money, and by the looks of the house, he thought she could afford it.

"You drive a hard bargain, Mr. Armstrong. I say you're hired. Can you start now?"

"Yes, ma'am. I'm ready."

The Armstrong Family

William's parents had grown up in Tennessee. Fred, his father, was born a free man in 1867. His mulatto complexion told the story of one whose parents held a higher status than most before the Civil War. Fred was a barber in 1910 in Logan, Oklahoma, and owned his house free and clear. He could read and write. His parents taught him how to talk with respect to white people. Mama taught him that you get more bees with honey than vinegar.

William was born in Oklahoma—the fourth son, with three older brothers. By 1920, his father was working as a janitor, but it wasn't enough for a growing family. Many black folks had moved north to Gary, Indiana, to work in the steel mills during the war and the steel strike of 1919. With the Immigration Act of 1921, the supply of foreign workers that the steel mills needed had dried to a trickle. That meant more opportunity for blacks and Mexicans for good-paying jobs.

The school William attended was a segregated one in Logan, Oklahoma. When he came to Gary, he enrolled in unsegregated Frobel High. He was lost. He had always been interested in things other than schoolwork, and it showed. He had a fascination with machines and was always a good-natured boy, causing very little trouble growing up.

His school days were over in December of 1922, as he didn't have enough credits to finish the 11th grade. Fred, his father, started working as a barber when he came to Gary. By September 1922, he had a job at the mill. William knew his mother and father would be proud of him getting the job as a chauffeur. *This is going to be a swell job*, he thought. *At least I'm making some money.*

Friday, February 9, 1923—First Day of Work

"OK, William, time to go to work," Harry said. "Do you know your way to Indiana Harbor?"

"Yes, sir. Out Fifth Avenue, turn onto the Gary Road, then up Cline Avenue."

"That's right, William. Let's get in the machine."

Off the three of them went to the Indiana Harbor National Bank. They were back at 3 p.m. in time to pick up the children at Emerson and Horace Mann schools. Emerson was on the other side of Broadway, but Horace Mann was just being built off of Fifth Avenue. It started with kindergarten and first grade in temporary buildings just a few blocks from their house at 647 Buchanan. The kids could walk, but Nettie said it was winter and too cold for them, especially for the baby, Cecil, only 7 at the time.

At 5 p.m., they were off to the Diamonds' house at 837 Monroe St. for Sabbath dinner. All the streets in Gary west of Broadway are named for U.S. presidents in order, starting with Washington. Most of the family would be celebrating the Sabbath with Nettie's five children. Harry's seven siblings would be there as well. It was a family affair, if not a little tense. The house was much smaller than Nettie's, but they managed.

Lena, 21, was the third Diamond child and Harry's younger sister. She saw William, the new chauffeur, standing by the India blue Hudson sedan. These dinners always reminded the Diamonds just how poor they were in relation to Nettie and her family. The only car they had was an old Ford Model T that ran only part of the time.

"What a swell car you have there, Nettie," Lena said.

"Why, thank you, Lena. It was my anniversary gift to Harry. I certainly hope he likes it."

"If he doesn't, you can give it to me," she offered. They both thought that was funny.

"My, look at the time," Nettie said. "It's 6:30, and I have to get these children ready to go to Chicago tomorrow." It was a polite way to exit. They all piled into the Hudson for the short ride back to the house.

After they got home, Harry said to Nettie, "William and I are going out for a little drive." Nettie gave no answer, as she was use to his nighttime trips. She knew he was either gambling, drinking, or seeing other women. It was too much to hope he had changed.

When they got in the Hudson, Harry said, "William, take me to 500 Washington Street." When they got there, Harry went into the building and came out with a very petite, heavily painted young woman. "William, head down Ridge Road to Hobart." He dropped them off at the old Berghoff Inn, the site of the failed cabaret. "Pick us up in about two hours," Harry said.

It was a cold night, so William drove back to Gary and spent time with his friend Louis. When the two hours were up, William was waiting for them outside Berghoff's. They found him there when they came out, and he drove them back to Gary.

"We're going to drop you off at your place, William. Then I'll take the car," Harry said.

"I'm staying with my friend Louis at 1717 Washington tonight, Mr. Harry."

When they got there, they dropped off William and Harry moved to the driver's seat. "Come by the house tomorrow about 9 o'clock, and don't tell my wife anything about what we did tonight," cautioned Harry.

"Yes, sir, Mr. Harry." Harry drove to the young lady's apartment, and they both went in. He left about 1:30 a.m. and drove home. Everyone was sleeping, except Nettie. She pretended she was asleep as he got into bed. *He hasn't changed one bit*, she thought. She could smell the perfume of another woman on Harry. She had smelled it before.

Saturday, February 10, 1923—Trip to Chicago

Will was at the house bright and early Saturday morning. It had snowed the night before, and there was a dusting of snow on the ground. Louis, Will's friend, had dropped Will off at the house. Will came in the back door and took his place down in the basement by the furnace. He barely had time to warm up when Nettie invited him up to the kitchen to have something to eat. He was as famished as any growing 17-year-old boy. He ate anything she put in front of him while the family got ready to leave.

The three boys, older sister Pearle, baby Fay, Nettie, and Harry all got in the machine. "This is why I got this model with the two pop-up extra seats," Nettie said. "Now the whole family can fit at the same time."

"We're off to Chicago, Bill. Do you know the way?"

"Yes, sir, I knows it," he said, never taking his eyes off the road. They drove into downtown Chicago and the Loop, stopping at the Morrison Hotel. Here is where the family got out.

Back seat showing pop-up extra seats, making it a seven-passenger car.
From original Hudson literature.

"Be back here at 5 o'clock, Bill. We will be out front," said Harry. This was the second time Mr. Harry called him Bill, and William liked it. Harry was becoming more of a friend than his employer. Pearle was going to her music lesson in the building around the corner. Harry was meeting with Diamond Louie to pick up some stones for Abe Ottenhiemer. Nettie did some shopping with the boys while carrying baby Fay. They all met back at the Morrison for a late lunch in the Grill Room. William kept busy moving the car around the Loop, as he could not park in one place for any length of time. He memorized the streets as he explored the Loop. He then drove the family back to Gary, getting home by 6 p.m.

"Nice driving, Bill. You really handle the Hudson well, even on these slippery roads," complimented Harry. After everyone was back home and supper was finished, Harry asked Will, "Bill, could you take me over to the Elks Lodge at Sixth and Washington?"

"Sure thing, Mr. Diamond," Will said. Harry and his friend Nick were trying to locate some women. After a few phone calls, they gave up and just had some drinks at the club.

"I'll drop you off at Louis's apartment, and I'll see you tomorrow around noon," said Harry.

Sunday February 11, 1923

William was at the house at 11:30 and went downstairs by the furnace to keep warm. The day was just warm enough to rain, but it was more like sleet than rain. Before he had a chance to settle in, Harry called him up to take Nettie and him to Rothschild's Restaurant for dinner.

They were back home by 2 p.m. At 3 o'clock, Nettie and the boys went to the Orpheus Theater on Eighth Avenue between Washington and Broadway to see the movie *Flesh and Blood* with Lon Chaney. (This was a hand-cranked silent film.) The plot was a crime melodrama with Lon a convict hiding out in Chinatown. He assumes the identity of a cripple in order to track down the businessman who framed him 15 years earlier. He discovers his daughter has fallen in love with the businessman's son. That's when he gives up his plot for revenge. His love of his daughter and her happiness was more important than revenge.

The family came home after the movie. Then William took Pearle to see the later show that evening. Pearle walked to the Diamonds' house after the show. During this time, the decorators, Mr. Ferrer and his son, were calcifying the walls at 647 Buchannan while Nettie and Harry were selecting wallpaper.

At 8:30 p.m., William drove the decorators home, as the weather had turned ugly. It was a cold stormy night, with the rain turning to ice when it hit the ground. He picked up Pearle (she had walked to the Diamonds' house after the show) and brought her home.

By 9 o'clock, Nettie went to bed. That's when Harry had Will drive him to Washington Street to pick up the young lady. "Bill, I want you to drive us to Hammond. Drop us off and be back in two hours," Harry said.

"OK, Mr. Harry. I be goin' to the show at the Parthenon. Dey has five vaudeville acts playin'."

Will picked them up two hours later and drove back to Gary. By 11:30 or midnight, Harry dropped William off at 16th and Washington, Louis's apartment. He stayed with his friend that night. Harry took the car and girl and left.

Monday, February 12, 1923

Today is Lincoln's birthday, Will thought, *a good day for the Republicans and all the Negro people.* Harry had taken the car and driven to Indiana Harbor. At 8:30 a.m., William was at the house burning the scrap wallpaper down in the basement. Later in the morning, he drove Harry and Nettie to Indiana Harbor to Anna Fishman's house on Grand Boulevard. Nettie stayed with Anna, and Will drove Harry back to Gary and the Elks Lodge. At 12:30 p.m., Will drove Harry back to Indiana Harbor to pick up Nettie. Her son Bernard went with them, as he loved to ride in the new car and there was no school in honor of Lincoln's birthday.

As Nettie came out of the house, she slipped on the ice and turned her ankle. That evening at 9 o'clock, Will drove Harry and the girl from the Washington St. Hotel to Chicago. He left them on the corner of LaSalle, opposite the Fort Dearborn Hotel. This hotel was built to serve businessmen in Chicago. It was a low-rate economy hotel. Harry and the girl entered, and Harry got a room for two nights. Harry would bring her back to the hotel tomorrow. This way she would be out of town when Harry executed his plan. They didn't have much time, as Will was to pick them up in three hours.

"Dolly, there's something big going to go down in a few days, and I don't want you involved. We only have a few more days together, and I want them to count. I'll tell you more tomorrow night. Right now, let's pretend this is our last night together." They were ready for Will on the corner of LaSalle Street right on time.

Tuesday, February 13, 1923

William took the children to their schools and then picked up Nettie. They went to Indiana Harbor to get Anna to go to Chicago. Nettie wanted to talk to her broker and discuss the Durant Motor check to see if it cleared Harry's account. She was never sure what Harry really did. She also wanted to talk with her attorney about the offer Harry made about adopting the children. The broker said the check had cleared. Now Harry could write her a check for the same amount. Her attorney warned her not to go ahead with the adoption. If so, Harry would inherit everything even if the will said something different. He suggested giving him a set amount, maybe $20,000 ($285,000 in 2017 dollars).

She and Anna talked about Nettie getting a divorce from Harry. Nettie thought there might still be a chance to fix things. After all, there was baby Fay to think about.

Abe Ottenheimer, attorney and bank vice president, American State Bank.
Courtesy of Calumet Regional Archives, Anderson Library, Indiana University Northwest

William arrived back in Gary and took Harry to breakfast. Harry picked up a $60 check from the real estate agents Hall & Somers for the rent on one of Nettie's properties. At 10:30, William drove Harry to Indiana Harbor Bank to deposit the check and then to East Chicago. Harry had a court date in East Chicago for a speeding ticket. His attorney, Abe Ottenheimer, was there to defend him.

Abe was also the vice president of the American Savings Bank. "Harry, did you know that Nettie has a couple of notes overdue at the bank? Will you tell her she needs to come by and pay them or renew them?"

"Sure will, Abe. Oh, by the way, I just got a couple of real nice stones. Are you interested?"

"As a matter of fact I am," said Abe.

"I'll bring them by tomorrow, when we come in to settle up on the notes. By the way, you remember the $17,000 check I deposited the other day?"

"How could I forget? With a check that size, you got everyone's attention."

"Well, just let Nettie know it was a mistake on the part of the bank that it got into my account instead of hers. It will really get me out of the doghouse."

"Consider it done, Harry."

"Here's another deposit for her account, $300." Harry handed the cash to Abe.

At 4 o'clock, William drove Harry back to Gary from East Chicago. "Bill, let me show you a shortcut to Cline Avenue. Keep going on Chicago Avenue, about eight blocks past the Calumet Drugstore, then turn right onto Parrish Avenue."

"Yes, sir, Mr. Harry."

"See that jog to the left? Take it. It's the old Gary Road that runs into Cline Avenue." It was a desolate area, and a macadam road that was very rough, with lots of potholes. They passed the pumping station before the road met Cline Avenue. At Cline Avenue, Will took a right, passing the Cudahy packing plant, then over the wooden bridge that crossed the Greater Calumet River. Will then took a left onto Fifth Avenue and then Buchanan to the house.

Later that evening, when Nettie got back from Chicago, she talked to Harry. William was downstairs in the basement, but the door to the kitchen was open so he heard the argument. "Harry, I discussed the adoption of the kids with the attorney, and I think we're going to leave things the way they are for now. I'm writing another will, and I'll leave you $20,000 should I die before you."

"Thanks Nettie. At least I get something to take care of the kids."

"I don't know what you mean," Nettie said. "The kids will have their own money, Harry."

"When I was at the American Bank today, Abe Ottenheimer said you have two notes that are overdue and we need to go in and pay them or renew them."

"I don't know how that can be, Harry. I've been giving you the checks to pay them. I hope they haven't ended up in your account."

Harry's face started to turn red. "I make one mistake, and I'm not even sure it was me that put the check in the wrong account, and you accuse me of stealing from you. There's just no pleasing you, is there?" Harry said, with a disgusted look on his face.

"You can prove it to me now, Harry. Write the check for $17,000. It will go a long way to making me believe you're telling the truth."

Harry pulled out his checkbook and wrote out the check. He threw it on the table. "Feel better now?" he asked.

With that, he called down the basement stairs, "William, I'm ready to go." He grabbed his long chinchilla winter coat and headed out the back door with William. "Let's go by Washington Street and pick up the girl. We're going to Chicago."

When they got to the apartment Harry handed William an envelope. "Bill, can you put your father's address on this? I'm planning on taking out some insurance on you so if you get hurt you'll get paid and I won't get sued. If you die, your father will be the beneficiary. Just want to be careful," Harry explained.

Bill took the pen and put his father's address on the envelope. He wrote F.G. Armstrong, 2304 Broadway, Gary, Indiana. Harry's mind was racing ahead. *When I kill him, it might as well be me that collects on his insurance. No*, he thought, *too risky. I just hired him five days ago. Besides it really wasn't in the plans.*

Just then, Dolly came out of the apartment—this time with a suitcase. Will dropped them off at the same corner on LaSalle in the Loop. Harry and Dolly walked across the street to the Fort Dearborn Hotel. When they got to the room, Dolly was ready for an explanation. "Look Dolly, I want you to get out of town tomorrow. I don't want you to be nailed by the police."

"What would the police want with little ol' me?" she asked, flipping her hair and batting her eyes.

"OK, here's the skinny. I'm gonna knock off the old lady and the chauffeur tomorrow. Got it all set up to frame the chauffeur for the murder."

"You mean you gonna kill Will, that nice colored boy?"

"That's the ticket, sweetheart. Then I get all the old dame's dough. She's writing a new will that hasn't been filed yet, so I have to do it tomorrow. I know the cops will be looking at everyone and everything in my life to try to pin it on me, but I'm too smart for them. You know I studied law for a few months at Valparaiso University. I know how these guys think, and they ain't too smart. Anyway, I want you to go to Louisville, Kentucky, and lay low at the Steelbach Hotel on Fourth Street. I've wired them some money and a reservation under the name Abe Levy. I'm giving you five C notes ($500, which was $7,000 in 2017 dollars) to tide you over till I come down and get you. Register under Mrs. Levy. If you have to leave the place, just give them a forwarding address and tell them to tell your husband where you are when he comes to town. Whatever you do, don't call, write, or telegram me—no matter what you read in the papers. I'll meet you there, babe, after things cool down around here. I'll need to dump them kids on someone, and we'll have a new life together."

"Oh, Harry, I thought you would never get free of that awful woman. Now I know you really mean it."

"OK, doll, we still have a few hours for you to show me how much this means to you."

Three hours later, Harry was on the corner but not Dolly. "Guess you're wondering where Dolly is, Bill?"

"Not my business to ask, Mr. Harry."

"She's planning to do some shopping tomorrow, so I got her a room for the night," Harry volunteered.

The weather on the way back was getting colder by the minute. This happens in Chicago when a blast of cold air comes down from Canada. The cold winds scream across Lake Michigan, and everyone walks backward to keep their faces from freezing in the wind. Harry had heard that Hammond was having trouble with their water intake out in Lake Michigan. Needles of ice were forming in the water intake, and the water pressure was going to zero. Not good if they had to fight a fire. They needed a diver to open up the intake pipe. Only one diver was willing to do the task. He was successful and got paid $50 ($700 in 2017 dollars).

When they got home, Harry said, "Bill, I think you had better put some chains on the Hudson. This cold weather will make the roads icy tomorrow."

"I take cares of it, Mr. Harry," Will answered.

By the next morning, the temperature was down to -5 degrees, and any moisture on the roads had turned to ice.

CHAPTER 15

Wednesday, February 14, 1923— Valentine's Day

William was at the house early and was in the basement warming himself by the furnace. Putting the chains on the Hudson in this weather made him enjoy the warmth of the furnace. It was bitterly cold outside, with an overcast sky and a strong north wind.

Nettie was in the kitchen getting breakfast for the children, but Harry was still in bed.

"William, the children are ready for school," Nettie called down to him in the basement.

"I's ready, Miss Nettie."

Nettie let the children out the front door. William met them at the car. They all got in. Lloyd, the oldest boy, got in the front seat next to William. The others fought over the two extra pop-up seats in the backseat. They first stopped at Horace Mann School to drop off Cecil. The school was just being built, and portable buildings were being used as the schoolrooms.

"Where's your lunch at, Cecil?" William asked.

"I don't know," he replied.

"Well, you just get along now. I's be bring'n it to you later."

"OK, Mr. Will," he said, as he got out of the Hudson and went off to school.

The next stop was Emerson, which was across town on the other side of Broadway. The three older children all had their lunches. Will was glad he had the chains on the machine, as the melted snow and ice of a few days ago was now as hard as crystal and slippery. When he got back to the house, Nettie was ready to go to the kosher meat market at 15th and

Emerson School, Gary, Indiana. *Courtesy of Wikipedia*

Washington. Nettie knew just what she wanted. It was a quick trip, but the heater made the Hudson toasty warm.

Harry was up by 8:30. Will drove him to breakfast at Seventh and Broadway at the grill across the street from the Tribe of K, a stationery store. Will waited for Harry to finish breakfast. Then Harry went to the barber shop between Seventh and Eighth for a shave.

"Bill, here's 5 cents go pick me up a paper at the Tribe of K."

"Sure thing, Mr. Harry." Will came back to the barber shop with the paper.

Harry finished his shave, paid the barber, went out the door with Will, and got back in the Hudson. "Take me to the Sydney Hotel, Bill." It was on Fifth and Washington, the same hotel where he picked up Dolly. Will saw Harry go in, meet a man, then come out. "Let's go over to Steve's Place at 16th and Washington," Harry said. Steve's Place was a soft drink parlor that was a cover for a saloon: soft drinks in front, hard liquor and beer in the back.

Steve was behind the bar. When he saw Harry, he signaled for a relief man and took Harry into his office. "OK, boy, are you ready to do the deed?" he asked.

"Yeah, I think I got it all worked out. Just need to get the nigger to write the letter."

"What letter?" Steve squinted his eyes, like he didn't understand.

"I got to frame the nigger so's I'm gonna have him write a letter that says he's got the money and diamonds. I'm gonna make him think the letter is for a joke on another kid's dad."

"Do you think he'll fall for it?" Steve asked.

"I can read him like a book. He'll do anything I say," boasted Harry.

"Now let's go over the shooting again. If you gut shoot dem, dey will die slowly, bleed to death inside. If you shoot dem in the head, you gotta get da brain, so go through the eye. Your 32 caliber doesn't have the punch of a 38, so get real close to dem. Of course, a shot to the heart will kill dem quick. If that doesn't work, finish the job by breaking dere skulls. Use the gun handle; it's heavy. You're not goin' chicken out, Harry, are ya?"

"No, I got a lot of details runnin' through my head right now. Just wanted to see you before I did it."

"Where you keeping the heater (gun)?"

"It's in a side pocket of the driver's door. Easy for me to grab around the side of the seat."

"Remember, it only has five shots. Don't use dem all on the dame." Steve slapped Harry on the shoulder as he exited the soft-drink parlor.

Harry was back in the Hudson and had Will drive him to the police station and the real estate office of Hall & Somers. He wanted to get as many alibis as possible showing he was just going about his business on a normal day.

They stopped in front of Slocum's drugstore. "Bill, here's a nickel. Go in and buy a tablet of paper." In only a few minutes, he was back in the car. "Bill, I want you to address this envelope." He handed the envelope over to Will with a pen. "Address it to Mr. Mcheil Levy, 836 Connecticut St., Gary, Indiana.

Mcheil had a grocery over on Connecticut Street and seven kids. The oldest was Abe, 33. He also had a son named Bill, who was 21.

The letter Harry was about to dictate could have been plausible to William—just in case he questioned Harry about the people.

"Bill, take that tablet you bought and write this letter. I would have had the children do it, but I forgot. It's a trick a Jewish boy wants to play on his parents. The boy left home a few days ago with only $11 in his pocket."

Bill put the tablet on the steering wheel and wrote as Harry dictated. Will wrote the letter in his own hand as best he could.

> Dear Folks,
>
> I am leaving Gary with a new car, several thousand dollars worth of diamonds, and some cash. Mr. Charlie has promised to buy the car and diamonds from me. I am leaving Gary for good. You will hear from me later on.
>
> Your devoted son,
>
> Will

"You need to date the letter back one day, Bill—to the 13th."

Will handed the letter to Harry. Harry put it in the envelope Will had addressed. Will noticed that there was a one cent stamp on the envelope when postage was two cents for a letter, but he didn't say anything. He backed the machine out onto Fifth Street to the post office. Harry went in and then came back out. Will thought Harry had mailed the letter, but Harry had put the letter in the envelope Will had addressed to his father the night before and put it in his own breast pocket.

"Bill, we're not that far from home. I need to take the car. I will meet you back there in about half an hour." Will got out of the car, pulled his coat up around his neck, and headed back to the house.

Harry drove to his parents' house on Monroe to talk to his dad. "OK, Pop, I'm ready to get things going. Did you get Nettie's safe open and all the bonds and stocks?"

"Here they are, kid."

"Did you get rid of the safe?" Harry asked.

"I had some of da boys drop it in the Calumet River. Ve von't be seeing that safe for a long time. Vhat you gonna do vit all dem bonds?"

"I'm gonna mail them to myself. If you mail general delivery, they just hold your stuff at the post office until you pick it up."

"Your mother and I love you, Harry, so be careful." His mother Esther, his sister Ruth, and his dad gave him a big hug.

"You all know about picking up the kids from school?"

"Ruth is going to get them in the Model T."

Harry took the envelope with the stocks and bearer bonds and addressed it to go to Louisville Kentucky General Delivery to be picked by Abe Levy. He then went back to the post office and mailed it.

Harry drove the Hudson back to the house and turned the stop cock off on the heater line. "OK, everyone, it's time to go," he said, as he entered the house. "Nettie, we need to drop off the baby and the maid at my parents' house. The heater isn't working in the Hudson. I just took it to the garage, and they couldn't fix it."

"That's strange. When William took me to the market, it was keeping the machine nice and warm," said Nettie.

"I don't know. These new cars always have bugs in them, but the baby will be fine with Mama. Do you have the stones?"

"They're right here in my beaded bag, alongside your check," she said. He cringed when she brought up the check. Last night's argument was still fresh in his mind.

They all got into the machine, bundled up against the cold, with Nettie in her heavy fur coat. Harry sat behind Will. Nettie was on his right side, the maid and baby next to her. They dropped off the maid and baby Fay, then went down Fifth Avenue to the Horace Mann School to drop off Cecil's lunch. Will went into the school. Harry and Nettie stayed in the Hudson.

While they were waiting, Harry leaned forward and pulled the gun out

Downtown Gary, showing Goodman's Department Store and Tribe of K, 1923. *Courtesy of Stephen G. McShane, archivist, Calumet Regional Archives, Anderson Library, Indiana University Northwest*

of the driver's door side pocket and began to load it. "What are you doing?" Nettie asked.

"Can't be too careful these days. A lot of people know I'm in the diamond business and may want the stones. Lot of guys are getting bumped off in Chicago, and I don't want to be one of them. I'm just being prepared to defend us."

Will got back in the car. Harry kept the gun in his lap. "To Indiana Harbor, Bill," Harry ordered.

The Trip to Indiana Harbor via Gary Avenue

They left the school and went down Fifth Avenue, turning right onto Cline Avenue. Nettie picked up the argument from where they left off last night when Harry stormed out of the house. "*A geshenktn ferd kukt men nit in/af di tseyn* (don't look a gift horse in the mouth), Harry."

"*Es iz nit dayn gesheft* (it's none of your business) what I do with my money," he shot back.

"I do when it's my *gelt* (money)," Nettie replied.

"*Vos ret ir epes* (what are you talking about)?"

"I'm through giving you 'loans.' From now on, it's going to be just like our marriage agreement said. What's mine is mine; what's yours is yours. I thought you would be different after

Baby Fay Diamond, *The Times*, June 2, 1923. *Courtesy of* The Hammond Times *and Newspaper Archives*

the birth of our baby, but all you care about is Harry. Tomorrow, I plan to file the new will and you get $20,000. That should be enough to keep you in flappers for the rest of your life."

Harry was silent. He knew what he was about to do, and now he had good reason. They were just passing the Cudahy packing plant. "Bill, turn here," Harry said.

"Why turn here?" asked Nettie.

"It's shorter," he said.

Will turned left onto Gary Avenue, also called the Gary Road. It was macadam and very rough with potholes that were filled with refrozen melted ice from the day before. The road was covered with a topping of windswept snow. It was hard to tell where the side of the road was. Will kept to the left, as he knew from the day before that the right side had more potholes.

When they got halfway between Cline Avenue and the pumping station, Harry said, "Bill, I think you lost your right rear chain."

"I'll check, Mr. Harry." Will pulled the Hudson to a stop on the left side of the road and got out, closing the door behind him. He walked back a ways looking for the chain behind the machine and then turned and saw Harry looking back at him through the back rear window. Will gave him a sign that the right rear tire had its chain in place.

As he walked back to the right side of the Hudson to inspect the chain, he heard a "Bang," then he heard Nettie scream, and then another "Bang." After the second bang, he knew he was hearing gunshots.

Harry had the gun in his lap and held it against Nettie's stomach, firing through her fur coat. The next shot was under her left eye into her brain. This shattered the left eye socket, dislodging her eye. The bullet to the stomach cut through her intestines and lodged in her spine. Blood started flowing out her nose and mouth. Will ran to the passenger side as Harry was stepping onto the running board and opened the door.

Will asked, "What's the matter with Mrs. Diamond?"

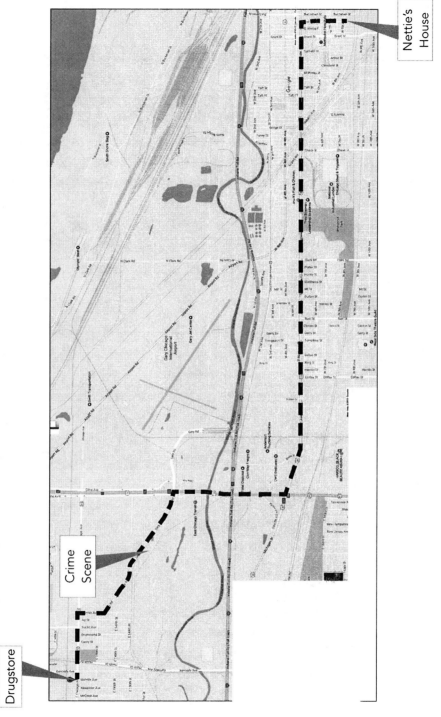

Map of Gary and East Chicago. Route of Nettie and Harry, and William Armstrong. Scene of shooting. *Courtesy of Google Maps*

Current look of crime scene on Gary Road. *Courtesy of Google Maps*

"Nothing. Get in the car," Harry said, as he opened the back "suicide door." (The back doors of the Hudson were hinged in the back, not the front as cars are today.)

Nettie was hollering, "Harry, what did you do it?"

Will reached to open front door; then "Bang," he was shot point blank under his left temple, with the bullet exiting his right cheek. Will fell back out of the Hudson, and his feet lay slightly under the machine between the front and back wheels. While he lay under the machine, Harry hit him over the head two or three times with the butt of the gun. Harry then opened the back door. With his foot on the running board, he started to beat Nettie over the head. One, two, three, four, five times. Nettie lost count.

"You're my husband. Why are you killing me?" she pleaded.

Harry heard nothing, except he knew she was still alive. Her thick luxurious hair softened the blows but not enough to keep her skull from fracturing. Blood ran down her face and covered her dress and fur coat.

"Why are you beating me so?" she cried. "I'll leave you. I'll give you what you want. Just don't kill me, Harry." He hit her again. One, two, three times. She lost count, but it was 15 times, and the handle of the Smith and Wesson was now broken.

Nettie lay over to one side and passed out. Harry reached into the pocket of her fur coat and took the beaded bag with his check and the diamonds. He then picked Will up from under the Hudson and put him in the passenger side of the front seat. Will started to crawl toward the steering wheel. He wanted to start the machine and get away.

Harry said "lay down." He went around to the driver's side, opened the door and, with his left hand on the steering wheel, starting beating Will again with what was left of the gun handle. Will was lying motionless, playing possum. Harry reached over and slipped an envelope inside Will's breast pocket. He then took Will's left hand and put his fingers around the gun and tried to make him squeeze it. Will started to relax his grip, and Harry took the gun back and started hitting him again.

"Damn you. I got you now," he said. Will covered his head. The blows of the gun broke the fingers on his left hand and put holes in his chauffeur's cap.

"I wants to live," Will said. "What you committin' murder for?" Will raised up on the passenger side of the front seat. He backed up against the door. "Mr. Harry, don't you hit me no more."

Harry pointed the gun at Will. "I'll shoot you again," he warned.

Nettie came awake and yelled from the backseat, "Will, take the pistol; take the pistol!"

With that, Will took his left leg, putting his foot against Harry's chest. The adrenaline was coursing through his body. He kicked Harry clear out of the machine. At the same time, Will's left elbow broke the passenger window from the force of the kick. With his uninjured right hand, he opened the door, jumped out, and immediately fell down. He got up and started to run back toward Cline Avenue.

Harry had to get back in the Hudson and climb over the gears to get to the other side of the car to give chase. Will had a head start, but Harry ran after him. Harry lost his Stetson hat somewhere along the road.

Just then, two cars came toward Will, seeing him covered in blood and yelling "Murder!" with his hands up in the air. They didn't slow down; they just put on the gas. Harry gave up the chase and went back to the Hudson.

Will flagged down a truck that picked him up. "Harry Diamond shot his wife and me," he said to the driver, William Eggers. "Take me to a doctor."

"Where is he?" Eggers asked.

"It's that Hudson standing there now. Don't go by. He'll kill you." William got in. Just then, Harry started the Hudson and sped toward East Chicago. Something was wrong with Eggers' truck's carburetor, and he couldn't get up any speed.

Coming from East Chicago was a Ford Touring car that Eggers flagged down and transferred Will. It was driven by Lloyd W. Parsons, the manager of the Illinois Telephone Company. He had with him three men just getting off a shift, and they were all going to dinner. He turned his machine around and headed back to East Chicago about two miles away. As they got close to the phone company on Chicago Avenue, they passed the Hudson, which was precariously parked in front of the Calumet Drugstore.

The telephone company was a few blocks farther west. Parsons called the doctor, George F. Bicknell, and the police. Leo McCormick, a traffic policeman, was in the area when Mr. Parsons' call came in, and he went directly to the telephone company. He saw Will sitting on a settee covered in blood with a pool of blood gathering at his feet.

Harry had been taken to the East Chicago Jail, while Will was waiting at the telephone company. The chief of police called and asked Officer McCormick to check for an envelope that Harry said was on Will. There was none.

Dr. Bicknell arrived, examined Will, and found the bullet had entered his left cheek under the zygoma and exited under the right eye. He had him remove his cap, which was soaked with blood. He found multiple scalp lacerations to the top and back of his head. Several fingers on his left hand were broken. He called an ambulance for Will. They

TOP:The Gary Road crime scene 2017. *Personal collection*
LEFT: Front seat of 1923 Hudson. *Courtesy of Hostetlers Hudson Auto Museum, Shipshewana, Indiana*

transported him back to Gary and the Mercy Hospital. Dr. Bicknell got in his own car and followed the ambulance to the hospital. Will would spend 19 days in the hospital.

Harry and Nettie at the Calumet Drugstore

Harry fled the scene down Gary Avenue toward East Chicago. *Why am I in a hurry?* Harry thought. *Steve said a shot to the gut would have them bleed out and die. She should be dead by the time we get there.*

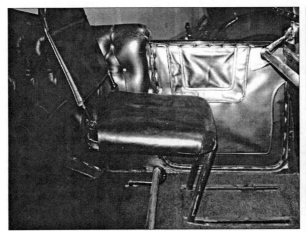

LEFT: Pop up extra seat. *Courtesy of Hostetlers Hudson Museum*
RIGHT: Nettie's view from back seat of 1923 Hudson. *Courtesy of Hostetlers Hudson Auto Museum, Shipshewana, Indiana*

There was silence in the backseat. On one curve on the Gary Road, he heard Nettie's body slip from the backseat and land on the floor. Then he heard, "Harry, why are you killing me? You can have all the money. Just let me live for my babies. Don't you care about your baby?"

Harry spoke, "I'll get all the money anyway. You didn't file the new will yet. I'll tell them the nigger shot you and I shot the nigger."

"You know you shot me, not William. I'll tell everyone the truth."

"Oh no, you won't," he said. As they were nearing the drugstore on Chicago Avenue, he slowed down. Harry turned in his seat, reached over the back, and fired one more shot into Nettie. At the angle she was lying, it entered her stomach area again, causing more damage to her intestines, but it also got a lobe of her liver and her spleen.

"Ooooh," she moaned in pain, as the bullet met its mark.

Harry made a sharp left turn across traffic on Chicago Avenue into Melville Street, putting the passenger side of the Hudson against the curb opposite the front door of the drugstore. Frank Simbolmos was driving up Melville Street and was almost hit as the Hudson came to a stop. He thought he had heard a shot but wasn't sure. Frank owned the Central Garage on Melville and lived just 300 feet from the drugstore. Always curious about what was going on, he throttled down his Ford and came to a stop across the street. He saw Harry jump out of the Hudson and run in the front door of the pharmacy.

Harry saw Hershel Canan. "Somebody call a doctor and the police. A nigger shot my wife, but I think I shot the nigger." Harry was then out the door. Frank saw Harry carry someone out the back door of the Hudson and into the drugstore. Frank waited a bit before he went in.

Hershel took two nickels from the register and went to the pay phone. He called Dr. Townsley and the East Chicago Police. His assistant pharmacist, James Storer, went to the front of the store and saw Harry drag Nettie from the car. Storer held the door open, and Harry brought Nettie in and threw her down on the terrazzo floor.

Harry started for the back of the store. Storer followed. "It seemed like he wanted to wash his hands. I asked him to wash his hands behind the prescription case. Instead, he turned and put his hands on me and said, 'I shot the nigger, and I hope I killed him.'"

Storer separated from him and went to the front of the store. At about the same time Frank Simbolmos had seen the Hudson stop in front of the drugstore, Thomas Kochis was walking home. His job at the railroad freight house was west of the drugstore. He also thought he heard a shot and then saw the Hudson pull in front of the store. He too saw a man in a light brown chinchilla coat run into the store and then come out and carry a woman's body into the store. He waited a bit before he entered the drugstore.

Inside, Harry walked back and knelt down by Nettie. "Honey, I didn't mean to do it." Nettie answered, "You're a liar. You shot me for my money."

No one else was in the store, and Canan was on the phone. Canan came over to Nettie after he made the calls. Nettie said, "Do what you can for me. Don't believe what Harry says. Harry shot me and also the colored boy. He knows it was not the colored boy that shot me. Don't believe that. I'm in my right mind. I recently made my will and left him $20,000. He also has $17,000 of my money in his account that is not his."

The floor was covered with blood. When Harry brought Nettie in, he also brought in snow and ice, which was melting on the floor, causing Nettie to lie in cold slush. You could hardly recognize it was the face of a person, with all the clotting blood on her face and in her hair.

Kochis and Simbolmos came in and talked to Canan. Simbolmos ordered a few soft drinks and watched the scene unfold. Then both men went over to Nettie on the floor. Simbolmos had known Nettie from the time she was married to Sam. She recognized him, which was amazing, as she could see through only one eye and her face and head were covered in blood.

She remembered him as the local gossip, so was sure her story would get out. "Don't believe anything that Harry Diamond tells you. It's not true. Everything I tell you is true. Oh, how he did beat me over the head with that gun and shoot me." She paused. "Oh my, I didn't think he would do such a thing when I made a will the day before that gives him $20,000."

The men could not believe how strong her voice was. Harry came over and knelt down and tried to kiss her.

"I don't want nothing to do with you, Harry. You are my husband, but you did shoot me, not the colored boy."

Simbolmos left the store. He had seen and heard enough. He went out to his machine he had left running to keep it warm on this very cold day.

In about eight minutes, the police were there, Hiram Kerr and Ed Knight, a former police sergeant and now bailiff for the East Chicago City Court. Knight heard the call at the station and picked up Kerr, and the two of them came out together. Knight knew Harry, or at least he had seen him in the East Chicago Court too many times to count. He saw him as a fancy Dan who thought he was too smart for the law. Now here he was, crossing paths with him again.

Dr. Townsley, also the deputy coroner of Lake County, came in following the police. Nettie saw him come in. "Dr. Townsley, I'm in my right mind and I know what I'm saying. I want you and everybody to know that my husband shot me."

"I don't care about that, Nettie. I'm here to take care of you."

Harry had been watching and moved in closer. "No, honey, I didn't shoot you. The Negro shot you."

She said, "No, he did not; you shot me yourself."

Canan went behind the prescription case and down the stairs to the basement to get a cot for Nettie. Harry followed but stopped at the head of the stairs and took the beaded purse from his pocket. He reached up and wedged it in the transom over the door to the basement stairs. Canan came up with the cot.

Dr. Townsley said, "Will one of you men help me move her to the cot behind the prescription case?" Ed Knight volunteered, and both he and Dr. Townsley moved Nettie onto the cot behind the prescription counter.

"Dr. Townsley," Nettie said, "do all you can for me." He used a towel to wash her face and hands and inspected her stomach for the bullet wounds. "Get the best doctor in Chicago. I believe I'm going to die; I'm badly injured."

Dr. Townsley knew she was in serious condition, as she was vomiting fecal matter. This meant her intestines had been ruptured by one or more of the bullets.

"Mr. Storer, call 271 for an ambulance. She needs to go to the hospital," Townsley said.

Harry was now behind the prescription case. "Harry, why did you shoot me? Why did you beat me over the head with the gun?" Nettie still spoke with amazing strength.

"I got a fit," Harry replied.

Policeman Kerr heard this confession, grabbed Harry, and took him out from behind the prescription case and set him on a chair in the middle of the store. "You're under arrest for attempted murder," Kerr said.

Harry faked a seizure, slipping off the chair but not so quick as to hurt himself. Officer Kerr grabbed him by the nape of the neck and put him back on the chair. It was not a gentle move. Harry knew not to try that trick again. He stayed upright in the chair until the paddy wagon came and took him to the East Chicago Calaboose.

Nettie's Ride to the Hospital

The ambulance came, and Nettie was carried out. She was hardly recognizable as a human being. There were blood clots on her face, beneath the eye, and abrasions on her head. "She looks in very serious condition," observed Storer.

Dr. Townsley rode in the ambulance with Nettie. "Doctor, what do you think about my condition. Am I going to die?"

"I don't know how serious your wounds are, Nettie." He had served in WWI and saw many gunshot wounds. He feared the worse, as Nettie had been vomiting in the drugstore and now in the ambulance. This was not a good sign, as the vomit was the contents of her intestines. "Do you have any preference of doctors I should call?" Townsley asked.

"I don't know of any. I trust you to use your discretion. Do you think I have a chance?" Nettie asked.

"Your vomiting tells me your intestines have been injured, and that is very bad. Are you sure there is no doctor you want me to call?"

"You can call Dr. Craig of Gary." Nettie found herself thinking of her first husband, Moshe. *This is what he must have felt after he was shot in the stomach*, she thought.

After the x-rays in the hospital, Dr. Townsley's assistant, Dr. Yarrington, talked to Nettie. "What did the x-rays show you, doctor?"

"It's not good, Nettie. Your intestines are severed in many places. We'll do everything we can, but I don't think you'll survive."

Nettie broke down. "Oh my babies. I'll never see them again. I'll never see what their lives will be like." The anesthesia took hold, and Nettie was silent.

The doctors both agreed that if the experimental blood transfusions they both saw during WWI were available, maybe she would have a chance.[1] With this much loss of blood they couldn't believe her will to live was so strong.

February 14, 1923—Nettie Goes into Surgery

They started the operation at 2 p.m. and finished at 4 p.m. Nettie's strength pulled her through the operation, much to the surprise of the doctors. She still had things to do. She just couldn't die yet.

They found nine perforations of the intestines, with two almost completely severed. Three inches of the small intestine had to be removed and connected together with a Murphy Button. The lower lobe of the liver was perforated, as was the spleen, and there were two holes in her stomach. One bullet was lodged in her spine. The other was found in her intestines. The bullet to her head went through her left nasal bone and fractured the bones of the left eye socket and ended up in her skull, not entering her brain. They left this bullet in her skull. Shaving her hair revealed fifteen lacerations to her scalp, some as long as two inches. One broke the suture of the parietal and frontal bones, which could not be reconnected.

The anesthesia was wearing off about 5:30 p.m. People were already in her room when she came back from surgery. Lena, Harry's sister, left her job early at the wholesale grocery where she worked as a stenographer. She first went with her father to the jail in East Chicago where Harry was being held. After they talked with Harry, the East Chicago police told her that Nettie had been taken to Mercy Hospital. She took Joseph home and went directly to Mercy Hospital and Nettie's room.

One of the nurses remembered her leaving, taking Nettie's blood-stained fur coat with bullet holes in it. She told her she was taking it home to get it cleaned. It was never seen again.

Harry at the East Chicago Jail

Harry was placed in the East Chicago Calaboose, or city jail. He said very little. He was brought in by Hiram Kerr and Edward Knight. He had $27 in cash and a diamond ring on his little finger. They took both for safe keeping. Officer Kerr had retrieved the gun, a

---

1 Blood transfusions didn't become commonplace until the 1930s after there was blood typing and methods to keep the blood from donors viable.

32 caliber Smith and Wesson. It was in the front seat of the Hudson, its handle broken. He gave it to Chief Struss.

"Is this your gun, Harry?" the chief asked.

"It is," Harry replied. The chief wrote down the serial number and noted the blood on the broken handle of the gun. There was still one live bullet in the chamber with four spent shells in the gun. He took them out and put them in an envelope. They took Harry and put him in central lockup, but not before he had a chance to talk to Lena, his sister, and Joseph, his father. They had arrived at the jail at almost the same time as Harry and the officers. They knew things had not gone as planned, and they feared the worse. The chief left them alone to talk.

"Tings didn't go so good for you Harry," his dad said.

"I'll be all right. Just had a fit, and I don't know what happened," Harry said, thinking the officers were listening to his conversation. Harry quietly whispered, "Get over to the house, find the new will, and destroy it."

"OK, Harry, ve vill go over to da house. Ve need tings for da baby," he said. "Ve need to get back to the house now. The children vill be coming home from school. Ve love you, Harry." With that, they were gone.

Officer Timothy O'Neil talked with Harry about 5 p.m. Harry asked, "Have you caught the nigger that shot my wife? Did you find anything on the colored boy, Armstrong? Did you find any stones? How's Mrs. Diamond? What am I doing here? What have I done wrong?" Harry questioned.

"She's in pretty bad shape," O'Neil replied. "We're sending Officers Lewis Edmonds and Callahan to the crime scene tomorrow morning to search for evidence."

The Kids Come Home from School

Pearle, Lloyd, and Bernard had waited for William to pick them up after school for the past hour, but no one came. Pearle said, "I guess we need to start walking home. We can go by the Diamonds' first. It's only eight blocks. We can warm up before we walk the rest of the way home."

"Good idea," Lloyd said. "It's only going to get colder."

Cecil was outside waiting for William at the Horace Mann School when he heard his name. "Cecil, over here." It was Ruth in the old Model T. He ran over to the flivver.

"Where's Mr. Will, Ruth?"

"I don't know. All I know is they told me to come pick you up and take you to our house." This, of course, wasn't the truth, but she had to get them all together before she would tell them the news. When Ruth pulled up in front of the house, the other three kids were just arriving.

"Let's get in the house. We're freezing," said Bernard.

The door opened, and there stood Esther Diamond holding baby Fay. They all seemed to push through the door at the same time to feel the warmth of the house. Once inside, Esther said, "Take off your coats, kids. You're going to have supper here tonight."

"Why?" asked Pearle.

Ruth spoke up. "Because your chauffeur killed your mother today. That's why."

"Who told you?" Pearle asked.

"Who cares who told me? That's the truth," Ruth said. "Lloyd, do you have your key to the house?"

"Yes," he said.

"Well, give it to me. I have to go to your house and get the baby's clothes and food."

Lloyd reached into his pocket and gave Ruth his key. When Ruth got to the house, her first job was to find the unfiled will. Lena told her that Harry insisted it must be destroyed. She had no problem finding it on the desk in Nettie's bedroom. She took it down to the furnace and burned it. She next picked up the things for the baby but couldn't help looking in Nettie's jewelry box. She helped herself to a few items. She and her sister and mother would be back tomorrow.

Anna Fishman had heard the news at 5 p.m., and it didn't take her long to head to Nettie's house. She had to see what was happening to the children and her best friend Nettie. She got to the house on Buchanan. It was dark. Not a light was on.

She then went to the Diamonds' house and found the children. They were so happy to see her. She was so close to the family that they all called her Aunt Anna. "Children, your mother is in the hospital. I'm going over to see her."

"See?" Pearle said, looking daggers at Ruth. "She's not dead, just in the hospital."

"Esther, can they stay here tonight?" asked Anna.

"Of course, they can. We have plenty of room on the floor."

"Children, tomorrow you will all come to my house until we can get things straightened out," Anna said.

"Is it true that William shot mom?"

"I don't know, Pearle, but we will all know soon enough. I'm going over to the hospital now."

"I'm going too," Pearle said, as she put on her coat.

"I guess that's OK. You're over 12, and that's the age limit they tell me for visitors." They were out the door in a flash.

Nettie in the Mercy Hospital

When they got to Nettie's room, she had just come out of the anesthesia. Harry's sister Lena had already been in the room but was now gone.

"Nettie," the nurse said, "do you know who is here at your bedside?"

"Yes, it's the dearest friend I have in the whole world, Anna. Anna, can you imagine Harry shot me? I afraid I'm going to die, and I worry about the children. Promise me you'll look after them and take care of everything?"

Nettie overheard the doctor and nurse talking that she had not responded to the stimulant. She was given 1/30 grain of strychnine and caffeine. and later, morphine sulfate and adrenalin chloride.

"Did you hear that, Anna? Do you know what that means? That means death. That means I'm going to die." Pearle was sitting next to Anna and heard everything. "Anna, I made out a will a few weeks ago and left everything to Harry. Two days ago, I changed it and only gave him $20,000, but that will is not filed. It's still on my desk at the house."

"I think you ought to get a lawyer, Nettie, and make a new will," Anna suggested.

"So you do know I'm going to die, don't you?" Nettie said, with desperation in her voice.

"Give me the name of the attorney you want me to get," Anna said.

"Call Mr. Sweeney. He's done work for me before."

Anna left the room and called Sweeney and explained the urgency of the situation. He was there within the hour.

"Hello, Nettie. I came as quick as I could. Anna says you want to make a new will."

"That's right. I don't want that lying husband of mine to get a cent of my money."

Nettie dictated her new will to Sweeney, indicating who would receive assets of the estate. She gave her first son, Edward Noah Sachs Zauderer, $2,000; Fay Diamond, $3,000; and Pearle, Lloyd, Bernard, and Cecil Herskovitz the remainder of her estate. "I appoint J.G. Allen, vice president of the Indiana Harbor National Bank, to be the executor of my will."

Anna and Pearle left about midnight. Pearle went home with Anna. Joseph talked with Lena that night and arranged for her younger sister Fannie to go into Chicago tomorrow. She would take Nettie's fur coat to a man he knew on Maxwell Street who would buy the coat.[2]

---

2 The Maxwell Street Market was on the west side of Chicago where in the 1920s, Eastern European Jews ran an open-air market. You could buy anything new or used, legal or illegal. It was an extension of the peddler culture from the old country.

And thereupon State's Exhibit No. 6 was read in
evidence and the same is in the words and figures following, to-wit:

State's Exhibit No. C.

Statement of Mrs. Nettie Diamond, Feby. 15th, 1923,
9:10 a. m.

My name is Mrs. Nettie Diamond. I am the wife of Harry
Diamond. We live at 647 Buchanan Street, Gary, Ind.
Yesterday we left our home in our Hudson sedan at about
10:30 a. m. Wm. Armstrong, a colored boy, was driving the
car. We were going to East Chicago. I had in my possession
a $17,000.oo check which I was going to deposit in the
American State Bank of East Chicago. This check was from
the sale of Durant motor stock which had been in my possession. Near the waterworks at East Chicago Mr. Diamond
told the colored driver to get out and see if one of the
chains were off. Armstrong got out of the car when Mr.
Diamond started to shoot me. The first shot when into my
abdomen. How many shots he fired into me I do not remember. He then stepped out of the car and shot some more.
I then heard Armstrong say, "Man alive, what are you committing murder for?" Harry then got back into the car and
beat me over the head with the gun. Harry then drove the

car to the Calumet drug store, East Chicago, and he said to
me, "Honey, tell them the nigger shot you." What became of
the $17,000.oo, I don't know. I make this statement know-
ing I am going to die.

                    (Signature)   MRS. DIAMONd.

Witnesses:
Miss Teressa J. Schamm, R N (Reg. nurse)
Miss Mae Gallager, (R N)
C W Yarrington   (Signature) Mrs. N. DIAMOND
Dr J M Craig
Wm. J. Linn

    This statement taken by Capt. W. J. Linn and officer
A. H. Windmueller of the Gary Police Dept."

Nettie's dying statement to the police. *Trial transcripts, Indiana
Supreme Court Archives*

CHAPTER 16

Thursday, February 15, 1923— Nettie Dies

Anna and Pearle were at the hospital the next morning about 9:45 a.m. Captain William J. Linn of the Gary Police Department was just leaving Nettie's room. He had just taken her statement describing the incident the day before, when Harry shot and beat both her and William Armstrong.

Officer Arthur Windmueller wrote the statement by hand. More than once, Nettie said, "I'm going to die." He had her sign the statement twice, once as Mrs. Diamond and then again as Mrs. Nettie Diamond. Nettie was awake and still talking when Dr. Townsley came in the room at 10:45 to check on her. It was about 11 a.m. when she said to Anna, "Anna, I can't fight anymore. Please take care of everything—the children, everything—because I will have to leave them."

At 12:30 p.m., she died. She was 37 years old—almost 38, as her birthday was March 15. Pearle watched her mother die. They were both in a state of shock when Anna got to the Diamonds' house and picked up the rest of the children. They stopped by the house on Buchanan. Pearle had her key. Anna went up to Nettie's bedroom and looked for the will Nettie said was on her desk. It wasn't there, but she had made a new will in the hospital. They picked up some of their clothes and other items they thought they might need. Baby Fay was left with her grandmother, Esther. Everyone else went home with Aunt Anna. She now had to enroll the children in the East Chicago schools, where they had been before the move to Gary. There was so much to be done—the funeral and Nettie's estate. Other people—the Diamond family—had plans for some of Nettie's estate: Joseph and Ruth used Lloyd's key to enter the house that Thursday night.

DEPARTMENT OF HEALTH - GARY, INDIANA

Certificate of Death

This certifies that, according to the records of this office

Name ......NETTIE DIAMOND...................died ..FEBRUARY 15, 1923......

DATE

at..MERCY HOSPITAL.................address..................................

Age at death ...33...... Sex ...F.. Race WHITE................ ..MARRIED...........

MARRIED / SINGL

Name of Husband or Wife ......HARRY DIAMOND.....................

Primary cause of death was ......HOMICIDE BULLET WOUND OF.........

.....INTESTINE FROM REVOLVER.....................................

Signed by........E. E. EVANS...

PHYSICIAN OR HEALTH OFFICER   ADDRESS

Place of burial or removal ....FORREST PARK, ILL...................

CEMETERY ADDRESS

Date of burial ..2-19-1923........ H. WEINSTEIN................

FUNERAL DIRECTOR ADDRESS

Filed ...3-15-1923...... Volume ......6........ Page ..62...

DATE

W. J. WHITE

HEALTH COMMISSIONER

HEALTH COMMISSIONER
CITY OF GARY, IND

DATE FEB 28 2012

Nettie's death certificate, which misstated her age as 33; she was really 37 years and 11 months old when she died. *Courtesy of ancestry.com.*

The Crime Scene

That day, February 15, about 10 in the morning, Officers Edmonds and Callahan went to the area they thought was the crime scene on the Gary Road. There, about 50 feet from Cline Avenue, they found a blood-stained envelope. It was still sealed and addressed to William's father. They also found a soft gray Stetson hat belonging to Harry. He lost it as he ran after William. They brought the evidence back to the station and turned it over to Officer O'Neil.

Later that day, the evidence was turned over to Captain Linn of the Gary Police. The captain went to Mercy Hospital to get William's statement. They paused to say hello to one guard who had been stationed outside William's room.

"Good afternoon, William. I'm Captain Linn of the Gary Police, and this is Officer Windmueller. Are these your parents?" William's parents had been with him all night after he was admitted to the hospital.

"Yes, sir," replied William. His father stood up and shook Captain Linn's hand.

"William, we're here to get your statement about what happened over on the Gary Road yesterday."

"Yes, sir," William answered.

"Just take your time and go over everything from start to finish. Officer Windmueller will write it all down."

William relayed the story from the time he showed up at the Buchanan house to when he was brought to the hospital. The story matched Nettie's perfectly.

"William, we found this envelope at the area where the shooting occurred. Do you recognize it?"

"Yes, dat's my handwriting and my father's address."

Officer Linn handed the unopened envelope to William's father. "This is addressed to you, so you may open it," he said. He opened the envelope and took out the letter from inside, looked at it, then handed it to the captain.

Captain Linn handed it to William. "Look at this letter, William. Is that your handwriting?"

"Yes, dat's da letter Mr. Harry had me write as a joke. He said a Jewish boy wanted to play a joke on his parents."

"It's dated February 13, 1923. Is that when you wrote it?" Captain Linn asked.

"No," said William. "I wrotes it on da 14th, but he axed me to date it on da 13th."

"Thanks, William. You get better now. We will need your testimony at the trial. We'll keep a 24-hour guard on your room. You're a pretty important fellow now that Mrs. Diamond has died."

A look of sadness came over William. "That nice lady died? I knows what it was like to be shot and beat over da head, but Harry shot and beat her more dan me. Why do you have a guard at my door? I ain't going nowhere," William said.

"It's not your leaving we're worried about," said the captain. "It's Harry's friends. They may not want you to testify. We want to keep you safe." He patted William's hand, the one without the broken fingers, reassuring him that he was safe. The two of them left the hospital, but not before talking to the guard outside William's room.

Thursday Night, February 15, 1923—Robbery

Ruth had the key to the house on Buchanan, and she and her father Joseph had plans for Nettie's estate. The timing didn't work out because Nettie didn't die on Wednesday; as Harry used to say, "That woman has nine lives." As soon as they heard she had died at noon on Thursday, they put their plan into action.

The children and Anna Fishman had visited the house that afternoon and had taken some of their clothes back to her place on Grand Boulevard in Indiana Harbor.

That night it was the Diamonds' opportunity to ransack the house. Joseph, Ruth, Lena and mother Esther entered the house that Thursday night, and the neighbors said the lights were on all night. They took everything of value, including all the clothes the children hadn't taken with them to Aunt Anna's house. The women found Nettie's silk lingerie. The court set its value at $2,000 ($28,000 in 2017 dollars). They even stole the deceased Dr. Herskovitz's fur-lined coat. They boxed everything that they didn't want to keep at their house.

On Friday morning, the 16th, they mailed the box weighing 65 pounds to a Mrs. Peter Hoss, 847 King Place, Chicago, Illinois, via American Express. This activity didn't go unnoticed. On Saturday, the 17th, Nettie's brother-in-law, Marcus Herschcovitz,[1] an attorney, got a search warrant for the Diamond house, as well as for The Standard Bottling Company where Nettie's safe was kept.

---

1 Marcus never spelled his name the same as his other brothers. He did things his way all his life.

CHAPTER 17

February 16, 1923— Harry Is Charged with Murder

Harry was brought into the East Chicago City Court. Edward Knight, the bailiff, who had been at the drugstore and helped Dr. Townsley move Nettie's mutilated body onto a cot, was there doing his job. Dr. Townsley, who was also the deputy coroner, charged Harry with first degree murder of Nettie Diamond, to be held without bail, on behalf of the state of Indiana. He testified that Nettie had told him Harry had shot her and the Negro chauffeur, and that Harry had beaten them both over the head with the handle of his gun.

Druggist Herschel Canan also testified that Nettie had told him the same story as she lay grievously wounded on the floor of the drugstore. Special Judge H.C. Carrol was in the process of reading the findings. Just then, the courtroom went into total darkness. It was 6 o'clock that winter evening, and no light was coming through the windows. The bailiff, Edward Knight, pulled his gun from its holster, expecting the worst. He was ready. A hush fell over the courtroom, and then everyone seemed to be talking at once. Captain Tim O'Neil grabbed ahold of Harry. Thirty seconds later, the lights went back on. Everyone breathed a sigh of relief, and Edward Knight holstered his revolver. It was thought to be a plot by Harry's friends to break him loose, but it turned out someone in the outside hall had turned the switch off to the courtroom lights by mistake. Nevertheless, everyone was now on guard to secure the prisoner against a jailbreak. Harry, charged with murder, had little to lose and much to gain if he should break out to freedom.

February 19, 1923—Harry Transferred to Crown Point Jail

Harry was transferred from the East Chicago Jail after his court appearance when he was charged with first-degree murder without bail. He was to be transferred to the Lake County Jail at Crown Point, Indiana. As he was leaving the jail, he was met by Joseph and Esther. Harry was all smiles. "Don't worry, Mom and Pop, I'll soon be out of this *little* scrape."

"Ve found da best lawyer ve could Harry, Charles Erbstein[1] of Chicago, to lead your team," Joseph said.

Esther tried to hug Harry, but the officers kept her at a distance. They didn't want to take the chance that she would slip Harry a gun.

Under heavily armed guards, he was put into the middle car of a three-car convoy. This was a high-powered vehicle. Captain Tim O'Neal was in charge, assisted by Officer Muha and Court Bailiff Edward Knight.

They arrived without incident. At the county jail, Harry found he was the only prisoner. Here he would wait until his trial. He knew Nettie's funeral was the next day and pleaded with the sheriff to let him attend. It is said that he offered the sheriff $1,000. The bribe didn't work; Harry stayed in jail.

Dora Loses Her Voodoo Dolls

It was early Saturday morning February 17 in St. Louis. Dora was on a rampage. "Where are my dolls, Joseph? If you've done anything to them I'll put a curse on you." Dora had threatened this before, but the look in her eyes made Joseph very uneasy. He joined in the search.

They had been having a rodent problem, and Joseph halfheartedly commented, "Maybe they were carried away by a rat?"

"Don't tell me no stories. Just keep looking," Dora ordered.

---

1   Charles Erbstein was a well-known attorney for mobsters in Chicago. A friend of gangster James Colosimo, also known as Big Jim, he ran brothels and saloons in Chicago. Erbstein had his own nightclub in Elgin, Illinois, the Purple Grackle. He was just starting his own broadcasting station, WTAS, in 1922 and turning over his cases to assistants, which probably was the reason he ultimately didn't take the Diamond case.

"There they are," Joseph said, as he peered under the bed.

"Where are you?" Dora asked.

"Here in the bedroom. I see them under the bed."

Dora rushed into the bedroom, got down on her hands and knees, and looked under the bed. There in the center almost out of reach were her precious voodoo dolls of Harry and Nettie. She reached under the bed and brought them out. "Look what happened to Nettie!" She showed the doll to Joseph. The rats or mice had pulled all the straw stuffing out of the body, and one had even chewed on the head. The Harry doll was untouched.

"I think the older Nettie doll had drier straw," said Joseph. "The rats or mice liked it better."

"I don't think so," said Dora. "These dolls are magic." Just then, the morning papers came along with the mail. Saturday was when Dora got a week's worth of *The Hammond Times* to check on Nettie and Harry. She tore apart the envelope, eager to see the headlines. There on the Wednesday edition: "**Woman's Husband Is Accused**. One of the victims died. The other, a chauffeur, was shot in the head." As she read further, she saw it was about Nettie Diamond.

In the next paper, on page 2, there was a box in the middle of the page: "**Late Development in Diamond Case**. Nettie Diamond still alive at Gary Hospital. Harry Diamond, her husband, is being held on an open charge."

Then the headline she was looking for: Friday, February 16: "**Diamond Accused of Murder**. Coroner Townsley ordered alleged slayer held for trial."

Nettie had died. Dora couldn't contain herself. She started running around the room screaming, "Nettie is dead, Nettie is dead!" She was clutching her voodoo dolls, talking to them. "Oh thank you, Harry. You did what Mama asked. You killed Nettie. She robbed Mama of the only love of her life. You killed Nettie."

Joseph knew something was wrong when the celebration stopped and Dora sat on the floor in the corner, never letting go of her dolls. After four days of this, he called the St. Louis Sanitarium and had her committed. When the attendants took her away, she was still saying, "Harry good. Killed Nettie for Mama. Nettie dead, Nettie dead."

Joseph contacted Sister Mary and told her about Dora. She said, "Som time da magic so powerful, it jump on you. Miss Dora no use magic for good, only bad. Bad magic more powerful, hard to control. It gots Miss Dora now."

CHAPTER 18

February 20, 1923—
Nettie's Funeral

It was another sad day for Nettie's children—first the loss of their father in 1916, and now their mother. Pearle was now 13, Lloyd 11, Bernard 10, and Cecil 8. Aunt Anna Fishman ordered a car from a rental agency for $30 ($420 in 2017 dollars) for her family and all the children to attend the funeral. Among those attending were Nettie's close friends Mr. and Mrs. Barinoff, Marcus Herschcovitz (he kept this different spelling of his name) and his wife Sophia, Dave Herskovitz, Mrs. E. Buchstaber, Mrs. Zimmerman, and Mr. and Mrs. Kirkendorfer. It was held in the Jewish section of the Waldheim Cemetery in the Weinstein Chapel, 3536 Roosevelt Road, Chicago.

Nettie was not laid to rest next to Sam. It's Jewish law that a woman can't be buried next to a previous husband if she has remarried. She was buried in the section called the Progressive Order of the Pioneers, while Sam was buried in The Independent Order of B'rith Abraham.

When they got to the cemetery, the boys stayed in the car while Pearle went to the burial plot with the rest of the family. Someone came by the car and handed the boys some candy bars.

"Oh, Pearle, it's so good to see you again," said her Aunt Rose from New York. "Just think how lucky we all were to see each other this past summer." Pearle remembered how much fun she had had visiting New York and meeting all her cousins. Coming with her Aunt Rose were her cousins, Florence, 17, and Louis, 19.

The funeral was the first time Lloyd got to meet this side of the family. They were always a mystery to him, his cousins that his mother talked about from New York. Now he got to meet two of his first cousins.

When they got back to Indiana Harbor, Rose got to talk with Anna. "Anna, last summer when Nettie came to New York, she mentioned the problems she was having, getting Harry to be a good husband. I told her that after the baby was born, things should change. I've never seen a Jewish man that didn't take care of his family."

"I know, Rose, and I feel so bad because at first I should have been more vocal in my doubts about the relationship. Nettie really needed a man around with all her real estate dealings, but this man was no good. She probably told you he is the son of a man she knew in our home town that was a *gonif* (thief), Joseph Finkelstein. I think he was behind the whole affair. He has a nose for other people's money, and he used his son to get it. Nettie's love was for her children. That was the only thing on her mind with her dying breath. I will do my best to see that they're taken care of."

"Thank you so much, Anna. I know Nettie would approve."

Edward Sacks of Houston

Bad news travels fast. "Look here in the paper, Edward," his wife Dora said, showing him an article in the Houston paper: "**Bootlegger Murders Wife for Her Money**."

Edward read the article. He couldn't believe his eyes. It was about his beloved sister Nettie. Self-preservation took hold. "This could be dangerous if we get involved, Dora. With the recent immigration act, they are deporting undesirables back to Europe. If Nettie was involved with breaking the law with bootleggers, we could be deported. I'm sure the bank can be trusted to look after her children. Besides, we have our hands full right here."[1]

---

1   This branch of the family never again communicated with Nettie's children. Nettie had made a number of trips to Houston when Edward's children were born. She made a point to give them American names. It wasn't until the late '70s when the author's father Bernard attended a principal's convention in Houston that by one lucky phone call, he found his cousin, Seymour Sacks, who was born the same year he was. This was the first branch of the family that was found, as Nettie's sister Rose never again contacted the family. In 2015, through a lucky break doing genealogy research, we found my cousin Ann Mitnick. She is the granddaughter of my Great Aunt Rose and a treasure trove of family history.

CHAPTER 19

Pretrial Events

February 24, 1923—Ruth and Joseph Diamond Charged with Grand Larceny

As a result of the search warrant asked for by Marcus Herschcovitz, Ruth and Joseph Diamond were charged with grand larceny. Ruth was taken from Gary to the jail in Crown Point. She was released after she posted a $1,500 bond. Joseph was nowhere to be found. Several days later, he was found hiding out at Nick's place in Hobart. He did not resist the arrest. Joseph was to be tried on the same charge as Ruth but with a separate trial. He too had to post a $1,500 bond.

The box containing Nettie's clothes and those of some of the children was on display in the courtroom. The box that had been sent to Chicago via American Express was also recovered. The children were in court and were asked to identify Nettie's clothes and other items in the box. Nettie's safe was still missing.

March 2, 1923—73 Gary Officials Charged with Conspiracy

Seventy-three Gary officials—from the mayor, Roswell O. Johnson, to the sheriff, Hut Olds—were charged with violating national Prohibition laws. William M. Dunn, judge of the city court, and Dwight M. Kinder, prosecuting attorney of Lake County, were also part of this group. Fifty-five were convicted. Their sentences ranged from one day to two years in jail, and fines of up to $10,000 were levied. These were the men responsible for enforcing the law, but when they confiscated illegal liquor, instead of disposing of it, they sold it. Many of Gary's most prominent citizens were involved, as were many of its saloon keepers. Harry's friend and partner, Matt Buconich, was one of these arrested in this raid.

March and April Events before the Trial

On March 1, it looked like Harry's problems just kept following him. He and Abe Rosen, his partner in The Standard Bottling Company, were sued for back rent of $300 ($4,200 in 2017 dollars). William Armstrong was released from Mercy Hospital on March 17 but heard his life was in danger. He asked and was granted police custody at the jail in Valparaiso, Indiana, as he also awaited the trial.

William J. Murray, attorney for Nettie's estate, searched the home on Buchanan Street for valuable papers and found none. He did get Nettie's rings and other valuables from Dr. Yarrington at Mercy Hospital. Murray and J.G. Allen, the executor of the estate, took several trips to St. Louis. They looked for safety-deposit boxes in Nettie's name and anything related to Edward Noah Sachs, her child from her marriage to Louis Zauderer.

Harry had changed the beneficiaries on both his and Nettie's $5,000 ($69,600 in 2017 dollars) life insurance policies. Now the beneficiaries on both the policies would be his parents, not Nettie or her children. J.G. Allen executor took issue with these changes. He pursued it in court but lost on appeal. All the money, $10,000, ($138,000 in 2017 dollars) went to Joseph and Esther Diamond.

On April 11, Harry again pleaded not guilty, and his attorney asked for a change of venue from Lake County. The change was granted. He would be tried in Valparaiso, in Porter County. The bank sold the new Hudson for $1,650 to John Bucnowski on April 26. Bucnowski was the pharmacist who ran Nettie's Red Cross Pharmacy on Cedar Street. He was a man always looking for a bargain, and he could overlook the car's history; after all, the damage had been repaired. The Hudson was a depreciating asset for the estate. J.G. Allen got the court's permission to sell it.

In April, Pearl "Pepe" Herskovitz, grandmother of the Herskovitz children, died in New York City. Their Uncles Marcus and Dave and Aunt Ettie went to the funeral. The children now had only one living direct relative—their grandmother, Mary Sachs, living in New York. She was ill and couldn't come to Nettie's funeral. She died in 1929.

The Boys Discuss a Plan to Spring Harry

The trial hadn't started yet. With all the problems Joseph was having with the grand larceny charge, the boys missed a few opportunities to spring Harry when he was in the East Chicago Jail. They had some men on the payroll on the inside, but they had no plan on what to do if Harry got out. Harry was now in the Crown Point Jail. His friends and father felt the sentence of death and the "electric cure" was a real possibility.

Joseph had just made bond from the grand larceny charge and was free at the moment. He and his oldest daughter, Ruth, had ransacked Nettie's house—both before and after she died in Mercy Hospital. Joseph was kept on ice for two days at one of Nick Slade's many hideouts. The Gary police got an anonymous tip and picked him up and put him under arrest.

The four of them—Abe, Steve, Matt, and Joseph—were meeting in the back room of Steve Buconich's soft drink parlor/saloon to talk about Harry. They had to devise a plan to spring him. "I don't know about that boy of yours," Matt Buconich said. "He's always thought he was smarter than everyone but can't seem to keep from gettin' nailed. Remember the robbery of the Excel Company? If it wasn't for his old lady's money, he would have spent time in the hoosegow (jail)."

"The jury did find him not guilty," said Steve.

Matt continued: "He likes to think he's in charge and never makes a mistake. I think he's more interested in his hair and clothes than anything else. He has trouble following through on the details. That's why we had problems at the roadhouse."

Abe chimed in: "Remember the case where he bribed two guys to say they bought liquor at Nettie's drugstore to try to break the lease? I've been watching that boy grow up, and sometimes I think he has as much concentration as a fart in a pickle barrel."

"Vhat's my boy you're talkin' about," said Joseph. "Ve gots a bigger problem now. Nettie is dead, but not the nigger chauffeur. Maybe kill the chauffeur?" Joseph suggested.

"I don't think we can get to the nigger now. He's holed up at da Valparaiso Jail," said Steve. "We can try to get a gun to Harry, like the Tommy O'Connor case. That's where a guy smuggled one in using a guy's wooden leg."

"You know a guy with a wooden leg?" asked Nick, with a laugh. "Maybe we can get him a saw if we can't get him a gun. Then let him cut his way out."

They all agreed it was going to be hard, but they wouldn't give up thinking of ways to help Harry. "If only he had shot and killed the nigger as he was running away. He still had

Valparaiso Jail. *Courtesy of Wikimedia Chris Light-own work, cc By-SA 4.0*

two slugs left in the gun. He did plant that letter on the chauffeur, so just maybe that's gonna help," said Steve. "I still want to know why the hell he couldn't kill Nettie. He put three slugs in her at close range," Steve added.

"Harry use to say that woman is like a cat; she has nine lives," said Matt. "Did any of you guys teach him to shoot?" No one volunteered an answer.

"Dere's still a chance he might get off. I'm gettin' the best lawyers from Chicago and Hammond," Joseph said. "Charles Erbstein from Chicago and Joseph Conroy, the 'Little Giant,' from Hammond. Conroy's got a record of getting niggers off murder charges. If he can do dat, maybe dere's hope," said Joseph.

The meeting ended, but they all agreed to go to the trial. Maybe there they would think of some angle to free Harry.

Klan Rally in Valparaiso

Harry had been transferred to the Valparaiso Jail from the Lake County Jail in Crown Point after April 11, when his attorneys asked for and received a change of venue for the trial. Joseph was there the first day Harry was transferred. He came every morning after that and gave Harry words of hope and cheer to get him through this ordeal. Armstrong was moved from this jail to an undisclosed location.

Joseph kept telling anyone who would listen that Harry was out of his mind, having an epileptic spell when he shot Nettie. "He didn't know what he was doing," Joseph said.

The weekend before the trial was to start, there was a massive gathering of 20,000 Ku Klux Klan members in this rural town of Valparaiso. The KKK had become very strong in Indiana in the 1920s. This was partially due to the large influx of Eastern European Jews, Mexicans, and Negros who were attracted to the industry in northern Indiana. The Klan was so strong in this region that it almost bought Valparaiso University, and the governor of Indiana was a Klansman. The parade of the sheeted and hooded Klansmen back and forth along the street outside Harry's cell made him very unsettled.

"Sheriff Pennington, please come here," Harry called out from his cell. There was the sound of a clank of the prison door.

The sheriff came over to Harry's cell. "What's the problem, Harry?"

"I'm worried about all those Klansmen out there. Could they break into this jail and lynch me?"

The sheriff saw the irony of the situation: this cold-blooded killer afraid for his own life from a mob. The sheriff couldn't resist: "I suppose they could overpower me and break into the jail. These doors were not built to stop a mob."

"Well, could you at least stay back here with me until they are out of town?"

"If that will make you feel better, I could do that, but then who's going to watch the front door?"

"Don't you have any extra deputies that could come to the jail tonight? Do they know you have a Jew in here?"

"Don't rightly know, Harry, but if you don't keep your voice down, the Klansmen will hear you through the bars on your cell window."

Harry became quiet. By Monday morning, the Klan members were gone.

Valparaiso Jail cell now part of the Museum. *Courtesy of Wikimedia Chris Light-own work, cc By-SA 4.0*

Harry (right) goes to court, *The Times*, June 2, 1923. *Courtesy of The Hammond Times and Newspaper Archives*

CHAPTER 20

Harry Is Tried for Murder

Monday, May 21, 1923—The Trial Starts

The jury selection took some time, as the first two groups of 40 men were selected and rejected by the attorneys. Harry was ready for his first day in court. He was well-dressed, showing an air of confidence. His hair was well-oiled and combed back and cut in the "sheik style." He wore a three-button small-check suit, tan oxford shoes, a blue shirt with a soft collar, and a knit tie. He made sure his sisters had brought him all his clothes from the house. He was no stranger to a courtroom or a jury—he had been there many times before and had always come up with the winning hand.

Tuesday, May 22, 1923—The Second Trial Day

A new group of 50 men was selected, and 12 of them needed to be seated as jurors to begin the trial.

The attorneys for Harry were a team led by Joseph Conroy, known as the "Little Giant," because he was only five-foot-three. (Mob lawyer Charles Erbstein—Joseph's first choice to head Harry's defense team—had declined to take the case.) Conroy was assisted by attorneys William Mathews and Frank B. Parks. Attorneys for the state of Indiana were special prosecutor William J. McAleer and prosecuting attorneys F.R. Marine and John C. Stevens. Both Conroy and McAleer were from Hammond and had crossed paths many times before. They did not like each other.

The judge, Hannibal Hamlin Loring, knew this and was ready for the battle to keep them in line. McAleer repeatedly objected to the long verbose questions Conroy proposed to the jurors. "You're grandstanding, Conroy," McAleer said.

"Well, you're just trying to railroad Diamond to the electric chair," replied Conroy.

"You're just a pettifogger, Conroy," said McAleer.

"Take your seats," Judge Loring directed the attorneys.

They finally got their jury, all farmers.

A Drunk Wanders into Town

Tony Celino got off the interurban train in Valparaiso on Tuesday, May 22, while the trial was in session. Tony appeared so ostensibly drunk that he almost overdid the act. He continued to stagger around town until the police picked him up.

"Hey there, fella," the officer said, "have you been drinking?"

"Why, no sir. Why do you ask?" he said, slurring his words.

"Maybe it's because you can hardly stand up?" That's when Tony slumped to the ground. "I think what you need is a little time to sleep this off." He called the paddy wagon, and off they went to the jail.

They put him in the cell that Harry was occupying, as it was the only one that was made up with sleeping mattresses. They left him and went back to the front office. Tony didn't waste any time. He quickly untaped the saw blade from inside his leg. Using a string, he suspended it in the sewer pipe in the cell. Abe Rosen had borrowed Tony from the Italian Chicago mob. He was a specialist in disguise. He had wanted to be an actor, but the mob paid more. For this job, he was getting a c-spot ($100, which was $1,400 in 2017 dollars).

When Harry got back from court, he found Tony in his cell. "Brought you a little company, Harry. I knew you might be lonely," Deputy Sheriff Lefrance said.

Tony was lying on the bottom bunk pretending he was asleep. As soon as the deputy left, he whispered to Harry: "The boys sent me. I put a saw blade in your sewer pipe. They told me you should use it if the verdict goes against you. Cut the bars, but not all the way through on the back side, so the guards don't see the cuts. They plan to break you out before you would go to the big house in Michigan City."

Just then, Deputy Lefrance came back to the cell block and saw Tony having a conversation with Harry. He knew then it had been a trick. This guy was not a drunk at all. Maybe a

L–R: Joseph H. Conroy, defense attorney; Stephen Carboy, court reporter; W.J. McAleer, prosecuting attorney. *Courtesy of The Hammond Times and Newspaper Archives*

Judge Hannibal H. Loring, presiding Circuit Court judge. *Courtesy of The Hammond Times and Newspaper Archives*

reporter who wanted to get in close to Harry and get a news scoop? Maybe something else? He unlocked the cell door and brought Tony out and took him to Sheriff Pennington. The sheriff realized the drunkenness was a bluff. After he searched him, he threw the man out.

Tony didn't waste any time getting back on the interurban train to Gary to pick up his money. The sheriff's department kept a close eye on his movements, but they were no match for Tony. He gave them the slip.

"Did you know that guy?" Sheriff Pennington asked Harry.

"Never saw him in my life. I think he was a plant for the state to get me to confess," said Harry.

The sheriff discussed this with his staff. One of the deputies said, "If he was a plant by one of Harry's friends, we need to look at the similarities between this case and the Carl Wanderer case."

Another deputy said, "Remember the Tommy O'Connor case, where a gun was smuggled in a guy's wooden leg?"

Sheriff Pennington wasn't taking any chances. They made a thorough search of Harry's cell but found nothing. Just to be sure, they doubled the guard.

Wednesday, May 23, 1923—The Trial

In his opening statement, McAleer said, "Harry Diamond planned and executed the murder of his wife for the purpose of ridding himself of her and inheriting her fortune. He expected to place the blame for the crime upon Armstrong, the chauffeur. Mrs. Diamond was shot twice in the abdomen and once in the head. Armstrong was shot once in the temple exiting out his cheek. Both were beaten over the head with the butt of Diamond's gun. The shooting took place in Diamond's automobile between Gary and East Chicago on February 14 of this year. We're asking for the death penalty."

Conroy, speaking for the defense, said, "Armstrong planned the whole crime with his colored friends from the Majestic Garage. There were two other Negros in a Ford car that followed the Diamonds that day with the intent of robbing them. Armstrong pulled over on Gary Avenue, saying a chain was off. Then Harry had an epileptic fit and was unconscious. Armstrong took this opportunity to shoot Nettie. Harry awoke from his fit and got the gun away from Armstrong and shot him. His accomplices robbed Nettie of the money and diamonds she was carrying. The state is also working on finding a woman

The jury in the Harry Diamond murder trial, 1923. *Courtesy of* The Hammond Times *and* Newspaper Archives.

from Gary that Harry was seeing. Harry had taken her to various resorts, and they had shared joy rides together. She disappeared at the time of Nettie's death. The state is also trying to find securities of $40,000 to $50,000 ($560,000 to $700,000 in 2017 dollars), which the bank knew were in Mrs. Diamond's possession."

Thursday, May 24, 1923—William Testifies

The state's star witness, William Armstrong, was to testify this day. The police had kept him in protective custody since he was released from Mercy Hospital. He had been in the Valparaiso Jail, but they moved him in the night to another secure location. Today in the front row of spectators were the who's who of bootleggers from the Northwest section of Lake County. Whether it was done to intimidate William or just keep track of the trial, no one knew. Scattered among the spectators were deputy sheriffs, fully armed.

Attorney Conroy grilled William for hours, going over every detail of his testimony. He asked William, "Did you see Harry shoot you?"

William answered, "No. If I seen he was gonna shoot me, I would have ducked."

Conroy continued, "Did you think Harry was your friend?"

William answered, "Not after he done shot me and hit me over da head with the gun."

It was McAleer who came to William's aid, saying, "The boy is tired. I think we should give him time to rest." Judge H. H. Loring agreed.

During the entire cross-examination, Conroy never got William to change his story—or make a mistake. He continued to suggest that others were involved and that William was part of a plot to rob Nettie and Harry. The jury didn't buy the story.

On this day, the deathbed statement by Nettie to William J. Linn, captain of the Gary Police, was read. Her statement matched that of William's.

Attorney McAleer said, "Harry Diamond should face the death penalty for premeditated ruthless murder for the purpose of robbery."

"Little Giant" attorney Conroy jumped to his feet. "I object, your honor. The woman was dying, and she knew it. She was not in her right mind. Her testimony should be stricken from the record."

"Conroy, are you crazy?" asked McAleer.

"What did you say?" Conroy was on his feet waving his arms at McAleer.

Because of his diminutive stature, McAleer was still looking down on him. "You're not deaf. You heard me," said McAleer.

Calumet Drugstore. *Courtesy of Google Earth*

"I object if the court please," said Conroy. "I object to the special counsel for the state—I repeat, the special counsel for the state—saying that I'm crazy."

"I didn't say you were crazy," stated McAleer. "I merely asked you if you were."

Judge Loring pounded his gavel to bring the courtroom to order. "Counsel will refrain from personal remarks," he ordered.

All this bad feeling had started the first day of the trial with McAleer calling Conroy a "pettifogger." The court adjourned until Friday.

Friday, May 25, 1923—Herschel Canan Testifies

Next to testify was Herschel Canan, 39-year-old druggist and proprietor of the Calumet Drugstore. He was the first to see Harry Diamond when he burst into the drugstore and asked someone to call a doctor and the police: "Harry went back out to his machine and brought his wife into the drugstore. Harry said, 'A nigger shot my wife, and I shot the nigger.' As his wife lay on the floor, he thought she was dead, but she came to and Harry said to her, 'Honey, tell them the Negro shot you. Don't tell them I shot you.' Nettie said, 'You're a dirty liar. You shot me yourself. You've got my money, and you shot me for it. I can forgive you for shooting me, but I can't forgive you for beating me over the head with that gun.'"

Conroy asked him if she said anything else.

"Yes. She said, 'Harry shot me and also the colored boy. He knows it was not the colored boy that shot me. Don't believe that. I'm in my right mind. I recently made a will and left him $20,000.'"

Thomas Kochis and Frank Simbolmos also had a chance to testify that they heard Nettie say the same thing, that Harry did the shooting and beating, no one else. James Storer, a clerk at the drugstore, was the one who held the door open when Harry brought Nettie in and threw her to the terrazzo floor. He too heard her statements that it was Harry who committed the crime.

Monday, May 28, 1923—The Trial

Police officer Hiram Kerr and court bailiff Edward Knight testified that Nettie had told them the same story: Harry shot Nettie and the chauffeur, William. Kerr was the officer who put Harry under arrest. That was when Harry faked a fit and fell to the floor. Harry had said he didn't remember anything, as he had a fit in the car. Next was Dr. Frank Townsley, the deputy coroner for Lake County and Nettie's doctor. He told the court Nettie's condition when he saw her in the drugstore. This was shortly after the police had arrived.

Conroy asked, "What did Mrs. Diamond say to you?"

"When I walked in, she said: 'Dr. Townsley, I'm in my right mind and I know what I'm saying. I want you and everybody to know that my husband shot me.' That's when Harry came over to her and said, 'No, honey, I didn't shoot you. The Negro shot you.' She said, 'No, he did not; you shot me yourself.'"

Townsley also told the court about their conversation in the ambulance. Nettie asked him, "Am I going to die, Doctor?" on the trip to the hospital. He also described for the court her wounds and the fact that he recovered only one of the three bullets that were in her body. That ended the court session until Tuesday morning, May 29.

Tuesday, May 29, 1923—Trial Continues

The state called James C. Storer again to the stand. He was the first person to see Harry and Nettie, as he held the door open when Harry brought Nettie's bloody body into the drugstore. "Tell us again what you saw when you held the door open for Harry," inquired attorney McAleer.

"He brought a body in through the door and threw her down on the floor in front of the prescription counter."

"Did I hear you correctly? Harry threw her to the floor?"

"That's correct. She was not laid down but thrown down on the terrazzo floor."

"Did they have any conversation?"

"Yes. After the lady regained consciousness, she said, 'Harry, you shot me. Why did you do it?' Harry replied, 'I know I did it, but I didn't mean to do it. Honey, don't tell them I shot you. Tell them the nigger did it.'"

"How did she look?" asked McAleer.

"Her hair and clothing were a mass of blood. Her right eye was hanging out from its socket. I've never seen a human being so battered and gory and still be alive," he said.

Wednesday, May 30, 1923—The Trial

Testimony was heard from Captain O'Neal and Chief Charles Struss of the East Chicago Police Department. They were cross-examined by the defense attorney Conroy.

"How many times did you hit Mr. Diamond in the face while you were questioning him?" Conroy asked Captain O'Neal.

"None," was his reply.

"When Mr. Diamond asked to go to his wife, didn't you say. 'You're going to hell,' and then you hit him in the face?"

"I did not."

"Didn't Harry have a diamond ring on one of his fingers?"

"I believe so," said the captain.

"Didn't you ask him for it?"

"No."

"Didn't you hit him again as you were trying to get it off his finger?"

"No."

"Where is that ring now?"

"I don't know."

Chief Charles Struss was next, asked about the gun used in the crime. Harry admitted to the chief that it was his gun. Chief Struss found one bullet in a chamber and four empty shell casings in the other cylinders. He also found the handle of the gun broken on both sides and covered in blood.

Officer Edmonds had gone to the crime scene the next day and found the letter William had written, dictated by Harry. He also found a gray Stetson hat. That ended the testimony for the day.

After this day of testimony, Harry didn't sleep well. Several times in the middle of the night, he used the saw hidden in the sewer pipe to cut the bars in his cell window. He was careful to make the cuts on the outside of the bars so the deputies wouldn't see them.

Thursday, May 31, 1923—The Trial

The state's first witness today was Dr. George F. Bicknell. He saw William Armstrong at the telephone company after he was shot. He was with him when Officer Leo McCormack came and took his statement. Then he went ahead of the ambulance to Mercy Hospital and met him there for treatment. He described for the court the bullet wound to William's temple, exiting out his cheek, and the lacerations to his scalp.

The attorney for Nettie's estate, William J. Murray, testified as to the value of the real estate holdings before she married Harry Diamond. In cross-examination, he testified

Anna Cohen Fishman, *The Times*, June 2, 1923. *Courtesy of* The Hammond Times *and Newspaper Archives*

that in the dozens of properties that Nettie owned, none were owned jointly with Harry Diamond.

Anna Cohen Fishman, Nettie's best friend, was asked to take the stand. She testified about the time she spent with Nettie in the hospital. Nettie had told her what she had said to Harry, "'I'll give you everything I have if you let me live and let me live for my children,' but he kept on beating me."

"I was right with her when she said, 'I can't fight anymore.' Fifteen minutes later, she died."

Anna also testified that while Nettie was in the hospital, her home was looted. Taken was $2,000 in silk lingerie ($28,000 in 2017 dollars) and $5,000 worth of clothing and jewelry ($70,500 in 2017 dollars). She also said that a large portion of Nettie's estate was in securities worth $40,000 to $50,000 ($560,000 to $700,000 in 2017 dollars). All were missing.

Attorney McAleer asked, "Do you know how much Mrs. Diamond weighed?"

"Yes, about 150 pounds," she answered.

"So at 5 feet, 4 inches tall, would you say she was of a stout build?"

"That would be true," Anna said.

"This means that she was at least 10 pounds heavier than Harry. I would think it would have been quite difficult to carry her from the car if he had just recovered from an epileptic seizure."

Conroy was on his feet. "I object to the statement. It's only an assumption by the state, not a fact."

"Objection sustained," said Judge Loring.

Captain Linn of the Gary Police Department was next. He told them he had taken Nettie's statement on Thursday morning, the 15th, about 9 a.m. The statement was all hers, not a result of questioning. Her statement matched with that of William Armstrong.

Thursday, May 31, 1923—Last Day for the State

Pearle Herskovitz was the next to testify. She was Nettie's eldest child with Sam Herskovitz and 13 years old. She had been at her mother's bedside on Wednesday afternoon, the day of the shooting, and on Thursday, the 15th, when Nettie took her last breath. Pearle was now a freshman enrolled in East Chicago Washington High School in Indiana Harbor. She was living with Anna Fishman. She told the court that Harry pursued her mother for six months before they were married.

"Is that the man you're talking about? Harry Diamond?" McAleer motioned over to Harry sitting with his attorneys.

"Yes, that's the man."

"Why won't you look at him, Pearle?"

"He has the power to put a spell on you. He did this to my mother too. I don't like him looking at me," complained Pearle.

Pearle Herskovitz, age 13, *The Times*, June 2, 1923. *Courtesy of* The Hammond Times *and Newspaper Archives*

"Will the defendant stop staring at the witness," Judge Loring directed.

Harry looked down at the table in front of him.

"Continue, Pearle," said McAleer. "Tell us what life was like in the house after your mother married Harry."

"After the marriage, he was never at home but stayed out to all hours of the night. One year before the shooting, I overheard an argument between Mother and Harry about the fact that he wasn't working and was not a good father figure. Harry was always asking my mother for money. He would get me to go to her and ask for a check. When my mother would give it to him, and it wasn't enough, he would tear it up and throw it in her face. 'What are you doing with the money?' my mother would say. 'You're not working, just squandering the money away. It's time to stop.'"

"What did he say after she told him to stop that behavior?" asked McAleer.

"He would not say anything."

"Were there any other arguments?"

"Many. He would be riding around, and Mother would say, 'Harry, what are you doing all day? You don't work any. You are running around with the car. You are running around with other women. If you don't stop it, I don't need you. I got along without you before I married, and I can get along without you after.' Harry answered, 'I will go if you give me $10,000.'"

"Was there any conversation between them about the maid?"

"Yes, we had a maid. She was about 21 or 22, the flapper type, and very good looking. The maid told Mother that Harry had given her $40 ($560 in 2017 dollars) to buy a dress. Harry denied it. Mother didn't believe him and let the maid go."

"Do you remember any disagreements your mother and Harry had about you children?"

"Yes, he would tell Mother that the children ought to eat in the basement. 'That's good enough for them,' he would say. He would also complain about the cost of the clothes for the children, always asking, 'How much did that cost?'"

"How many times did this happen?"

"Many, many times."

Attorney McAleer entered Nettie's new will into the record. After paying all her debts, she bequeathed the following: "Edward Noah Sachs $2,000 ($28,000 in 2017 dollars), Fay Diamond $3,000 ($42,000 in 2017 dollars). The rest of the estate is given to the following four children. All the remainder of my estate real, personal, and mixed of every kind to share and share alike: Pearle Herskovitz, Lloyd Herskovitz, Bernard Herskovitz, Cecil Herskovitz. I appoint J.G. Allen, Vice-President of the Indiana Harbor National Bank, to be the executor of my will. Signed Nettie D. Diamond, February 15, 1923."

The state now rests. It was now the defense's turn to try to prove Harry's innocence.

Friday, June 1, 1923—The Defense Begins Its Case

The first thing the defense did was ask the court to disallow all statements made by Nettie when she was on the floor in the drugstore. They reasoned that at the time the statements were made, Harry was not within hearing distance and, therefore, had no way to defend himself. There were also parts of the testimony by Storer, Hershel Canan, Dr. Townsley, and Thomas Kochis that they wanted removed. The motion was overruled by the court and the defense accepted it.

This day, the defense brought forward medical doctors. They used their testimony to try to convince the jury that Nettie was not in her right mind. They wanted to disallow statements where she told witnesses at the drugstore and in the hospital that Harry did the shooting.

The first doctor was Dr. C.W. Packard.

Q. What is your name?

A. C.W. Packard.

Q. Where do you live?

A. Gary, Indiana.

Q. How long have you lived in Gary?

A. Sixteen years.

Q. What is your profession?

A. Physician and surgeon.

Q. How long have you been practicing as physician and surgeon?

A. Since 1897.

Q. Are you a graduate of any school or college?

A. Yes.

Q. What medical school?

A. The State University of Iowa.

Q. Are you a regular homeopath or allopath physician?

A. Regular allopath.

Q. In your practice, have you had to deal with gunshot wounds to the head or abdominal region?

A. Yes.

Q. I call your attention to the condition of Nettie Diamond on the 14th day of February. Assume aged 35 to 38 years old, five feet, five inches tall, and received a bullet wound from a .32 caliber revolver in three different places. One below the left eye, fracturing the eye socket, and two bullets, one entering the abdomen near the navel and the other three-quarters of an inch to the left of the navel. Would a woman with these wounds make statements which you could have confidence in or have reliability placed?

Objection by the state: "This is a hypothetical question that does not contain all the facts. It is for the jury to decide if she was of sound or unsound mind."

A. I would say that she probably would be of unsound mind.

Q. Assume this woman makes a written statement in the presence of police officers doctors and nurses. She signs the statement in a scrawled signature and dies three hours later. In your opinion, would she be of sound or unsound mind?

A. I would say she was probably of unsound mind.

Cross-examination by Mr. McAleer was next.

Q. You said she probably was of unsound mind.

A. Yes, sir.

Q. If she was lying on the floor, using the name of the party that shot her, and when he denied it, this woman said, "Don't believe him; he shot me." And she would call another party by name and the doctor by name and name the party who shot her said. "No, I did not; another man shot you." She says, "No, you shot me" and said "I'm mentally sound; I know what I am talking about, you shot me." Would you say she was of unsound mind at that time?

A. She possibly would be.

Q. Possibly be, possibly be what?

A. Unsound.

Q. How would you say she would possibly be when she would say all that? I am possibly of unsound mind?

A. Yes, sir.

Q. And so are you?

A. Yes, sir.

Q. Anybody is possibly of unsound mind?

A. Yes, sir.

Q. We are all unsound a little bit?

A. Yes, sir.

It was obvious that this witness was never going to say Nettie was of sound mind. It didn't take long for attorney McAleer to find out why. As he continued his questioning, it was revealed that the opposing attorney, Conroy, had represented him in four malpractice suits.

The next witness was Dr. Antonio Georgi. Dr. Antonio Georgi was 61 years old and had been practicing in Gary for the last 16 years. He ran his own hospital in Gary.

Q. What school or college are you a graduate of?

A. The University of Italy, 1891.

After given the same information about Nettie, her wounds, and her testimony, he too said she was of unsound mind.

Attorney McAleer did the cross-examination.

Q. Doctor, we are all more or less of unsound mind, are we not? None of us are of sound mind?

A. I think 99 percent are unsound.

Q. About 1 percent are of sound mind?

A. Yes, sir.

Q. If she told the people in the drugstore how her husband shot her, would you think she was crazy?

A. Yes, sir.

Q. If she talked to her attending physician and said, "How could you do it? Harry, how could you take me away from my little baby?" you would say these were the words of a crazy woman?

A. Well, not sound mind.

The courtroom erupted in applause and laughter. It was so obvious to them that these doctors were going to say only what attorney Conroy wanted, that it was a waste of time. Attorney Conroy stood up to make a motion to clear the court. The judge overruled his motion.

McAleer continued questioning Dr. Georgi. He brought up the fact the he was just recently in this court for a malpractice suit with Mr. Conroy as his attorney.

Q. You practiced for a long time without a license?

A. Why, not very long.

Q. You knew nothing about this case?

A. I read about it in the newspapers.

Q. You never saw this woman, but you think she was of unsound mind?

A. Yes, sir.

The next doctor for the defense was Dr. E.H. Miller. He was 32 years old and had been practicing one year. He too thought Nettie to be of unsound mind. No amount of questioning could get him to change his mind. Next doctor was E.L. Schaible. He treated Harry for epilepsy in 1916. He was the doctor that sent Harry to the Mayo Brothers Clinic in Rochester, Minnesota.

Q. Is a patient totally unconscious during an epileptic attack?

A. Yes.

Q. If Harry had grand mal epilepsy, wouldn't he have a localized sensation, known as the aura, before an attack?

A. Yes, that is true.

Q. Can you describe what happens to the patient after an attack?

A. A frothy saliva escapes from the mouth, and he goes into a sort of coma after the convulsions have ceased.

Q. How long would a patient sleep after an attack?

A. It varies, but usually hours.

Q, Would the patient be weak?

A. Yes, very weak.

Lena Diamond, Harry's younger sister, was next to testify. She was also called Leonita and Leona. She was working as a stenographer for a local grocery store. She testified about seeing Nettie, Harry, and the baby at Friday night Sabbath supper at her parents' house. She also saw William Armstrong, the chauffeur, standing by the car.

Harry's mother, Esther, was next to be called to the stand. She was dressed in black, and her eyes were red and swollen from crying. She gave information about Harry's fits. After his treatment, they became very infrequent. She said he hadn't had one to her knowledge since he married three years ago. When released from the stand, she ran to Harry and sobbed violently on his shoulder. This show of emotion was not lost on the people in the courtroom.

Afternoon, June 1, 1923—Harry Diamond Takes the Stand

Harry sat attentively in his seat all morning. Various people were called by the defense. He appeared ready, in his words, "to explain everything" with his testimony. He appeared his usual cocky self, ready to undergo a personal grilling. During a recess in the morning, he told bystanders, "I love those children. When I'm set free, the first thing I'm going to do is adopt them."

It didn't take much to get Harry to tell his story. After graduation from high school, he spent two months at Valparaiso University law school. He quit that and worked in the tin mill for 30 cents an hour. He worked there for almost a year and a half. He was overcome with sulfuric acid at the tin mill and then quit work. "I spent time at the Mercy Hospital. I was spitting up blood and having spells. I had to go to the Mayo Clinic in Minneapolis to get cured. After my time in the hospital, I started The Standard Bottling Works. We made extracts from alcohol. I got a government permit for 573 gallons a year. I used to take orders for saloons to get whiskey from Chicago distributors. I never made any deliveries of whiskey. My problem was I was getting too prominent, so I stopped taking orders for whiskey."

Q. Were you arrested for transporting alcohol?

A. Yes, once, in this court in 1922. We had 10 barrels of alcohol on a truck, but I was acquitted.

Q. When you slowed down the illegal alcohol business, did you do anything else?

A. Yes, I sold diamonds, which I bought in Chicago, wholesale.

Q. How much would you say you made a month on the diamonds?

A. About $29,000 a month ($280,000 in 2017 dollars).

Q. Did you do any other type of business?

A. In 1921, I was a silent partner in a road house in Hobart.

Q. How did you get involved with the road house?

A. They were buying near beer from us, and couldn't pay their bill. In exchange for the bill, I became a one-third partner.

Q. Was it successful?

A. We had to close it, and it went into receivership. I had to appear in this court with Judge Loring.

Q. How many children did your wife Nettie have?

A. She had four. Pearle was 13, Ruth was 12, Bernard 10, and Cecil 8. (The attorney did not pick up on the fact that Harry could not name the children. The second child was Lloyd, whom he did not mention at all. Ruth was Harry's younger sister.)

Q. Did you and Nettie have any children?

A. Yes, a little girl named Fay, July 21, 1922.

Q. Who paid for the properties that were purchased in Gary? Three houses on Pierce Street and one at 647 Buchanan?

A. I paid for everything.

Q. You paid for everything? But your name does not appear on the titles.

A. I don't know why.

Q. You said you were always giving her money to play the stock market. How much money do you think you gave her?

A. About $35,000.

Q. Do you have any of the cancelled checks to show you had given her money?

A. No, I don't seem to have them.

Q. How old were you when you married Mrs. Diamond?

A. 21 years old.

Q. How old was Mrs. Diamond?

A. 29 years old. (She was really 34 years old.)

Q. There was a revolver used in the crime. Was it your revolver?

A. No.

Q. Did you ever tell a police officer that it was your revolver?

A. Not to my knowledge, no.

Q. Do you know the colored boy who goes by the name William Armstrong?

A. I do.

Q. Where did you meet the colored boy you hired as your chauffeur?

A. I really don't know.

Q. On February 14, Valentine's Day, what time did you get up?

A. About 8:30 a.m.

Q. Did Armstrong take you uptown?

A. Yes, he took me to the grill for breakfast, then for a shave.

Q. Was he waiting for you after your shave?

A. No, the car was not there.

Q. How long did you wait?

A. Two or three minutes.

Q. Did you at any time give Armstrong money to buy a tablet at Slocum's Drugstore?

A. No, sir, I never did.

Q. Did you ever ask him to get a paper or direct him to write a letter?

A. No, sir, I never did.

Q. At any time, did you talk to this man about writing a letter?

A. Never.

Q. I call your attention to state's exhibit No. 2, the envelope and the address to Mr. F.J. Armstrong, 2304 Broadway, Gary, Indiana. Look at it and tell the jury if you have ever seen this envelope before.

A. Never.

Q. Did you at any time try to put this envelope into the breast pocket of Armstrong?

A. No, sir, I have never seen that envelope before.

Q. Did you ever talk to Armstrong about insurance?

A. No, never.

Q. Where did you go after the barber shop?

A. We went home.

Q. Did you go to the Stanley Hotel?

A. No, sir.

Q. Did you go to the post office?

A. No, sir.

Q. Did you go to a place called "Steve's Place"?

A. I don't know of a place like that.

Q. When you and Armstrong got home, what was said?

A. He said, "We have to get some gas and oil before we go." I bawled him out and told him why didn't he get that when we were uptown? I gave him $3 and told him to go back and get some gas and oil.

Q. How long was he gone?

A. He was gone about 35 minutes.

Q. When he came back, what did you say to him?

A. I asked him where he had been. He said he got the gas and oil, but the heater was on the blink. He stopped and tried to fix it.

Q. What was said when he came into the house?

A. I asked, could the heater be fixed, and he said no. He said, "I would not take the baby, Mrs. Diamond. It's pretty cold outside." We left the baby with the maid.

Q. Did you tell him where you were going?

A. He knew where we were going.

Q. Did you go to the Horace Mann School first?

A. Yes, we had to drop off a lunch for one of the boys.

Q. Did anything happen there?

A. Yes, when he came out of the school, there was a red Ford coupe 150 feet back of our machine. A man was by the radiator, and Armstrong waved his hand at the fellow.

Q. Was that a white man or a colored man?

A. A colored man.

Q. How far did you go before anything happened?

A. Shortly after we left the school, two men in the Ford coupe passed us and gave Armstrong some sign.

Q. How many men in the Ford?

A. Two.

Q. White or colored?

A. Both of them niggers.

This finished the testimony until next week.

Tuesday, June 5, 1923—Third Day for the Defense

Harry Diamond took the stand and his attorney Conroy resumed his examination.

Q. What money or valuables did your wife have with her that morning?

A. She had $300 in cash and five stones.

Q. Where did she have them?

A. In a beaded purse.

Q. Did your wife have with her a check for $17,000?

A. She did not.

Q. Did anything else happen on your trip?

A. As we passed the Pennsylvania tracks we passed the Ford coupe, and Armstrong turned, kept looking back and turning his head and almost hit another machine.

Q. Did the Ford coupe pass you again?

A. Yes, before we got to Cline Avenue.

Q. Were they white or colored?

A. Two colored men.

Q. Did anything happen when they passed you?

A. They looked back, and I told Armstrong, I says, "Give me that gun out of the pocket." He reached on his side and gave me the gun.

Q. What did you say to your wife?

A. I said in Jewish, "It looks mighty funny."

Q. What did your wife say?

A. She said, "I don't know," and looked a little frightened. She spoke in Jewish.

Q. Did you or Armstrong say anything when you came up to the turn on Gary Avenue?

A. No, no one said anything.

Q. Then what happened?

A. We went a little way on Gary Avenue and then he stopped the machine, and I said, "What's the matter?" Then I keeled over, and when I come to, I heard the woman moaning, and I heard someone say, "Oh, leave the rings and run." I grabbed Armstrong by the overcoat and attempted to pull him up on the transom and throw him out. Then I heard Mrs. Diamond say, "For God's sake, honey, help me." I grabbed the gun out of his hand and shot over his head. He tried to throw me out of the car. He tried to get away from me and kicked the front window of the car out and pulled away from me, and upon that Mrs. Diamond said, "Kill him, Harry; kill him." I jumped past Mrs. Diamond and got in the front seat of the car, and as he came out on the radiator I shot at him. Then he fell down on the ground. I beat him with the gun, and he tore away and run five or six feet, and I heard Mrs. Diamond again calling for help, "Help me, honey, help me." I climbed back in the car, and she slid, fell partway back on the seat.

Q. Take your time; take your time, Harry.

A. She says, "Honey, honey, I am going to die." I spoke to her to cheer her up. And she says, "Honey, listen. Why, why?" And she repeated, "I am going to die; I am going to die." I says, "Keep still and I will get you to a doctor in a little while." She said, "Harry, I want to die in my own building. Take me to the drugstore." I sat her up in the seat and I kissed her, and I got out of the car and got in the front and started the car. After I started towards Calumet, we got by the South Shore tracks. All of a sudden, she screamed, "Honey, kiss me, I'm dying," and she slipped to the floor. I stopped the car and I got back and picked her up in my arms and both of us cried. She said again, "Harry, I'm going to die." I says, "No, honey, you're not going to die." She says, "Honey, take care of the children and the baby." We both started to cry there and I was trying to realize myself. I wanted to get to the drugstore as soon as I could. I wanted to help her all that I physically could do and proceeded to the drugstore, and there was blood coming from her mouth and I tried to wipe it away with my handkerchief and I failed to stop the flow of blood. I placed her back in the seat and just about as we got to the road, she hadn't spoken a word until we got to the brick road on Chicago Avenue. When all of a sudden she spoke up, and said, "Harry, if I die, you will die. Honey, I can't go alone. I can't go alone and leave you running around with other women. I have been jealous of you all the time, and you know I love you." And I says to her, "You're not going to die." And then she says, "I'm going to say you shot me and the Negro did not shoot me."

Q. What did you do when you got to the drugstore?

A. I run out and into the drugstore and I says, "For God's sake, Canan, call a doctor and the police. Some Negro shot Mrs. Diamond and I shot one of the Negroes." I run out and lifted the body of Mrs. Diamond and carried her into the drugstore. I then kissed her and I got a fit myself. I guess I got a fit, because I found myself on the cement floor.

Q. Where?

A. In the East Chicago police station.

Q. Harry, when did you have your last spell?

A. February 8.

Q. Where?

A. In the Crown Point Jail.

Q. How many attacks did you have that day?

A. Three during the night.

Q. Did you mean February or April 8?

A. April 8, three days before they brought me to the Valparaiso Jail.

Q. How many attacks would you say you have in a year?

A. I can't say; sometimes half a dozen in a day, then none for three or four months.

Q. I call your attention to three insurance policies, referring to the questions that you have had no apoplexy or fits. You said you had no apoplexy or fits.

"Objection," said attorney McAleer.

"The policy stands as a record by itself. If permitted to answer, he would say he signed the policy, as the agent told him it did not make any difference if he had fits," said Conroy.

"I withdraw my objection," said McAleer.

A. I signed the policy and said I did not have apoplexy in order to get the insurance.

Q. Was there any discussion about where the benefits of the policy should go?

A. Yes, I wanted my benefits to go to the children, but she wanted them to go to her instead.

Next was the cross-examination by McAleer for the state.

Q. You started working at the mill after you got out of school?

A. Yes.

Q. What salary were you getting there?

A. Thirty cents ($5.60 in 2017 dollars) an hour.

Q. How much would you make every week?

A. $18 to $21 ($335 to $375 in 2017 dollars) if I worked on Saturday.

Q. How long did you work there?

A. About a year and a half.

Q. When you quit your job at the mill, you went into the hospital?

A. Yes, I was treated for epilepsy by Dr. Schalbie at the Washington Park Hospital.

Q. How much did it cost?

A. I don't know. It cost $50 ($932 in 2017 dollars) to see him.

Q. Can you give the jury an idea of how much you paid for your treatment?

A. I don't know. It may have cost $200 or $300, and it might have been $500 ($9,327 in 2017 dollars). I don't know.

Q. You paid this out of your earnings?

A. Yes, sir.

Q. Did you pay Dr. Schalbie $1,000 ($18,650 in 2017 dollars)?

A. Yes, more than that.

Q. How much money did you have when you started in the bottling works?

A. I know I had $1,700 ($26,800 in 2017 dollars) when I started in The Standard Bottling Works.

Q. How old were you when you started The Standard Bottling Works?

A. Twenty.

Q. How long after you left school did you start The Standard Bottling Works?

A. I started the Standard Bottling Works during April 1918. I just got out of school.

Q. So about a year after you got out of school, you started The Standard Bottling Works?

A. Yes, sir.

Q. You only got 30 cents an hour in the mill?

A. I did not. I was first a laborer then I run up and got charge of the metal room. I was the foreman in the black plating department.

Q. And they gave you a bonus?

A. Yes, sir. I had a man working under me.

Q. Who did you organize The Standard Bottling Works with?

A. Abe Rosen.

Q. When did you go into the "booze" game?

A. I don't know.

Q. Give us an idea?

A. In the early part of 1920.

Q. What did you do in the "booze" game?

A. I took orders for whiskey and never delivered a gallon in my life.

Q. Where did you get the booze?

A. I didn't get it. It was delivered by men from Chicago. They came from Halsted Street and Blue Island.

Q. Would you call in your orders?

A. I don't know. I would generally meet them at the Morrison Hotel. I would call number 870 at the Morrison.

Q. Where did you go to meet the bootleggers?

A. They came to Chicago. I would give them directions where to go when I met them at the Morrison Hotel.

Q. What kind of whiskey would you get?

A. Anything they wanted. Sunny Brook, Johnnie Walker, Waterville, and Frasier.

Q. What did you order?

A. Nothing, I've never tasted a drop in my life.

Q. How much did you sell a case?

A. $125 ($2,100 in 2017 dollars).

Q. How much profit would you make?

A. Between $15 and $25 ($210 to $350 in 2017 dollars).

Q. How long were you in this business?

A. About three years.

Q. Did you report your profits on your income tax?

A. No.

Q. So you committed perjury?

A. I did.

Q. You were also in the diamond business? Where would you meet these thieves?

A. Yes, I bought them from two men at the Morrison Hotel and the Sherman House in Chicago.

Q. How long did you deal with these diamond thieves?

A. I didn't say they were thieves.

Q. You would not buy anything from a thief?

A. No, they were representing a diamond house in New York, Tapper and Tapper.

Q. As far as you were concerned, these men were doing legitimate business?

A. I did. Both of us were.

Q. Was the whiskey business a legitimate business?

A. It was the way I worked it.

Q. Did your wife participate in the whiskey business with you?

A. Yes, sir.

Q. Didn't you say yesterday she did not? Was not that your answer?

A. May I… I cannot answer that question that way. I can answer it if you give me a fair chance.

Q. Do you know whether you did or not? Yesterday you said she was not.

A. I will have to explain a thing to clear myself.

Q. I just wish you would answer the question.

A. My memory is no friend… If one is in jail so long, it deadens the brain.

Q. You think your brain is dead now?

A. I don't know what you are talking about.

Q. Did you know yesterday what you were talking about?

A. I did.

Q. You can't recall yesterday whether you said your wife was in the whiskey business with you or not?

A. I don't know what I said yesterday to that question.

Q. Do you know what you said in regard to other questions?

A. I don't know. The way you shoot them at me, I might not be able to tell.

Q. At the cabaret in Hobart, did they sell whiskey?

A. No, just soft drinks.

Q. Did you ever bring any of your booze there?

A. No, I did not.

Q. Did they have girls there that would serve whiskey?

A. The girls there were entertainers.

Q. How many entertainers?

A. I don't know, six or eight.

Q. I think you said yesterday they sold booze there. And they couldn't pay for the beer you delivered?

A. No, I didn't say I sold booze there.

Q. How do you remember so distinctly when you could not remember that you said yesterday that you your wife was not in partnership with you?

Objection for defendant and sustained by the court.

Q. Is your memory getting a little better now?

A. Just the same.

Q. Did your wife put any money into The Standard Bottling Works?

A. Never, not a penny.

Q. If she didn't, then how do you explain this check drawn on The Standard Bottling Works and signed by Nettie Diamond for $80?

Objection by defendant.

Q. I want to ask one question. I'm entitled to ask this question. You have in your hand checks amounting to $2,240. They were paid and signed by Nettie Diamond?

A. Yes, sir.

Q. Did Mrs. Diamond ever give you any money?

A. What do you mean by "give"? Do you mean present?

Q. Just answer the question.

A. That's not fair to me unless he could explain the word "give."

Q. Did Mrs. Diamond ever give you any money?

A. Yes, sir, she did.

Q. In 1921, Mrs. Diamond gave you checks amounting to $7,880.57 ($109,790 in 2017 dollars)?

A. I don't know.

Mr. Conroy: "I'm objecting to this line of examination."

The court to Conroy and McAleer: "Both of you be seated and keep still."

When order had been restored, McAleer resumed his line of questioning.

Q. Mr. Diamond, did you do a great deal of business for Mrs. Diamond?

A. No.

Q. Did you handle any of her business?

A. I may have collected a few rent checks.

Q. What bank did you run your business?

A. Indiana Harbor National.

Q. Was Mr. Packard in that bank?

A. No.

Q. Did you ever deal with the Packard Bank?

A. I did.

Q. How long did you deal there?

A. I guess I have a couple of dollars there yet.

Q. A short time before your wife was shot, did you kite any checks?[1]

A. Yes.

Q. You kited checks, did you?

---

1   Kiting checks is a crime involving writing a check on an account with insufficient funds and depositing it in another account and then writing a check on that account and depositing it in the first account to cover the check written on the first account. The kiter obtains an illegal interest-free loan.

A. Yes.

Q. That's another crime?

A. It's no crime as long as you make the checks good.

Q. How often did you kite checks?

A. I don't know.

Q. You were put out of the Packard Bank for kiting checks, were you not?

A. No. I think I have a couple of dollars still in that bank.

Q. Your wife took you over to that bank and recommended you?

A. She had a purpose, yes sir.

Q. When you got married, you were still living at home?

A. Yes, sir.

Q. You lived upstairs over the drugstore with your wife?

A. Yes, in Calumet.

Q. You carried a gun in the car all the time?

A. No, I had one in the house.

Q. Was this the gun here? (Harry was shown the 32 caliber Smith and Wesson).

A. No, it was not.

Q. Did you say in the presence of the chief of police, "That is not my gun"?

A. I did.

Q. Didn't they show you a gun in there?

A. No.

Q. Didn't they show you the blade, the handle of it?

A. No.

Q. Didn't they show you the cracked handle?

A. No.

Q. Didn't you say, "This gun is mine; it's my gun"?

A. No.

Q. Did you get your gun out of the car?

A. No.

Q. Did Captain O'Neal beat you up?

A. He took a crack at me.

Q. Did it leave any marks?

A. I had a sore jaw.

Q. Did he leave any marks?

A. A little cut here.

Q. How long were you in a fit after the car stopped?

A. I don't know.

Q. Did you kill your wife before you were in a fit?

A. I never killed that little girl or touched her in my life.

Q. After you got out of your fit, you killed her then?

A. I never touched that girl in my life.

Q. What did you see when you woke up?

A. I saw a shadow, a form.

Q. How can you see a shadow when there was no sun shining?

A. That may be a shadow. I mean a form.

Q. After you saw the shadow, what did you do?

A. I grabbed the gun out of Armstrong's hand and pounded him over the head.

Q. You want to tell the jury that while Armstrong had you covered with the gun, you reached over and took it out of his hand?

A. I reached over this way, as he was right there. He was shooting or attempting to shoot, and I reached over that way and grabbed the gun.

Q. Let me get this straight.

A. I am lying on the floor and he is trying to pull me over the wheel, pulling that way with the gun in this position (indicating) in his hand and leveled this way, and I grabbed the gun like this and hit him over the head.

Q. Then you grabbed the gun and shot him twice?

A. No.

Q. What did you do when you grabbed the gun?

A. I beat him over the head.

Q. You didn't beat your wife at all?

A. I did not. I never touched that girl in my life. I loved her too much (crying).

Q. After you beat him, what did you do?

A. When he started to pull away, Armstrong opened the door and got outside. Then Mrs. Diamond said, "Kill him, kill him." Then he got around in front of the radiator, and I shot at him.

Q. Did you shoot him?

A. I understand that he was shot at that time.

Q. Then what happened?

A. I saw him running down the road and I followed him five or six feet after him.

Q. Is this the same gun that you had there that you shot him with?

A. Yes, sir.

Q. Then you took your wife to the store?

A. I did.

Q. Do you remember talking to a clerk, Storer? Do you know him?

A. I never met him.

Q. Do you remember him being there?

A. I never seen him until he came here, to my recollection.

Q. Do you remember the time, Mr. Diamond, you remember of your wife accusing you, saying you shot her? Didn't she say that in the store?

A. I don't know. I collapsed in the store.

Q. You carried her in the store?

A. Yes, sir.

Q. How much did she weigh?

A. Both of us were weighed the Saturday previously, and Mrs. Diamond weighed 145 pounds and I weighed 164 pounds.

Q. Didn't you lean over her and say, "Honey, say the colored boy shot you"?

A. I don't know what happened in the store.

Q. When you were taken to the Crown Point Jail, didn't Dr. Blackstone attend to you?

A. Yes, Dr. Blackstone.

Q. Have you taken any fits since you got down to this jail?

A. No.

Q. Did you see Mr. Murray and Mr. Allen in the jail at Crown Point, and didn't you tell them that your wife had $19,000 in cash and two five-carat diamonds in her purse?

A. No, sir.

Q. Didn't you see little Pearle in jail?

A. Yes, she came down to see me.

Q. Didn't you say to Pearle that day, "Pearle, I know where the diamonds are and I am getting them for you whether I live or die," or words to that effect?

A. No, sir.

Q. What was the value of the five diamonds you had?

A. About $2,300 ($32,300 in 2017 dollars).

Q. Did you apply for life insurance for $25,000 that you didn't get?

A. I never applied for any life insurance for Mrs. Diamond.

Q. You heard Mr. Gillman testify the other day?

A. Yes.

Q. You say you never applied for any life insurance for her?

A. No, sir. She did her own talking.

Q. Was life insurance talked with Gillman?

A. Yes, sir.

Q. Was it not arranged that there was to be $25,000 life insurance taken out on the life of your wife and each of you to be the beneficiary?

A. No, sir.

Q. Gillman lies when he says that, does he?

Objection by Mr. Conroy.

Q. Did you make application to any other life insurance company on or about the 7th of February, 1923, seven days before the shooting?

A. I made…

Q. Did you, or did you not?

A. I cannot answer that. You are not putting the question fair to me. I made application for myself, and Mrs. Diamond made application for herself.

Q. In what company?

A. The Lincoln National Life.

Q. And you received a reply stating they would not issue any insurance for you or your wife?

A. Yes, sir.

Q. The letter was directed to you, was it not?

A. I don't know.

Q. They advised you they were not going to issue any policies for you or Mrs. Diamond on February 7, 1923, did they not?

A. Yes, sir.

Q. You had a lot of money in 1922, did you not?

A. No, sir.

Q. You had been bootlegging and running the cabaret?

A. The cabaret cost me $6,000.

Q. You didn't have any money?

A. I had money all the time, and I was always broke.

Q. You made application for insurance to the Rockford Life Insurance Company on September 13, 1920, and November 26, 1920. They asked you if you were engaged in the manufacture or sale of beer, wine, or malt, or liquor. You answered "No."

A. I don't know if that question was in the policy.

Q. When you said in your application that you were not in the liquor business, you did not tell the truth?

A. I still maintain I have not been in the liquor business.

Q. Listen. Have you now or have you ever been engaged in the manufacture or sale of beer, wine, malt, or any other liquor and the sale of them? You did not tell them about bootlegging, did you?

A. The agent told me what to say.

Q. You didn't tell?

A. No, I did not.

Q. The agent would put a lie in your mouth?

A. He wanted his commission.

Q. You never answered the question. Did the agent tell you to tell a lie, an untruth?

A. He wanted his commission.

Q. You were examined by a medical man?

A. Yes, sir.

Q. Didn't he ask you whether you ever had fits?

A. I presume so.

Q. Did the doctor tell you to answer a lie?

A. No, he did not.

Q. Did he ask you whether you had apoplexy?

A. He did.

Q. You told an untruth or a lie, didn't you?

A. I did. I was under instructions.

Q. He asked you, "Did you suffer any ailments, disease of the brain, and nervous system," and you said "No," didn't you?

A. Yes, sir.

Q. Then he asked you if you were ever engaged in the manufacture or sale of spirits or liquor. You answered "No," didn't you?

A. Yes, if that's in the policy.

Q. You told an untruth again there, didn't you?

A. Yes, sir.

Q. When did you tell the truth?

A. I think I told you what I meant.

Objection by Mr. Conroy. Sustained.

Q. When did Armstrong give you the gun?

A. You mean the time when I told him, when I reached down and got it?

Q. Yes.

A. When I passed by these fellows.

Q. Did he give you the gun?

A. He did not. He gave me some excuse.

Q. You drove after all this shooting, after you shot Armstrong and pounded him on the head, then you drove the car?

A. Yes, sir.

Q. To the drugstore?

A. Yes, sir.

Q. And carried your wife in all alone?

A. Yes sir.

Q. And then you had another fit?

A. I collapsed.

Q. Was there any collapse in addition to the collapse in the car?

A. I would not say, because I don't know. I know I keeled over. I was all in, I presume.

Q. What were you doing before you got married?

A. Running the bottling works.

Q. Were you a driver?

A. Yes, sir.

Q. You were driving a truck?

A. Yes, sir.

Q. And delivering?

A. Yes, sir.

Q. Mrs. Diamond told you she was not going to say the Negro did the shooting and beat her?

A. Yes, sir.

Q. How many times did she say this about the Negro beating and shooting her, and she was not going to say that. How many times did she say that?

A. I don't know.

Q. You know that you're trying to cover that up, Diamond?

A. No.

Q. You know you're not telling the truth?

A. I am telling the truth.

Diamond leaped from his chair. "I am, I am!" he shouted. "I've bared my life to tell the truth."

"Look at him," McAleer said, looking at the jury box. "Is that a picture of a loving husband?"

Objection by Mr. Conroy.

Judge Loring said, "Will the bailiff secure the defendant."

Reexamination of Harry Diamond by his attorney, Conroy.

Q. Look at these photographic copies of your insurance policies. Is that your signature at the bottom?

A. Yes, sir… I don't know.

Q. Did you fill out the answers to these questions, or did someone else fill them out?

A. Somebody else done that.

Q. Are these policies still in force?

A. Yes, sir.

Q. In August of 1918, you conferred with Dr. Graham whether or not you would be accepted for any army or naval service? Did you or did you not?

A. Yes, sir.

Q. Were you examined for military service?

A. Yes, sir.

Q. Were you accepted or rejected?

A. Rejected.

Re-cross-examination by Mr. McAleer.

Q. Do you remember talking to Mrs. Fishman and Pearle outside your cell in Crown Point?

A. Yes, they came down to see me.

Q. Do you remember Mrs. Fishman saying, "We are having a hard time trying to locate Mrs. Diamond's bonds"? You said, "I know where they are, and I'll get them for you."

A. No, no discussion of bonds at all.

Q. When your wife said, "If I'm going to die, you will die too," do you remember?

A. Do I have to go over that again?

Q. Just relate what it was.

A. "If I die, you die. I'm not going to lay in the ground and let you run around with other women."

Q. She knew what she was talking about at that time?

A. What?

Q. At the time she told you, "If I die, you die." That's what I want to know. Was she rational then?

A. She was.

William J. Murray was re-called by the state and re-examined by Mr. McAleer.

Q. Do you know Harry Diamond?

A. I do.

Q. Were you down to see him in jail?

A. I was.

Q. Did he say in the jail cell that his wife had $19,000 in cash and five two-carat stones and that the East Chicago Police got them?

A. Yes, sir.

Cross-examination by the defense and Mr. Conroy.

Q. Are you the attorney for the estate of Nettie D. Diamond?

A. I am.

Q. Why did you go down to the jail?

A. Harry Diamond wrote and asked Mr. Allen and myself to come to see him.

Q. Was not the subject in reference to real estate?

A. Real estate and bonds and money.

Q. Was this about a real estate transaction?

A. No. We asked him about a $17,000 check from Durant Motor Stock. He said there was no check; that she had $19,000 in cash. In her pocketbook, she had the money and two diamonds.

Q. Didn't he say she had $300 and two diamonds in a mesh bag?

A. No, he said $19,000.

The court adjourned until Wednesday, June 6, 1923.

Wednesday Morning, June 6, 1923—Closing Speeches in the Diamond Murder Case

The room was filled to the doors with spectators. Many came early to get a seat and brought their dinner. Mrs. Esther Diamond, mother of the accused, and her daughter Ruth entered from the hallway. Esther was dressed all in black. Sheriff William Pennington and Deputy Sheriff William Forley brought Diamond into the courtroom. One motherly old lady sitting in the front row of the spectator seats looked up from her knitting but didn't miss a stitch. She had been there since 8 o'clock. A pretty young lady, also in the front row, said to the man next to her that she had a fluttering feeling because she was excited. It was 9 o'clock, and Judge H.H. Loring, looking much like President Harding, entered, took the bench, and called the court into session.

Esther, sitting next to Harry, leaned over to him and said, "Harry, I'm praying hard for you, my boy."

"Don't worry one bit, Mother. I'm sure the result will please us," Harry replied.

The jury, all farmers, filed in. Most of them were in shirt sleeves. The state began its argument. The state and the defense each got three hours to present their cases.

First was John C. Stephen, deputy prosecutor from East Chicago. He reviewed the courtship of Harry and Mrs. Diamond and the events leading up to the murder. He discussed the evidence of William Armstrong, the chauffeur.

Frank Parks opened for the defense. He spoke loudly. He worked on the emotions and sympathies of the jury. Parks described Diamond's conduct throughout the entire affair as above reproach. He said that Diamond, coming out of a stupor in which he was lying at the bottom of the auto, sprang into action, wrested a revolver from the assassin, William Armstrong, and shot him. "Diamond did everything he could for his poor dying wife. He took her to a drugstore, called doctors and police, which is more than any other living man did. There were eight men in the store and not one did a thing. Then Diamond collapsed. There's not a man on the jury who would not have collapsed under such an ordeal. Just think, gentlemen, to have your wife murdered before your eyes and be helpless to prevent it, to have an encounter with a Negro and then have your wife tell you on the way to help that she blamed you for the murder. Is it any wonder that Diamond collapsed? Diamond has done all he could in this trial. He has sat in the witness box and looked you square in the eye and told the truth. He has a little child to raise and a poor old mother to care for." Harry dabbed a handkerchief to his eyes. "Diamond has told the truth, and no man's liberty is safe when you cannot believe him under oath if his story is not contradicted. Men who sometimes violate the law are often proved to be the best to their families. Such is Harry Diamond."

F.B. Marine spoke next for the State. He was followed by William Matthews for the defense. The afternoon was reserved for the leading attorneys, and then the big guns were to be fired.

W.J. McAleer is the final attorney for the state: "Gentlemen of the jury, you have seen and heard these past two weeks the testimony of witnesses for both sides of this case. It is up to you to decide who is telling the truth and who is lying. We are asking you to inflict the death penalty upon a self-confessed bootlegger, check kiter, and perjurer who has committed the most dastardly murder that was ever perpetrated on this earth. He is a contemptible character, a man that admits that he made from $100 to $500 a night on eight women in the notorious resort he operated in Hobart. Where did he get the diamonds he sold? He got them from sneak thieves and holdup thugs. Here is a bootlegger and a man who kept women for hire, marrying a woman who had four children and who was 16 years his senior (really 13 years). Did he love that woman? No, he didn't, he loved the money."

McAleer pointed at Harry. "He hated her," he shouted, "and he killed her!"

"You lie!" cried Harry, half rising from his chair and glaring at the prosecuting attorney.

"Look at him," said McAleer to the jury. "Just look at his vicious face. If he had a gun, he'd kill me. Can you for one minute believe a single word he said? He wants you to believe him against the dying declaration of his poor wife and the testimony of the colored boy. He says the police lie when they say he told them this gun, splattered with the blood of his dying wife, belonged to him. He can't tell you what became of the money and the diamonds. How easy for him to plant them after the crime and send one of his sisters to get them. How easy it would have been for him to tear up the anti-nuptial agreement if he had been successful in killing his wife and the colored boy. Now Diamond says he saw Armstrong signal to two Negroes in a Ford. Joe Conroy doesn't believe that story himself. I know who made it up. Attorney Matthews did. Where is Matthews?"

A voice from the crowd said, "He has left the building."

McAleer continued, "Diamond carried his dying wife into the drugstore and threw her on the floor. He thought she was dead, but she regained consciousness. There in the presence of Storer, the drug clerk, she accused her husband of killing her, and he replied, 'I know I did, but I didn't mean to do it.'" McAleer was just getting started. "What about the letter that was found on the road near the scene of the crime?" Looking at Harry, McAleer said, "It's stained with the blood of your wife from your own fingers, Harry. The colored boy told the truth. Diamond dictated that letter. It came from the shrewd crooked brain of Diamond, a brain that has been running in criminal channels for years. Would the colored boy write to his parents that he was leaving town with an automobile and diamonds and several thousand dollars? Wouldn't they know he was a thief if he did? Diamond tried to place that letter in the colored boy's coat, and it dropped out as the little fellow ran for his life. Didn't Diamond ask the police if they found anything on Armstrong? Remember Mrs. Diamond's pitiful plea to this human brute: 'Oh, Harry, you shot me and shot me and shot me, and you pounded me over the head and pounded me over the head. Why did you do it? How could you separate me from our seven-month-old baby?'" Speaking to the jury, he said, "Remember that and then KILL HIM! Diamond said she wanted to take him to heaven, so she accused him of killing her so that he would go to the electric chair! Do you believe that story? Could any man believe it? If Diamond had been innocent of killing her, would she have wanted to take away the father of her little babe and rob her of her only protection? If he had been innocent, she would have said in her dying statement, 'Harry, take care of the children for me.' There was never in your life a time when responsibility rested so heavily upon you. You are sworn to do your duty and uphold the law. It's a disagreeable duty, but my God, men, what else can we do with this creature except kill him? My heart goes out to his poor old mother, but she'll be better off without a son like him. I say that the good people of Indiana are watching to see if we are going to do our duty. For the sake of decency and law and in the name of womanhood, stand by your guns and kill him. Society demands that he go to the electric chair and suffer death."

Harry glared at McAleer from his seat at the defense table. His boastful tone and ill-mannered behavior on the stand were now not in his best interests. The spectators were on the edges of their seats as McAleer finished his statement. What could Conroy say to convince the jury that Harry Diamond was innocent? Joseph Conroy didn't get the nickname the "Little Giant" for losing cases. As difficult as this case was, it wasn't impossible to spin a tale that the jury would believe, or at least have a reasonable doubt. The difference would be life imprisonment and maybe parole or the electric chair.

Joseph Conroy Speaks for the Defense

"Gentlemen of the jury, you have heard the testimony. Now I will explain why my client is innocent of the horrible murder. Harry fell in love with Nettie, and the difference in age was not a factor. This is true when one really loves another. As a young man of 21, he took on the responsibility of Nettie's four young children. This is asking a lot from such a young man. This is why from time to time he had to leave the house and seek solitude elsewhere. Most of the time, he just went to the Elks Club to be in the company of other men. I admit that some of his business dealings were not exactly legal, but we have to remember he was trying to provide for a big family. This was the way he found to make enough money to provide for them. His wife was involved in his illegal business as well. She loaned him money to buy the illegal diamonds and wrote checks for The Standard Bottling Company. She was even involved in a perjury action to break the lease on one of her drugstores to allow it to be a front for illegal whiskey sales. Being older than Harry, she understood the business world better than he did and gave him advice. She used him to carry out stock transactions in Chicago. It was her idea to hire William Armstrong as their chauffeur. When he came to the house, he saw that they were wealthy and held out for a higher salary. He knew that they were in the diamond business, as he took them to Chicago on buying trips. He also knew that Harry carried a gun in the car, and that's when he and his buddies devised a plan to rob and kill them. Harry said he saw a red Ford coupe with two Negroes in it following them on the day of the murder. It was unfortunate that Harry had a fit and didn't see what happened. He used all his strength to fight off Armstrong and try to get Mrs. Diamond to safety. It was because of his history of fits that he was unable to fight for our country in WWI. He loved Nettie and would never hit her or shoot her. It was his money that bought their houses and Hudson car. He loaned her $35,000 to play the stock market. With all the money he was making, he had no need for her money so no reason to kill her. Look at him and his mother and sister. This is a family man that only loves his family, not a cold-blooded killer."

Conroy described the terrible death Harry would suffer if sent to the electric chair. Conroy became very dramatic. Mrs. Diamond, mother of the defendant, swooned and had to be revived with smelling salts by her daughter. He turned on Mrs. Anna Cohen Fishman, lifelong friend of the slain woman. She was not a witness to the case but sat at the side of Pearle Herskovitz, the orphaned daughter of Mrs. Diamond. "Mrs. Anna Fishman has influenced the testimony of Pearle because of her hatred of Diamond."

McAleer interrupted. "That argument is unfair. Mrs. Fishman is a kind woman and a mother to the girl."

"These enemies of Harry Diamond," Conroy continued, "have given hearsay evidence that would convict Christ himself." When referring to Diamond's mother, Conroy broke down and wept. "The defense now rests."

Judge H.H. Loring read the instructions to the jury before they were escorted out of the courtroom to deliberate Harry's fate.

The Court Empties; the Jury Deliberates

The crowd began to work its way out the door. The people seemed to regret that the trial was over. (They would return early next morning to wait on the courthouse lawn until word came that the jury had reached a verdict. Then they rushed upstairs, fighting each other to be the first in the courtroom to hear the verdict.)

W.J. McAleer and Joseph Conroy were talking to each other, but they did not appear to be very friendly.

Harry was talking to his father, a little man with dark circles under his eyes and a worried countenance. Harry's sisters were standing near. The father and one of the sisters had been indicted by a grand jury at Crown Point for stealing the slain woman's clothes from her home. They were not worrying about that now; they were worrying about Harry.

Mrs. Diamond had her handkerchief to her eyes. She was hardly able to walk and leaned heavily on the shoulder of one of her daughters as she left the courtroom. She had heart trouble, and it was rumored that she might not live long.

Two uniformed police entered the room. The deputy sheriff snapped one link of the handcuff on Harry's left wrist and the other link on his own, and then he and Harry started for the jail. There Harry would remain alone throughout the night. Would he pray that he may be spared, hopeful in knowing that a conviction meant the electric chair?

All around the town, groups gathered asking each other the question. In a barbershop, on the main street, a customer told the barber the latest developments of the trial. At the Elks Club, members gathered around the bar to drink near beer and speculate on the verdict. It was zero hour for Harry Diamond.

Wednesday, June 6, 1923—The Verdict

The courtroom was jammed with spectators. The jury had spent only four hours in deliberation. The defendant's mother and sisters and the attorneys for the state had gone home. Harry's father, a little man, sat with his head in his hands swinging from side to side. Harry sat between two of his attorneys nervously locking and unlocking his fingers. His skin was yellow. The jurors had been brought into the room.

Judge H. H. Loring asked the jury, "Do you have your verdict?"

Amos Richmond, who had been selected foreman, stepped from the jury box. "I have here your verdict, gentlemen," said the juror. He handed Judge Loring a paper folded in the center. Not a person in the throng moved. It was still—the stillness of death. The judge began to read. He appeared to be under great strain: not since 1837 had there been a penalty of death inflicted in Porter County. "We the jury," he began, "find the defendant, Harry Diamond (Harry slumped forward in his chair), guilty of murder in the first degree, as charged in the indictment, and fix the penalty at death."

Harry seemed to shiver as the last word was read and turned a deadly white. His head fell forward. He began to whimper and whine like a little boy. His father cried and came toward him. The father fell on the boy, his arms around him, and sank to the floor. They held each other in a tight embrace, both crying.

"Oh, father, this is terrible, this is terrible," whimpered the doomed man. The little old man could not speak. He was no more than five-foot-three tall and wore trousers that bagged at the knees and a coat that was far too large. His head was bald, and he looked tragic.

The court discharged the jury. The stillness of the crowd broke, and there was the sound of feet and a roar of conversation. Judge Loring rapped for order. The sheriff and his deputies walked to Harry and laid their hands on his arms. He arose uncertainly. The handcuffs clinked on his wrists, and he walked bareheaded with unseeing eyes from the courtroom down the stairs and across the street to the jail. He seemed not to hear the questions of reporters.

It was dark in the big cell room. There were no other prisoners. The deputy sheriff snapped the iron gate behind the condemned man. Harry stood with his hands gripping the bars. "My God, Bill," he said to the deputy sheriff in a broken voice. "My God, turn on the light. Don't leave me in the dark." The sheriff switched on the light. Harry sank to his knees beside the cot and buried his face in his hands. He was motionless as the sheriff left for the night.

William Leaves the Courtroom

William Armstrong came out of the courthouse. His hands were in his trouser pockets. He wore a black derby hat that was cocked on one side of his head. He walked with a rhythmic swing to his steps. He was whistling a lively tune and kicking pebbles as he rambled across the courthouse lawn. He grinned as he passed one of the attorneys for the defense under an arc light. "Ah guess you won't have to bother about trying me now," he said with a broad grin, tipping his hat. "Ah's goin' to be Mister McAleer's chauffeur, ah spect."

Thursday, June 7, 1923—Judge Passes Sentence

It was the next afternoon before Judge Loring again called the court to order. It was time to pass sentence upon Harry Diamond, the wife slayer. Harry was brought into the courtroom handcuffed on each side to a deputy sheriff. Another was in the front and one in the rear, plus two more policemen. The handcuffs were removed as he stood before the judge's bench. Harry was pale, and there were large circles beneath his eyes. He appeared dejected and weak, but composed.

"Mr. Diamond, do you have anything to say?"

"I do not."

Attorney W.J. McAleer was present for the state, and Joseph H. Conroy for the defense.

"It is the judgment of this court," the judge said to Harry, "that you suffer death by electricity according to the verdict of the jury, which you heard yesterday. I set the day of your execution in the electric chair at Michigan City for the 12th day of October, 1923."

Harry's father and mother had been sent out of the courtroom before the sentence was read. Esther said, "I can't believe that my boy has been sentenced to death. He was always wonderful to me. I don't believe there was ever a boy in the world who was so good. My Harry never smoked or chewed tobacco or drank liquor. He was a model son and always treated me with the greatest of love and respect. Death. Why can't they take me instead of my boy?"

They stood in the hall. When Attorney McAleer passed out of the courtroom, Mrs. Diamond made a plea for her boy. "Don't kill my boy; don't kill Harry!" she pleaded.

"I'm very sorry for you, Mrs. Diamond," said McAleer, "but Harry killed his wife, and he didn't give her a decent killing either. He beat her to death while she pleaded for her life. He made those four little children orphans. He killed the mother of his own baby. I conducted this case fairly, Mrs. Diamond, and I am sorry for you."

Mrs. Diamond turned away without saying anything. She went to her husband, who was sitting in a chair in the anteroom. The little old man presented a picture that wrung the hearts of spectators, looking like a *karabeinik* (country peddler). Little did they know that he was at the center of the whole plot, from beginning to end. He always used others to do his dirty work. This time it was his son, and he now knew that was a mistake. Harry just had not been up to the task.

Attorney Conroy was talking to Jerome Bartholomew, one of the jurors and an old friend. "You made a good fight, Conroy," said Bartholomew, "but there wasn't a chance for him. He killed her and deserved to die for it. We stood ten for death and two for life imprisonment on the first ballot, and the other two swung over. It never was a question of guilt or innocence—just a matter of death or life. We knew he was guilty."

Another member of the jury said, "The defense did all that it could, but it didn't have a leg to stand on."

CHAPTER 21

After the Trial, Harry Waits

Motion for a New Trial

Judge Loring now gave the defense 30 days to file a motion for a new trial.

Attorney Conroy announced that Harry and his family had exhausted their resources. "I plan to proceed all the way to the Supreme Court if the friends of the Diamonds come to their aid financially," Conroy said. "It was rumored that three members of the Ku Klux Klan were on the jury." The source or truth of the rumors could not be ascertained. There was one Catholic on the jury. Conroy said, "Harry Diamond was sent to death because he is a Jew."

Harry's father and mother expressed the same opinion. "Harry would never have been convicted if he wasn't a Jew," his father declared.

Attorney McAleer stated that the defense already changed venues for the trial and they accepted the jury. The fact that juries in Porter County had freed several Negroes tried for murder indicated that Porter County juries were not prejudiced.

The Boys Meet Again: Plan to Spring Harry

Joseph called Nick Slade, Abe Rosen, and Steve Buconich to discuss Harry's situation. They met in the back room of Steve's soft drink parlor. "I don't know vat ta do, boys. My Harry is certainly gonna fry if ve don't gets him out of jail," said Joseph.

"Ya, it sure looks bad for da boy," agreed Steve.

"I say we try to spring him before they take him to the big house in Michigan City. That's his only chance," suggested Nick.

"I know he has that saw. Let's hope he's been cuttin' dem bars. Let's get someone in to see him and find out if he's ready to break out," Abe said.

"My boy is very 'fraid of da electricity." Joseph knew that Harry was very upset. Just the thought of the electricity going through his body as described by Attorney Conroy at the trial was truly frightening.

"I got it," Nick said. "How's about sending a barber in to cut his hair? He could let us know if he's ready to break out."

"Great idea," said Abe. "I know just the barber for the job. I'll get right on it."

This made Joseph feel a little better. All hope was not lost. Maybe, just maybe, Harry could beat the rap with an appeal. If not, they would try to spring him. "Boys, I'm all tapped out. If ve are goin' get an appeal for Harry, ve needs money."

They all reached into their pockets and threw some bills on the table, enough for Harry's appeal, for now.

June 10, 1923—The Barber Comes to the Jail

Nuncio was Harry's barber from Gary. Abe Rosen made sure he would be able to get in to see Harry, as he called the jail in advance. Nuncio could be trusted and would let Harry know the day for the breakout so he could get the bars cut. Sheriff Pennington checked him out before letting him in Harry's cell. He counted the scissors that he took in and emptied his bag to be sure nothing but barber supplies were in it.

"Got your barber here, Harry. He's gonna make you look real nice for the boys in Michigan City." (That was the state prison, the next stop for Harry.)

"When are they gonna move me, sheriff?"

"I think next Saturday, the 23rd," Sheriff Pennington answered.

Nuncio was getting his tools unpacked. He brought with him an electric clipper. The only socket was in the light bulb that hung in the middle of the corridor. "Come over here, Harry, and help me plug in these clippers. I can't reach the socket."

"Are you sure this will work in this socket?" asked Harry. "Do you think I want to get electrocuted?" They both got a laugh out of that.

While Nuncio worked, he whispered to Harry that the boys wanted to know if he was working on the bars. Harry nodded a yes and said, "I'm almost through the first one."

"Looks like they plan to move me on Saturday, the 23rd."

"I'll let them know."

"Tell them I'll be ready on Friday, the 22nd. They have guards watching me almost day and night, so I can't work very fast. Thanks for coming, Nuncio. Tell my father I'm OK. I hope this is not the last haircut you'll give me," Harry said with a smile, his spirits a little brighter today.

Tuesday, June 12, 1923—Esther Diamond Pleads with the Court

Esther was carrying baby Fay in her arms when she appeared before Judge Loring in circuit court. "Please give my boy a new trial, judge," she pleaded.

"Mrs. Diamond, I cannot give your boy a new trial. It's a matter of the law and Harry's attorney to file for a new trial."

Esther left the courtroom crying. "It's terrible; it's terrible," she told Joseph, who was waiting in an outer room. "They can't," she kept repeating. "I can't see what we're going to do. We have no money, and I heard it takes $300 ($4,200 in 2017 dollars) to file an appeal for a new trial. Now I must go over to the jail and tell poor Harry that there won't be a new trial, that the law must take its course, and that a new trial will come only if there is a legal reason."

Harry was to be moved to the Michigan City Penitentiary in one week to await results of efforts by Attorney Joseph Conroy for a new trial, or possibly an appeal.

June 15, 1923—Attorney Conroy Files Bill of Exceptions

The defense team led by Conroy filed a bill of exceptions with the court. Harry Diamond saw the article in the newspaper. "Looks like they may not fry me after all," he said to the deputy outside his cell door. "Says here the motion will be filed July 1. The judge ordered the clerk of courts to set the motion for the first Tuesday in September. You might have me for a guest for a while longer." Harry's spirits were exceptionally high now that he saw the wheels in motion to save his life.

"Don't think so, Harry," replied the deputy. "Got a note today that they are taking you out of here on Saturday, the 23rd, to the big house. You can make some new friends there," he said sarcastically.

Harry was quiet. The breakout was set for Friday, the 22nd. *Just in time before they move me*, he thought. *If I stay in prison and get life or break out and maybe get killed, which would be better?* He spent the afternoon thinking about his options.

June 18, 1923— Harry Foils His Own Escape

All was going well on sawing the bars off the outside window of the cell. Harry would wait until late at night when everyone was asleep and the deputy had left his watch on the cell, thinking that Harry was asleep. That's when Harry would get the blade out of the sewer trap and do the sawing. He worked from the outside of the bars. He felt he could squeeze through the opening if only two bars were cut. Harry had one bar cut completely through top and bottom, forgetting that he was not supposed to cut it all the way through, so that it would look untouched from the view from the front of the cell. He tried to balance the bar in the window.

Monday night, the deputy came to check on him before handing off his shift to another deputy. "How you doing tonight, Harry? Less than a week to go before you take the trip," he said. He then took hold of the cell door and shook it to check the lock. Just then, the bar fell out of the outside window with a "clank clank" as it hit the floor. The deputy looked up. "What's that?" he said, with a startled look on his face.

"What?" said Harry, as he moved his body in front of the cell window to block the deputy's view.

"I thought I heard a metal bar hit the floor. Move aside, Harry." Harry didn't move. The deputy called for reinforcements. Two more deputies came to his aid. They grabbed Harry while the other found the cell bar on the floor.

"Let's move him to another cell until morning," one said. "Sheriff Pennington can do a thorough search then. Let's post a man outside the jail tonight."

In the morning, they searched Harry's cell and found the saw blade in the sewer trap. Pennington called Attorney W.J. McAleer, the special prosecutor, and told him what happened. McAleer in turn filed a petition to the circuit court for immediate removal of Harry to the state penitentiary at Michigan City.

McAleer said, "If Harry gets out of jail, he'll be the most desperate man ever at large in Indiana. He would kill at sight."

Harry knew all his options to break out were over.

June 21, 1923—Harry Moves to Michigan City

"Get your things together, Harry. We're about to go on a little trip," said the deputy through the cell bars.

Harry moved to the back of the cell. In his mind, this was the end. He didn't want to go to the penitentiary. He had taken all the bromide that Dr. Parker had given him for his epilepsy and mixed it all together. This overdose should surely kill him. He put the bottle to his lips and drank as much as he could. Almost immediately, he appeared weakened and almost dropped to the floor. The deputies entered his cell and deputy Sheriff Forney handcuffed Harry to himself and led him out of his cell.

"Well, boys, it's all over with me now. I haven't the money to fight the case. My family has spent all they have on my trial costs. It's tough to have to die for something I didn't do. I say now I'm innocent of the crime charged to me and for which I must forfeit my life. If I had done the deed, I surely would tell it now, before I die. Tell the Elks Lodge to advance the money to bury me, as my family hasn't the necessary cash. I'm all through, I can't fight anymore."

Harry didn't appear like the man at his trial. His bravado was gone. He was gaunt and had lost the spring in his step. "Come along now, Harry," one deputy said, as they almost had to shove him along to keep pace with the sheriff. He entered the automobile for his ride to Michigan City. During the ride, he took sick and vomited on himself. Maybe it was the bromide he took in his cell, hoping to end his life. Even his attempt at suicide was unsuccessful. He would now wait for an appeal or his death by electrocution.

July 2, 1923—Motion for a New Trial

Joseph Conroy and his team received word from Judge Loring today. The appeal to get Harry a new trial was denied. Now they would try the Indiana Supreme Court.

August 29, 1923—Nick and Matt

Even without Harry, the bootleg whiskey business in Indiana continued. Nick Slade and Matt Buconich were arrested in Gary at the request of Sheriff Pennington of Porter County. Nick was charged with the shooting of Deputy Sheriff W.B. Forney in a liquor raid. It was thought that Matt Buconich was the "brains" behind the gang of bootleggers. This all happened when Sheriff Pennington's posse approached a still making the bootleg liquor. Deputy Forney was expected to recover.

September 4, 1923—The Children and School

Pearle was living with Mrs. Anna Cohen Fishman and was enrolled at Washington High School. The three boys were living with their Uncle Marcus Herschcovitz and his wife, Sophia. Cecil and Bernard were attending Washington Elementary, and Lloyd was attending Washington High. The boys, especially Lloyd, were having problems adjusting to their new situation without a mother or father. Lloyd would be 13 in November. Bernard was 11, and Cecil was 8. The trial was fresh in everyone's memory, and the boys were teased about it. This led to numerous fights, especially for Lloyd.

September 18, 1923—Conroy Appeals to the Indiana Supreme Court; Governor Gets Involved

Attorney Conroy sent an appeal to the Indiana Supreme Court. This delayed Harry's execution indefinitely until they had a chance to rule on the motion. It was now September 18, 1923. Harry got the news in prison.

"I always knew I might beat this electrocution," he said. "You just have to get good lawyers if you want to get off." He was in much higher spirits. Indiana Governor McCray gave Harry a 60-day reprieve on October 1, just 11 days before his scheduled electrocution. Defense team member McMahon confirmed the Supreme Court stay of execution until April 4, 1924. It was extended again until November 14, 1924

April 10, 1924—Matt and Steve Buconich Arrested

The government was starting to crack down on the soft drink parlors acting as fronts for the sale of illegal alcohol. They arrested Matt and Steve Buconich in their parlor at 21 West 11th St. in Gary, Indiana.

May 26, 1924—Nettie Gets a Tombstone

After much deliberation, the bank finally gave the authority to buy a headstone for Nettie and get it engraved. The expense was $313 ($4,300 in 2017 dollars). It was Anna Fishman and Pearle together who decided on the wording.

"Anna, Mama was so different from other women," Pearle said. "She was the only one in her family that graduated from college, and being a pharmacist was special."

"That's right, Pearle," Anna agreed. "Growing up, she was never afraid of anything. Life was an ever-changing experience for her. She was a survivor. She knew it was a man's world we live in. I've never told you this, but in the old country she tried to pass as a boy and attended my brothers' *yeshiva*. She tried her best to be the mother to you and your brothers, even though at times she was unconventional. I think I know just the person from our Jewish history that Nettie would represent."

"Who is that, Aunt Anna?" asked Pearle.

"It's Deborah, the fourth judge of Israel. She was unique as the first and only woman judge of Israel. She had the difficult role violating all stereotypes about biblical roles for women. She had to work with men who found her very unusual. Deborah's primary weapon was words, and Nettie couldn't stop talking even when she was dying. No one could keep her quiet. She wanted justice, just like Deborah."

They decided to inscribe the tombstone with the Hebrew words "Nacha Devorah Daughter of Yahshua." Yahshua was a mortal with a direct connection to God.

Nettie's tombstone. Nettie—who was always careful to conceal her real age— would probably be dismayed to see her tombstone erroneously listing 39 as her age at death. She was born in March 1885 and died in February 1923, at age 37 years and 11 months. *Courtesy of the Waldheim Cemetery Company*

Summer, 1924—Uncle Marcus Throws the Boys Out

It was the summer of 1924. The three boys, Lloyd, Bernard, and Cecil, had been living with Marcus and his wife this past school year. The tension in the house was obvious. The boys had never had a father figure in their lives. Sam, their father, died when they were very young. Harry, if anything, was a very poor role model as a father. He paid so little interest in the children that at his trial, he could not remember all their names. When asked to name them, he forgot Lloyd.

Uncle Marcus, the attorney, had a short fuse and he showed it at work. On several occasions, he called out the opposing attorney to settle the matter in the street. The bank was paying them for boarding the boys. At times, he didn't feel they appreciated what he and Sophia were doing for them. One of those times happened when they were having dinner. Sophia did not keep a kosher[1] house and would serve pork. This night, Lloyd said to Bernard, who had gotten up from the table before the meal was over, "Why don't you come back and eat the rest of this junk?"

Marcus had heard enough, and criticizing his wife's cooking was one insult too many. He went into a rage. He got up from his chair and went over to Lloyd and jerked his seat out from under him. Lloyd fell on the floor. "If that's how you feel about the food around here, then the three of you can get out," he said. From the sound of his voice, they all knew they had poked the bear one too many times.

Marcus Herschcovitz. *Family collection*

The boys all headed for the front door with Uncle Marcus right on their heels. Lloyd was the first to say something. "Please, Uncle Marcus, let us back in the house. I'm sorry. We really aren't that bad, are we?"

"I've made up my mind. You boys will have to find another place. I don't want you in my house ever again. I'm through with the likes of you." He had fought for them and gotten the Diamonds convicted for grand larceny when they ransacked Nettie's house, and this was the thanks he got: three ungrateful spoiled brats with a trust fund at the bank. He was through with them. Marcus and Sophia had raised one daughter. Violet was now 20. Raising three boys was not what they had expected. As

---

1 Kosher is the term used to describe the dietary laws often observed by Jews. They began as a way to prevent illness before refrigeration or glazed dishware. Meat and milk items were eaten on separate plates to decrease contamination. Animals were killed in a kosher manner, and certain foods were not eaten as they were felt to be unclean. Pork was on this list; it was associated with trichinosis, a disease contracted by eating undercooked pork.

much as Sophia wanted to help Nettie's sons, they just didn't seem to appreciate what they were doing for them.

The boys had no choice but to walk down the street to Aunt Anna Fishman's house, where Pearle was living. When the three of them arrived, Lloyd knocked on the door. Anna answered the door. "What are you boys doing here?" she asked.

"Aunt Anna," Lloyd said, "Uncle Marcus threw us out. Can we stay here at your house for the night?"

"Of course, Lloyd. You and your brothers can stay here tonight. Tomorrow I'll go over to Marcus's house and talk with him. Then we can figure out where you will stay."

"Thank you so much, Aunt Anna," Lloyd said.

Bernard and Cecil did the same.

The next morning, Anna went to see Marcus and Sophia. It became very clear that they did not want the boys back. She gathered up their things and took them back to her house. She would now figure out where they would live the rest of the summer. She would talk with Mr. Allen at the bank tomorrow. The next day, they went to the bank and talked with Mr. Allen about where they could live. Aunt Ettie would take Cecil; Bernard would live with Uncle Dave. Who would take Lloyd? Mrs. Zimmerman, a close friend of Nettie's and now a widow, had an extra room for Lloyd, at least for the summer.

Mr. Allen in his dual roles as bank vice president and executor of the estate had a decision to make. "Mrs. Fishman, I think it best for the boys to leave town and attend a boarding school. I know of one that is highly recommended for its academic excellence. My boss, Colonel Riley, sent his nephew there. It's run by the Jesuits in Wisconsin. I think the boys need a father in their lives, and who better than the Jesuit brothers?"

The die was cast. Lloyd and Bernard set about enjoying the rest of their summer. The activity this summer was tennis. Bernard really loved the game—Lloyd not so much.

September 1924—Lloyd and Bernard Go to Boarding School

Mr. Allen accompanied the boys on the train ride to the school. It was almost a 300-mile trip, so they had plenty of time to talk. Mr. Allen told them as much as he could about the school. The tuition was $100, and room and board $400 for each of them. The name was Campion Jesuit High School in Prairie du Chien, Wisconsin. The school was located on over 100 acres near the confluence of the Wisconsin and Mississippi Waterway, which connected the Great Lakes with the Mississippi River.

Jewish boys in a Catholic School could not be a good fit. As expected, the boys did not adjust well to their new environment. It was academically challenging, but they kept to themselves, making few friends. They always had complaints about the food, especially Bernard. Pork was frequently on the menu, and the boys wouldn't eat it. It also reminded them of the time Sophia, Marcus's wife, served it to them on their last night in his house. By the end of the school term, Bernard had gone from pudgy to skinny.

October 31, 1924—Harry Diamond Is Not Insane

The "Little Giant" Joseph Conroy wasn't done with schemes to free Harry, or at least save his life. He petitioned the court on October 20, 1924, claiming that Harry was now insane. "Judge, you can't execute an insane person," argued Conroy.

"We will take your motion and give you a ruling within the month," the judge said.

Conroy didn't have long to wait. On October 31, 1924, the petition was denied. Harry was sane.

CHAPTER 22

Harry Diamond
Is Executed

November 13 and 14—The Execution

Harry Diamond prison photo.
Courtesy of the Indiana State Archives

On November 13, Edward Fogarty, the warden of the Indiana penitentiary, went to Harry's death cell. "Harry, I'm here to tell you they're going to put you to death at midnight tonight." The warden left and Harry returned to his cot.

Harry spoke to the guard outside his cell. "I've just one chance left, just a one in a thousand chance to get a stay from the new governor. My folks and attorney are in Indianapolis now working on it."

The guard didn't answer, and Harry went back to his cot.

Attorney Conroy was making one last appeal to the new governor of Indiana to stop Harry's execution. Both Harry's father, Joseph, and his mother, Esther, were waiting for Governor Branch in his outer office to plead for the life of their son. They were alternately crying and consoling each other. Joseph made sure both he and Esther were wearing old clothes, just like he did at the trial to get the sympathy of the jury and now the governor.

Governor Branch arrived, and Joseph and Esther were admitted to his office. "Please sir," they pleaded, "can you change the death sentence to life imprisonment?"

"I'm sorry, I can't do that," he said.

"Can you give him a stay of execution? Our attorney needs time for further investigation of Harry's mental condition."

"You folks must understand that the courts have decided that Harry is sane. I can do nothing," the governor said. The one in a thousand chance was now gone.

Joseph and Esther called Fannie in Gary and told her the news. She and her younger brother David went to Michigan City to see Harry one last time. It was 3:30 in the afternoon when they arrived at the prison. They were admitted to Harry's cell block. Fannie was clinging to the bars of the cell and was sobbing pitifully. "Harry," she said, "Mom and Dad talked with Governor Branch. He wouldn't grant a stay of execution. There's no hope for a reprieve."

Harry patted her hand. "It's cut and dried, sis. I'll take my medicine. I'm not afraid of the electric chair."

"What can I do, Harry?" Fannie asked.

"Take the kid and go back to Gary, and don't let the folks come here. I don't want any of you to be here when it happens. Tell Mother and Dad I love them, and tell Mother I'm sorry I brought this disgrace upon her. I didn't know what I was doing when I killed Nettie. I was having an epileptic fit." Then he brought Fannie close to the bars and whispered, "Tell Pop to check out the transom over the door that leads to the basement at the drugstore." In a louder voice, he said, "Is Rabbi Hyman coming to see me?"

"He'll be here. I know," said Fannie. The rabbi was from Gary and the synagogue where Harry attended as a boy. Nothing more was said. Fannie and her brother lingered for several minutes. They kissed Harry through the bars of his cell and left.

Where's the Rabbi?

All afternoon, Harry waited for the visit from Rabbi Hyman. He asked if he would be admitted as soon as he arrived. The Rev. A.W. Wood, prison chaplain, came—but Harry did not appear to be interested in talking to him.

In the evening, Harry ate the normal prison fare. "Well, I guess I'll get my first electrical treatment tonight," he said to the guard, laughing. There was no mirth in the laugh. Harry whistled a tune to keep up his spirits. The rabbi still had not arrived by 9:30 p.m.

Harry stretched out on the cot in his cell and fell asleep. He was awakened at five minutes to midnight. The door of his cell was opened, and two guards entered. In the corridor stood the warden, the chaplain, the prison physician Dr. F.H. Weeks, and a practicing physician from Michigan City, Dr. J. J. Kerrigan.

The warden had posted guards at the power house and another where the power entered the prison execution chamber. There was a rumor that an attempt might be made to interfere with the execution. They doubted the rumor, but they were not going to take any chances. This was a matter of safety.

Harry got up unaided and straightened his coat collar and tie. He looked at the men standing in the corridor and said, "Where's Rabbi Hyman?"

"He didn't come," replied Fogarty.

"God!" exclaimed Harry. It was his only display of emotion.

"Are you ready?" questioned Fogarty.

"Must I go now?"

"Yes."

Harry picked up the comb that hung from a chain on the wall of his cell and parted his hair carefully. He brushed his well-fitting blue suit. "I'm ready," he said, stepping out of the cell. He walked to the execution chamber unaided. He entered smiling, but it was not a pleasant smile—it was more tragic, more ghastly, and more horrible than the most anguished expression could have been.

In the lobby of the prison was Rabbi Hyman, excitedly begging the guard for admittance. He had not been notified until late because he had been away from home. "I must see Harry before the execution."

"It's impossible," said the guard.

Harry was being led to the execution room, and it would be over in a minute. The little rabbi's eyes were wet with tears, but he was not without spirit. "Can't a man make peace with his God before they kill him in Indiana?" he demanded.

Harry Diamond gazed at the electric chair a moment. As he sat down, he pulled the legs of his trousers a trifle as though to keep the knees in the crease. Undoubtedly, he was unconscious of the act. The chaplain offered a prayer to God for the soul of Harry.

"Have you anything to say?" asked Warden Fogarty.

Harry shook his head. The smile was blanched. He was resigned and beaten. The braggadocio of the trial and of long weeks in prison had broken him. He sat in the electric chair as helpless as a baby. He seemed unable to so much as raise his hand as the black cap was pulled over his head. What was he thinking? Was it about the day he murdered his wife and shot William? Was it what he wanted to tell the rabbi?

Harry was strapped in the chair. There was a pause of barely a second during which the warden, the physicians, and the two guards stood motionless looking at the silent figure in the chair. Then, at a signal from the warden, a guard pressed a button. Two thousand three hundred volts of electricity passed through Harry. His body strained at the strappings and, after a brief convulsion, became tense and rigid. There was no burning flesh as the interlocked oil switch method was being used. Next followed a shock of 500 volts, and finally another shock of 2,200 volts. The first volts were sent through his body at four minutes after midnight November 14, 1924. He was pronounced dead by the physicians at 12:10 a.m.

Out in the lobby, the rabbi ("the little man in the cloth of the church," as one newspaper called him), was praying on his knees. The room was filled with newspaper men awaiting the news of Harry's death. At 12:14 a.m., Warden Fogarty came through the prison gates and announced that he was dead.

Harry's uncle from Waukegan, Illinois, Lewis Berger, who was married to Harry's mother Esther's sister, stepped forward and claimed the body, which was being placed in an undertaker's wagon.

Rabbi Hyman and Berger trudged through the night to the undertaker's room. The streets were alive with townspeople gossiping about the ninth execution to the credit of the great state of Indiana. The rabbi and the uncle entered the undertaker's office and were escorted back to the room where the body of Harry Diamond, still warm, was lying on a slab.

Berger went back to the officer with the undertaker to make out the papers. Harry's remains would be shipped to Chicago for burial. He would be buried in the same cemetery as Nettie. Rabbi Hyman was alone with the earthly remains of Harry Diamond, 26 years old, one month shy of his 27th birthday. He died without confessing to the public and without making peace with his maker.

It was 15 months to the day since he had committed the murder of his wife Nettie. With her last dying breath, she had told the authorities and anyone else who would listen how Harry had killed her. She now reached out beyond the grave and received justice. Could she rest in peace, or not, until the whole story of what happened to her surviving family was told?

Harry's Parents Arrive Home from Indianapolis

Defeated, Joseph and Esther had arrived home before midnight Thursday, the 13th, just hours before Harry's execution. They had planned to get the new governor of Indiana to stay Harry's execution but had failed. Now their oldest son was dead. Esther now held a deep resentment toward Joseph, knowing that he had orchestrated the whole affair, dating back to the old country when Nettie spurned him and he never got over it. He had sacrificed his eldest son to try to settle old wounds. Nettie was dead. So was his son. He was now no closer to getting Nettie's fortune. He should have known better. Harry was not up to the task of carrying out Joseph's plot. As parents, they had given him everything they didn't have growing up. The sun rose and set on their boy Harry. Unfortunately, Harry developed no humility—just an oversized ego that could not be satisfied. Like his father, money was his obsession. Harry thought he was a *macher* (big shot, a man with contacts) and smarter than everybody. In truth, he was really a *menuvel* (a person always causing grief, someone who just can't get things right).

With Harry gone, there would forever be a missing part of the family they could never recover.

CHAPTER 23

The Children, Now Orphans

Life at the Boarding School after the Execution

Lloyd and Bernard heard about the execution of their stepfather while in school. There was an article in the local paper, and it didn't take long for the other boys at the school to find out that Lloyd and Bernard were part of the family. This led to further disciplinary problems, especially for Lloyd. The boys made up their minds that after this school year was over, they would not come back to this place. They longed to go home to East Chicago.

"Bernard, let's break out of this place. I have some money for bus tickets," said Lloyd. Bernard agreed with his older brother.

It was after Christmas and exceptionally cold—so cold that the Mississippi River had frozen over. Lloyd's plan was to get across the river to the city of Marquette on the other side, get on a bus, and head back home. They started across the river after supper under the cover of darkness. They hoped to be across the mile-wide river by the time bed check took place. It was tricky going, crossing the river ice. They heard creaking sounds as the ice seemed to move beneath them. They were careful to give a wide berth to any open leads in the ice. They could feel the water flowing under their feet. If they fell through, it was certain death in the icy water, being trapped under the ice.

Bernard started to think this wasn't such a great idea, but it was too late; they were more than halfway across. "It's a good thing we brought these sticks with us to test the ice," Bernard said, as he tapped the ice with his stick ahead of himself. By the time they reached the other side, there was a full-scale hunt for the boys. They got into the town of Marquette, but the Jesuit brothers had anticipated their plan and found them at the bus station. That was the last attempt they made to get back home. When they finished the year, they were determined not to return.

Drugstore Robbery?

Officer McCormick was walking his beat. As a service to the community, he would check the doors of the businesses on his route. Tonight he noticed the back door to the Calumet Drugstore was ajar. It had been pried open. It was now 11 p.m., November 27, Thanksgiving evening. He called A.J. Gavolis, who came down to the store. They both entered through the back door and began checking for any signs of a robbery. Everything looked in order, but the door to the basement was open and there was a chair in front of the door. They checked the basement, but all was in order. Officer McCormick said, "I've never seen a break-in where nothing was taken."

Harry's family now had Nettie's beaded purse and the diamonds. Attorney McAleer was right about Harry's always knowing where Nettie's purse was located. In his last few words, Harry had told his sister where the diamonds were hidden.

Baby Fay Gets Adopted March 1925

In March of 1925, Gertrude Fay Diamond was legally adopted by her grandparents, Joseph and Esther Diamond. This was one week after Nettie's estate paid $3,000 ($42,000 in 2017 dollars) to Fay's account and $2,000 ($28,000 in 2017 dollars) to Edward Noah Sachs, the two half siblings of the Herskovitz children. They were mentioned in Nettie's last will as she lay dying in the hospital. This would not settle Fay's account if Joseph had anything to say about it.

Joseph Diamond hired an attorney and opened the succession and sued Nettie's estate for more money. As a result, Fay got a monthly allowance of $15 ($263 in 2017 dollars), $5 more than the other children received. In addition, Fay would share in the entire estate equally with her Herskovitz half siblings.

In July of 1925, the ring that was taken from Harry when he was arrested the day of the shooting was returned to the estate. It was J.G. Allen, executor of the estate, who sued the East Chicago Police department to get the ring back. He personally delivered the ring to the Diamond family. Its value was estimated at $600 ($8,400 in 2017 dollars).

May 1925—Lloyd and Bernard Return to East Chicago

When the school term ended, Mr. Allen had arrived at the school and escorted the boys back home. They talked on the trip home, and Mr. Allen found that Lloyd had developed a much better attitude. The school and the Jesuits had done their job.

When they got home, Cecil was living with Aunt Ettie. Bernard moved back to Uncle Dave's, but Mrs. Zimmerman had died the past year, and Lloyd stayed with Aunt Anna Fishman temporarily. Lloyd's reputation for not being told what to do was still fresh in the minds of his uncles. The next school year was fast approaching, and he had to find a place to stay.

He went to the Indiana Harbor Bank to talk to Mr. Allen, the trustee. "Mr. Allen, I need to find a place to stay before school starts. Aunt Anna says she just doesn't have the room and can only keep Pearle," Lloyd said.

"Lloyd, if you can't find anyone to take you, I see only two choices for you," Allen replied.

Washington High School, Indiana Harbor, Indiana. *Courtesy of Calumet Regional Archives, Anderson Library, Indiana University Northwest*

"What's that?" Lloyd asked.

"It's going back to the boarding school or to reform school," he said, with the tone of a banker. That was more than Lloyd could take. He went out into the lobby, sat in one of the overstuffed chairs, and started to cry. He just couldn't go back to the school in Wisconsin.

Just then, Aunt Ettie came into the bank and saw Lloyd. She went over to him. "Lloyd, why are you crying?" she asked.

"Mr. Allen said boarding school or reform school if I don't find a place to live," Lloyd said, as he wiped the tears from his eyes.

"Well, you just come with me. All I have is a day bed in the living room, but that will have to do." She opened the door to Mr. Allen's office. He looked up from his desk. Before he had a chance to say anything, Ettie said, "Mr. Allen, Lloyd is going to stay with me." Ettie thought, *Pepe took me in after my mother died. I can do the same for her grandchildren, my nephews.* Pepe died in April just two months after Nettie was murdered.

He smiled back at her and said, "Thanks, Ettie. I'll make sure the bank adds his support to your account." That seemed to end the crisis, and Lloyd and Aunt Ettie left the bank. Lloyd had to be tested when he re-entered Washington High in the fall. His boarding school education allowed him to skip a grade, and he entered as a senior—in the same class as his older sister Pearle.

CHAPTER 24

Wills and Estates

August 1925—Harry Diamond's Last Will and Testament

On Harry's last day alive, he wrote out his will in the presence of Walter Daly at the prison. His mother Esther submitted it for probate on August 4, 1925. In his will, he gave his mother his diamond ring and his father his diamond stickpin. In keeping with Harry's professed love for Nettie's children, which he said at his trial, he gave them the following, showing his true feelings: "To Pearle, Lloyd, Bernard, and Cecil Herskovitz and Edward Sachs, I give and bequeath the sum of five dollars ($5.00), to be divided evenly among them. To my daughter, Gertrude Fay Diamond, I give and bequeath all my personal and real property remaining in my estate." All he had in his estate was one piece of property valued at $500 ($7,036 in 2017 dollars).

May 1926—Joseph Diamond Continues to Sue Nettie's Estate

Before he was put to death, Harry changed the beneficiary on two $5,000 ($140,000 in 2017 dollars) insurance policies. He made his father and mother the new beneficiaries. Mr. James G. Allen, executor, thought that Nettie's estate should get the money and challenged him in court. The U.S. Court of Appeals ruled in Harry's favor. That didn't stop

Allen. He was a man on a mission and fought for the ruling to move to the next higher court. During this time, he and Joseph Diamond developed an intense dislike for each other. Allen was always on guard protecting the estate from the attorneys hired by Joseph.

Joseph Diamond Plans a Hit on James G. Allen

It seemed that every time Joseph tried to get more money out of Nettie's estate, Allen blocked his move. Allen used the assets in the estate to file motions with the court and pay attorneys' fees. The attorney usually appointed to work for the estate was James Murray. He had intimate knowledge of all of Nettie's holdings. He was also the one who signed her death certificate.

This time, Joseph met with his longtime friend and partner, Abe Rosen. "Abe, I gots a problem vit da guy at da bank. I needs to get him off da estate. Maybe an accident vould do it?"

Abe always knew the right man for the job. He had connections deep within the Chicago mob. "You want him killed or just roughed up enough to not be able to work?" Abe asked.

"I don't care, as long as he's out of da bank," said Joseph.

"I'll get a tail on him, and we'll see where he goes and how he travels. How much do you have to spend?" asked Abe.

"I can spend a C spot." ($100 in 1928 was $1,400 in 2017 dollars.)

"Consider the job done. I'll let you know when I need the money."

That was all Joseph had to do. Getting others to do his dirty work was his specialty. With Allen gone, Joseph's attorneys said they could work with James Murray, the bank's attorney, who had political ambitions and would "play ball."

A Tail Is Put on Allen

Abe Rosen had just the guy to tail Allen. This man blended into the crowd so well that no one, especially Allen, would notice him. He found that Allen was making biweekly trips to Chicago to work on the Diamond case with the appellate court. Every Tuesday and Thursday, he would take the New York Central Railroad to downtown Chicago, then the 5:30 Danville train number 13 back to Indiana Harbor. The passengers at the Indiana

Harbor station had to walk across six sets of tracks after they arrived at the station. There were always several trains stopped on these tracks switching between engines, as they made up a freight delivery. It would be easy for someone to come up behind Allen and make it look like he had been hit by a train.

Bruno was just the man for the job. He was a giant of a man, almost six-foot-four and very large-boned. He had worked in the stockyards in Chicago but was now out of work. He weighed over 280 pounds, and it had been his job to hang the sides of beef on hooks as the cows were slaughtered. He had six kids at home, so making a $100 for "a little bump" was easy money, and he needed it. He worked with the tail one day to identify the pigeon (target), and then it was time to strike.

BANKER, BADLY INJURED, BELIEVED TRAIN VICTIM

HAMMOND, Ind., Oct. 26.—J. G. Allen, vice president and cashier of the Indiana Harbor National bank and one of the most prominent bankers in the Calumet region, was found with broken ribs, broken arm and serious internal injuries on a switch track near the New York Central depot last night. It is believed he was struck by a switch engine as he alighted from a Chicago passenger train at the Indiana Harbor depot. He is at St. Catherine's hospital in East Chicago in critical condition.

Article on J.G. Allen and his accident, *Hammond Lake County Times*, October 26, 1928. *Courtesy of Newspaper Archives*

October 25, 1928—James G. Allen Has an Accident

The day of the "hit" was October 25 when Allen got off the train. It would be dark. Wearing dark clothing, even at his size, Bruno would be hard to see. He hid between two rows of boxcars parked on the last two tracks, farthest away from the station platform. He carried with him a small suitcase filled with iron bars. The plan was to swing the suitcase into Allen as he passed the last line of boxcars. It would look like a boxcar hit him.

Allen, with briefcase in hand, got off the number 13 train. The train was on the opposite side of the station platform from where he was going. It was only a short walk from the station to his home on the Indiana Harbor side of the tracks.

Bruno watched from the shadows as Allen came toward him over the tracks. Allen was walking toward a streetlight, and its light was shining in his eyes. Just as he passed, Bruno came around the boxcar and swung his suitcase into Allen's body, hitting him on his right side and throwing him across the tracks. Allen, at only 155 pounds, was an easy target for Bruno. Allen passed out from the blow and lay on the ground.

Bruno turned away and started back across the tracks. A train backing into the intersection saw him about to cross the tracks and blew its whistle. Bruno reversed his course and walked alongside the train, pulling his cap down to conceal his face, and slipped out of sight.

Allen was first spotted by Ernest Pearson, a fireman for the Baltimore and Ohio Railroad. He noticed Allen about 10 feet away from the tracks. It looked like he'd been hit by a train. Ernest was riding on a switcher that was backing up, with its coal tender leading the engine. The light on the coal tender caught the image of Allen on the ground.

"There's a man lying along the track," Ernest hollered to the engineer. He stopped the train. The engineer and the conductor got off the train and went over to Allen. By then, a man from the mill was there too.

"What hit you?" the conductor said.

"I don't know. Whatever hit me didn't have a light or make any noise," Allen said.

"Are you hurt?" the engineer asked.

"My right arm hurts," he said.

"Is there a doctor you want us to call?" said the engineer.

"Just let me lie a bit," Allen said. He then started to get up on his knees, and the two men helped him to his feet. "Wait a minute. I want to see where I am," Allen said, a bit confused. "Oh, I see now," he said.

The engineer, conductor, and mill man took Allen to the mill clock house on the Indian Harbor side of the tracks, on Block Avenue. "Is there a certain doctor you want?" asked the engineer.

"Yes, Dr. Teagarden," Allen replied.

They called Dr. Teagarden, but he didn't answer.

"Do you want us to notify any of your folks and tell them what happened?"

"No," said Allen.

They couldn't get Dr. Teagarden but did get Dr. Cotter and Dr. Niblick. Dr. Niblick arrived at the clock house and saw Mr. Allen about 7:30 p.m.

"Where do you hurt?" Dr. Niblick asked.

"I hurt all over," Allen said.

"Do you want me to call an ambulance?" asked the doctor.

"I can sit in your car, and I will go out in that," said Allen.

They helped him into the doctor's car, and he took him to St. Catherine Hospital. It took several hospital employees to get him out of the car when they arrived at the hospital. At the emergency room, Allen complained of a lot of pain to his left chest and abdominal region.

Dr. Niblick called Dr. Robinson and turned the case over to him. When they undressed him at the hospital, he still had his pocketbook and other items. Robbery was ruled out.

Mrs. Allen was called to the hospital. Dr. Robinson's examination found a fracture of the right clavicle and right scapula and a contusion to his left thorax and right abdominal region and middle abdominal region.

The next day, Captain Knight of the East Chicago Police came to get Allen's story. This was the same Captain Knight who was with Nettie as she lay dying in the Calumet Drugstore.

"Can you tell me what you think happened?" Captain Knight asked Allen.

"I thought I saw a boxcar about one foot from me, and I jumped forward to get away from it. The next thing I remember is two men helping me up and walking me to the clock house."

Allen spent the next two weeks in the hospital. He seemed to be progressing well until the morning of November 11 when he had a very sudden distress in the left thorax, in the region of his heart. Within 15 minutes, he was dead. He was 65 years old and left a wife and 13-year-old daughter. The autopsy showed death from a cardiac embolism, probably from thrombosis of the pulmonary vein to his lung due to the accident.

Joseph got more than his money's worth. Bruno was not paid to kill Allen, just cripple him. Seventeen days after the accident, Allen was dead. November 11, 1928, attorney William J. Murray petitioned the court to become both the executor and attorney for Nettie's estate. Joseph got the attorney his people wanted. It was the green light to again attack Nettie's estate.

Indiana Harbor Bank and Nettie's Estate

None of the Herskovitz children were of legal age; they had been completely dependent on the decisions of the bank's executor, James G. Allen. After Allen's death, attorney William J. Murray took Allen's place as executor and attorney in December of 1928. He managed all the economic affairs for the children. The bearer bonds and stocks estimated at $40,000 to $50,000 ($563,912 to $703,646 in 2017 dollars) that Harry had mailed to himself in Louisvile, Kentucky, under an assumed name were never found. Both Allen and Murray searched Chicago banks for Nettie's accounts. They even took a few trips to St. Louis, where they found a safety deposit box in her name.

After Allen's death, Murray came to a final valuation in November 1929. This was necessary to determine estate taxes:

	1929 Valuation	In 2017 Dollars
Value of personal property	$16,620	$233,892
Value of real estate	$79,550	$1,119,501
Total gross value of estate	$96,170	$1,353,393
Deductions, debts, mortgages, etc.	$53,540	$753,464
Total net value of estate	$42,670	$600,491

At this time, the only heirs to get any cash were Fay Diamond, $3,000, and Edward Noah Sachs, $2,000. The four Herskovitz children had a tax value in the estate of $9,407 ($132,384 in 2017 dollars) each. The federal tax exception was $50,000, so they were exempt. The Indiana inheritance deductible was $5,000. The estate had to pay inheritance tax on $4,407 for each of the four children. The tax rate was 1 percent. Each had to pay $44.07 ($620 in 2017 dollars).

Allen and Murray needed cash to pay the bills of the estate. To do this, Indiana Harbor Bank took mortgages on most of Nettie's properties. They used the rents from the properties to pay the mortgages. During the economic downturn, after the stock market crash of 1929, the estate lost most of the property to the bank. When the bank ended its services to the estate on October 30, 1930, there were only seven properties left: The Calumet Drugstore Building rented for $300/month, and the house at 647 Buchanan rented at $70/month. Three other properties remained that did not have mortgages, and there were two more properties with mortgages. Lloyd Herskovitz took over as the executor of the estate before he graduated from law school in 1932.

	Fair Market Value ($100 in 1929 equal to $1,400 in 2017 dollars)	Mortgage
Lot 2 Blk 36 O.T. Indiana Harbor (still in Estate in 1934)	$7,500	$2,580
Lot 19 Blk 64 O.T. Indiana Harbor	$6,000	$0
Lot 1 Blk 10 S.W. 28th East Chicago (Calumet Drugstore)	$20,000	$6,000
Lot 6 Blk 51 ReSub O.T. Indiana Harbor	$7,000	$3,750 Foreclosed
Lot 16 Blk 10 3rd Add, Indiana Harbor	$1,000	$0
Lot 30 ReSub Blk 20-21 4th Add	$2,600	$1,500
Lot 35 ex. S. 28ft Blk 4-4th Add, Indiana Harbor	$4,250	$2,500 Foreclosed
Lot 14 Blk 10 3rd Add, Indiana Harbor	$1,000	$0

Gary Property	Fair Market Value ($100 in 1929 equal to $1,400 in 2017 dollars)	Mortgage
Lot 8 Blk 2 Gary Land Co. 2nd Add	$6,500	$3,300 Foreclosed
Lot 7 Blk 2 Gary Land Co. 2nd Add	$7,300	$3,300
Lot 6 S. 1/2 Blk 2. Gary Land Co. 2nd Add	$7,400	$3,500 Foreclosed
Lot 6 S. ½ 5 Blk 2 Gary Land Co. Lot 12 N ½ 13 Blk. 5 Gary Land Co. 2nd Add (This was the house at 647 Buchanan)	$9,000	$5,860

In March of 1928, the bank decided to sell all the jewelry in the estate ($100 in 1928 was valued at $1,400 in 2017 dollars):

1 diamond ring	$300.00
1 diamond wedding ring	$15.00
1 gold chain	$2.00
1 diamond bar pin	$125.00
1 diamond scarf pin	$75.00
1 ruby scarf pin	$.50
3 unset rubies	$.50
1 Pathfinder watch and fob	$2.75
1 Hampton watch	$5.00
1 pair of cuff links	$2.50
Total	$528.25

On March 10, 1928, the bank bought the following stocks for $1, saying they had no value. No one knows what happened to these stocks, now in the name of the Bank.

Stock Name	Shares
Twin Tube & Rubber Company	10
Hughes-Weatherford Oil Syndicates	200
Great American Chemical Products Co.	5,000
Gary Motor Truck Company	40
United Owners Supply Co.	1
Orion Pharmaceutical Co.	2
The Lester Offsets	1
Auto Parts Company (preferred)	10
Barnhart Coal Company	10
Blackstone Petroleum Company	500
Gaston, Williams, Wigmore, Inc.	10
Gulf Oil Company	550
Commonwealth Mortgage company (preferred)	6
Commonwealth Mortgage company (common)	3

Stock Name	Shares
Allied Oil Corporation	200
Indiana Trust & Savings Bank	2

Nettie's Cash Assets	
American State Bank of East Chicago	$113.11
Citizens Saving Bank, Indiana Harbor	$88.36
Proceeds, Redmond & Company stockbrokers	$3,554.45
Proceeds, McNulty & Company stockbrokers	$441.08
Proceeds, Redmond & Company stockbrokers	$175.00
Note Wm Weiss	$19.90
Life insurance policy, Mutual Benefit Life Insurance Co.	$8,730.04
Sale of Hudson auto	$1,650.00
Ruman note paid	$400.00
Mrs. H. Ruskin note	$319.01
Dividends Blackstone Petroleum Company	$15.00
Balance from Sam Herskovitz estate	$300.00
Sale of buffet	$50.00
Sale of piano, cabinet, and rug	$100.00
Proceeds of sale of household goods	$628.00
Sale of china cabinet	$31.00
Total	$16,614.95

Disbursements from Estate	
National Garage, auto to funeral	$26.00
Meyers Central Drugstore	$23.45
Lake County Ice & Coal	$47.50
Spire Coal Co.	$69.63
S. Schwarzbach, grading and care of grave	$16.00
J. W. Brissey, attorney's fees	$300.00

Disbursements from Estate	
Hydrex C. Store Chicago	$36.88
Chicago Trust, safety deposit rent	$8.00
S. Berliner, tombstone	$308.00
Dr. Townsley, professional services	$750.00
H.L. Wheaton, clerk, copies of will	$4.50
Cash paid for car storage, W.J. Murray	$5.00
J.G. Allen, cash paid for filing will and copies	$11.00
J.G. Allen, trip to St. Louis	$36.63
Notes interest paid to banks Indiana Harbor National	$2,961.39
American State Bank	$4,082.23
Citizens Trust & Savings	$2,528.89
J.G. Allen, executor's fee	$400.00
W.J. Murray, attorney's fees	$500.00
Weinstein Bros, funeral expenses	$869.25
M. Herskovitz, cash paid to rabbi	$15.00
W.C. Huber, ambulance and auto	$40.00
Chicago Telephone Co.	$27.68
S. Levin & Co., note and interest on Hudson auto	$401.85
Balance at "The Fair" store	$500.00
Simon Bros., balance on Victrola and records	$81.55
Illinois Electric Company, balance on electric cleaner	$8.75
W.J. Murray, attorney's fees	$300.00
E.L. Shaver, storing and repairing Hudson	$38.10
Max Friedman, balance insurance on car	$7.94
Van Liew & Funkey, buffet and piano, etc.	$150.00
Mrs. Sizer, auto to funeral	$30.00
Safety deposit rent	$5.00
Murray and Allen to St. Louis, Missouri	$77.29
Dr. Yarrington, professional services	$100.00
Mercy Hospital	$57.00

Disbursements from Estate	
Dr. Evan, death certificate	$3.00
W.S. White, secretary bd. of health certificate	$3.00
S. Levin & Co., note and interest, Hudson auto	$380.76
J.A. Sweeney, attorney making will	$50.00
J.G. Allen, traveling expenses	$7.84
Kliott & Hurley, judgments superior court	$243.37
Edward Sachs legacy as per will	$2,000.00
Fay Diamond legacy as per will	$3,000.00
I.H. National Bank demand note	$100.30
J.G. Allen, executor's fee	$600.00
W.J. Murray, attorney's fee	$700.00
Box rent I.H. Bank	$5.00
Louis Stebbins, appeal bond	$25.00
Strall & Tonkup, appeal bond	$10.00
Louis A. Stebbins, balance fees and cost	$206.00
Champlin Law Ptg. C. brief superior court	$160.60
J.G. Allen, executor's fee	$2,000.00
J.W. Murray, attorney's fee	$4,000.00
Campion Boarding School costs (2 boys for 1 year)	$1,000.00
Monthly stipend to relatives for care of children	$55.00
Total disbursements	$29,364.38

This was $12,759.43 more than Nettie had in cash assets. The balance came from mortgages on the remaining property.

The executor J.G. Allen received $3,000 ($42,318 in 2017 dollars). The attorney W.J. Murray received $5,000 ($70,364 in 2017 dollars). Together, their fees represented almost 20 percent of the net value of the estate. J.G. Allen received a salary from the bank of $7,200 ($101,325 in 2017 dollars), plus a yearly bonus. This extra money from the estate was icing on the cake.

By the time the four Herskovitz children graduated from high school, they were essentially without liquid funds. They received a living allowance during their high school years of $10/month, which continued when they entered college. The income from the remaining two rental properties went to paying their notes, to avoid foreclosure. Some funds came from second and third mortgages on these properties.

These cash assets were used to pay the bills and other obligations of the estate. There was never enough money to give the Herskovitz heirs any monetary funds beyond a monthly allowance given to the families with whom they were living.

Joseph Diamond Sues for Double Indemnity

Joseph was never one to give up on a chance to make money at the expense of others. Harry had signed over two $5,000 insurance policies to his parents on March 31, 1923—one for Nettie, with the proceeds going to her children, and one for himself, with the proceeds going to Nettie. The bank via Allen failed in getting the courts to honor the original beneficiaries. Instead, the courts ruled in favor of Joseph and Esther Diamond. These policies had a double-indemnity benefit if the person named on the policy died by accident. Joseph wanted to have the insurance company pay this benefit.

Joseph hired Benjamin C. Bachrach and Walter Bachrach, two attorneys from Chicago, to represent him. These were high-powered, high-priced attorneys who worked with Clarence Darrow on the Leopold and Loeb case in 1924. Walter Bachrach submitted to Federal Judge Charles E. Woodward a claim for $12,648 ($182,413 in 2017 dollars). He said, "Harry was strapped to a chair by unknown persons, shocked by electricity against his will. This within the meaning of the insurance policy constituted an accident." Their argument was that Harry did not go willingly to his death. It was an accident that he committed the murder because he was insane while having an epileptic fit.

The insurance company stated that the policy would not pay the additional benefit if the insured's death resulted from any violation of the law by the insured. The insurance company said that Harry's intentional, malicious, and felonious undertaking resulted in the consequence of his death. The attorney for the insurance company said that Harry killed his wife and knew that under the law of Indiana, death was a possible result of his act. When he killed his wife, a court found him guilty. This meant he caused his death by his own hand, just as if he had placed a gun to his own head and killed himself. Suicide is not an accident; neither is death at the hands of the law. If the insured had been acquitted, there would have been no cause of action on the policy.

Joseph and Esther lost this case but appealed all the way to the U.S. Supreme Court, where they lost again in 1931. They did collect the $10,000 in insurance ($144,000 in 2017 dollars) on these policies. Fay had received $3,000 ($42,318 in 2017 dollars) as settlement in the will. Through the efforts of her grandfather, Joseph Diamond, Fay shared in the remaining assets of the estate, and Joseph sued to receive a monthly stipend of $15 ($211 in 2017 dollars) until February 1, 1935. This was 33 percent more than the other children received. This amounted to $1,800 ($25,900 in 2017 dollars). In 1941, Lloyd paid $345 ($5,600 in 2017 dollars) for Fay's tuition to the Chicago Academy of Fine Arts plus $55 in fees, and he restarted her $15/month stipend during her school year. Fay continued to refuse final settlement of the estate until January 3, 1945, getting $2,530 ($35,192 in 2017 dollars). In total, she received $17,573 ($302,280 in 2017 dollars).

CHAPTER 25

Nettie's Surviving Legacy: Her Children and Grandchildren

N ettie had given birth to six children with three different husbands. Five of those children received college educations. Edward Noah Sachs Zauderer was the only one not to finish school or have children that lived. The five other children produced 12 grandchildren. All were college educated—many with advanced degrees in medicine and law.

Following is a brief summary of Nettie's children, their lives, and their contributions to America. I'm sure Nettie would have been proud. This was her real legacy to America, the country that she loved.

Nettie's Children:

Pearle Dorothy Herskovitz Baskin (born September 16, 1909, died December 29, 1998)

Pearle was Nettie's first child with Sam Herskovitz. Nettie tried her best to give her everything, including music lessons in Chicago. She was her mother's daughter, as was seen when she took the stand against Harry Diamond in Nettie's trial. She was only 6 years old when her father, Dr. Samuel Herskovitz, died and 13 when Nettie was murdered. Pearle graduated from East Chicago High School in 1927. She was active in the Home Economics Club, the French Club, and the Debating Team. She was the editor of the *Anvil*, the

LEFT: Pearle Herskovitz, high school graduation, 1927.
Courtesy of yearbooks.com.
RIGHT: Pearle Herskovitz, Baskin College graduation,
1930. *Courtesy of yearbooks.com.*

yearbook for the school. She was a founding member of the U.X.I. debating team, the first all-female team at the high school; its name translated is "You against I." After graduation, she attended Rockford College for girls, transferring to the University of Illinois, graduating in 1930. She returned to East Chicago, living with Anna Fishman, and taught Spanish at Washington High School in 1931. She and Dr. Lester Baskin were secretly married in 1931. She lost her job when a school board member found that she was married. At that time, female school teachers could not be married. In 1933, she and Lester bought a Model T Ford and set out for the West. They ended up in Tacoma, Washington, where Lester took a residency in medicine. Lester's younger brother was the "Baskin" in the Baskin-Robbins Ice Cream Company. Pearle and Lester had two children, a boy and girl. Pearle was a founding member of the Tacoma Philharmonic. She and her husband helped secure the old National Bank of Washington Building as a home for the Tacoma Art Museum. When she died, she had four grandchildren and one great-grandchild.

Justin Lloyd (Herskovitz) Hurst (born November 22, 1910, died November 24, 1988)

Lloyd was Nettie's first son by Sam Herskovitz. He was 5 years old when his father died and had just turned 12 when Nettie was murdered. His time at Campion Academy served him well. He skipped a grade and graduated with his sister from East Chicago High School in 1927. While in high school, he was in the Webster Literary Society, Latin Club, and the Debating Team. This was the same team his sister Pearle was on; she took the negative side, and he the affirmative. He enrolled at Indiana University when he was 16 and graduated from law school in 1932. Times were tough, especially after the 1929 economic collapse. There was little left of the estate. The bank had taken most of the property for failure to pay the mortgages. Lloyd was paying $3 a week for his room at college; it was more than he could afford. His landlady, Mrs. Hensley, said he could stay rent-free and pay her back later. Lloyd followed through on his commitment. He remembered this as the first act of kindness he was shown. In the summers, he would work at the steel mill in East Chicago. It was Dr. Schlafer who may have been the father figure in his life. He was the head of the Intramural Athletic Department at Indiana University. He gave jobs to athletes but hired Lloyd to do stenography for his correspondence courses. He gave him a room in his home and $50 a month. It meant working 112 hours a month. This allowed Lloyd to be self-supporting in the years 1931–32. Lloyd never forgot him

Lloyd Herskovitz Hurst, high school graduation, 1927. *Courtesy of yearbooks.com*

Lloyd Justin Hurst
East Chicago
LL.B. Law
Sigma Alpha Mu; Debating Team '30; Bryan Prize '30; Vice-President Senior Law Class; Student Board of Editors of Law Journal; A.B. I. U. '30

Lloyd Herskovitz Hurst graduation from law school, 1932. *Courtesy of yearbooks.com*

L–R: Bernard and Lloyd Hurst, 1940. *Personal photo collection*

and established a scholarship in his name while they were both still living. Dr. Schlafer participated in awarding the prizes until his death, when he was in his 90s. Lloyd's sons continue support for the scholarship. Lloyd also set up a scholarship to be given to a graduate of his fraternity, Sigma Alpha Mu, at Indiana University. He changed his name from Herskovitz to Hurst February 13, 1932. After graduation, he delivered mail when by chance he saw a sign for a job at an insurance agency. He did practice law for a few years before making a career of real estate and insurance. He married Lillian "Lynn" Steiger April 10, 1939. Together they had three sons and seven grandchildren. The last part of his career, he developed and managed a chain of restaurants. He was most proud of his philanthropic work supporting many local and national charities. He felt his most important contribution was funding a chair at Ben Gurion University, "The Lynn & Lloyd Hurst Family Chair in Local Government." It was a life well lived from a very difficult beginning. He, like his brothers and sisters, lived the American dream that Nettie had for all her children.

Bernard (Herskovitz) Hurst (born January 30, 1913, died February 15, 1981)

Bernard Herskovitz Hurst, high school graduation, 1929. *Courtesy of The Anvil Yearbook*

Bernard was Nettie and Sam's second son. He was 3 years old when his father died and had just turned 10 years old when Nettie was murdered. He graduated from Washington High School in 1929. (East Chicago High School changed its name in 1928.) He lived with his Uncle Dave Herskovitz during his high school years. He was very active in school activities, National Honor Society, Weekly Anvil, Senior Class Play, Debating Team, Puppets Club, Webster Literary Society, Latin Club, and the Tennis Team. His skill on the tennis court earned him a position on the Indiana University Tennis Team. He played for three years, always in the number-one position. He started college with the goal of becoming a physician, like his father, but found he was better suited for education. After graduation, he applied for a teaching position in the East Chicago Public Schools. He was turned down because his sister Pearle had been fired for breaking the rule against teaching while married. He

Bernard Herskovitz Hurst, Indiana University Tennis, 1931. *Personal photo collection*

had to get a job selling tires in Gary, Indiana. The following year, he got a teaching position—only after the school board member who fired Pearle lost her spot on the board. He first taught at an elementary school and then the high school. He taught science, physics, and chemistry, but also was the coach for the tennis team. He continued to play competitive tennis and win both local and state tournaments into his 40s. He always felt being left-handed gave him an advantage. After receiving his master's degree in education in 1940, he became the principal of Washington Elementary in Indiana Harbor. This was the same school he had attended after the death of his mother. An innovative educator, he started both the first bilingual and gifted student classes in East Chicago. He married June Van Vliet on June 16, 1940. It was June who encouraged him to legally change his name from Herskovitz to Hurst on May 11, 1942. This was two years after they were married and almost one year after the birth of their first child. Bernard and June had two children, a boy and girl, and two grandchildren. June, like "Bernie," was also a school teacher, and together they were a great team for over 40 years. Bernard was very active in the community, teaching Sunday school, and later was superintendent of the East Chicago Public School System. He was president of the Lions Club and a member of both the Elks and Moose lodges. In later years, he tried to

Dr. Cecil Hurst, WWII. *Family photo collection*

locate members of his family. Bernard found the Sachs (now spelled *Sacks*) branch of the family in Houston, Texas. These were his first cousins, children of Nettie's brother Edward. He passed on his interest in finding his roots to me, his son.

Cecil (Herskovitz) Hurst
(born July 4, 1914, died January 4, 1954)

Dr. Cecil Herskovitz Hurst, medical school graduation, 1937. *Courtesy of yearbooks.com.*

Cecil was the youngest of the Herskovitz children. He was only 20 months old when his father died and 8 years old when Nettie was murdered. He lived with his Aunt Ettie Baranowsky after Nettie died. He graduated from Washington High School in 1931. He participated in many of the same activities as his older brothers—Puppets, Drama Club, National Honor Society, Latin Club, Webster Literary Society, and the Debating Team. After high school he went to Indiana University and played football his freshman year. He graduated in 1935 with a B.S. in anatomy and physiology. At that time, he had changed his name from Herskovitz to Hurst. He continued on to medical school—the boys had discussed that one of them should follow in their father's profession. Since Bernard didn't, it was up to Cecil to go to medical school. He finished in 1937. He moved to Washington State to do his internship, living near his sister Pearle. Cecil entered the military February 5, 1941, stationed at Fort Thomas in Newport, Kentucky. He married Lucille Feist August 28, 1941. They had three children, two boys and a girl. He was in an orthopedic residency at the University of Washington when he died while preparing for an operation. Cecil died tragically at age 39, January 4, 1954, in Seattle, Washington, of a heart attack. He was the first of the brothers to die, but all would die of heart ailments.

Edward Noah Zauderer Sachs
(born July 30, 1905, died May 2, 1972)

Edward was Nettie's first and only child with her second husband Louis Joshua Zauderer. He was born in St. Louis, Missouri, with a number of congenital birth defects. Based on his characteristics, it is possible he had Cornelia de Lange Syndrome, which may have been first described in 1916 but was not named until 1933. Edward was left in St. Louis at the St. Louis City Sanitarium in 1908, where he was cared for and educated. He had signs of mental retardation, the result of his birth syndrome. He moved from St. Louis to Chicago after Nettie's death. In 1930, he was a boarder with the Glickman family in Chicago and was working as a salesman. In July of 1930, he married Molly Glickman, a book binder two years his senior. They had one child in 1935 that was stillborn. In 1940, he was working on a labor gang. Mollie predeceased him by nine years. At the time of his death, he was working as a shipping clerk. He was being treated for a heart problem when he died.

Gertrude Fay Diamond (born July 21, 1922, died May 17, 1998)

Fay Diamond, college graduation. *Courtesy of yearbooks.com.*

Fay was Nettie's sixth child, and her only child with Harry Diamond. She was almost 7 months old when Nettie was murdered. After Nettie's death, she was adopted by her grandparents Joseph and Esther Diamond. By 1935, Esther had moved to Detroit, Michigan, with Lena, one of her daughters, and granddaughter Fay. Joseph remained in Gary. It is said that Fay knew nothing of her real mother or her father and the murder, but as a teenager, she found a scrapbook that one of her uncles kept that told the story. She studied at Wayne State in Detroit and later attended the Art Institute of Chicago, all paid for by Lloyd from Nettie's estate.She studied sculpture at the Rhode Island School of Design and graduated from the Drexel Institute of Technology in Pennsylvania with a degree in art. Fay refused to settle with Nettie's estate until January 1945, delaying the final closure. She married Arthur Freedman in 1946, and they had two girls. They moved to Philadelphia in 1953 when her husband accepted a position at the Wharton School of Business. Fay taught art for 45 years at the Community Arts Center in Wallingford. Many of her works are on display in Philadelphia museums. Fay died of heart failure.

Nettie's Grandchildren:

The grandchildren Nettie never got a chance to know continued her pursuit of education and her fearless determination to succeed in America.

Among her 12 grandchildren are 10 who have achieved these advanced degrees:

- An Otolaryngologist
- A Gastroenterologist
- A Biochemist
- A Vascular Surgeon
- An Orthodontist
- A Psychologist
- Two Orthopedic Surgeons
- Two Attorneys

Some of these grandchildren have also pursued additional advanced degrees, and some have taught in universities and medical schools, lectured, and published articles as well as books in their areas of education as well as other subjects.

They and their families live all over the United States, from Maine to Washington to Michigan, Oregon, Louisiana, Florida, and California, keeping Nettie's American dream alive from coast to coast.

She would be proud of their accomplishments.

CHAPTER 26

The Adults
in the Family

David Herskovitz
(born February 4, 1875, died May 23, 1937)

David Herskovitz, New York, 1902. *Courtesy of the Louise Walsh collection*

David emigrated from Romania, arriving in New York in August 1900, the last member of the family to leave Romania, as he was serving in the army. He had learned the tin smith trade before he came to America. His first marriage was to Lina Braizig in 1902 in Ohio. He married Esther Greenberg in December of 1905; they had three children, Joseph in 1907, Leo in 1909, and Pearl in 1910. David became a naturalized citizen in 1910. He and Esther divorced in 1912. He next married Pauline Dorachinsky in August of 1923, the same year that Nettie was murdered. Nettie's son Bernard lived with his Uncle Dave. Because he was left-handed, Bernard couldn't master the tin smith trade, as the tools were all designed for the right hand. David died in 1937 of a stomach ailment for which he had been treated a year prior to his death.

Marcus Hershcovitz (Herskovitz)
(born October 6, 1879, died January 1, 1937)

Marcus was the only one in the family who refused to spell his name like the others; all his life, he did things his way. He immigrated to America in May of 1900 from Romania.

Marcus Herschcovitz.
Family collection

The second child in the family, he was a bookbinder by trade, but it didn't take him long to get educated and become an attorney. He married Anna Harris in 1900 and had his first child, Violet, in 1903. He married again in 1907, wedding Sophie Feinberg. Marcus was his own man and had a bit of a temper. In 1912, he got into a fight with another attorney whom he called a liar. Marcus won, but they were both arrested; the judge dismissed the charges. His next altercation was in 1915 with L.C. Saric, an attorney and realtor. The judge adjourned the court and let them take their quarrel outside. Within 10 minutes, they returned with Saric looking like he had fought with a bearcat. Marcus also fought for Nettie's children after she was murdered, and he was the one who pressed charges against Joseph and Ruth Diamond, landing them in jail for stealing Nettie's property the day she died. It's no wonder that he threw the boys out of his house after Lloyd complained about the food; I'm sure he felt they didn't appreciate what he had done for them. In 1925, he survived a serious auto accident when a Ford truck ran into his Chevrolet coupe. Only the driver of the truck was treated by a doctor, but both "machines" were total wrecks. Later in life, he donated 334 volumes in the Romanian language to the East Chicago Public Library. Bernard and his wife June spent time with Marcus's widow after he died, but Bernard's brother Lloyd would have nothing to do with the family. (Lloyd may have been more like his Uncle Marcus than he would ever admit.) Marcus died of a heart attack at 57 years of age.

Ettie Herskovitz Hillel Baranowsky Alter (born November 8, 1881, died August 30, 1951)

Etta, or Ettie, was the third child in the Herskovitz family and the only girl. She was the daughter of Pepe's sister Pauline Sibalis, who died during childbirth. Pepe raised Ettie with the rest of the family; the boys thought of her as their sister. She emigrated from Romania to New York on June 27, 1900, and married Newman Hillel, a watchmaker, in March of 1901. They moved to Connecticut and then to St. Louis, where Sam attended medical school. They had three children, Pearl in 1902, Sarah in 1903, and Jack in 1908. In 1912,

TOP LEFT:
Ettie as Midwife. *Courtesy of Louise Walsh collection*
TOP RIGHT: Ettie and Dr. Cecil Hurst, WWII. *Family photo collection*
BOTTOM LEFT: Marcus and Ettie Alter: True love at last. *Louise Walsh collection*
BOTTOM RIGHT: Ettie Sibalis Herskovitz Hillel Baranowsky Alter. *Personal photo collection*

Newman died of a heart attack. Soon after, Ettie and the family moved to East Chicago to be with Nettie and Sam. She worked as a midwife for Sam and his patients. She remarried in East Chicago, wedding Myer Baranowsky, seven years her junior. Ettie was always there for Nettie's children and raised Cecil after Nettie's death; she also allowed Lloyd to stay at her house after he returned from the academy. She divorced Myer in 1936 and moved to Detroit, Michigan, with her daughter and son-in-law. Her last move was to California, where her son Jack was living. There she was married for the last time, to Marcus Alter, her first love from her hometown in Romania; he was a printer in San Francisco, and by chance they found each other at the Frances Hotel. Her last marriage was for love, just what Emma Goldman had advocated so many years ago in St. Louis. Ettie died of a heart ailment in 1951 at the age of 69, living longer than any of her siblings.

Anna Levin Cohen Fishman
(born February 24, 1884, died September 4, 1968)

Anna was Nettie's best friend and was there for her in life and in death—their lives were entwined. She had four boys with her first husband Barney Cohen, who died in 1913. Her children were Cecil in 1900, Isadore in 1903, Lloyd in 1909, and Irving in 1910, born 18 months after Lloyd. In 1920, Anna married Morris Fishman, a boarder in her boarding house who was six years younger than she. Anna was with Nettie as she lay dying in the hospital and promised to take care of her children. Pearle, Nettie's oldest daughter, lived with Aunt Anna until she married Dr. Lester Baskin. Anna was also there when Uncle Marcus threw the boys out and she gave them a place to stay, until they found other places to live. Things were not always easy for her. In April 1924, the U.S. district attorney tried to close down her saloon and poolroom for one year for a violation of the Prohibition law; though he was not successful, Anna did have to pay a fine and cease selling alcohol. In 1937, as she and Myer were headed to Bloomington, Indiana, for her son's graduation from Indiana University, they hit a hole in the road, flipped their car, and were trapped underneath. She suffered a broken collar bone but no other serious injuries; an ambulance took her to the hospital in Bloomington, but she missed her son's graduation. She was like a mother to Pearle, who never forgot her kindness. Anna lived the rest of her life in the same house in Indiana Harbor.

CHAPTER 27

The Diamond Family

Joseph A. Diamond
(born June 21, 1878, died December 11, 1941)

Joseph was the father of Harry Harold Hyman Diamond, his eldest son, who murdered his wife Nettie Diamond. Joseph married Esther Brown almost as soon as he moved to Louisville, Kentucky, from New York City after emigrating from Lithuania. Together, they had seven children.[1] During his life, he worked a variety of jobs, learning his trade on the Lower East Side of New York under mob boss Monk Eastman. He then moved to Louisville, Kentucky, where he set up shop as a pawnbroker. This was similar to being a peddler, as his father had been in the old country. After being caught stealing in Louisville, he got a job as a salesman selling men's furnishings. By 1911, he was very deep in debt and left town for Gary, Indiana. In Gary, he again worked as a salesman selling men's clothing. Next, he was a partner in operating The Standard Bottling Company with his son and Abe Rosen. This put him in the bootlegging business. After his son Harry was electrocuted for killing Nettie, the bottling company was closed. In 1930, he worked as an electrician in the steel mills. About 1935, his wife Esther, daughter Lena, and granddaughter Fay left Joseph in Indiana and moved to Detroit, where son David and his wife had moved earlier. Joseph's last job was that of a motor inspector in 1940. Joseph, who was never one to miss a chance for additional funds, put in a claim for Social Security in November of 1941, but he died before he could collect. He was living with his youngest son Julius when he died in December 1941.

---

1 Only five of Joseph and Esther's seven children played roles in Nettie's murder. The two youngest, Albert and Julius, were only 9 and 7 years old at the time of the crime and were not involved.

Esther Brown Diamond
(born May 1874, died February 28,1965)

Esther married Joseph in Jefferson, Kentucky, and gave birth to her first child, Harry Harold Hyman Diamond, on December 25, 1898. He was the first of seven children. Her last child was born in Gary, Indiana, when she was 41 years old. She was supportive of her husband and knew from the start that he didn't obey the law. It started in Kentucky when he stole a chicken and the family ate the evidence. She and Joseph adopted Nettie's and Harry's daughter Fay and continued to live off Nettie's estate until Fay turned 21 and was no longer receiving a living allowance. After the death of her fourth child, Fannie, in 1932, Esther moved to Detroit with Fay and her daughter Lena in 1935. During Harry's trial for murder, she won the crowd's sympathy for her seemingly frail condition; all were told she didn't have long to live. Esther did have an operation for gallstones in 1923, but she lived another 41 years, dying at age 90. She was never able to read or write English, and she never held a job, according to the census.

Harry Harold Hyman Diamond
(born December 25, 1898, died November 14, 1924)

Harry was the first child of Joseph and Esther Diamond. They raised him in such a manner that he was very egocentric. He was the first one in their family to be born in America, and they did not want to deny him anything. His obvious ego showed in high school, where under his graduation photo it was written, "Harry has such a good opinion of himself." During high school, he worked at Goodman's Department store but was fired for stealing clothes. He dropped out of Valparaiso Law School after two months, saying, "There's not enough money in law." His jobs after that at the steel mill all ended with problems. He complained of not being paid enough, and he inhaled sulfuric acid fumes at one of his jobs. This landed him in the hospital suffering from epileptic fits. Starting The Standard Bottling Company put him in the bootleg whiskey business. He was not always one step ahead of the law and wound up in court numerous times. Selling hot diamonds was another one of his scams. The ultimate criminal activity was his part ownership and participation in a roadhouse where liquor and women were for sale and hire. All this culminated in his murdering his wife, Nettie, whose fortune he expected to receive. Unfortunately for Harry, his plan failed, as both his victims lived long enough to tell the true story. For Harry, bad luck was always caused by others, but in truth, it was Harry who couldn't get things right. He was electrocuted for his crime on November 14, 1924.

Ruth (Rebecca) Diamond (born August 23, 1899, died July 20, 1986)

Ruth was the second child born to the Diamonds. Ruth was directly involved in the theft of Nettie's property the day she died. She was charged with grand larceny along with her father in 1923. She married Stanley Warren Smith August 11, 1931, when she was 32 years old. In April 1945, she divorced him and then moved to Detroit, Michigan, to be with her mother and sister Lena. Detroit is also where she died.

Lena (Leona) Diamond (born February 10, 1901, died February 1987)

Lena was the third child in the Diamond family. She worked as a bookkeeper in various businesses. She moved to Detroit after her younger sister Fannie died in 1932. There she lived with her mother and niece Fay. She never married. It appears she outlived everyone in the family except her younger brother Elbert, who died in 1994. When she died, she was living in Pennsylvania near her niece Fay.

Fannie Diamond (born September 15, 1906, died September 1932)

Fannie was the fourth child in the Diamond family. She, like her older sisters, was involved in the theft of Nettie's possessions—in particular, Nettie's bullet-damaged fur coat. She disappeared to Chicago when the police wanted to question her. She was 18 years old when she and her younger brother went to the prison to see her brother Harry the afternoon before he died. Fannie worked as a saleslady. She was the second child to die after her brother Harry, dying of a heart ailment at only 25 years of age.

David Diamond
(born September 20, 1911, died February 1968)

David was 13 when he went with his sister Fannie to see their older brother Harry in prison on the day Harry was put to death. By 1935, David was married and living with his in-laws in Detroit, Michigan; that was probably the reason his mother and sister left Gary, Indiana, to live in Detroit after they were no longer under Joseph's influence. In 1943, David served in the military during WWII.

CHAPTER 28

The Rest of the Story: People and Property

William Armstrong (born August 7, 1905, died August 27, 1970)

William Armstrong, 1923.
Courtesy of The Hammond Times *Newspaper Archives*

William was born in Oklahoma and came to Gary, Indiana, with his family when his father, a barber, sought work in the steel mills. William didn't make it through high school; he dropped out and began working in a pool hall and auto garage. His first chauffeur job with Harry Diamond was almost his last. Being a light-skinned mulatto in 1923 allowed him many opportunities. After Nettie's death and Harry's trial, he started working as the chauffeur for the winning attorney, William McAleer. William married Eudora Reaves August 29, 1929. In 1930, he was driving a truck for a dry-cleaning company. In 1940, William worked as a clerk. In October 1940, he married Clemette Lloyd; she was his wife until his death in 1970. The circumstances of his death concerned a domestic dispute. On August 27, 1970, William showed up at the house of Mrs. Martha Cornell, his former girlfriend. When he entered the house, he hit one woman and then chased Mrs. Cornell out the back door. She ran into her yard with William close behind. He shot at her twice but missed. When his shots missed, he caught up to her and began to pistol whip her about the head. That's when the police arrived and ordered him to drop the gun. He refused. They fired five shots, hitting him in the heart and killing him instantly. It is interesting to note that he died while shooting and beating his girlfriend with his gun, as Harry did to Nettie. The difference was that the police witnessed the act this time and ended his life saving hers.

William Murray
(born November 4, 1879, died December 23, 1959)

William Murray, judge and attorney for Nettie's estate.
Courtesy of The Hammond Times *and Newspaper Archives*

William Murray was the attorney who supplied the information on Nettie's death certificate. He was also appointed by the bank to be the attorney for Nettie's estate. He took care of the Hudson after the murder and may have found the buyer for the machine, the pharmacist who ran Nettie's Red Cross Pharmacy. After the death of James G. Allen, he was both the executor and attorney for the estate. It was he who dealt with Joseph Diamond and his attorneys who broke the will that Nettie wrote on her death bed. Murray was the executor of the estate during the time that most of the property was lost due to nonpayment of their mortgages, and all the stock was sold to the bank for one dollar. He became a judge on the criminal court as a Democrat in 1932 and was on the bench in 1934 for the John Dillinger case. (The John Dillinger gang killed an East Chicago policeman as they robbed the First National Bank and Trust of East Chicago. Dillinger escaped the jail at Crown Point and was later shot to death.) Murray was running for re-election at age 80 when he died of a heart attack.

James Gaylord Allen
(born March 31, 1862, died November 11, 1928)

Nettie asked James Allen to be the executor of her estate as she lay dying in the hospital. He had been her personal banker, and she trusted him. Records show a detailed accounting of his expenses and those of the estate. He fought for what he thought was right and resisted the attempt by Joseph Diamond to break the will to allow his granddaughter Fay an equal share of the estate as her half siblings. He was successful in protecting the estate until his death when William Murray took over the executorship. The stress of the trial was so great that after it was over, Allen went to the Martinsville Sanitarium in Indiana to

J.G. Allen, bank vice president and executor of Nettie's estate. *Courtesy of* The Hammond Times *and Newspaper Archives*

recuperate. He confronted Joseph Diamond every time he tried to attack the estate. Because of this, Joseph decided to hurt him with a staged accident when he got off the Danville Number 13 train from Chicago on October 25, 1928. It looked like he had been hit by a railcar, but in truth it was a hit man. Allen died November 11, 1928, from a cardiac embolism of the left ventricle and pulmonary thrombosis of the left lung, complications from the attack. He had been the vice president and treasurer of the bank and the first president of the East Chicago-Indiana Harbor Clearing House association of banks. He left a wife and teenage daughter. He tried to give fatherly advice to Lloyd and Bernard when no one else was there for them.

William J. McAleer
(born July 1867, died December 26, 1942)

W.J. McAleer was the lead prosecuting attorney for the state of Indiana against Harry Diamond. He was born in Canada. As a youth, he was a harness horse enthusiast, winning many trophies and purses. To put himself through school while still in Canada, he turned to boxing. He was an amateur light-heavyweight and later turned professional. He could compete with many of the top boxers of his day. Later in his life, he took up golf. Here too he was competitive with many who were much younger. When he came to Indiana, he went to school at Valparaiso University to get his legal education. He practiced law in Lake County for almost 40 years and was very involved with the Republican Party, serving as a district chairman.

Joseph H. Conroy
(born January 20, 1872, died December 30, 1948)

Joseph Conroy was Harry Diamond's defense attorney. He was nicknamed the "Little Giant" for both his size, just over five feet tall, and the nature of his cases. He took cases that looked impossible, pitting the client against the state or large institutions. He and his mother moved to Valparaiso after his father died when he was just 6 years old. He went to both college and law school at Valparaiso University. He began practicing law at the age of 19. Always at odds with the attorney William J. McAleer, he organized a Lawyer Guild in 1937. His intent was to wage war on conservative groups to which McAleer belonged. He said the guild would align itself with labor groups. Conroy was a lifelong Democrat, and McAleer a Republican. The "Little Giant" survived a burst appendix and had surgery in 1940 for a tumor on his bladder. He died of prostate cancer.

Judge Hannibal H. Loring (born December 23, 1862, died December 26, 1936)

Hannibal H. Loring was the judge in the Nettie Diamond trial. He had to keep order in the court and control the two opposing attorneys, Conroy and McAleer. He was the fifth of five children growing up on a farm in Grant County, Indiana. He farmed until he was 18. He then taught school for three years. In 1882, he came to Valparaiso and entered Northern Indiana Normal School, now Valparaiso University. He graduated from the teacher program. He taught school for two years, became a principal in 1899, and then became superintendent of the Porter County Schools. He went back to Valparaiso Law School to get his law degree, later becoming the circuit judge for Porter County. In January 1927, four years after Nettie's trial, Judge Loring retired as judge of the Porter circuit court. He was now president of the State Bank of Valparaiso and in partnership with his son Bruce in the practice of law. When the country suffered an economic collapse and a banking crisis in 1933, his bank was the only Valparaiso bank to remain open. This was the same year he received extortion letters for $5,000, threatening to kill him, but he did not pay. He died three years later at home, 10 weeks after an abdominal operation in Chicago. No one had a bad word to say about him or his life. He was a man of principle who always kept his word and cared about others.

Harry's Friends

Nick Slade, Steve Buconich, and Matt Buconich, Harry's and Joseph's friends in crime and the bootleg business, all died natural deaths. Nick died of a ruptured aortic aneurism at age 43 in 1935. Steve died at age 52 in 1933. His younger brother Matt died of pneumonia at age 66 in 1945. Abe Rosen (Harry's father's partner in crime and the not-so-silent partner in the Bottling Company) died at age 72 in 1959.

CHAPTER 29

East Chicago Banks

Banks played a central role in Nettie's life and death. One bank managed Nettie's estate and distributed funds for the care of her children after her death. Things came to a head in Nettie and Harry's marriage when Harry deposited her Durant stock check in his account at the American Bank and Trust. The event was covered up by the bank attorney Abe Ottenheimer, the vice president of the bank and a customer of Harry's for stolen diamonds. The Indiana Harbor National Bank was in charge of Nettie's estate through both its vice president James G. Allen and its attorney William Murray. It may interest the reader where those banks are today.

The American Bank and Trust

This bank was capitalized in 1909 with $61,000 ($852,000 in 2017 dollars). Like all banks in the Depression in the '30s, it fell on hard times and looked for another bank with which to merge. In September 1930, the president of the bank, Hazel K. Groves, disappeared for two weeks. He returned home a victim of amnesia. He was on his way to a conference with the board of directors to ratify a merger with another bank. He last remembered being at Cedar Lake, Indiana, until he was found at a Peoria, Illinois, hotel. When he awoke in the hotel, he called his brother Harry to come pick him up. He remembered nothing but was not robbed, as he still had money on his person. His automobile, a coupe, was missing. To prevent a run on the bank, it closed and state bank examiners were asked to come in and go over the books. They found some irregularities but withheld publication. In October of 1930, the bank remained closed pending negotiations for a merger with the East Chicago State Bank. In April of 1931, Groves was named in an affidavit for charging overdrafts. The state closed the American State Bank September 19, 1931. On December 24, 1931, a trial was set for Groves in Lake County criminal court; there is no mention of Abe Ottenheimer, who may no longer have been with the bank. Abe died in 1937.

The Indiana Harbor Bank

Indiana Harbor National Bank handled all of Nettie's estate—first through its vice president James G. Allen and then exclusively through William Murray, the bank's appointed attorney. This bank ended its services to the estate in October 1930, when Lloyd Herskovitz began managing what was left of the estate. In December 1931, the chairman, Colonel Walter J. Riley, merged two of his banks—Indiana Harbor National Bank and the Union National Bank of Indiana Harbor— in an effort to make them stronger. In November 21, 1958, the Union National Bank of Indiana Harbor merged with the First National Bank of East Chicago. Walter J. Riley II, the president of the First National Bank of East Chicago, died in 1990. He had attended the Campion Academy at the same time Lloyd and Bernard attended. He was named for his uncle Colonel Walter J. Riley, who founded the bank in 1909. In 1993, this bank was merged into the National City Bank of Indiana, which was bought by the Peoples National Bank.

CHAPTER 30

The Properties Left in the Estate

Home in Gary, Indiana, at 647 Buchanan

This is the house that the family was living in when Nettie was murdered. The house was rented at $70/month ($989 dollars in 2017 dollars). This helped cover the mortgage to prevent its foreclosure by the bank. When Lloyd took charge of the estate, he had the property transferred to him from the bank with a quitclaim deed in 1935. He mortgaged the house several more times before he sold it in 1936 to Allen J. Frantz. Originally built in 1915, it was on a lot measuring 125 by 45 feet. The house itself was two stories with a finished basement. It had four bedrooms, one full bath, and one half bath. This gave it 2,664 square feet of living space. There was a detached garage with an additional 360 square feet. It was last sold in 2014 for $32,000.

Calumet Drugstore at 723 Chicago Ave., East Chicago, Indiana

This was Nettie and Sam's first real home, where they lived in the 10 rooms above the drugstore they built in 1910. The building was 30 by 65 feet. It was approximately 4,000 square feet, as it had two floors. The drugstore and Sam's office were on the first floor, and the family lived on the second floor. There was a staircase outside the back of the building that went all the way to the roof. The roof was where Bernard tested the theory that cats had nine lives. He told the story that as an 8-year-old, he took the family cat to the roof and dropped her off nine times and she lived. He said that after each drop, it became

447

2nd floor
Patio

Calumet Drugstore. *Courtesy of Google Earth*

more difficult to carry the cat to the roof. The drop was only one story, as he dropped her off above the patio area on the second floor where the maid hung the laundry. Lloyd and Bernard also used the roof as a vantage place to watch people cross the empty lot across the street from the drugstore. They had dug holes in the ground and then camouflaged them for those who took the shortcut across the lot. The drugstore building, as the family called it, remained in the family until just a few years before the deaths of Bernard and Lloyd. Each of the Herskovitz children, or their children, had a divided 25 percent interest in the building. It may have been a reminder to them of their earlier happy lives, when their father and mother were alive and the family was all together. The building was saved from bank foreclosure, as it always had an income stream. In 1923, the first-floor drugstore rented for $300/month ($4,240 in 2017 dollars). I remember as a teenager painting the back staircase and repairing the chimney brickwork with my father, Bernard. I also re-member the basement with its asbestos-covered pipes that sent hot water to the building's radiators for heat. The coal bin, no longer used, was a storage area. The building had many tenants. The last I remember on the second floor in the old apartment area was a dental office. When the dentist retired, he moved to Florida and left all his equipment for us to remove. That's when I learned just how heavy an old dental chair could be. The building was sold to John Robert Wilhelm in 1979 for $20,000, the same dollar amount that the building was valued at the time of Nettie's death, 56 years earlier. The difference was that in 1923, $20,000 was equivalent to $282,725 in 2017 dollars; not all real estate increases in value, as the city had been in decline for many years. The building was sold with the provision that the buyer would buy it over a period of six years. In 1985, Mr. Wilhelm had completed his payments and was given a warranty deed. Before it was executed, we (the owners) had to pay off the mortgage. The mortgage was now owned by Mrs. Takles, widow of Gus Takles, the holder of the first mortgage of $10,000. Mortgages seemed to follow all the real estate. This sale represented the last of Nettie's original property.

Sam and Nettie. *Family collection*

About the Author

Dr. Robert V.V. Hurst

I should have known that it was my job in the family to tell the story of my Grandmother Nettie's life: I grew up in the town where she was murdered and spent time in the exact spot where she lay dying from her wounds in the family drugstore. None of her other grandchildren, to my knowledge, had such an intimate relationship to her physical location, and so my aunts and uncles confided in me with stories and information about the family that they had never told their own children.

My father Bernard—Nettie's third child with my grandfather— was left an orphan at age 10, and as an adult he sought answers about his family's history. (Eventually he located the Houston, Texas, branch of our family, but despite his efforts many unanswered questions remained for me to pursue.) I mention that my father was the third child—that's important, because as a third-born, he had a natural curiosity about his family history. (Third-borns have an innate sense of all their family interrelationships and look at life differently than do their older siblings; they see the artistic side of things and the bigger picture of humanity in all its forms.)

Why do I say that? I was fortunate enough to become an orthodontist, and over the years I became inquisitive about the birth orders of my patients. Interesting parallels emerged when I began observing that although children came from the same family, they did not act the same. This led to my book about birth order, *Life's Fingerprint: How Birth*

Order Affects Your Path Throughout Life. When I began researching Nettie's life and murder, having this information allowed me to see my ancestors, like my patients, expressing their birth-order traits.

Working as an orthodontist, I must wait years to see my patients' end results. This gave me the patience to persevere through 6 years of sometimes frustrating research looking into Nettie's life. Some findings were truly astounding but fit with her birth order traits. The wait and the journey were well worth the effort.

CPSIA information can be obtained
at www.ICGtesting.com
Printed in the USA
FFOW01n0047171217
44083043-43351FF